THE POLITICS OF GENDER IN
ANTHONY TROLLOPE'S NOVELS

The Politics of Gender in Anthony Trollope's Novels

New Readings for the Twenty-First Century

Edited by

MARGARET MARKWICK
University of Exeter, UK

DEBORAH DENENHOLZ MORSE
College of William and Mary, USA

and

REGENIA GAGNIER
University of Exeter, UK

ASHGATE

Published by
Ashgate Publishing Limited
Wey Court East
Union Road
Farnham
Surrey, GU9 7PT
England

Ashgate Publishing Company
Suite 420
101 Cherry Street
Burlington
VT 05401-4405
USA

www.ashgate.com

British Library Cataloguing in Publication Data
The politics of gender in Anthony Trollope's novels : new readings for the twenty-first century. – (The nineteenth century series)
   1. Trollope, Anthony, 1815–1882 – Criticism and interpretation 2. Sex role in literature
   I. Markwick, Margaret, 1945– II. Morse, Deborah Denenholz, 1949– III. Gagnier, Regenia
   823.8

Library of Congress Cataloging-in-Publication Data
The politics of gender in Anthony Trollope's novels : new readings for the twenty-first century / edited by Margaret Markwick, Deborah Denenholz Morse and Regenia Gagnier.
   p. cm. — (The nineteenth century series)
  Includes bibliographical references and index.
  ISBN 978-0-7546-6389-8 (alk. paper)
   1. Trollope, Anthony, 1815–1882—Criticism and interpretation. 2. Gender identity in literature. 3. Sex role in literature. I. Markwick, Margaret, 1945– II. Morse, Deborah Denenholz, 1949– III. Gagnier, Regenia.

  PR5687.P55 2009
  823'.8—dc22

2008051709

ISBN: 978-0-7546-6389-8

Mixed Sources
Product group from well-managed forests and other controlled sources
www.fsc.org Cert no. SA-COC-1565
© 1996 Forest Stewardship Council

Printed and bound in Great Britain by
MPG Books Ltd, Bodmin, Cornwall.

Contents

The Nineteenth Century Series
General Editors' Preface

The aim of the series is to reflect, develop and extend the great burgeoning of interest in the nineteenth century that has been an inevitable feature of recent years, as that former epoch has come more sharply into focus as a locus for our understanding not only of the past but of the contours of our modernity. It centres primarily upon major authors and subjects within Romantic and Victorian literature. It also includes studies of other British writers and issues, where these are matters of current debate: for example, biography and autobiography, journalism, periodical literature, travel writing, book production, gender, non-canonical writing. We are dedicated principally to publishing original monographs and symposia; our policy is to embrace a broad scope in chronology, approach and range of concern, and both to recognize and cut innovatively across such parameters as those suggested by the designations 'Romantic' and 'Victorian'. We welcome new ideas and theories, while valuing traditional scholarship. It is hoped that the world which predates yet so forcibly predicts and engages our own will emerge in parts, in the wider sweep, and in the lively streams of disputation and change that are so manifest an aspect of its intellectual, artistic and social landscape.

Vincent Newey
Joanne Shattock
University of Leicester

List of Figures

Notes on the Contributors

Steven Amarnick, Associate Professor of English at Kingsborough Community College, City University of New York, curated the exhibit "Anthony Trollope: The Art of Modesty," at the Fales Library, New York University. He has written on many aspects of Trollope's career, including such topics as Trollope and anti-Semitism, Trollope's rivalry with Dickens, his advanced conservative liberalism, and his visits to the United States, and is currently preparing a new edition of *The Duke's Children* which restores Trollope's cuts.

Helen Lucy Blythe is Assistant Professor of English at New Mexico Highlands University. She has published on Trollope in *Nineteenth-Century Contexts* (2003), and her book manuscript *Shadowy Resting Places for the Imagination: The Rise and Fall of the Victorian Colonial Romance* deals in part with Trollope's use of "New Zealand" as a site for aesthetic, utopian, and satirical reflections on English culture. She is interested in Trollope's late works for what they reveal about his attitude towards the colonies as well as the seat of empire.

Mary Jean Corbett is the John W. Steube Professor of English and Affiliate of Women's Studies at Miami University in Oxford, Ohio. She is the author of *Representing Femininity: Middle-Class Subjectivity in Victorian and Edwardian Women's Autobiographies* (Oxford, 1992) and *Allegories of Union in Irish and English Writing, 1790–1870: Politics, History, and the Family from Edgeworth to Arnold* (Cambridge, 2000), which includes a chapter on the Irish fictions of Anthony Trollope. Her new book, *Family Likeness: Sex, Marriage, and Incest from Jane Austen to Virginia Woolf*, will be published by Cornell in 2008.

Regenia Gagnier is Professor of English, Director of Research, Director of the Centre for Victorian Studies, Director of the Migrations Research Network, and Senior Fellow at the ESRC Centre for Genomics in Society (Egenis) at the University of Exeter and a critical theorist and cultural historian of Victorian Britain. Her books include *Idylls of the Marketplace: Oscar Wilde and the Victorian Public* (Stanford, 1986), *Subjectivities: A History of Self-Representation in Britain 1832–1920* (Oxford, 1991), *Critical Essays on Oscar Wilde* (Boston, 1991), and *The Insatiability of Human Wants: Economics and Aesthetics in Market Society* (Chicago, 2000). She has just completed a study of individualisms in the nineteenth century and is beginning a literary anthropology of freedom and choice.

Lauren M. E. Goodlad is Associate Professor of English and member of the Unit for Criticism and Interpretive Theory at the University of Illinois, Urbana-Champaign.

She is the author of *Victorian Literature and the Victorian State: Character and Governance in a Liberal Society* (Johns Hopkins University Press, 2003), the co-editor of *Goth: Undead Subculture* (Duke University Press, 2007), and the co-editor with Julia Wright of "Victorian Internationalisms," the Winter 2008 special issue of *Romanticism and Victorianism on the Net (RaVoN)*. She is at work completing *The Victorian Geopolitical Aesthetic: Literature, Internationalism, and "the South."*

Nathan K. Hensley is a PhD candidate in English at Duke University, specializing in Victorian literature, empire, and critical theory. He received his MA from the University of Notre Dame, and has published a review essay in *The Minnesota Review*.

Margaret Markwick is an Honorary Fellow at Exeter University, and has been writing widely about Trollope for several years. *Trollope and Women*, (Trollope Society and Hambledon Press, 1997), was her first full-length study of the novels, and her latest book, *New Men in Trollope's Novels: Rewriting the Victorian Male*, was published by Ashgate in 2007.

Elsie B. Michie is Associate Professor of English at Louisiana State University. She is the author of *Outside the Pale: Cultural Exclusion, Gender Difference, and the Victorian Woman Writer* (Indiana University Press, 1993), and has published on Mary Shelley, the Brontës, Elizabeth Gaskell, George Eliot, Jane Austen, Margaret Oliphant, and Anthony Trollope. Most recently, Michie edited the Oxford *Jane Eyre* (published March 2006) for its Casebook series. She is currently completing a book entitled *The Vulgar Question of Money* that links political economy to the woman of wealth in novels of manners from Austen to James.

Deborah Denenholz Morse, Inaugural Distinguished Professor for Teaching Excellence at the College of William and Mary and Professor of English, is the author of the first feminist study of Anthony Trollope, *Women in Trollope's Palliser Novels* (UMI Research Press, 1987; rpt Boydell and Brewer 1991), as well as a co-edited anthology (with Regina Barreca), *The Erotics of Instruction* (UPNE, 1997). Her collection of essays, *Victorian Animal Dreams: Representations in Literature and Culture*, co-edited with Martin Danahay, was published by Ashgate in 2007. Her new book, *Narrative and Tolerance in Anthony Trollope's Fiction*, is under contract with the Ohio State University Press. Professor Morse has published articles on Anne Brontë, Maxine Hong Kingston, Mona Simpson, Elizabeth Gaskell, Anthony Trollope, A. S. Byatt, Elizabeth Coles Tayler, and Kay Boyle, among others. In December of 2003 Morse was on National Public Radio to discuss the work of A. S. Byatt.

Christopher S. Noble is Associate Professor of English at Azusa Pacific University in Southern California, where he teaches composition, British literature, and literary theory. He has lectured and published on such topics as the nineteenth-century elegy, Victorian spirit photography and mourning rituals, Coleridge's conversation poems, and the intersection between literary gender theory and religious identity. His current project analyzes conflicting representations of widowhood in Victorian literature, and includes chapters on Frances Trollope's *The Widow Barnaby* (1839) and Tennyson's *In Memoriam* (1850).

Robert M. Polhemus is the Joseph S. Atha Professor in Humanities at Stanford University, where he served for nearly a decade as Chair of the English Department. He studies nineteenth-century British literature (especially the novel), twentieth-century British fiction and visual arts, including film. His work centers on fiction and art as a means to express the longing for some kind of faith in the last two centuries, and in representing, shaping, and determining belief. His books include *The Changing World of Anthony Trollope* (University of California, 1968), *Comic Faith: The Great Tradition from Austen to Joyce* (Chicago University Press, 1982); *Erotic Faith: Being in Love from Jane Austen to D. H. Lawrence* (Chicago University Press, 1990), and the recent *Lot's Daughters: Sex, Redemption, and Women's Quest for Authority* (Stanford University Press, 2005). He is presently writing a book on the tensions between religion and art, *A Device to Root Out Evil*, and one on Woody Allen.

Kathy Alexis Psomiades is Associate Professor of English at Duke University. She is the author of *Beauty's Body: Femininity and Representation in British Aestheticism* (Stanford 1997) and co-editor with Talia Schaffer of *Women and British Aestheticism* (University Press of Virginia, 1999). She has been the recipient of an NEH fellowship, and a Kaneb award for undergraduate teaching at the University of Notre Dame. Her current book project, *Primitive Marriage: Victorian Anthropology and the Novel*, examines the intersections between the novel and anthropology in the second half of the nineteenth century.

David Skilton is Research Professor in English at Cardiff University, where he was Head of the School of English, Communication and Philosophy 1988–2002. He is author of *Anthony Trollope and His Contemporaries* (Longman and St. Martins, 1972, Macmillan, 1996), *Defoe to the Victorians* (Penguin, 1985) and *The Early and Mid-Victorian Novel* (Routledge, 1993). He was General Editor of the Trollope Society and the Pickering and Chatto edition of Trollope's novels, and has edited numerous Victorian works for Oxford University Press, Penguin, and Everyman, among others, including the Penguin edition of *An Autobiography* (1993). He writes on the art and literature of London, and is part of a large project on Victorian illustrated literature.

Jenny Bourne Taylor is Professor of English at the University of Sussex. Her work includes *In the Secret Theatre of Home: Wilkie Collins, Sensation Narrative and Nineteenth-Century Psychology* (Routledge, 1988); (ed.) *The Cambridge*

Companion to Wilkie Collins (in press); (ed. with Sally Shuttleworth) *Embodied Selves, an Anthology of Psychological Texts 1830–1890* (Oxford, 1998), and (ed. with Martin Ryle) *George Gissing: Voices of the Unclassed* (Ashgate, 2005). She has also published various articles on the construction and significance of illegitimacy in nineteenth-century culture.

Anca Vlasopolos's nonfiction novel, *The New Bedford Samurai*, appeared in 2007, as did her poetry collection, *Penguins in a Warming World*. She published a non-fiction book, *No Return Address: A Memoir of Displacement* (Columbia, 2000; recipient of the National Writer's Voice Award for creative non-fiction; and of the Board of Governors and life achievement in arts awards from Wayne State University). Her scholarly publications include a book of literary criticism, entitled *The Symbolic Method of Coleridge, Baudelaire, and Yeats*, and over 30 scholarly articles and book chapters on nineteenth-century globalization, animal culture, British, French, Italian and comparative literature, theater, and film. She has published over 200 poems and short stories in literary print and online magazines; a short story was nominated for the Pushcart Prize. She has also collaborated with Christian Kreipke on two poetry-music compact discs and with James Hartway for the opera *Ke-Nu and the Magic Coals*, performed by the Michigan Opera, the Hilberry Theatre, and the WSU School of Music.

Acknowledgments

All of us who have written about Trollope owe a huge debt of gratitude to the great Trollope scholars who preceded us. It is no exaggeration to say that without the pioneering work of N. John Hall, Ruth apRoberts, R. C. Terry, Juliet McMaster, Robert Polhemus, and James Kincaid, we would all be still at the starting blocks. Deborah Morse would particularly like to pay honour to the brilliance and wit of Christopher Herbert, who first introduced her to Trollope's work. Indeed, we all have our lists of the commentators who have been instrumental in shaping our thinking about Trollope and whose names can be found in the bibliography at the end of this volume. And to this list we should add the editors of the new editions of Trollope's works that have been published in the last 25 years. It would not be possible to list them all, but John Sutherland surely deserves to be singled out.

We thank the Royal Holloway College, London, who identified the advertising material for Holloway's pills, and gave us permission to reproduce it, Boston Public Library for their permission to reproduce copies of two of their pictures of Kate Field, the Beinecke Library for the copy of a page of the original manuscript of *The Duke's Children*, and Sir Anthony Trollope for his permission to use it. David Skilton, one of the team at Cardiff responsible for the database of mid-Victorian wood-engraved illustration, and the Journal of Illustration Studies, has been a generous and helpful advisor with the presentation of illustrations in this volume. Thank also to John Plunkett, who gave his time and his expertise in preparing many of the scans.

For sponsoring the meeting that brought the contributors to this volume together in July 2006, we would also like to thank the College of William and Mary, Williamsburg, for their support and funding of Deborah Morse, the Centre for Victorian Studies and Department of English at the University of Exeter, and the British Academy.

And finally, we are, as ever, grateful for the computer technology skills of Charlie Morse and Chris Markwick, who did so much to marshal our scripts into a book.

Introduction

Margaret Markwick and Deborah Denenholz Morse

Trollope has always been one of his generation's most popular writers, with many of his novels continuously in print for 150 years, but his canonical position has not been as secure. Seasoned commentators have long quibbled about whether Trollope was worthy of serious study. Frederic Harrison found it necessary to apologize for including him in his 1895 survey of early Victorian novelists,[1] while Stephen Spender declared in 1974 that he had never read any of the Palliser novels, and, further, doubted whether any of his colleagues in the Department of English at University College London had either.[2] In 1976 Terry Eagleton wrote that Trollope's work "bathes in a self-consistent blandly undifferentiated ideological space," whose aesthetic is "an anaemic, naively representational 'realism', which is merely a reflex of commonplace bourgeois empiricism."[3] It is as though Trollope's very popularity has been his downfall, and even those who appear to be his staunchest supporters can hold diametrically opposing views. R. H. Hutton, the earliest commentator to offer a penetrating critique of Trollope's craft,[4] said in his obituary of Trollope that "His name will live in our literature … it will picture the society of our day with a fidelity with which society has never been pictured before in the history of the world,"[5] whereas Leslie Stephen, in 1901, wrote that he created "a general and peaceful world, oblivious to the intellectual, political and social revolution that was in the air."[6] By the 1920s Hutton's view was in the ascendancy. George Saintsbury praised Trollope for creating "real people"[7], and

---

[1]   Frederic Harrison, *Studies in Early Victorian Literature* 1895 (London: Edward Arnold, 1910), p. 183.

[2]   Quoted by James R. Kincaid, *The Novels of Anthony Trollope* (Oxford: Clarendon Press, 1977), p. 175, taken from a column in *The Radio Times* 24–30 (May 1974).

[3]   Terry Eagleton, *Criticism and Ideology: A Study in Marxist Literary Theory* (London: New Left Books, 1976), p. 181, quoted in Bill Overton, *The Unofficial Trollope* (Brighton: The Harvester Press, 1982), p. 1.

[4]   David Skilton's 1972 study *Anthony Trollope and his Contemporaries* (London: Longman, 1972), ch. 5, explores Hutton's critical analyses in detail.

[5]   R. H. Hutton, *Spectator*, 9 December 1882, lv. 1574, quoted in Donald Smalley (ed.), *Anthony Trollope: The Critical Heritage* (London: Routledge and Kegan Paul, 1969) p. 508.

[6]   *National Review*, 38 (1901), quoted by Donald D. Stone in R. C. Terry (ed.) *Oxford Reader's Companion to Trollope* (Oxford: Oxford University Press, 1999) p. 129.

[7]   George Saintsbury, *Essays and Studies by Members of the English Association*, pp. 41–66; quoted by Stone p. 130.

Virginia Woolf believed in Trollope "as we believe in our weekly bills".[8] But by the end of the Second World War, V. S. Pritchett was posting him back to Leslie Stephen's Arcadian dream; he declared that Trollope had become "one of the Great Air-Raid Shelters. [Trollope] presides over the eternal Munich of the heart, and Barchester has become one of the great never-never lands of our time."[9] Little wonder that, in 1971, Ruth apRoberts opened her magisterial study of Trollope with "There is something of a mystery in Anthony Trollope."[10]

Today, while Trollope still has a popular following, evidenced by the success of his dramatizations on television, and the regular appearance of adaptations on the radio, he is equally read for insights into how they lived then. We look to Trollope both to refute and to confirm—Janus-like—or otherwise complicate our view of the Victorian in his or her milieu. In the academy, the argument about Trollope today is about reading and interpretation as we interrogate the text from multiple perspectives. The concept "Trollope" now contains a range of different possibilities, possibilities that have been blown open over recent years. Today, Trollope is simultaneously the sociologist providing the raw material for every researcher's project, and the originator of a highly individualistic, esoteric, visionary take on issues such as colonialism, imperial power, the ethics of capitalism, liberalism, and gender. Thus he has become both the reflector of his times and a dissident voice subverting convention and inviting change.

This is never more evident than in the gender analysis of Trollope, for when we come to examine how the treatment of Trollope and gender has developed, we should start by recognizing that Trollope's treatment of gender issues has been seen as interesting for longer than gender studies have been seen as interesting. Kate Millett wrote *Sexual Politics* in 1970 and arguably changed forever the way that all disciplines across the humanities frame their critiques. In 1968, two years earlier than Millett, Robert Polhemus, in his originative work *The Changing World of Anthony Trollope*, used gender theory—before such theory was commonly articulated—to examine Trollope's conflicted feminism. In his chapter "Love and the Victorians: Thorns among the Roses," Polhemus explores a Trollope who exposes the "schizoid nature of love among the Victorians … He managed to get down the confusion and conflict about love which worried Victorian souls."[11] His extended examination of Glencora's impulsiveness, passion, and rebellion, and the way Trollope perceives these qualities as problematic within her stifling Victorian milieu, prepares the way for a generation of feminist analysis. As Polhemus says, "[Trollope] understood the feminine need for action, emotional outlet, and an

---

[8]   Virginia Woolf, "Phases of Fiction," *Collected Essays*, vol. 2. (London: Hogarth Press, 1966–77), p. 57.

[9]   V. S. Pritchett, *New Statesman*, (8 June 1946) p. 415; quoted by Stone, p. 130.

[10]   Ruth apRoberts, *Trollope, Artist and Moralist* (London: Chatto and Windus, 1971), p. 11.

[11]   Robert Polhemus, *The Changing World of Anthony Trollope* (Berkeley: University of California Press, 1968), p. 89 and p. 90.

Fig. 1.1   "Lady Ongar, are you not rather near the edge?" M. E. Edward's illustration for *The Claverings*, Chapter 27

end of intense repression."[12] He was followed in the 1970s by Ruth apRoberts, in her important article on *He Knew He Was Right* in the collection *The Victorian Experience: The Novelists*,[13] and by Juliet McMaster in *Trollope's Palliser Novels: Theme and Pattern*. While she posits no clear feminist agenda, McMaster's retelling of the plots and sub-plots foregrounds the action of his women.[14] Her new, insightful interpretation of this group of novels opened the way for more rigorous and specifically feminist critiques, and Deborah Denenholz Morse's was the first of these. In her exploration of Trollope's conflicted feminism, Morse shows that while Trollope sees the truth about women's lot, he also shrinks from endorsing the direct action of the activists of his time. She shows him, in spite of his insight, both as a man of his time in seeing marriage and children as a woman's best career, and as a man ahead of his time in admiring egalitarian marriage and portraying the disastrous effect on real men and women of conventional Victorian gender roles.[15] Morse was followed two years later by Jane Nardin's *He Knew She Was Right: The Independent Woman in the Novels of Anthony Trollope*. Mark Turner's recent review of Trollope criticism from 1987–2004 for the *Dickens Studies Annual* says of these two studies: "Taken together, Morse's and Nardin's books represent a particularly important moment for feminist readings of Trollope, which make his fiction complex and nuanced texts in which the role of women can never be taken for granted."[16] In 1990, Polhemus's illuminating chapter on Phineas in love in *Erotic Faith* complicated sexual politics with aesthetic and philosophical issues,[17] while Morse and Nardin's themes were reiterated by Margaret Markwick's 1997 study, *Trollope and Women*, which argued for a subversive Trollope, whose women are accorded space to achieve sexual expression and fulfillment. For increasingly, old truths about the Victorian woman have been examined and found wanting. Earlier feminist readings have now been superseded by works like Elizabeth Langland's *Nobody's Angels: Middle-Class Women and Domestic Ideology in Victorian Culture*, which re-evaluate and reconstruct the Victorian woman, whose greatest duty is no longer to suffer and be still.

By the mid-1990s, the field of feminist studies had broadened to the wider forum of gender studies encompassing the growing interest in forms of masculinity

---

[12] Polhemus p. 106.

[13] Ruth apRoberts, "Emily and Nora and Dorothy and Priscilla and Jemima and Carry," in Richard A. Levine (ed.), *The Victorian Experience: The Novelists* (Athens: Ohio University Press, 1976).

[14] Juliet McMaster *Trollope's Palliser Novels: Theme and Pattern* (London: Macmillan, 1978).

[15] Deborah Denenholz Morse *Women in Trollope's Palliser Novels* (Ann Arbor: UMI Research Press, 1987).

[16] Mark W. Turner "Trollope Studies: 1987–2004" *Dickens Studies Annual*, 37 (2006), p. 226.

[17] Robert Polhemus *Erotic Faith: Being in Love from Jane Austen to D. H. Lawrence* (Chicago: Chicago University Press, 1990).

and in gay and lesbian critiques. This is reflected in Turner's *Trollope and the Magazines: Gendered Issues in Mid-Victorian Britain* (2000). The previous decade had witnessed an explosion of examinations of masculinity (400 in ten years, according to Lynn Segal[18]), and Turner's study, which analyzes the masculinization of Trollope's prose when writing for periodicals targeting a male audience, has paved the way for further studies of Trollope's men, of which Markwick's 2007 study, *New Men in Trollope's Novels: Rewriting the Victorian Male*, is the latest.

The nature of our reading has also changed. Single-issue interpretation has less validity and is being displaced by multifaceted readings. We can see a clear illustration of this in Morse's work, where her original strong feminist voice is now tempered and coupled with the subtleties of new historicism and liberalism. This is evident in Morse's chapter in this volume, where she traces the influence of the Governor Eyre affair, following the 1865 Morant Bay rebellion, from the embedded themes of race and racism in *He Knew He Was Right*, and makes the firm connection between Trollope's construction of gender and his liberalism. Today's commentators look at the fine detail of the inlaid references to the political background, for no other writer of his age writes so compellingly in the present. Since the turn of the century, other critiques in Victorian studies—informed by discourses as various as race and queer theory and the history of liberalism—have merged with gender critiques to examine imperialism and its postcolonial legacy, the distortions wrought by capitalism and discriminatory legislation, liberal ideologies, racial codings and injustices, and marginalization. Commentators have increasingly turned to Trollope for their material in these fields, and again have discovered a conflicted Trollope, a Trollope who does not so much mirror the times he wrote in, as undermine the given view. Mary Jean Corbett is a cogent example of this, as she pins down the implicit references to Robert Peel's Encumbered Estates Acts to adduce Trollope's stance on Irish reform in the Trollope chapter of *Allegories of Union in Irish and English Writing 1790–1870*. Indeed, this study, published in 2000, is the exemplar for so much of the work being undertaken on Trollope in the twenty-first century, where the keynote Trollope studies are to be found in very focused short essays in books with broader concerns in these fields. Thus Lauren Goodlad devotes one chapter of *Victorian Literature and the Victorian State* (2003), her book-length study of liberalism, legislation, and political reform, to Trollope's representations of the Civil Service. Corbett's influential study is the direct inspiration for *Victorian Literature and Culture*'s issue dedicated to Victorian Ireland (March 2004). It is significant that of the 13 Irish essays published, 4 are on Trollope's use of Irish tropes. Additionally, Corbett's identification of Trollope with post-colonial theorizing signalled his potential for broader studies in this field.[19] Lisa Surridge's argument in *Bleak Houses* on the legal underpinnings of

---

[18]   Lynn Segal, *Slow Motion: Changing Masculinities, Changing Men*, 1990 (London: Virago Press, 1997), p. xii.

[19]   Though in this field, as in so many others, it is important to notice that Polhemus was there first, in 1968. His chapter on *The Macdermots of Ballycloran* examines at length

domestic violence in *He Knew He Was Right*, Elsie Michie's work on the gender of capitalism, Kathy Psomiades's work on aesthetics, and Jenny Bourne Taylor's analysis on nineteenth-century psychology equally inform the construction of so much of the recent work on Trollope. This is all cogently demonstrated by William A. Cohen's chapter, "Trollope's Trollop," in *Sex Scandals: The Private Parts of Victorian Fiction* (1996), in which Cohen looks at the "economy of gender relations" in *The Eustace Diamonds*, and more recently, in Mark Forrester's essay on gender anxiety in Trollope in *Imperial Desire: Dissonant Sexualities and Colonial Literature* (2003).

Amanda Anderson's recent essay, "Trollope's Modernity," perhaps epitomizes these shifts in reading and interpretation. In this essay, she uses Lionel Trilling's aesthetic explorations in *Sincerity and Authenticity* to understand Trollope's codes of honor. By examining Trollope's concepts of honesty in *Barchester Towers* and *The Way We Live Now*, she uncovers the limitations of Trilling's thesis—that it reduces, rather than enlarges the Victorian moral ethos. She detects in Trilling a sense that "the Victorians lack the spirit of freedom to relinquish sincerity and the idea of being true to oneself in the society that underwrites it." In demonstrating that Trollope fails to fit into the generalizations of Victorian literature that Trilling identifies in Matthew Arnold, Charles Dickens, and George Eliot, Anderson subtly manages simultaneously to use Trollope to critique Trilling's application of liberal humanism, and Trilling to critique Trollope, again uncovering a conflicted Trollope. As she concludes: "There is a genuine tension between his liberalism and his persistent valuing of traditional forms of life in the face of what for him are the negative dimensions of modernity," a twenty-first century articulation of the contradictions in Trollope identified earlier in feminist studies, and now drawn out as a major theme in decoding Victorian liberal humanism and its relevance to political processes today.[20]

The Politics of Gender, based on ideas emerging from the Exeter Trollope conference in July of 2006, recognizes Trollope's importance as source material for scholars working in diverse fields of cultural study. Trollope, more than any of his fellow novelists—such as the Brontës, Dickens, Collins, Hardy, even Gaskell and Eliot—is being studied as source material by commentators from such wide and dissimilar disciplines, as well as by literary critics. This book draws together the threads of this very diversity, and finds unity in the themes. Thus, imperial and postcolonial studies are examined from economic, cultural, aesthetic, and demographic angles; gender-sensitive analysis exposes Trollope's own critique of the influence of capitalism; Queer Studies, the Law, new constructions of archetypes, and re-critiquing of classical feminism address Trollope and sexuality; and Victorian understandings of psychology bring new approaches to narrative theory.

---

the interaction between the English colonial rulers and a demoralised peasantry. "The Macdermots," he says "is one of the most powerful indictments of colonialism written in the nineteenth century" (Polhemus, p. 16–17).

[20]   Amanda Anderson, "Trollope's Modernity," *ELH*, 74.3 (Autumn 2007), pp. 509–34.

Alongside contributions by established Trollopians, such as Markwick, Morse, Polhemus, and Skilton, and by leading cultural historians, such as Bourne Taylor, Corbett, Gagnier, Goodlad, Michie, Psomiades, and Vlasopolos, are essays by young emerging scholars—Amarnick, Blythe, Hensley, and Noble—the next generation of Trollopians. It is also significant to notice how often these commentators turn to lesser-known texts to locate their theses. Thus while in this volume you will find analyses of the cornerstone works, such as the Palliser novels, the Barchester chronicles, *He Knew He Was Right*, and *The Way We Live Now*, there are interesting explorations of *Lady Anna*, *Ralph the Heir*, *Castle Richmond*, and *Is He Popenjoy?*. Our contributors also make wide use of Trollope's travel writings and his short stories, both very under-explored territory. And Helen Lucy Blythe locates her examination of colonial aspiration in that unclassifiable tract, *The New-Zealander*.

The first part, on Sex, Power, and Subversion, opens with a new essay from Robert Polhemus, who applies the thesis of his great work *Lot's Daughters* to Trollope, both as a man and as a writer. To this end, Polhemus takes two of Trollope's short stories, one early, one late, and examines them in the light of Trollope's deep attachment in the last 20 years of his life to the young and beautiful American feminist journalist and lecturer, Kate Field. This is followed by Kathy Alexis Psomiades's examination of Victorian theories of anthropology set against Carole Pateman's classic feminist critique of liberalism. Her analysis of *He Knew He Was Right* opens up the subtleties of the impact of the Second Reform Act on Trollope's intuition of human society and culture. Jenny Bourne Taylor considers Trollope's relish for the ambiguities of the legal boundaries between legitimate and illegitimate birth in his late fiction, examining *Ralph the Heir*, *Lady Anna*, and *Is He Popenjoy?* in the light of contemporaneous litigation and George Eliot's *Felix Holt*. Margaret Markwick seeks to establish a liberal Trollope, open-minded and tolerant of difference, in her exploration of the indicators of homoeroticism in the novels.

Part 2, Imperial Gender, is a group of essays by Deborah Denenholz Morse, Lauren Goodlad, Mary Jean Corbett, and Helen Lucy Blythe examining Trollope's views on colonial development and the West Indies, India, Ireland, and the Antipodes, respectively. Morse, in her essay, which could well be read alongside Psomiades', posits a Trollope who expounds a strong critique of British imperialism. She identifies Trollope rethinking his ideas of Empire following Governor Eyre's massacre of Jamaican rebels, and offers a close reading of *He Knew He Was Right* to repudiate the Victorian legal framework of masculine control of the female body. Goodlad's essay is a multifaceted and virtuoso exploration of the nexus of several discourses: the histories of the annexing of Indian states after the dissolution of the East-India company in 1858; the treatment of Indian Princes such as Prince Azeem Jah at the hands of the British legislature; Trollope's own fictionalized Indian Prince, the Sawab of Mygawb; and the commodification of Lucy Morris. This is followed by Blythe's study of "Catherine Carmichael," a late and little-known short story set in New Zealand. She locates her analysis of the gendered aesthetics of the new colony in the context of that other little-known text, Trollope's Carlyean discourse, *The New-Zealander*, written in 1857, though not published till 1972, where he postulates a Britain of the future, in ruins, visited by the young, beautiful glitterati from New Zealand, a trope he borrowed from Macaulay.

This leads to a third section, Genderized Economics, which examines the connections between money, capitalism, and class, with essays by Nathan Hensley, Elsie Michie, and Chris Noble. Hensley tracks the gendering of speculative wealth from Defoe's "Lady Credit" to current Western foreign and economic policy, and finds Trollope critiquing their value judgments in *The Way We Live Now* with great pertinence for the state of international affairs today. Michie's researches have uncovered the originals for Martha Dunstable's Oil of Lebanon fortune; she exposes the hype of Holloway's pills, and the light it throws on Miss Dunstable's locus as a touchstone of honesty. This is followed by Chris Noble's examination of financial independence and widowhood. This essay unpicks Trollope's masculinization of married women without husbands through four very different widows, Eleanor Bold in *Barchester Towers*, Mrs Greenow in *Can You Forgive Her?*, Emily Warton in *The Prime Minister*, and Madame Max in the Palliser Novels.

The final section, the Gender of Narrative Construction, has essays by Steven Amarnick, David Skilton, and Anca Vlasopolos. Amarnick compares the manuscript of *The Duke's Children* with the published version to uncover an original where the primary plot is the emerging manhood of the young Lord Silverbridge, and which is a longer, discursive novel with intriguing shifts in Trollope's conceptualization of masculinity. Skilton, reaching back to his 1973 *Trollope and his Contemporaries*, gives an historical examination of the Victorian process of reading, and uses George Lewes's and R. H. Hutton's writings on realism and the ideal to show Trollope's innovation in breaking down the separation between the characterization of men and the historical conventions of the analysis of women. Vlasopolos examines the writing of two pieces of Trollope's shorter fiction, "Mary Gresley" and *Sir Harry Hotspur of Humblethwaite*, to expose a darker Trollope critiquing the cultural Victorian "Law of the father," and the fatal results of the pursuit of this feminine ideal. Regenia Gagnier's Afterword examines the cultural differences between readings of Trollope in Britain and Europe, and in North America. She rereads *The Prime Minister* from Ferdinand Lopez's point of view, and considers his treatment at the hands of the British upper classes in the context of her work on philosophical anthropology, to produce a radical and illuminating analysis of this great novel of liberal politics.

Looking back on the history of Trollope criticism, it is probably true to say that each generation finds in Trollope the Trollope they wish to find. In the twenty-first century we recognize that he is not merely holding a mirror to his times; he is one who comments on that reflection, and advances personal, often controversial, and sometimes subversive ideas about his times that resonate with twenty-first century liberal ideologies.

PART 1
Sex, Power And Subversion

Chapter 1
(A)genda Trouble and the Lot Complex: Older Men-Younger Women Relationships in Trollope

Robert M. Polhemus

Trollope was fascinated by the drive for female agency, voice, and authority in his changing world. He offers a provocative, highly nuanced, complex, and telling engagement with gender in his fiction and life, no matter how disturbingly ambivalent and even wrong-headed that wide-ranging engagement can sometimes appear. I want to look at Trollope and gender in relation to what I call the Lot complex, the ongoing human drama of varying desires and mutual attraction between young females and older males. My subject is older men/younger women relationships and how they come to figure in some of his most interesting and best work.

I

In *Lot's Daughters* (2005), I identify and analyze this Lot complex and try to make clear how, as it develops in history, it pervades, generates, and illuminates life, language, literature, and art.[1] I didn't discuss Trollope there, but I want to now: he and the Lot complex fit together beautifully. As I read the Lot syndrome in the Victorian and modern world, it represents, in various ways, the drive or compulsion, in an age of growing female emancipation, to preserve, adapt, and/ or expropriate the traditional paternal power to sustain, regenerate, define, and transmit life and civilization—the patriarchal seed of culture. And that's what I see in Trollope. His fiction pulses with the sometimes muted but insistent rhythm of women's quest for authority.

Let me begin with a short reprise of the extraordinary Genesis 19 description of the Lot family's rescue from God's fire-and-brimstone obliteration of Sodom and the aftermath featuring Lot, his wife, and, most notably, his daughters: Lot, the equivocal, God-fearing, tippling, unwittingly incestuous survivor of the Sodom holocaust and nephew of Abraham, is the patriarch in the closet, so to speak (more precisely, in the cave). A good but flawed man, in desperate crisis he offered up his virgin daughters as a bribe to the vicious Sodomites if they would spare the

---

[1] *Lot's Daughters: Sex, Redemption and Women's Quest for Authority* (Stanford: Stanford University Press 2005).

designated agents of God who had come to judge the sinfulness of the cities of the plain. Those angels, however, reveal themselves, blind the wicked men and save the Lot family from destruction by whisking them out of town. But then Lot's wife famously disobeys God's order not to look back and gets zapped into a pillar of salt. Lot's daughters think their father is the only man left, and together they plot to take responsibility to "preserve seed of our father" (Gen. 19:32) and repopulate their world. Right or wrong, the decision of these women to act—to assume agency—for the sake of humanity's future has momentous implications. They conspire to get him drunk to blot out the incest taboo and arouse his lust; then, in a dark cave, they lie with him on successive nights and get pregnant.

The incestuous seed of Lot, preserved through the elder daughter's action, is Moab, and that means her progeny eventually includes not only the marginal races of Israel's foes, but also the virtuous Moabite daughter Ruth, whose marriage to the Israelite Boaz legitimizes and redeems the older man/younger woman bond and issues in her glorious great-grandson King David, David's genealogical line, and eventually—depending on your perspective—Jesus Christ, the Word incarnate, and thus Christianity itself.

Out of this lore comes *the Lot complex*, a dynamic configuration of wishes, sexual fantasies, and symbolic imagery that has worked to form generational relationships and structure personality, gender history, religious faith, social organization, and art.[2] The patterns and figures of the *Lot* story can form an explanatory grid for reading familial and gender relationships—and thus for reading Trollope. What you can see figured in this Scripture are desires that shake the world: the desire of women to control the actions of men to whom they traditionally have been subject; the desire of both men and women to project on others wishes, thoughts, and deeds of their own that might cause guilt; the desire of men to preserve themselves, conquer time, remain potent, and keep on wooing the future.

Trollope wrote so much that only one in a million readers of English fiction can take it in and none in a million can remember it all. To write about him is to realize how much inevitably must be left out or qualified. I mean to illuminate the main general features of the Lot complex that I see driving his creative life—those crucial development of older men/younger women interactions and needs that mark his novels—but to do so, I must let parts stand for the whole: I'm going to focus on two of his short tales "A Ride Across Palestine" and "Mary Gresley" and also on Kate Field, the real young woman, who was the principal "Lot's daughter" in his imagination.[3] Those stories and that young woman in his life have great

---

[2]   By the term "complex," I mean a condensation in human psychology of personal and social experience, images, drives, motives, and impulses that can be seen both to form and represent a pattern.

[3]   Another such figure, in the last years of his life, was his niece Florence Bland, who is almost surely the inspiration for Mary Laurie in the very fine short novel, *An Old Man's Love* (1884).

symbolic, typological force in showing and stressing what came to matter so profoundly in his fiction.

II

Trollope's "A Ride across Palestine" stands as his literal version of a Lot-country, Lot complex story.[4]   Part travelogue, part shaky pilgrims' progress in gender relations and sexual candor, it opens with the narrator, a middle-aged, practical Englishman, touring "the Holy Land" alone (Trollope, when he made the same journey in 1858, was 43). Traveling *incognito*—"if the reader will allow me, I will call myself Jones" (p. 231),—the narrator says that he was facing, both literally and figuratively, "the wild unlimited sands, the desolation of the Dead Sea, the rushing waters of Jordan, the outlines of the mountains of Moab" (p. 230). That landscape, steeped in the tormented history of faith, he says "was one which did lead to many thoughts" (p. 259).

A good-looking, young gentleman, hearing that "Jones" was traveling to the Dead Sea" and identifying himself only as "John Smith," asks to travel with him: "He seemed to be very bashful and half ashamed of what he was doing" (p. 232). Though normally standoffish with men, "Jones" confesses "I was attracted by John Smith" (p. 232). "It looked as though he had determined to hook himself on to me" (p. 244).

In a key exchange, Smith asks the older man if he's married, and the narrator equivocates: "Now the fact is that I am a married man with a family; but I am not much given to talk to strangers about my domestic concerns.... 'No,' said I" (p. 245). (Trollope's biographer Victoria Glendinning suggests that he liked to flirt on his many, far-flung travels, and did not always admit to being married.[5]) Smith later asks Jones, "Do you dislike women?" "No, by Jove! I am never really happy unless one is near me—or more than one"(p. 262).

Trollope describes their journey to the Dead Sea (the Sea of Lot), featuring the older man's solicitous care for appealing youth. "I would have done almost anything in reason for his comfort" (p. 247). When they read the Dead Sea, Jones goes swimming and tries to get Smith to join him. "'The Dead Sea waters are noisome,' Smith refuses, and says metaphorically, 'and I have been drinking of them by long draughts'" (p. 260). I find the symbolism of the narrator's post-marital plunge into the Sea of Lot revealing, to say the least. You can feel the splashes of that immersion again and again in Trollope's fiction to come.

The two enjoy an easy camaraderie, and Jones teaches the tenderfoot Smith about traveling through rough country. At one point, the narrator falls asleep

---

[4]   *Tales of All Countries*, Second Series (New York: Arno Press, 1981), pp. 228–86. The tale was first published under the title "The Banks of the Jordan" in *The London Review* in January, 1861.

[5]   Victoria Glendinning, *Anthony Trollope* (New York: Knopf, 1993), p. 238.

with his head resting on the young man's leg: "He then put out his hand to me, and I pressed it.... I thoroughly hate an effeminate man; but, in spite of a certain womanly softness about this fellow, I could not hate him." (p. 261–2). On the way to Jaffa, Smith suddenly disappears when he sees a stern old man coming towards them. This patriarchal figure questions Jones, but then moves off. Smith, frightened to death, comes out of hiding and tells Jones that the man's after him. Then comes another key passage: "So I sat ... and talked to him ... and I again felt that I loved him. Yes loved him!... I did love him.... I felt a delight in serving him ... though I was almost old enough to be his father." (p. 272).

In Jaffa, before the youth can get away, the rigid old man shows up again. He turns out to be Sir William Weston, Smith's "odious" guardian and uncle, "unforgiving towards all offenses" (p. 274), and he seizes *her*, because the youth, it turns out, is really Julia Weston, a lovely young *woman*. When the uncle charges the narrator with "eloping with his niece", Jones is flabbergasted (like Lot waking up in the cave?). "I traveled here with a companion dressed as a man; and I believed him to be what he seemed" (p. 277). But there's more: the guardian rages at the girl, "What! He has gone off with you; he has traveled through the country with you, hiding you.... He shall give me his promise that he will make you his wife" (p. 280). And Trollope says that Julia would have agreed, "without dismay" (p. 280). The narrator equivocates and claims he's innocent—hasn't done anything wrong. The uncle talks of a dowry, but "Jones" then has to tell them that he can't marry the girl because he has a wife: "I deeply regretted that I had thoughtlessly stated to her that I was an unmarried man." (p. 279).

Oops! Or as the Airline Ad famously says, "Wanna get away?" This story, then, partakes of a *Lottish* old-wives' tale. Just before he wrote it, Trollope opined in *Framley Parsonage* (1861), "I will not say that the happiness of marriage is like Dead Sea fruit—an apple, which, when eaten, turns to bitter ashes in the mouth.... Nevertheless, is it not the fact?" Praising Julia Weston's attractions, "personal and mental, I bowed to my fair friend, who looked at me ... with sad beseeching eyes. I confess that the mistress of my bosom (his *wife*, that is, left behind somewhere, no doubt a pillar of the community, of whom he tells us nothing), had she known my thoughts at that one moment, might have cause for anger" (p. 282). Jones then becomes defensive about lying: "It seemed as though I had cruelly deceived her, but," says he, "I was the one really deceived" (p. 283).

The tale ends without any agenda for the young woman—no reference to her future whatsoever—but we do get, in the narrator's rueful last words, a new seed of moral consciousness: "I had been deceived, and had failed to discover the deceit, even though the deceiver had perhaps wished that I should do so. For that blindness I have never forgiven myself" (p. 286). That sounds like the rationale of a modern Lot—and it is. The tale ends up focused on *his* mind—*his* future—but what that guilty gender blindness might or should lead to, the narrator doesn't say.

The story ends, then, with the puzzling aimlessness of this young woman's shadowy agency. It's incomplete. The pun in my title, ("A)genda trouble", might sound a bit glib and stale—maybe it is—but I mean it to be precise and serious.

I want to stress a link in Trollope's work as whole between "gender troubles" and the tough challenge of finding a suitable, flexible, hopeful agenda for young women especially, but for older men too in their relationship to those women— agenda meaning "things to be done, items to be considered, vocational concerns and opportunities to be addressed and acted upon, and plans for a successful future to be carried out."

What makes it such an important Trollope Lot story is the quick, clear way it sets before you the dynamic tension between *he-knew-he-was-right* and *can-you-forgive-her?* (to adapt his famous titles). It moves, that is, from oppressive surety to uneasy wonder, from the old patriarchy to the edge of a surprising new daughterland with its fragile, inconclusive quest for opportunity and freedom and its painful, confusing conflicts over shifting gender definition and sexual desire. You have here both a realistic and symbolic narrative in which a young woman takes action by trying to gain the advantages of male identity so that she can escape from *he-knew-he-was-right*—"he" being, the realm of the eponymous old patriarch Weston)—only to land indecisively in *can-you-forgive-her*, an ambiguous, psychological and cultural condition—potentially progressive, but still part of a man's world where success and happiness for women depend upon their power to both seduce aging male desire and sublimate it into favorable patronization. That kind of female odyssey is common in Trollope's fiction, but, as in this story, it can be a dangerous affair.[6] Nevertheless, from the time he wrote "A Ride Across Palestine" (July 1860) to the end of his life the idea of deep, erotically tinged, potentially benevolent, hard-to-categorize relationships between older men and younger women fed his art.

III

In the Palestine "Ride," the older man enjoys the historical continuity that he finds visiting biblical sites, despite all the present-day folly and trouble he finds there, but the young woman wants to get away as fast as she can from space so tainted by patriarchal irresponsibility. That difference matters. Like *The Warden* (1855) and *Barchester Towers* (1857), this story, far removed as it seems from those novels, takes place in the changing territory of faith—its setting permeated and defined by religious associations. That fact can stand as a trope for the historical setting not only for Trollope's early, break-through Barsetshire fiction, but for all his work — a changing world shaped by its secularizing, kinetic heritage of faith and women's hope for respect and authority. If religion is, as William James said, "the belief that there is an unseen order, and that our supreme good lies in adjusting ourselves

---

[6]   Trollope's friends Thackeray and George Smith, editors for *Cornhill*, turned the story down because of its racy sexual implications, and when it appeared in the *London Review*, it *did* draw a shower of outraged letters. See N. John Hall, *Trollope: A Biography* (Oxford: Clarendon Press, 1991), p. 207.

harmoniously thereto," and if Lot's daughters showed the will to act on behalf of a divine order as they saw it in chaotic circumstances of male arrogance, failure and weakness, then it's easy to see the overriding historical reason for the Lot complex gender tensions in Trollope's novels set in the milieu of institutionalized faith.

As a gender allegory, the early Barset world is both autobiographical *and* sociological. In general its women are stronger and sharper than its men. Its authority is nominally patriarchal, but a Lot complex hangs over Barchester (the romantic hero Arabin, for example, is saved by two of the novel's daughter-figures, Eleanor Bold and Madeline Vesey-Neroni; and you can argue that the strongest love story in all of the Barset chronicles is between Eleanor and her mild father, Mr. Harding). In *Barchester Towers* nobody has a good word for the ambitious Mrs. Proudie, but, when you come down to it, why indeed shouldn't *a woman* be Bishop of Barchester instead of her weak, incompetent husband of little faith? Trollope's remark about Arabin, the most intellectual and serious clerical figure in *Barchester Towers*, provides the basis of an *apologia* for Mrs. Proudie: "He liked to have near him that which was pretty and amusing, but women generally were little more to him than children. He talked to them without putting out all his powers, and listened to them without any idea that what he should hear from them could either actuate his conduct or influence his opinion." At the heart of the Lot complex hypothesis is a sense—an image—of the primal importance and model of the father-daughter tie, and generalizing, you could say that power relations between the sexes until very recent times would best be symbolized, not by a mother-son relationship, nor a husband-wife relationship, but by the synecdoche of a father-daughter relationship. Nowhere has that been more evident than in the paternalistic organization of religion. Women would seem especially well suited by history and experience for high pastoral calling, and yet no vocation has been more resistant than the world's collective priesthood to letting women in. A case could be made that, though she's dictatorial, the world needs a Mrs. Proudie as Archbishop, Pope, or *Duce*, to make the trains of progress and women's liberation run on time.

In Trollope's family life, of course, the patriarchal structure broke down. His mother was stronger, more energetic, more joyous, and more capable than his father, and that was crucial in shaping Anthony's character and imagination. His neurotic father, though intellectually gifted, could not cope with the world, and Frances, his wife, had to take over. She left 12-year-old Anthony behind in the spirit-blacking factory of his father's fecklessness, went to America for four years, and came back to become a famous writer of the snidely derogatory, hugely popular, *Domestic Manners of the Americans* (1832). But her American trip was an emotional disaster for him. It was a big reason why his (a)genda problem with the Lot complex germinated and his conflicted views about proper roles for females took shape. He saw women needed vocational opportunity, but the exercise of such agency could hurt. They had to have their own agendas, but carrying them out might mean painful trauma for boys. The mother who didn't pay enough attention to you, neglected you, and, turning hard, left you behind

Fig. 1.2   Photograph of Kate Field, taken by Elihu Vedder in Florence, where she and Trollope met, in 1860, the year of their meeting.

might have to be left behind herself, consigned to the past for the sake of a future. In his autobiography, he tells you that his mother was a successful, admirable human being of courage, but he also says that she was anything but clear-sighted (especially about America explicitly and himself, implicitly, who, he knew, didn't come close to being her favorite child). He calls her an untrustworthy narrator, inaccurate in describing manners, morals, and fact, and intimates that she, whose genes obviously drove his astonishing energy and accomplishment, had a shoddy literary vision. No wonder that Trollope was hopelessly split on what came to be known as the Woman Question, but that split drove him to open up his fiction and imagine and represent contradictions and tensions in female characters that would shape modern psychological and communal reality.

IV

Allegorically, for Trollope studies, what the strange Palestinian tale of an aging man's weird baptism in the tainted sea of Lot can stand for is his coming emotional intimacy with Kate Field—Mary Katherine Feemie Field to be precise—the young, charismatic American woman barely half his age who would have a major effect on his imagination and art. His fictional Dead Sea pilgrimage shows how ready and willing he was to find her and get involved. Hardly two months after he finished a draft of the story, he met her in 1860 at his brother Tom's in Florence, where she had come to study classical music and voice. He befriended her, fell in love with her, mentored her, played the tough critic, wrote to her, visited her on his trip to America (1861–62), and found the basis for a lasting friendship all within the year of its publication. Field, an American paragon of domestic manners, intelligence, passion for the arts and idealistic feminism —"the American Beauty" to give her the epithet Trollope uses for Isabel Boncassen in *The Duke's Children*—was a Lot's daughter who drove his creativity and helped to preserve his literary seed over the last and most productive decades of his life.

Trollope had what the world calls a happy marriage. In 1844, at age 29, he married Rose Heseltine, a loyal, devoted, good partner and person who gave him the emotional security and support he needed to move successfully from a miserable youth into an amazingly productive middle age. But though she helped him immensely, she became for him a woman without flash. "My marriage," he says in truly deflationary prose, "was like the marriage of other people and of no special interest to any one except my wife and me."[7] Trollope was essentially a middle-aged novelist. His first commercially successful work was written by a man of 40, and by that time his feeling for his wife had undergone Lot's sea-change. An aging man (45–67) fascinated by all kinds of women, especially younger ones, and particularly by Field, produced the masterful output of fiction from 1860 to his death in 1882.

Relating an artist's life and work is a notoriously tricky thing to do and must always be hypothetical. Still, thinking about how, why, and what autobiographical signs appear in a novelist's work can help you see what generates it, how it functions, what needs it fulfills, how it touches and moves people, and why they might care about it at all. Whatever you think of biographical criticism and its psychological speculations, an autobiographical imperative has surely driven most literary art in modern times. Writers' projections of their own desires, conflicts, and obsessions usually give their work its deepest interest and meaning. And, in

---

[7]   *An Autobiography*, 1883 (London: Penguin, 1996), p. 50.

turn, that art can give shape to the direction of their actual lives and perceptions. Novelists may have love affairs and/or write about having love affairs, but both the love and the story come out of real, fusing mental processes. The Palestine "Ride" concludes by showing how susceptible Trollope or any man his age might be to a beautiful, bold young woman who needs him.

After Trollope met and fell for Kate Field, he was much more interested in creating broadly feminist, strong-minded, witty, sharp young women who want to attach themselves to the knowledge and power of older men. Victoria Glendinning says shrewdly of Trollope, "In later life he met intelligent, exciting young women whose ideas of themselves did not include clinging or doglike wifeliness, and with fascination he began to write them into his novels. At the time he married Rose, he could not have entered with such acuity and sympathy into the hearts of such women" (p. 149). Field was the ace of those hearts. With the low-key, understated nature of his *Autobiography* in mind—especially those cool passages about his mother and his wife—I want to look at Trollope's well-known tribute to Kate Field, and I want to de-familiarize it:

> There is an American woman, of whom not to speak in a work purporting to be a memoir of my own life would be to omit all allusion to one of the chief pleasures, which has graced my later years. In the last fifteen years she has been, out of my own family, my most chosen friend. *She is a ray of light to me from which I can always strike a spark by thinking of her* (emphasis mine). I do not know that I should please her or do good to any one by naming her. But not to allude to her in these pages would amount almost to a falsehood. I could not write truly of myself without saying that such a friend has been vouchsafed to me. I trust she may live to read the words I have now written, and to wipe away a tear as she thinks of my feeling while I write them" (p. 201).

At the end of the nineteenth century, Field's adoring biographer Lilian Whiting wrote "Of all the expressions ever made regarding Kate Field in life or in death, this sentence of Mr. Trollope's stands out, '*She is a ray of light to me from which I can always strike a spark by thinking of her.*'"[8] It's a wonderful thing to say about her, and, written to appear posthumously, a surprisingly straightforward avowal by a married man of that inevitably problematic "L-word", *love*. It's also a very personal word to her—an "inside" message, even—because as a 15-year-old she had written the following sentence to her beloved father and later no doubt shared it with Trollope, her ultimate writing teacher and confidante (as she so obviously did with so much of the language of her journals and letters that Whiting used to make her *Record*): "You don't know how I long to get hold of some one who will *strike fire....*"[9] Trollope's *ray-of-light* sentence also describes—epitomizes—just

---

[8]   Lilian Whiting, *Kate Field: A Record* (Boston: Little, Brown, and Company, 1900), p. 573.

[9]   Whiting, *Kate Field*, p. 309.

how she functioned as a muse for him. Her remembered brightness could set off spark after spark. Says the disingenuous Trollope a few pages after that *sparkplug* for Field "If the rustle of a woman's petticoat has ever stirred my blood … of what matter is that to a reader?" (p. 232). But it matters a lot.

Kate Field was a multitalented, magnetic figure. She sang well, wrote engagingly, acted, followed the arts, and pursued intellectual interests in many fields. Eventually she made for herself a career as a "pioneering" woman journalist and a public lecturer, when lecturing was a lucrative profession in America for star performers. And yet, overall, her life lacked the focus of true vocation that greatness demands—agenda mastery. She began as a consummate Daddy's girl. Whiting says, "She was very fond of the companionship and comradeship of men."[10] Older men just went gaga over her, including such literary lions—besides Anthony—as his brother Thomas Trollope, Walter Savage Landor, Robert Browning, George Henry Lewes, Henry James (both Sr. and Jr.!), Charles Dickens, Whitelaw Reid— and on and on. But women also—famous ones, like Elizabeth Barrett Browning and George Eliot—praised and liked her. In "Miss Ophelia Gledd," the 1863 short story, inspired by Kate and a sleigh ride Trollope took with her in Boston, the narrator, describing his snowy trip with Ophelia, gets at the kind of aura Field had: "[I] could not but think how nice it would be to drive on and on, so that nobody would ever catch us. There was a sense of companionship about her in which no woman that I have ever known excelled her. She had a way of adapting herself to the friend of the moment which was beyond anything winning."[11]

From Whiting's 1899 *Kate Field: A Record*, with its scads of journal entries, it's easy to see why: Kate is funny and frank: told that uniquely talented, rich, intriguing Henry James Jr. was enthusiastic about her, she writes succinctly, "Barkis is willin'"; meeting George Eliot, she notes: "Miss Evans, or Mrs. Lewes, is a woman whose whole face is of the horse make; but there's something interesting about her.… I liked Mr. Lewes, too, who is a very ugly man."[12] She can be naïvely girlish and vain: "People think me so full of passion and truth"[13]; but more typically, she's responsible, honest, and self-deprecating: "My poor mother's eyes failed … she cannot work. It is my duty to do my best.… But have I any talent? I fear not."[14] She has strong feminist sentiments: "Well, they pretend to say that God intended women to be just what they are. I say that He did not, that men have made women what they are, and if they attribute their doings to the Almighty, they lie."[15] She also had the kind of crap-detecting common sense that appealed to Trollope and to Dickens too: "I went to [Bronson] Alcott's Conversation on *Theism and Christianity*, my first experience in these unique entertainments. Mr.

---

[10]   Whiting, *Kate Field*, p. 190.
[11]   "Miss Ophelia Gledd," *Tales of All Countries*, Third Series (New York: Arno Press, 1981).
[12]   Whiting, *Kate Field*, p. 101.
[13]   Ibid., p. 96.
[14]   Ibid., p. 67.
[15]   Ibid., p. 69.

Alcott is to me incomprehensible.... Carlyle calls him the acorn-eating Alcott".[16] She's a candid social star with a big, sweet, ego: "Henry James Jr. remained until night. We had a good long talk about everything under the sun and some things above it. I lay on the sofa rather exhausted. When I'm excited I do not realize how much vitality I throw off."[17]

Kate Field was a great source for the glorious fictional projections of "the American girl" you can read in *He Knew He Was Right*'s Caroline Spalding, *The Duke's Children*'s Isabel Boncassen, and in Henry James's own famous Isabel in *A Portrait of a Lady*. She was a formidable soul. A daft anecdote in the spiritualist Whiting's little book of tribute to Kate, shows the kind of impression she could make. After Field died in 1896 in Hawaii, Whiting says she was visited in her Paris quarters by Kate. They communicated, and Whiting, later working with a medium who wrote down messages from "the other side," "entreated" Kate, "tell me of your life in the new conditions."[18]

"It's very simple and natural.... I read and study and cultivate my mind. I hear beautiful music and noble lectures, and enjoy art in the drama and paintings." And she adds, showing she's in a heaven all orators and professors might envy, "I lecture, myself, and my audiences are far more intelligent and clear-headed than they were in your world," a fate devoutly to be wished.[19]

Both her parents were theater people in St. Louis, but her beloved actor-writer-father died when Kate was 17. Devastated, she confided in her journal how much "the death of the only one whom I adored" haunted her.[20] And later she added, "where shall I find a second father? Oh how I need his counsel."[21] At 19, the girl writes, "I sometimes think it is a great misfortune that I was not born a boy, for then any and every employment would be open to me, and I could gain sufficient to support my mother and self."[22] "Oh if I were a man! There is not an ambition, a desire, a feeling, a thought, an impulse, an instinct that I am not obliged to crush. And why? Because I am a woman, and a woman must content herself with indoor life, with sewing, and babies." In Trollope's *He Knew Hew Was Right*, his novel in which the influence of Kate Field seems most explicit, he gives his admirable heroine Nora Rowley those sentiments precisely: "The lot of a woman, as she often told herself, was wretched, unfortunate, almost degrading. For a woman such as herself there was no path open to her energy, other than that of getting a husband.

---

[16]   Ibid., p. 202.

[17]   Ibid., p. 211.

[18]   Lilian Whiting, *After Her Death: The Story of a Summer* (London: Gay and Bird, 1904), p. 151.

[19]   Whiting, *After Her Death*, p. 153.

[20]   Whiting, *Kate Field*, p. 66.

[21]   Ibid., p. 75.

[22]   Whiting, *Kate Field*, p. 66.

Fig. 1.3   Kate Field, painted by Frank Millet in 1881.

Nora Rowley thought of all this until she was almost sick of the prospect of her life."[23]

How well Trollope and Field knew each other, how often they were together, what such times were like, what happened to her letters to him and missing journal entries, how intimate they were are still matters of conjecture. Speculation that he fell deeply, but innocently in love with her—intimate friendship, cross-generational soul-mating, but no sex—is most likely true. His conclusion to a July 1868 letter to her when they had been much together that spring in America conveys the overall nature of Trollope's connection to her: "Give my kindest love to your mother. The same to yourself dear Kate ... with a kiss that shall be semi-paternal—one third-brotherly, and as regards the [small] remainder, as loving as you please." It's diplomatic; it's neither improper, nor scary, but it implies anxious, nuanced, barely suppressed erotic feeling.

What counts most about that relationship can be seen in Trollope's work and the evolution of the Lot complex in Victorian times. In his letters (hers to him are missing), he criticizes her work frankly, doesn't pull his punches, gives her strong support, keeps patronizingly telling her to get a husband, but seems assured that their relationship thrives on candor. It seems so strong it doesn't depend on flattery on either side. It's easy to see how much at ease they were with one another. Trollope's passionate purple passage of posthumous prose did not come out of hot air. Gary Scharnhorst argues that "Field deliberately concealed the precise nature of her relationship with Trollope even after his death .... Their intimacy was sacrosanct and confidential, never to be publicized or even divulged."[24]

Trollope did not try to transpose Kate directly into his work (except maybe in "Miss Ophelia Gledd") or create characters just like her, but he used her continually. Neither *Phineas Finn*'s Madame Max Goesler, glamorous young widow of a rich, old, Jewish banker and the social-climbing adored-one of the elderly Duke of Omnium, nor Lady Mason, *Orley Farm*'s graceful siren for Victorian senior citizens superficially resembles the American girl their author was so interested in the years he invented them. But Field surely got him thinking about the force of attraction between older men and younger women and what it could do—and Trollope's way of deep thinking was through his fiction.

Kate confided in him, and no doubt he was fascinated by, and learned from, her own agenda problems—namely, what's more important, love-and-marriage or career? How should a young woman with brains, intellectual and aesthetic interests, good looks, charm, high ambition, and a real sense of her own exceptionalism, choose a vocation—or a husband? Should she marry at all? Who, why, and when? How much faith should she put in love? How much talent did she need to have, if she wanted to write—or sing—or act? What if the person you love or think it wise to marry doesn't want to marry you? What if a rich man does? Whom could

---

[23]   *He Knew He Was Right*, 1869 (London: Penguin, 1994), ch. 4, pp. 34–5.

[24]   See Gary Scharnhorst, "Kate Field and Anthony Trollope: the Gaps in the Record," *Victorian Newsletter*, 109 (Spring 2006): 21–3.

she trust, how can you smooth the way in finding out what the world is like and negotiating it? She needed the counsel, the support, the unselfish love of a wise good father-figure who wouldn't exploit her, and Trollope was sometimes her man and mentor—and her student.

What this preternaturally sensitive novelist did was to take in and shape what they said to one another, what she made him feel, what he found out about her, what problems she faced, what she wrote and asked him to look at, what he saw in her—whatever her presence, her virtues and faults, her erotic appeal and his memories of her suggested—and then fold all that he could use of that into his fiction. It's not that she *is* the silly feminist ideologue Wallachia Petrie, "the American Browning," in *He Knew He Was Right*. It's that there would be no Wallachia without her, just as there would be no Caroline Spalding or Nora Rowley. What he got out of their relationship was the need and impetus to imagine such characters as vital expressions of the reality in her and in his world with all its expanding possibilities.

The time when contact and communication between them is most evident—1860–61 in Florence and America, 1868 in America, 1873 in London—corresponds to, or immediately precedes, fiction by Trollope that probes and represents issues, behavior, and subjects churning in her life and in his imagination. *Orley Farm* (1862), for instance, written just when he met and took so feelingly to Kate, features Lady Mason, a Lot's daughter made to marry a man three times her age, and then, when betrayed, widowed, and in legal trouble—but still beautiful and seductive—driven to depend upon Sir Peregrine Orme, a good man 30 years her senior who loves her. The sign of the Lot complex is all over the novel. Says Orme, "If you will take me for your husband, as your husband will I stand by you. If you cannot—then I will stand by you as your father."[25] And Trollope writes that her middle-aged, long-married, lawyer, infatuated with her, "seeing that Lady Mason wept, and seeing that she was beautiful, and feeling that in her grief and beauty she had come to him for aid, his heart softened towards her, and he put out his arms as though he would take her to his heart—as a daughter" (p. 108).

V

Trollope's deceptively modest, subtly moving short story "Mary Gresley" (1869), written and published shortly after he returned from post office business and seeing Kate Field in America, can stand as a *locus classicus* of the evolving, benevolent Lot complex and older-man-younger woman "intercourse "in the Victorian and modern world.[26] It's written in a pleasant, "we're-men-of-the-world" tone, but

---

[25] *Orley Farm*, 1862, Introduction by John Mortimer (London: The Trollope Society, 1993), p. 318.

[26] "Mary Gresley" *An Editor's Tales*, 1870 (New York: Arno Press, 1981), pp. 49–97. "Intercourse" is Trollope's word here: "but still there came to us from our intercourse with her much of delight mingled with sorrow" (p. 51).

it's very sad and brave in the way that it cuts through superficiality about gender troubles. In it, Trollope's autobiographical imperative surrounding Kate, the gender-agenda problem for an impoverished young woman of literary talent, the sacrifice of women to a patriarchal religion tainted with pathology, and a dialogue with a great feminist writer, Charlotte Brontë, and her most famous novel, all remarkably come together. What Brontë did in *Jane Eyre* was to marry the Lot complex to modern social history, love, and the marriage plot of the English novel— an act of imagination that still reverberates, even for people who don't know the book. Trollope, in this story, with melancholy, enigmatic variations, does the same.

The narrator begins by describing "the girl or woman" Mary Gresley and the emotional relationship he has with her—how he sees her and what he feels for her. He does that before he gives any overt reason for their connection (*she needs money desperately; she wants to be a writer; can he advise her?*). The editorial "we" and "us" used by the editor-narrator looks at first to be a joky affectation to amuse readers, but rhetorically it winds up fusing the intensity of private experience into a broad public significance and giving the piece a universal flavor of *Lot* primer material in modern history:

> To be loved was to her all the world; unconscious desire for the admiration of men was as strong in her as in other women; and her instinct taught her. ... the gifts on which she depended ... were her softness, her trust, her woman's weakness, and that power of supplicating by her eye without putting her petition into words, which was absolutely irresistible. Where is the man of fifty, who in the course of his life has not learned to love some woman simply because it has come in his way to help her, and to be good to her in her struggles. *In love with Mary Gresley, after the common sense of the word, we never were, nor would it have become us to be so.... We were married and old* [emphasis mine]; she was very young, and engaged to be married, always talking of her engagement as a thing fixed as the stars.... She looked upon us, no doubt,—after she had ceased to regard us simply in our editorial capacity,—as a subsidiary old uncle whom providence had supplied to her, in order that if it were possible, the troubles of her life might be somewhat eased by assistance to her.... We regarded her first almost as a child, and then as a young woman to whom we owed that sort of protecting care which a greybeard should ever be ready to give to the weakness of feminine adolescence. *Nevertheless we were in love with her* [emphasis mine], and we think such a state of love to be a wholesome and natural condition.... But in our intercourse with Mary Gresley there was more than that. She charmed us.... When she would sit in the low arm-chair opposite to us, looking up into our eyes as we spoke to her words which must often have stabbed her little heart, we were wont to caress her with that inward undemonstrative embrace that one spirit is able to confer upon another. We thought of her constantly, perplexing our mind for her succour. We forgave all her faults. We exaggerated her virtues. We exerted ourselves for her with a zeal that was perhaps fatuous (pp. 52–4).

That passage is full of psychological complexity; it drips with paternal condescension, mutual need and vulnerability, openness, hidden eroticism, and intelligent kindness. It's especially useful for understanding Trollope, the unpredictable ways of love, and passionate, intergenerational attraction of great significance. The subtlety in him, not to be missed, and the contradictory nature of life, so much a part of his vision, come through in that delicately unconscious transition from "*In love with Mary Gresley... , we never were,*" to "*Nevertheless we were in love with her.*" Trollope's *Autobiography* may often seem guarded and impersonal, but in his fiction he gets very personal—sometimes even confessional. Mary Gresley's personality is hardly at all like Kate Field's, but the editor *is* like Anthony Trollope—motivated by a Lot complex and his autobiographical imperative.

The language of the editor may seem patronizing, but what the title character craves and needs in her era *is* a patron. She's 18, a poor, but precocious daughter of a medical practitioner's poor widow, and she's engaged to a poor, sick curate named Donne. Between them they haven't the money to marry. She has written a novel, and an old man of letters in her neighborhood, calling her work "promising," gives her an introduction to the editor-narrator. The trouble is that her beloved curate disapproves of novel writing on religious grounds. And he's so sick he has to be sent away to the South of England, where he can do no work, so she comes up to London with her mother and her novel, desperate to earn enough to wed. Before the editor sees Mary, he is cranky and wishes the old writer had told her: "Go, girl, and mend your stockings. Learn to make a pie."

Trollope is playing a game here, but it's a serious one. Elizabeth Gaskell's biography of Charlotte Brontë had come out, and in it you could read the infamous letter to her from Robert Southey. When Charlotte was 20, she wrote the Poet Laureate, pouring her heart out about her hopes and sending him some of her poetry. The great man replied, but with a wet blanket: "The day dreams in which you habitually indulge are likely to induce a distempered state of mind.... Literature cannot be the business of a woman's life, and it ought not to be. The more she is engaged in her proper duties, the less leisure will she have for it."[27]

The editor, though he tries to discourage Mary, feels her power over him and agrees to read her work. The novel is neither publishable nor salvageable, he thinks, but he finds the girl has real talent, besides being immensely appealing. He tells her that the work is good in its way, but no one will pay her for it. "But I shall try again at once" she says.... Currer Bell [Charlotte Brontë] was only a young girl when she succeeded." Says the patriarchal Victorian editor, "the injury which Currer Bell did after this fashion was almost equal to that perpetrated by Jack Sheppard" (p. 77). But by the end of their long interview, her will to succeed and her aura of grace persuade him to help her. He agrees to give her the best of his professional skill and attention in revising her work: in other words,

---

[27]   See Elizabeth Gaskell, *The Life of Charlotte Bronte*, 1857 (London: Penguin, 1985), pp. 172–3.

a respectable Lot mentorship—that boon of nineteenth and twentieth century positive sublimation, education, and female empowerment.

At first she resents his criticism, but he does have faith in her imaginative ability. He tells her she can be successful if she works at her art like an apprentice learning a vocation. And he does arrange for her "the publication of two short stories," for which she gets real money. He also befriends her mother. The Trollopean narrator slyly and with candid wisdom acknowledges and deals with his own incipient Lot's-Wife problem: "We had made a clean breast of it at home in regard to our heart-flutterings, and had been met with a suggestion that some kindness might with propriety be shown to the old lady as well as to the young one" (p. 81). Mary keeps working hard and effectively on her novel, but she worries about her absent lover's worsening consumption. Finally she tells the narrator that he is dying, and the older man gives her the money to go to him. Then he makes this editorial comment and self-correction about her talent, and it's revealing:

> We could not tell her how infinitely more important to our thinking was her life than that of him whom she was going to see now for the last time; but there did spring up within our mind a feeling, greatly opposed to that conviction which formerly we had endeavoured to impress upon herself,—that she was destined to make for herself a successful career." (p. 93)

But when she returns from seeing her dying fiancé, she says, "I will make no more attempt at novel writing." On his death-bed, the curate tells her that writing novels is "a misapplication of God's gifts" (p. 95). She burns her novel, "every scrap of it" (p. 95). The editor protests, but she answers, "Must he not know better than I do? Is he not one of God's ordained priests?.... He shall judge for me.... I do not want to write a novel now" (pp. 94–5).

The fiancé does die, and Mary does give up fiction. She goes home, apprentices herself to a "married curate" as "a female Scripture reader" (p. 96), and the narrator abruptly winds up his tale:

> From time to time we endeavoured to instigate her to literary work; and she answered our letters by sending us wonderful little dialogues between Tom the Saint and Bob the Sinner. We ... can assert, that though that mode of religious teaching is most distasteful to us, the literary merit shown even in such works as these was very manifest....

> At last, when eight years had passed over her head after the death of Mr. Donne, she married a missionary who was going out to some forlorn country on the confines of African colonization; *and there she died* [emphasis mine]. We saw her on board the ship in which she sailed, and before we parted there had come that tear into her eyes, the old look of supplication on her lips, and the gleam of

mirth across her face. We kissed her once,—for the first and only time,—as we bade God bless her!" (pp. 96–7).[28]

Some blessing! Note that her fate is just what Brontë makes clear would have happened to Jane Eyre, had she married the God-sure man St. John Rivers, followed him in his missionary calling and forsaken Rochester. Rochester and a positive Lot complex brought Bronte's heroine Jane her life, including, crucially, the vocation of writing the autobiography of Jane Eyre. The abstract logic of Trollope's story says something very like the logic of Charlotte Brontë's novel, but without the happy ending: *The fascination of the girl with the older man's power and experience, often flattering and energizing to him, and fascination of the older man's with the young woman's fresh appeal and hopeful mind must be recognized, acknowledged and dealt with as part of history's ongoing flow. This mutual attraction—this passion for communication, help, and love across gender and generation lines—has been, and is, so ripe for exploitation that it needs to be socialized, controlled, and made legitimate through new female agency and restricted patriarchal power.*

"We bade God bless her:" God didn't bless her, but a supportive editor and literary figure did. The strength of feeling at the end is very great, and it would not have been so if Trollope had not known Kate Field. What shouldn't be missed is that the vocational ambition of the woman in the story changes the narrator, changes the author, and changes the patriarchal feeling. The story is a powerful statement on behalf of vocation for women and on behalf of art in its recurrent conflicts with religion. It can be seen as a mode of discovery and enlightenment in pointing up the modern agenda problem for women making their way in the world and in tracking the history of Lot's daughters.

The working through of Trollope's Lot complex in literature and life is a process of patriarchal transition—a letting go of conventional past prejudices and a necessary embrace of a changing future for a daughterland. "A Ride Across Palestine" shows his erotic susceptibility to, and awareness of, the daughter figure in her mysterious, uncertain journey out of spiritual bondage. Kate Field and his feeling for her bring him new curiosity about and new sympathy for, young women in their quest for authority and fulfillment. "Mary Gresley" shows his alter-ego narrator trying to instruct and help a young woman—whom he can't help loving—in her need for vocation. Imagining the daughter-figure Mary's life and death bring him to comprehend and appreciate—or at least sense—the truly righteous vocation of a Charlotte Bronte and what it could mean—something his mother's career and behavior had not been able to do for him.

---

[28]   In the last letter Trollope sent to Kate Field upon leaving her in America in July, 1868, he wrote:" God bless you dear,—I wish I thought I might see your clever laughing eyes again … but I suppose not." And he added these words: "I wish I could have seen your dear old face once more, (before the gray hairs come. Or the wings which you will wear in heaven)—but I do not see how it is to be."

Such distinguished late Trollope fiction as *The Duke's Children* and *An Old Man's Love* (1884) support the desires and efforts of young women to choose what and who should count most in their own destinies and to even to oppose with justice the wills of well-meaning older men who love them. These books both chronicle and point to further stages of the evolution of agenda problems for women in their quest for authority. Forty years ago, writing about *The Duke's Children*, I said, "old men must bless or die despairing; fathers want to put some sort of lasting mark on the mutable world; sons must be free to move with the times." Those are very wise words—except for the glaring sexism, which left daughters out: *Agenda trouble*, as Trollope shows so well.

Chapter 2
He Knew He Was Right:
The Sensational Tyranny of the Sexual Contract and the Problem of Liberal Progress

Kathy Alexis Psomiades

Over the past decade, a central project of Victorian literary studies in the United States has been the re-examination and revaluation of Victorian liberalism. The history of the Liberal party; liberal attitudes towards the state; liberal self-cultivation; the enlightenment ideals of reason, discussion, and self-reflexivity—all have received extensive scholarly attention.[1] Yet the new liberalism studies have been remarkably silent on the Woman Question. How the liberal self might be gendered, or what feminism and liberalism might have to do with one another, seem to be questions best left to feminists interested in that sort of thing, or questions that already led to an exhausted impasse in the 1980s, or even questions that a revived enthusiasm for liberal universalism would put to rest.[2] Recent studies of Victorian literature and liberal theory, and of literature's relation to the historical development of the Victorian liberal state have tended to skirt what is surely one of the largest and

---

[1]   Even a partial bibliography of this work would include Amanda Anderson, *The Powers of Distance*, and in a more theoretical register, *The Way We Argue Now: A Study in the Culture of Theory* (Princeton: Princeton University Press, 2005); Lauren Goodlad, *Victorian Literature and the Victorian State: Character and Governance in a Liberal Society* (Baltimore: Johns Hopkins University Press, 2003); David Wayne Thomas, *Cultivating Victorians: Liberal Culture and the Aesthetic* (Philadelphia: University of Pennsylvania Press, 2004); Irene Tucker, *A Probable State: The Novel, The Contract, and the Jews* (Chicago: University of Chicago Press, 2000); and Elaine Hadley's as-yet-unpublished work, whose trajectory is suggested in "On A Darkling Plain: Victorian Liberalism and the Fantasy of Agency," *Victorian Studies* 48.1 (Fall 2005): 92–102.

[2]   One notable exception to the absence of thinking about relationships among liberalism, gender, and sexuality is Richard Dellamora's *Friendship's Bonds: Democracy and the Novel in Victorian England* (Philadelphia: University of Pennsylvania Press, 2004), which addresses the intersection of sexuality, religion, and politics in a variety of Victorian locations. Another is Wendy Jones's *Consensual Fictions: Women, Liberalism, and the English Novel* (Toronto: University of Toronto Press, 2005), which discusses bourgeois marriage as a form of voluntary association that necessitated conceptions of women's liberal agency and that thus was ultimately enabling to feminism.

most wide-ranging changes effected by liberal ideas: the change whereby gender ceases to seem a logical or valid criterion for determining eligibility to participate in the political process. This lacuna makes sense historically—part of the aim of the new liberalism studies is to get beyond the legacy of the 1980s and produce something new. But it also makes sense theoretically, since feminist theory is where some of the most powerful critiques of liberal universalism have emerged.

Anthony Trollope's *He Knew He Was Right*, begun in November of 1867 and finished in June of 1868, would seem a particularly good place to examine liberalism and gender. It has most often been read as centrally engaged with Victorian feminism—with the arguments about marriage that occurred around the Matrimonial Causes Act of 1857 and that John Stuart Mill brought to discussions around the second Reform Bill.[3] But if we see these arguments about women's economic and political agency as part of a larger discussion about broadening the ranks of liberal individuals, we can see how the novel uses the problematics of power and rule in relations of marriage and kinship to address larger questions of what it means to govern and be governed, and of how to allow for and yet contain the changes the progressive logic of liberalism would seem to demand.

In an 1861 review in *The Economist* of Mill's *Considerations on Representative Government*, Walter Bagehot defined liberalism as "the faith in the possibility, nay the duty, of constant political expansion—of drawing a larger and larger portion of the population into the circle of political duties that connect them with the government, give them a control over it, and interest them in what it does."[4] By 1869, the notion of an ever-increasing mass of liberal agents could be viewed rather less cheerfully by Matthew Arnold as the potential anarchy of too much liberal individualism, or "doing as one likes."[5] The Woman Question, the problematic of marriage laws and the laws governing women's economic and political agency, is one place where the tenets of liberal individualism and legal realities are graphically at odds. On the one hand, historically, Mill's defeated amendment to the Reform Act to substitute "person" for "man" was one of many events that raised the problem of representation and rule. As Catherine Hall, Keith McClelland, and Jane Rendell detail in *Defining the Victorian Nation: Class, Race, Gender and the Reform Act of 1867*, the problem of marital authority was discussed alongside problems of imperial authority posed by the Morant Bay

---

[3] Jones does the most sustained reading of the novel in relation to Mill's ideas on marriage and contract—her article "Feminism, Fiction and Contract Theory: Trollope's *He Knew He Was Right*," *Criticism* 36.3 (1994): 401–14, seems to form the core of the book's larger argument. Ruth ApRoberts also invoked *Subjection* and parliamentary speeches in "Emily and Nora and Dorothy and Priscilla and Jemima and Carry," in Richard A. Levine (ed.) *The Victorian Experience: The Novelists*, (Athens: Ohio University Press, 1976).

[4] Walter Bagehot, "Principles of Political Economy," in *Collected Works of Walter Bagehot*, vol. 6 (London: The Economist, 1974), p. 336.

[5] Matthew Arnold, *Culture and Anarchy and Other Writings*, ed. Stefan Collini (Cambridge and New York: Cambridge University Press, 1993).

rebellion of 1865, by anxiety about Fenianism, as well as by the demonstrations in Hyde Park that so troubled Arnold.[6] Women are thus one among many groups seeking political agency. On the other hand, theoretically, Mill's substitution of "person" for "man" demonstrates feminism's special critical relation to the problem of liberal universalism. Not merely one group among many, women are half of humanity, and their exclusion from the universal makes the lie of universalism uniquely visible.

In *The Sexual Contract* (1988), the feminist political theorist Carole Pateman launched what has become a classic feminist critique of liberalism. Pateman claimed that the social contract described by John Locke, Thomas Hobbes, and Jean-Jacques Rousseau, under which men agree to give up certain rights for the benefit of equality before the law is underwritten by a secret sexual contract that gives all men compensatory sexual access to women. Liberal society is thus divided into a private sphere in which men oppress women in the family and a public sphere in which gender-neutral liberal subjects engage in contractual relations. Women's access to such universal subjectivity is, however, compromised, since their unequal role in the home precludes the autonomy on which the liberal subject is predicated. Pateman's argument is that the sexual contract is always present in liberal social contract theory, from the initial debates about patriarchy between Locke and Filmer.[7] What I would like to suggest is that the theoretical narrative linking private marital relations and public political relations through lurid accounts of sexual violence is itself a modern phenomenon, emerging in 1860s liberal discourse in relation to the problem of mass democracy. In other words, it is no accident that the sensation-fiction story of the tyrannical husband, Victorian anthropology's sensational tale of the violent origins of primitive marriage in capture, and Mill's *Subjection of Women* should share with Pateman's 1980s feminist political theory this common story of primitive sexual and marital violence, for the 1860s lurid story of sexual violence is connected to the larger problem of violence and Reform. Trollope's *He Knew He was Right* is one of the places where this story of the sexual contract emerges. Tyrannical husbands, "foreign" wives, matriarchal family structures, aristocrats who fall for Americans (who always stand in, in Reform-era discussions of democracy, for democracy's excesses, not just feminism's), penniless spinsters, men who work for a living— these are the figures not only in a series of arguments about marriage and women's protection under the law, but also about larger issues of authority and consent, right government, and ways of thinking about collectivity and individualism.

This is not just Trollope's story and it is not just a literary story. By 1867, theoretical discourses existed that linked the power relations of marriage to power relations in the society at large as part of a developmental narrative. There was, in

---

6   Catherine Hall, Keith McClelland, and Jane Rendall, *Defining the Victorian Nation: Class, Race, Gender and the Reform Act of 1867* (Cambridge, UK: Cambridge University Press, 2000).

7   Carole Pateman, *The Sexual Contract* (Stanford: Stanford University Press, 1988).

other words, not just a metaphorical relation between marriage and other power relations, but also a historical relation made visible by theories about social progress. We can see some of this classically articulated by Mill:

> For what is the peculiar characteristic of the modern world—the difference which chiefly distinguishes modern institutions, modern social ideas, modern life itself, from those of times long past? It is, that human beings are no longer born to their place in life, and chained down by an inexorable bond to the place they are born to, but are free to employ their faculties, and such favorable chances as offer, to achieve the lot which may appear to them most desirable.... The social subordination of women thus stands out an isolated fact in modern social institutions; a solitary breach of what has become their fundamental law; a single relic of an old world of thought and practice exploded in everything else.[8]

Certainly this narrative about the status of women and the status of civilization did not make its first appearance in the 1860s. But it was newly theorized then in texts that today are seen as inaugurating the modern discipline of anthropology: Henry Sumner Maine's *Ancient Law* (1861) and John McClennan's *Primitive Marriage* (1865).[9] Together these two much-discussed texts became part of educated people's ideas about the emergence of society and marriage.

In *Ancient Law*, Maine put forth his famous theory that progress towards civilization was a matter of moving from a society of *status* to one of *contract*. In ancient society, Maine claimed, people lived in patriarchal family groups, governed by the father's law and holding all property as a group. The patriarchal family was a primitive social form, characterized by the subjection of women, group identity, and what would appear from the perspective of modernity to be tyrannical rule. Membership in the group was not voluntary, even the fiction of adoption still relied on the involuntary association of blood. Gradually, contracting workers replaced slaves, unmarried women were able to enter into contracts, parents no longer had power over children who were of age, except through contract: "The individual is steadily substituted for the Family, as the unit of which civil laws take account."[10] There is a radical disjuncture between the two kinds of society: insofar as remnants of the social relations of status still exist in civilized countries—slavery in the United States, married women's property law in England, to name Maine's most common examples—those societies are not truly civilized. By redefining marriage

---

[8]   John Stuart Mill, "The Subjection of Women," in Stefan Collini (ed.), *On Liberty and Other Writings* (Cambridge, UK, and New York: Cambridge University Press, 1989), p. 134.

[9]   For an account of Victorian anthropology's emergence see George Stocking, *Victorian Anthropology* (New York: Free Press, 1987).

[10]   Henry Sumner Maine, *Ancient Law: Its Connection with the Early History of Society and its Relation to Modern Ideas* (1861) (New York: Dorset Press, 1986), p. 140.

as an ancient social arrangement of status, like slavery, a holdover from a world without the benefit of contract, Maine primitivizes patriarchy. The laws governing "the proprietary disabilities of married females" he sees as "archaisms" that have "deeply injured civilization."[11]

John McClennan's brother, Donald, observed of Maine that his greatest innovation was to change "the Patriarchal theory" from "a theory of the source of sovereignty" to "a theory of the origin of society."[12] That is, he changed the speculative "social contract" discussions of the seventeenth and eighteenth centuries into a historical inquiry into law and social structure. But it remained to McClennan to put the organization of sex at that originary moment. Rather than beginning with fathers, McClennan begins with a world of chaotic and violent sex. McClennan sees culture beginning in rape—more in the sense of seizure than in the sense of forced sex, although the latter seems also to be implied. The reason for rape, or "marriage by capture," is the shortage of women caused by another violent act—female infanticide. The murdered baby girl and the raped foreign woman are the two figures of violence against women with which McClennan's story begins. In other words, for McClennan as for Carole Pateman, gender relations are inherently violent and tyrannical. This early violence lives on in the symbols of marriage like carrying the bride over the threshold. But primeval violence and tyranny do not, for McClennan, lead logically and directly to natural patriarchal tyranny. Primitive people have to figure out kinship, first by coming to understand maternity, then by tracing kin through matrilineage, then, finally, after a very long time, figuring out paternity and moving to patriarchal social organization. For Maine, the family group precedes the individual, and kinship/status is a form of pre-modern social organization without individuals. But for McClennan the discovery of blood/kinship/family is *part of the process* of modern individuation. McClennan's revision of Maine does away with the radical break between the status and contract stages of society, and makes sex—not just reproduction—the central motor of social formation. (Primitive men do not understand how reproduction works: only at a relatively late date and after much thought do they realize that sex makes babies.[13])

There are two narratives here—Maine's hopeful liberal-progressive narrative of a radical break with a primitive past (derived mostly in the 1850s), and McClennan's later narrative that by positing a more primitive and disorganized state than the patriarchal makes patriarchy progressive and allows for more gradual forms of transition between various kinds of past tyranny and progressive individuation. In both narratives, however, masculine tyranny belongs to an earlier stage of culture than does egalitarian monogamy—a stage of culture that Maine

[11] Maine, p. 131.

[12] John McClennan, *The Patriarchal Theory*, edited and completed by Donald McClennan (London: MacMillan, 1885), p. ix.

[13] John McClennan, *Primitive Marriage: An Inquiry into the Form of Capture in Marriage Ceremonies* (1865) (Chicago: University of Chicago Press, 1970).

sees as more primitive than McClennan does, but both see as gradually giving way to a world in which more and more social relations are egalitarian.

In a by now classic article on *He Knew He Was Right*, Christopher Herbert refers to the "conventionalized Victorian story of the tyrannical husband and the victimized wife" as a "literary institution."[14] And he sees the primary function of this story as the covering over of how closely bound together "patriarchal" and "companionate" modes of marriage actually were for the Victorians—a covering over of which Trollope's novel is critical. What I would like to add to this argument is that the story of the tyrannical husband is not just a story that acts to manage tyranny in marriage, but one that also acts to manage the larger liberal fiction in which tyranny as liberalism's other, is always somehow disappearing and hanging on. It is not just a "literary institution" but also one of the institutions of liberal social theory. That for the Victorians the tyrant is not, as it might have been in the seventeenth century, the father, but rather, as it will be for Pateman, the husband, is part of the process of the sexual contract's emergence. And in particular, in the 1860s, a theory of the links between various kinds of tyranny in the science of anthropology, a fascination with tyrannical husbands and rebellious wives in sensation fiction, and an equally strong fascination in Pre-Raphaelite art and painting with countering law with sex, indicates that eroticized tyranny/rebellion is a central way of talking about the violence of the state, and the violence of reform, without touching upon political violence.

The novel's tyrannical husband, Louis Trevelyan, is thus not just a figure for marital tyranny, but a figure for tyranny more generally. Elsewhere in this volume, Deborah Morse shows how Trevelyan's mismanagement of his authority over the dark, rebellious girl from the tropics he marries refers to Governor Eyre's disastrous mishandling of the events at Morant Bay in 1865. Not merely historically, however, but also theoretically, Louis is the reluctant embodiment of liberalism's outmoded other. He combines classic tropes of aristocratic decadence—he doesn't work, he becomes increasingly feminized, he dresses extravagantly and falls into a certain amount of alcohol and drug dissipation—with an overweening will to power. He uses the political language of mastery—"master," "command," "obey," "submit"—yet he is a man "absolutely unfitted by nature to have the custody or guardianship of others."[15] The novel's references to Shakespeare's *Othello* and traditional tragedy racialize and primitivize Trevelyan, but they also make clear that he is temporally out of step, caught up in a non-modern plot.

Critics have read Trevelyan's madness as an attempt to make a realist version of a sensation-novel plot device (often with reference to the much more sensational mad-tyrannical-husband novel of 1867, *Sowing the Wind*, by Eliza Lynn Linton), as referring to debates on sanity and legal culpability, and as making husbandly

---

[14]   Christopher Herbert, "*He Knew He Was Right*, Mrs. Lynn Linton, and the Duplicities of Victorian Marriage," *Texas Studies in Literature and Language* 25.3 (Fall 1983): 448–69, 449.

[15]   Anthony Trollope, *He Knew He Was Right* (Oxford: Oxford University Press, 1998), p. 257.

misuse of power something that only insane men would do.[16] Viewed in the light of liberal theory, his madness figures two kinds of anti-liberal irrationality. On the one hand, it figures the irrationality of the persistence of laws arising out of past social structures, in a present that runs on an entirely different logic—the irrationality to which Mill and Maine refer when they see existing marriage laws as anachronisms, relics of a past at odds with a modern way of looking at the world. On the other, it figures an irrationality that is liberalism's other—for rationality is a central attribute of the modern liberal subject. Through rational discussion in a public forum, the liberal subject solves problems and makes rational choices. What critic Jane Nardin said of women in this novel is also true for the newly enfranchised citizens Mill describes in *On Representative Government*: "Women in this novel do not necessarily mind being mastered, but they must be mastered through argument."[17] Argument, or rational persuasion, transforms obedience into rational consent.

Emily says that she will obey her husband "in anything reasonable" (p. 100). Her sister Nora counsels her:

> "Simply do what he tells you, whether it is wrong or right. If it's right, it ought to be done, and if it's wrong, it will not be your fault."

> "That's very easily said, and it sounds logical; but you must know it's unreasonable."

> "I don't care about reason. He is your husband, and if he wishes it you should do it." (p. 46)

The problem with even benign despotism, the classic liberal argument goes, is that it stunts the intellectual and ethical growth of a people. Nora's practical advice, which one has a hard time imagining herself following, asks Emily to give up making intellectual and ethical distinctions between right (true, morally good) and wrong (false, morally bad). Trollope's realism is based in such distinctions, and his character-driven art is all about the exercise of ethical agency. When it comes to self-determination, ethical decision-making, self-reflexivity (the qualities of liberal subjectivity), men and women in Trollope are essentially the same. The difference, however, lies in the positing of a natural desire to be dominated in the name of love. The very thing from which Emily recoils, Caroline Spalding lovingly embraces—she says to Nora about her husband to be Glascock: "I feel that all responsibility is gone from myself, and that for all the rest of my life I have

---

[16]   See, for example, David D. Oberhelman, "Trollope's Insanity Defense: Narrative Alienation in *He Knew He Was Right*," *Studies in English Literature*, 1500–1900 35.4 (Fall 1995): 789–806.

[17]   Jane Nardin, "Tragedy, Farce, and Comedy in Trollope's *He Knew He Was Right*," *Genre* 15 (Fall 1982): 306.

to do just what he tells me" (p. 767). She has, the novel implies, made her ethical choice in the choice of a good husband, and now can trust herself to her chosen ruler. Even Emily will humor Trevelyan in his delusions in the name of love, once his madness has become visible to all.

Sir Marmaduke Rowley, governor of the Mandarin Islands, is also identified with an older era of patriarchy that can, through love, be gently modernized. Unable to grasp how his own imperial authority works, and given to issuing patriarchal commands that his daughter Nora repeatedly works her way around, Sir Rowley is a figure of powers past. Patriarchal power over daughters who are of age is, as the novel insists on telling us, legally limited—Sir Rowley can't forbid Nora to marry who she chooses. Indeed Nora herself points out that the laws governing men's and women's right to self government are the same, at least for unmarried men and women, and asks that her father treat her like a rational liberal subject and an equal:

> Do listen to me, papa. I have listened to you and you ought to listen to me. I
> have promised him, and I must keep my promise. I shall keep my promise if he
> wishes it. There is a time when a girl must be supposed to know what is best for
> herself,—just as there is for a man. (p. 658)

Despite her invocation of rights here, Nora insists to Hugh that even though she is not legally compelled to do so, she will get her parents' consent to her marriage anyway, thus preserving the old familial forms, while asserting her right to choose her own husband. She thus manages better than her sister has to be a modern liberal subject, yet to gesture respectfully to the older traditional forms. Of course, this is a much easier operation when everyone realizes that the old forms no longer have any legal power.

Patriarchal tyranny and husbandly tyranny are equally outmoded and irrational but they can, the novel implies, be accommodated in a new world in which rational liberal subjects use womanly affection to gesture towards the past, while they move towards a more egalitarian and gender-neutral future. In Victorian anthropology, a universal matrilineal stage in which relations between women regulated social identity makes patriarchy seem relatively civilized. In *He Knew He Was Right*, women who take on masculine power act to produce a form of misrule that can easily be articulated as unjust and done away with, without threatening the culture by too precipitous an abandonment of traditional patriarchal or husbandly power.

To Hugh Stanbury and Brooke Burgess, young men without actual fathers, Miss Jemima Stanbury appears as the usurper of power even a father is no longer supposed to have. They repeatedly refer to her authority in the language of tyranny and slavery that liberal political theory classically uses against patriarchy (pp. 390, 408, 410, 678). If Dorothy Stanbury treats her like a true authority figure ("I would yield to her in anything that was possible to me" p. 390), Brooke, like Hugh, refuses to grant her any such power ("I won't ... and I don't think I should do any good if I did," p. 390). Miss Stanbury's power comes from money diverted from its proper patriarchal channels, and that diversion has an aura of sexual scandal—it is the money left to her by the first Brooke Burgess, the man who ought to have been her husband, but wasn't. This combination of sexual scandal and the interruption of inheritance through the male line makes her resemble anthropology's scandalous figure of the matrilineal stage of culture, when money doesn't flow from father to son because paternity is too difficult to determine in an era of promiscuous polyandry. Her marrying off of a kinder gentler Stanbury (Dorothy) to a better tempered Burgess (Brooke II) restores the natural order of things and the money and power to their rightful place. Indeed, she moves from matrilineal to patriarchal mother-figure as she ultimately makes Brooke II into Brooke I's son, one who inherits his "father's" money, his "father's" liking for Stanbury's and his "father's" reputation.

By positing a matrilineal stage before patriarchy, anthropologists both recivilized Maine's patriarchal family (which suddenly seemed more modern by contrast) and also primitivized a version of feminine power. For if Maine was right, and contract would come to determine relations between people, then a gender-neutral world opened up ahead. John Stuart Mill, for example, asked why the marriage contract was not more like the gender-neutral business contract, with the same rights and privileges on either side. As Sharon Marcus has recently noted, this vision of marriage as gender-neutral contract is often connected in Trollope to visions of female marriage.[18] In this novel, both Miss Jemima Stanbury and the American feminist Wallachia Petrie are seen as taking up inappropriately husband-like roles in relation to Dorothy and to Caroline Spalding. Whereas Dorothy speaks of obeying Miss Stanbury in the same way other women in this novel speak of obeying their husbands, and Caroline Spalding insists throughout the novel on her love for Wallachia and the fact that her husband doesn't really understand the woman, the novel depicts these women as unfairly usurping masculine power. Miss Stanbury herself wonders if Brooke is as attracted by Dorothy's looks as she has been herself—"it was your looks won me first, Dolly" (p. 689). Glascock speaks of himself as having won Caroline away from Wallachia, in a battle (p. 765). Women who substitute for husbands and fathers can thus be dispensed with in a way actual husbands and fathers cannot. The matrilineal usurper and the female husband can thus be safely deprived of an authority they never legitimately had in ways that male tyrants cannot.

Finally, in the free-for-all of the Gibson farce plot, marriage is a matter of gender warfare, where bad girls with chignons (which seem to represent both feminine and masculine appendages) have too much power. The violence that is specifically refused in the colonial plot (the Mandarins are not the West Indies), in the patriarchal plot (Sir Rowley doesn't curse his daughter), and in the Trevelyan plot (Louis doesn't beat his wife) appears in the form of the knife-wielding Camilla

---

[18]   Sharon Marcus, *Between Women: Friendship, Desire and Marriage in Victorian England* (Princeton: Princeton University Press, 2007). See especially ch. 6, "Contracting Female Marriage in *Can You Forgive Her?*," pp. 227–55.

French. That the eruption of this violence is labelled "French" is hardly accidental, since by 1860s France has stood for nearly a hundred years as a sign of the violence of democratic revolution, and the threat of sudden and dangerous change. Batted from one female-headed household to another (Stanbury to French), Gibson seems like matrilineal man, deprived of the privileges of masculine choice and power. He does in the end manage to assert himself enough to choose the girl who will accept his guidance (at least in regard to coiffure), but in no way is anyone in this parodic world to serve as an example.

In contrast with these various misuses and abuses of power are the novel's happy modern marriages, where fully developed self-reflexive liberal subjects freely consent to a social arrangement in which command and obedience are emptied of their meaning by affect, and self-regulation makes law irrelevant. Like the not yet fully liberalized political system, the marriage system is an old legal form inhabited by new subjects. What is desirable is that these new subjects should render the old legal forms irrelevant, without precipitous social change. Thus Hugh and Nora, the novel's natural radicals, entrepreneurial and self-reliant, can still inhabit the hierarchy of marriage, making it modern by his forbearance on matters of command, and her romanticized and eroticized pleasure in "submission." Whereas Brooke seems more commanding, and Dorothy more submissive than Nora, they also happily inhabit older social forms—indeed, insofar as they repeat and correct the story of Miss Jemima Stanbury and the first Brooke, they are both modernizing and traditional. Perhaps the most hopeful vision of the possibility of uniting traditional and modern can be seen in the case of Mr. Glascock (Lord Peterborough) and Caroline Spalding. If Trevelyan is a faux aristocrat, the marvellously named Glascock is the figure for the grace of aristocracy that should be preserved, the very thing that the hyper-democratic wish to get rid of at their peril. Whereas Nora, like the post-Reform nation, prefers other leadership, the American Carrie finds him irresistible. And Glascock, unlike Trevelyan, likes American women. If in the 1860s the French still stand in for the violence of revolution, Americans stand in for rapid and enthusiastic democratization. Wallachia Petrie gives voice to this spirit:

> "It is the instinct of fallen man to hate equality, to desire ascendency, to crush, to oppress, to tyrannize, to enslave. Then, when the slave is at last free, and in his freedom demands–equality, man is not great enough to take his enfrachised brother to his bosom."

> "You mean negroes," said Mr. Glascock, looking round and planning for himself a mode of escape.

> "Not negroes only,—not the enslaved blacks, who are now enslaved no more,— but the rising nations of white men wherever they are to be seen." (p. 529)

Wallachia Petrie's language here is a radical language of liberal reform that applies to all the forms of broadening the franchise the Reform Act brings up. Marrying Caroline, despite Lady Rowley's error, is not marrying Wallachia, but it implies a compatibility between aristocratic love of the past and a liberal progressive future, so long as the liberal progressive future is properly respectful.

These three marriages taken together and taken separately figure ideal progressive communities, in which modern subjects respect old forms, obedience is an act of love, and control is (to paraphrase the unnamed Governor who testifies on the happiness of Britain's colonies) "never more harsh and seldom less refreshing and beautifying than a spring shower in April" (p. 643). Indeed, for wives, far more than for colonies, "devotion and loyalty" are "quite a passion" (p. 643). In general, the novel disassociates violence and tyranny, preferring instead to associate violence with revolution. But in descriptions of all three courtships, Victorian anthropology's violent originary scene of marriage by capture is used to naturalize and eroticize male dominance by making it an object of feminine desire. In all three cases, male physical dominance is seen from the perspective of the female character who is turned on by it. Seized by Hugh, who tries and fails to kiss her, Nora reflects

> If a girl were to be subjected to such treatment as this when she herself had been so firm, so discreet, so decided, then indeed it would be unfit that a girl should trust herself with such a man. She had never thought that he had been such a one as that, to ill-use her, to lay a hand on her in violence, to refuse to take an answer. (p. 378)

This, seizure, however, is part of what makes her "the happiest girl alive" (p. 378). "He had been very violent with her, but his violence had at least made the matter clear. He did love her" (p. 380). Later, she uses explicitly political language: "But he got the better of me, and conquered me and I will never rebel against him" (p. 605). Similarly, when despite Dorothy's protests, Brooke "seized her in his arms and kissed her," "That is very, very wrong," she said, sobbing, and then ran to her room,—the happiest girl in all Exeter" (p. 489).

Finally, in the chapter titled, "Mr. Glascock is Master," Carrie finds herself similarly physically restrained:

> She felt that he was altogether too strong for her,—that she had mistaken his character in supposing that she could be more firm than he. He was so strong that he treated her almost as a child;—and yet she loved him infinitely the better for so treating her. Of course, she knew now that her objection, whether true or unsubstantial, could not avail. As he stood with his arm round her, she was powerless to contradict him in anything..."Be good to me," he said, "and tell me that I am right."

"You must be master, I suppose, whether you are right or wrong. A man always thinks himself entitled to his own way."

"Why, yes. When he has won the battle, he claims his captive." (p. 765)

Here love makes the abandonment of ones own judgment into a romantic imperative. The old forms of masculine power persist because modern women, even American ones, are aroused by them.

The sexual contract story eroticizes violence, making it sensational, visible, and embodied. In Victorian anthropology, marriage begins by capture; in Trollope, husbands-to-be seize wives; in Pateman, rape is at the beginning of culture. In the old social contract stories, what men fight about is property; in anthropology's sexual stories of origin, what men fight about is sex—they fight other men for access to women and they fight women for access to sex. Trollope's scenes of eroticized violence are not unique to him—they reference stories about the violence at the primitive beginnings of gender relations. We see more and more of these stories in the 1860s and later, I am hazarding, because of the need for something like the old social contract story to deal with the problem of power in mass democracy.[19] As the old grounds for participation in property are gradually eroded, sex/desire begins strangely to underwrite citizenship. It is finally feminine desire in Trollope that turns violence into something to be consented to. It is feminine desire, rather than rebellion against fathers, that links together the novel's men into a network of actual and metaphorical brothers-in-law.

In a way, then, we could say that the novel proves the justice of Carole Pateman's claims. In a time in which the social contract extends to more and more people, the novel's men—be they wealthy property owners or rising journalists—all have the right to control the distribution of women, and the right to control those individual women in private life after marriage. In return for not engaging in class warfare with each other, they all get to enjoy the perks of married life. But at the same time, the novel suggests that the difference between such a primitive arrangement to distribute women and the new arrangements that make the world modern is feminine desire. *Raptus* may be as old as the hills; what makes modern women different from their primitive counterparts is that they, like modern citizens,

---

[19]   Like Trollope and the Victorian anthropologists, Pateman began to write at a time in which new possibilities seemed to be opening up for democratic social arrangements. Her first two books, *Participation and Democratic Theory* (1970) and *The Problem of Political Obligation* (1979, reprinted 1985), dealt with precisely the problem of democratization—with whether participatory, rather than purely representative democracy, was realistic, and with whether participatory democracy naturally followed when you took political obligation seriously. *The Sexual Contract* shared with her first book a criticism of subordination and with her second an interest in the original contract, but it was written in the context of the economic neo-liberalism of the 1980s, in which those possibilities raised in the 1960s and 1970s seem to be shutting down.

Fig. 2.1   "Monkhams." Marcus Stone's illustration for *He Knew He Was Right*, Chapter 96

get to choose who carries them off. Nora refuses Glascock and chooses Hugh, Dorothy refuses Gibson and chooses Brooke. And they make these choices based not on external considerations of wealth or position, or even on moral qualities, but on the basis of a capricious and idiosyncratic desire that is implicitly erotic.[20] Glascock and Gibson are refused, Trollope's narrator implies, because despite the fact that they look like sensible matches for Nora and Dorothy, they don't turn these women on. What might be the different interests of conservative aristocrats who haven't read Mill, rich bankers, unpropertied journalists, and the idle rich become common interests through the desires of their women: Glascock, Burgess, and Stanbury, connected through channels of feminine desire, can come together to take care of Trevelyan and make the world safe for marriage again.

For several decades now, critics have argued that gender relations parallel political relations in Trollope, that marriage and politics alike in his novels involve power struggles. What I hope to have suggested here is that this is not just Trollope's idiosyncrasy, not even just domestic fiction's tendency to translate the political into the domestic and thereby contain and diffuse it, but that this is part of a general tendency in the era of the Second Reform Act to use marriage and gender to construct social and political theories about how human society and culture work. And these same social and political theories in turn shaped twentieth-century feminist theory.

---

[20]   Wendy S. Brown has commented that this desire, which because important to the Victorians because of its opposition to mere financial interest, winds up inadvertently giving to women a great deal of autonomy in choice (*Consensual Fictions*, p. 137).

Chapter 3
Bastards to the Time:
Legitimacy as Legal Fiction
in Trollope's Novels of the 1870s

Jenny Bourne Taylor

Philip the Bastard:
...............For he is but a bastard to the time
That does not smack of observation.

William Shakespeare, *King John* I. i. 207–8.

The vexed question of personal legitimacy—of what constitutes a proper marriage and thus legally sanctioned offspring, and what it means, more generally, to be a socially authorized member of a family or community—recurs throughout Anthony Trollope's work. Many of the novels of the late 1850s and 1860s, for example *Doctor Thorne* (1858), *Castle Richmond* (1860), *Can You Forgive Her?* (1865), *The Belton Estate* (1866), and *He Knew He Was Right* (1869), explore the legal, social, and emotional consequences of various forms of actual or alleged illicit liaisons; and the fall-out from unorthodox relationships can be the means of investigating the often contradictory claims of formal law, dynastic imperative, romantic love, and other kinds of emotional entanglements. It is a concern that is extended in *John Caldigate,* Trollope's late novel of 1879 that explores the consequences of a possibly bigamous colonial marriage; however in much of the work of the 1870s and early 1880s, particularly *Ralph the Heir* (1871), *Lady Anna* (1874), *Is He Popenjoy?* (1879), and his final completed novel *Mr Scarborough's Family* (1883), Trollope seems to be intrigued by the slipperiness of the legal boundary between legitimate and illegitimate birth itself. "'Nothing is more difficult to decide than questions of legitimacy,'" remarks the solicitor Mr Frick in *Lady Anna*, recalling a case in which "'they had to go back a hundred and fifty years and at last decide on the memory of a man whose grandmother had told him she had seen a woman wearing a wedding ring.'"[1]

In these novels, Trollope plays on the legal undecidability of personal legitimacy to probe a complex set of relationships between birth status and wider forms of economic, political, and symbolic power, as difficult questions concerning rightful authority are refracted through the uncertain figure of the bastard. It is no accident that these concerns surface in Trollope's fiction at this moment, for a series of

---

[1]   Anthony Trollope, *Lady Anna* [1874] (Oxford, World's Classics, 1990), pp. 222–3.

discussions about citizenship, subjecthood, political sovereignty, and the meaning of national belonging came together in the late 1860s and early 1870s, together with a wider set of intellectual debates about the nature and origins of civil society itself. In their different ways, these debates can all be seen as part of a renewed preoccupation with legitimacy in both its individual, private, and collective, political meanings—a concern shared by Trollope and other contemporary writers, who use the figure of the male bastard as a conduit to investigate forms of social and symbolic authority in a world in which the older interests of landed and dynastic wealth are coming under new kinds of cultural, economic and political pressure.

George Eliot, for example, explores these issues in *Felix Holt* (1866) and, more complexly, in *Daniel Deronda* (1876). *Felix Holt* explicitly places doubtful personal legitimacy alongside a crisis of political representation in the figure of the secretly spurious heir, the adulterine bastard Harold Transome, while *Daniel Deronda* makes subtle interconnections and contrasts between Daniel's imagined identity as Sir Hugo Mallinger's natural son, his uncertain position as a British subject, and the discovery of his Jewish descent. Indeed, although Daniel discovers a "higher" legitimacy by embracing a still un-formed future identity and renouncing his status as an English gentleman, he is able to do this, in part, because he has already occupied the subject position of a noble bastard.[2] The question of how symbolic legitimacy is created and sustained is central, too, to Tennyson's *The Coming of Arthur*—that part of *The Idylls of the King* that begins the cycle's internal chronology but was only published in 1869. Over the previous three decades Tennyson had transformed an enduring Celtic legend into an epic of Englishness, but in *The Coming of Arthur* he left his principal source Malory behind in order to submit Arthur's origins to a quasi-legal scrutiny by Guinevere's old father King Leodogran, making the undecidable nature of Arthur's authority inextricably bound up with his slippery position as a bastard.[3] The sections of the *Idylls* cycle published in 1859 had dealt with the effects of adultery on the stability of the realm, but *The Coming of Arthur* focuses on the broader question of legitimate power, as the mythological tropes through which sovereign authority is created and sustained are explored through a kind of medieval bastardy trial. Leodogran is given conflicting accounts of Arthur's origins, each involving a different notion of "higher" legitimacy; but ultimately there is no clear standpoint for Arthur's symbolic status: legal fiction, royal genealogy, even supernatural sanction are all mediated and provisional, held together by the anomalies and contradictions of an old man's dream.

---

[2]   For an important discussion of Deronda's nationality in relation to contemporary debates on naturalisation and Zionism, see David Glover's forthcoming *Literature, Immigration, Diaspora: A Cultural History of the 1905 Aliens Act.*

[3]   On the sources of *The Coming of Arthur*, see J. M. Gray, *Man and Myth in Victorian England: Tennyson's The Coming of Arthur* (Lincoln: The Tennyson Society, 1969).

Tennyson's Arthur played a key role in shaping a flexible medievalism by transposing a sixth-century story into a twelfth-century setting while endowing the characters with a specifically "modern" self consciousness, and the fictional reappearance of the bastard son at this moment also involves a complicated form of historical awareness. As Alison Findlay has argued, the male bastard had acted as a linchpin for the intimate relationships between patriarchal authority in the family and the state in Renaissance drama. His position both inside and outside the dominant structures of power made him a liminal figure *par excellence*—both natural and unnatural, either excessively vicious or virtuous—who performed the double role of subverting and upholding the structures from which he is excluded yet on which he ultimately depends.[4] Historically, this political ambivalence culminates in the figure of James, Duke of Monmouth, Charles II's eldest and favorite natural son whose doomed bid to seize the English throne from his Catholic uncle James II had sparked one of the crisis of succession that led to the Glorious Revolution of 1688. Monmouth, whose attempt to start a popular rebellion in the West Country had gained massive popular support, had based his claim for his "higher legitimacy" on the dual authority of his blood ties to his royal father, and his Protestantism. As Wolfram Schmidgen has suggested, his failed attempt marks the moment when the fictional bastard leaves the public stage, moving across social space as a mixed prototypically "modern" figure, both inside and outside the boundaries of the reconfigured nation state, in novels such as Henry Fielding's *Tom Jones* (1749) and Robert Bage's *Hermsprong* (1796).[5]

Indeed, representations of illegitimacy became privatized and increasingly "feminized" from the late eighteenth century. Although Edmund Burke presented the monstrous "mother who is not a wife" as the embodiment of the collapse of the natural political order in 1795, it was the sentimental figure of the ruined mother, often driven by desperation to infanticide, that dominated much radical rhetoric—in the writing of Mary Wollstonecraft and Mary Hays, for example, and in the melodramatic attacks on the poor laws in the 1830s and 1840s.[6] During the 1850s, the figure of the virtuous bastard is most likely to be female—think of Esther Summerson in *Bleak House* (1851) and Mary in Trollope's own *Doctor Thorne*—as the illegitimate daughter becomes the focus of explorations of how social and psychic inheritance is both internalized and resisted; a trope cleverly undercut in the contrasted virtuous and transgressive Vanstone sisters in *No Name* in 1862, as Wilkie Collins exploits the interplay of illegitimacy and imposture to emphasize the fictiveness of social roles and identities.

---

[4]   Alison Findlay, *Illegitimate Power: Bastards in Renaissance Drama* (Manchester: Manchester University Press, 1994).

[5]   Wolfram Schmidgen, "Illegitimacy and Social Observation: the Bastard in the Eighteenth-Century Novel," *ELH*, 69.1 (2002): 133–66.

[6]   See Josephine McDonagh, *Child Murder and British Culture 1720–1900* (Cambridge, UK: Cambridge University Press, 2003) pp. 80–88.

So while noble natural sons persisted into the early nineteenth century—a staple of both radical melodrama and "silver fork" fiction—by the mid-nineteenth century they often act as conduits of historical memory and imagination. Like Tennyson's Arthur, these figures stand both inside and outside their time, taking up the double-sided identity of the natural son and rendering it knowingly anachronistic. One of the most influential novels of the nineteenth century, Scott's *The Heart of Midlothian* (1818) had embodied this sense of anachronism it its double plot of illegitimacy: Effie Dean's seduction and trial for infanticide, and the story of her lost child, who survives to return as an unconscious force of retribution against his father—a wild, nameless figure who marks the limits of the incorporation of Scotland into a reformed Britain. And in 1852, William Makepeace Thackeray had returned to the traumatic years of British self-definition between the Civil Wars and 1688 in *The History of Henry Esmond*, a historical *bildungsroman* of the secretly legitimate son at the heart of an aristocratic Tory-Catholic family.[7] The return of the natural son in the late 1860s comes freighted with this sense of historicity, but reconfigures in the recent past of the present; and now the bastard is more of a hangover from an "older" patriarchal order that nonetheless contains within it the knowledge of change.

Trollope's supposititious children figure as sites of memory in various ways: they enact a process of cultural and literary reproduction; they literalize the transmission of psychic inheritance, and they are the means of unpacking the residual but still powerful ideological force of patrilineal legitimacy while playing on the long-standing recognition of its fictiveness. And this multifaceted identity enables illegitimacy to represent the uneven ways in which the boundaries of belonging within both the family and the nation were being negotiated across diverse fields and practices during the late 1860s within a broadly liberal consensus, in which the free, socially mobile, individual is seen as the crucial unity of the polity, but always within the framework of ambivalent newly dominant conceptions of civil society as comprising both mass society and the nation state within an increasingly complex global economy.

Natural-born subjects

In the disciplines of legal history and anthropology, the very meaning of "legitimate" descent was being investigated as an aspect of the family's role in the emergence of civil society. Henry Maine had posited an original primitive patriarchy in *Ancient Law* (1861), but had argued that the narrative of progress was marked both by the gradual move from "status" to "contract" in social relations, and by the replacement of agnatic descent (traced purely through the father) to

---

[7]   For a detailed discussion of *The History of Henry Esmond* in relation to mid-nineteenth-century political debates, see Pam Morris, *Imagining Inclusive Society: The Code of Sincerity in the Public Sphere* (Baltimore: Johns Hopkins University Press, 2004), pp. 86–110.

cognatic kinship, in which both parents are equally acknowledged. He emphasised that paternity was essentially a fictive construct, and saw the artificiality of the patriarchal family as the root of all legal fictions and the necessary precondition of systemic codes. Maine's historicist approach was framed within a progressivist narrative in which the emergence of modern feudal society was bound up with the emergence of testamentary freedom (the power of the individual to alter lines of inheritance) and the development of entail in response to this. His arguments were questioned by the liberal lawyer J. F. McLennan, who suggested in *Primitive Marriage* (1865) that social structures originated in exogamous marriage in which descent was traced through the female line. But Maine and McLennan, with the social theorist Walter Bagehot, all shared the mixed model of progress in which ancient mentalities endure as atavisms in modern cultures and symbolic forms that would gain increasing force through the rest of the century.[8]

These discussions highlighted connections between public and private forms of legitimacy that were implicit rather than spoken within a political culture which could no longer rely on heritable 'blood' for its ideological authority yet which still regarded dynastic marriage as the foundation of social stability—as debates around the 1857 Divorce Act had testified.[9] The extension of male suffrage with the passing of the Second Reform Act in 1867 marked a significant moment in a developing concept of citizenship and what it might mean within a mass society in which the state provides new mechanisms of social inclusion and exclusion.[10] But another key challenge to established notions of subjecthood in the late 1860s was posed over nationality itself, one aspect of this being the radical interest in Italian nationalism, the other closer to home.[11] Since the political union of England and Scotland in 1604 a person's legal status as a 'natural-born subject' of Great Britain had been conditional on being born within the realm (*jus soli*). That 'subjecthood' primarily took the form of indelible allegiance to the Crown, embodying a notion of feudal allegiance which had been under strain since the American War of Independence, and reached crisis point when, in 1867, Irish-born American citizens fighting the British Government during the Fenian uprising were arrested as traitors to the Crown. The ensuing diplomatic crisis (alluded to by Trollope in *He Knew He Was Right*) starkly dramatized the impossibility of reconciling an increasingly anachronistic notion of subjecthood with a modern international

---

[8]   See George W. Stocking Jr, *Victorian Anthropology* (New York: The Free Press, 1987), pp. 117–28; pp. 164–79 and Christopher Herbert, *Culture and Anomie: Ethnographic Imagination in the Nineteenth Century* (Chicago and London: Chicago University Press, 1991), pp. 60–65, and pp. 136–48.

[9]   See Mary Poovey, *Uneven Developments: The Ideological Work on Gender in Mid-Victorian England* (London: Virago, 1989), pp. 51–88.

[10]   Morris, *Imagining Inclusive Society*, pp. 3–5.

[11]   On the importance of Italian nationalism to British radical politics in the 1860s, see Margot Finn, *After Chartism: Class and Nation in British Radical Politics 1848-74* (Cambridge, UK: Cambridge University Press, 1993).

system of nation states, and the Naturalisation Act of 1870 that followed it made it possible for British subjects to renounce their nationality as well as loosening national borders by easing the naturalization of aliens.[12] However the heritability of nationality had repercussions too, which came to a head in the 1860s, not primarily on the political stage, but in the courts—in the tangled relationship between the natural-born subject, and the natural child; between the bastard, the "alien" in the family and the alien, the "bastard" of the state.

Illegitimacy held an odd place in mid-nineteenth-century liberal legal culture. Under English common law a child born of unmarried parents was indelibly *filius nullius* ("nobody's child"), and while under canon law (still in operation in Scotland) and European civil law children could become legitimate retrospectively if their parents married, the English child remained illegitimate for life. The English law regarding prenuptial children came under some scrutiny during the 1850s and 1860s: it was strongly attacked by the liberal lawyer J. S. Wharton, whose *Exposition of the Laws Relating to the Women of England* emphasized the responsibility of natural fathers irrespective of marriage in 1853, and it was condemned as a "'cruel law in a Christian country'" in Collins's *No Name* (1862).[13] It was questioned, too, in the Appendix of the 1868 *Report of the Royal Commission into the Laws of Marriage*, which attempted to iron out the incommensurate marriage laws of England, Ireland, and Scotland; but while the illegitimate child was widely seen as a victim, the boundary of legitimacy itself was rarely challenged, and the *filius nullius* rule of indelible bastardy stayed in place until the twentieth century.[14]

While the discrepancies between national marriage codes underlined bastardy's legal instability, the rule that allowed nationality to be inherited also made it dependent on legitimacy, and for children born outside the realm the two kinds of status were crucially connected. Their tangled relationship gave rise to the Legitimacy Declaration Act of 1858, a confusing and often contradictory statute that enabled the newly established Divorce Court to investigate cases of doubtful legitimacy alongside those of dubious marriage, and that sprang directly from the struggle of one man, William Shedden, to prove his legitimacy and with it his status as a British subject.[15] The Shedden case was a dramatic and

---

[12]   See the opening of Chapter 87, "Mr Glascock's Marriage Completed." On the implication of the Naturalisation Act (33 and 34 Vict. c. 14) see Ann Dummet and Andrew Nichol, *Subjects, Citizens, Aliens and Others: Nationality and Immigration Law* (London: Weidenfield and Nicholson, 1990), esp. pp. 71–92.

[13]   Wilkie Collins, *No Name* [1862] (Oxford: World's Classics, 1986), p. 98.

[14]   On the debates on marriage in the 1860s, particularly as a result of the notorious Yelverton case, see Rebecca Gill "The Imperial Anxieties of a Nineteenth-Century Bigamy Case," *History Workshop Journal*, 57 (2004): 58–78.

[15]   For a full discussion of the case and its implications, see Jenny Bourne Taylor, "Bastardy and Nationality: the Curious Case of William Shedden and the 1858 Legitimacy Declaration Act," *Cultural and Social History*, 4.2 (2007): 35–56.

longstanding dispute that echoes the inheritance plots of Scott and Stevenson as well as Trollope, and that demonstrated how the preoccupation with patrimonial inheritance both extended into colonial relationships and became destabilized by patterns of migration and colonial trade established a century before. Shedden's father, William Shedden senior, the heir to a large estate in Scotland, had moved to America on family business in 1764; he had settled into business and a household and had two children, William and Jean, but had only formally married their mother a week before his death, in 1798. William senior had left his personal property to his children; but the family estate was quickly claimed by William's cousin John Patrick on the grounds that William was illegitimate. The case was taken to Scottish Court of Session in 1804, then to the Lords in 1808 where Shedden (still a child) was defended by the youthful Henry Brougham. Shedden lost, but having made his fortune in colonial trade, returned to Britain to fight for his inheritance in 1848, and kept up his unsuccessful struggle, using up his fortune in the process, until the case was finally defeated in the Lords in 1869.

Shedden's case prompted a series of staged disputes over the meaning of legitimacy as it was re-enacted through the nineteenth century. "Legitimacy is entirely a creature of the law" Brougham maintained in 1808; while his opponent Samuel Romilly drew on natural law theory to argue that the status of legitimacy was universal, though the means of acquiring it might differ.[16] The case brought together a bewildering array of laws, as informal colonial partnerships and the discrepant marriage rules of England (and America as its former colony) and Scotland came up against inheritance claims based on nationality and domicile. Should William's position be judged by Scottish criteria, where the property was situated, and where he would be legitimate, or by English common law, which America, where he was born, still officially followed? How did his nationality affect his inheritance rights, since, bastard or not, he would be debarred from holding a tenured estate in Scotland as an alien, and he could only be a British subject (since he was born in America) as his father's legal son? Indeed, it was finally Shedden's nationality that confirmed his status as the case came again before the Lords in 1854 and 1869. Shedden may have been legitimate according to the custom of the country, as American society increasingly resisted the old *filius nullius* rule, Lord Cranworth the Lord Chancellor conceded in 1854: "but at the time of his birth he had no father. The consequence was that alienage attached upon him and attached upon him irreversibly."[17] Here the outworn notion of indelible allegiance at once drew meaning from, and reinforced, indelible bastardy.

---

[16] John Fraser MacQueen, *Report of Scotch Appeals and Writs of Error, Together with Peerage, Divorce and Practice Cases, in the House of Lords* (4 vols., Edinburgh: T. and T. Clark, 1855), vol. 1, p. 550.

[17] MacQueen, *Report*, pp. 612–13.

Noble sons and spurious inheritors: *Ralph the Heir*

This contradictory formation, in which illegitimacy becomes the arena in which older, anachronistic structures are held in position as class divisions and the boundaries of the nation are being actively redefined, is reworked in Trollope's late fiction, where the uncertain figure of the bastard highlights the competing claims of natural, legal and moral right. Trollope was familiar with Jacobean drama and reworks older traditions of the fictional bastard. But he also responds specifically to George Eliot's recently published *Felix Holt, the Radical.* Harold Transome (the unwitting adulterine bastard whose origins are quickly revealed to the reader, and who has turned himself into an alien by his long sojourn in Smyrna) is at once modern, with his radical political views, and profoundly conservative, with his patriarchalist views of women. It is Harold who both pulls the "political" and "inheritance" strands of the novel together and who (again unwittingly) reveals the ideological emptiness and illegitimacy of both.[18] But while the spurious heir is set against Felix's static monumentality and "higher" moral and cultural authority in an implicitly conservative rejection of the political sphere, Trollope's representation of illegitimacy is a more ambiguous representation of the tensions within what he describes in his *Autobiography* as his "advanced but still conservative" Liberalism.[19]

Trollope's late fiction amplifies contemporary liberal ambivalence towards legitimacy by representing bastardy as fictive and arbitrary yet also as rooted in a belief in the necessity of cultural rather than genealogical continuity. It is where and how the weight falls in this ambivalence that is significant: the child may be the innocent victim of the father's transgression, but this does not override the fact that, for Trollope, the father (and it is usually the father rather than the mother) *has* transgressed, and his sins *are* visited on the children, no matter how unjustly. Yet (and in contrast with Eliot) any notion of "higher legitimacy" is elusive in these late novels.[20] Trollope plays on the instability of illegitimacy to satirize fixed moral positions and to highlight how legal codes are rooted in social and economic interests. But if the comic tone of much of his narrative generates a sense of complicity, of shared values with an implied upper-middle-class reader, it also pulls the ground of that complicity away, as the use of irony and parody, and the deployment of multiple plots undercuts any overarching legitimising narrative framework.

---

[18]   See Catherine Gallagher, *The Industrial Reformation of English Fiction: Social Discourse as Narrative Form* (Chicago and London: Chicago University Press, 1985), pp. 219–67.

[19]   Anthony Trollope, *An Autobiography* [1883] (Harmondsworth: Penguin Classics, 1996), p. 186.

[20]   For a contrasting interpretation, see R. D. McMaster, *Trollope and the Law* (London: Macmillian, 1986), pp 1–32.

Indeed, *Ralph the Heir, Lady Anna* and *Is He Popenjoy?* each take up particular elements within *Felix Holt*: the relationship between legitimacy in the family and the polity at a moment of political reform (Harold Transome); the question of the unsanctioned daughter's claim (Esther Lyon); and the status of the mixed-race, dubiously legitimate son (little Harry). By reconfiguring these elements, Trollope highlights the inconsistency within the Burkean ideal of genealogical continuity as the basis of social stability—yet is unable to offer any alternative. While *Felix Holt* opens with a self-consciously historicising Preface and is set in the aftermath of the 1832 Reform Act, *Ralph the Heir* takes place in the immediate past (drawing on Trollope's own disastrous experience in the Beverley by-election), and sets the dispute over a name and estate alongside the political fall-out of the extension of the franchise in the mid 1860s. But while the ironizing tension in *Felix Holt* rests on Harold's formal legitimacy as an adulterine bastard (for illegitimacy within marriage was extremely difficult to prove legally), *Ralph the Heir* ironizes the notion of heirdom itself in the contrast of the legitimate and illegitimate cousins who share a name—"Ralph Newton"—and who, like the cousins Shedden and Patrick, both have a kind of claim to Newton Priory, one based on paternal genealogy and natural affection, the other on the vagaries of law. The novel juggles the well-worn literary theme of legitimate and illegitimate brothers by setting the feckless heir (the nephew of the present Squire) against the virtuous bastard. It follows the Tory Squire's fight for testamentary freedom as he schemes to reclaim the inheritance rights on the Newton estate, altered by entail by *his* father because of his own youthful indiscretion (in making an extramarital alliance with a foreign woman), so that he may bequeath the land to his much loved natural son.

Trollope plays on the legitimate/illegitimate opposition, first by complicating the grounds of distinction between the Ralphs: Ralph the legal heir ideologically delegitimizes himself by committing the sin (in conservative terms) of turning land into liquid capital by taking out endless post-obits against his expectations; and his claim is derived indirectly, through the artificial means of an entail. Ralph the noble bastard is presented as the ideal potential heir and the perfect English gentleman by blood and temperament, but is unambiguously both illegitimate and legally an alien: his mother was French, and died before his father could marry her, averting the kind of legal tangle of the Shedden case. Second, Trollope sets different forms of marriage, mixture and economic and political power against each other in a narrative focalized through three different kinds of conservative voices. The Squire, with his horror of household suffrage, uses his class position to overturn the law. The lawyer, Thomas Underwood, reluctantly stands as Tory candidate in the Percycross election, but is himself an absent father. Lastly, the more liberal Anglican rector Gregory, legitimate Ralph's younger brother, believes in moderate progress. The Squire's scheme to bequeath the property in what he sees as the natural succession is set beside the threat of class mixture in the novel's comic counter-plot, as the tradesman Neefit attempts to offer his daughter in marriage to legitimate Ralph, and both Underwood and the Radical tradesman Ontario Moggs are the victims of political corruption.

So on one level Trollope reinforces the consensus of these conservative voices: that the blurring of the lines of class is more threatening than the boundaries of formal legitimacy. But he also implicitly reassesses both Maine and Bagehot's analysis of how legal, economic, and social structures are reinforced by symbolic forms, and this sets those same voices in mutual tension. In tracing the Squire's fight for testamentary freedom (which is cut short by his death in a hunting accident) Trollope amplifies Maine's question in *Ancient Law*—"But what was the Family? The Law defined it one way, natural affection another, and in the conflict between the two the feeling ... grew up [in which] the dictates of affection were permitted to determine the fortunes of its object."[21] Illegitimate Ralph holds a central position as an emblematic force, a self-consolidating other who explicitly upholds the structures that exclude him but in doing so, forces the reader to question them. He is a fantasy of patrilineal identification striped of ambivalence, who initially regenerates the symbolic power of the landed gentry precisely because his claim is built (in Maine's terms) on an older agnatic rather than cognatic legitimacy—on the father's desire and status rather than the contractual confusions of marriage— but who finally concurs with Gregory's sense that "things would go terribly astray [if] the right heir [i.e. legitimate Ralph] was extruded."[22]

Bastard Ralph's story, told almost in tragic vein, is one of the strategies by which the other narrative, of political inclusion and social mobility, can be safely relegated to the comic realm. But the very duplication of the family name also makes "Ralph Newton" itself a tenuous identity (Ralph can only be "Ralph who was not the heir" (vol. 1, p. 129), "this other Ralph" (vol. 1, p. 171 and so on), so that in sustaining these forms, the novel eats away at the possibility of any higher-order authority that his subaltern presence may suggest. And this means, too, that the monumentality of Ralph the Bastard as upholder of the symbolic order is undermined both by his own belatedness and by his legitimate counterpart, whose chronic indeterminacy and deferral eats away at the novel's Tory consensus, just as his post-obits drain the estate. "For every Harry Esmond, there are fifty Ralph Newtons" muses the narrator (vol. 2, p. 339).[23] Finally Newton Priory is maintained as a piece of heritage culture in which "the broad-acred squire" is a "comparatively modern invention" (vol. 2, p. 252), as Ralph the Heir is married off for the sake of an invented lineage. Everybody ultimately survives by "growing into some shape of conviction from the moulds in which they are made to live" (vol. 2, p. 142).

---

[21]   Henry Sumner Maine, *Ancient Law* [1861] (London: John Murray, 1927), p. 238.

[22]   Anthony Trollope, *Ralph the Heir* [1871] (Oxford: World's Classics, 1990), vol. 1, p. 340.

[23]   On the almost nihilistic emptiness of "legitimate Ralph" see Christopher Herbert, *Trollope and Comic Pleasure* (Chicago and London: Chicago University Press, 1987), pp. 117–232.

Legitimacy and allegiance: *Lady Anna*

The relative claims of legal, moral, and natural right, and the question of what legitimate possession actually means depends on keeping the legal distinction between the two claimants intact in *Ralph the Heir*, though it is never finally answered. In *Lady Anna* and *Is He Popenjoy?* the instability of the law itself lies at the centre of Trollope's exploration of what it means to have a valid identity as residual structures and alliances come under increasing pressure of new forms of subjecthood and shifting patterns of affiliation. Opening in the 1810s in the aftermath of the French Revolution, then brought forward 20 years to the decade of the First Reform Act, *Lady Anna* (Trollope's favorite, and perhaps most sensational, novel) revolves around the disputed status of the daughter of Josephine McMurray and the Earl Lovell, in a celebrated case that, like *Shedden v Patrick*, spans two generations, two countries, and two branches of a family, and that rests on the almost improvable question of whether the wicked old Earl's previous liaison with an Italian countess had constituted a valid marriage.

Lady Anna plays on the correlations between valid birth, national affiliation and political allegiance, through this double historical lens, which sets up the novel's key inter-class relationship, then places it under strain. On first being declared illegitimate Anna and Josephine are taken in by the radical shoemaker Thomas Thwaite, an artisan steeped in the revolutionary culture of the 1790s who regards their claim to legitimacy (echoing the contemporary Tichborne case) as emblematic of the political claims of the poor and excluded; and the novel explores the consequences of that bond for the next generation in the 1830s.[24] The inheritance and political narratives are explicably blended here, and there are no other courtship and marriage plots to qualify the central drive of the story. But now Trollope transforms the legitimacy plot by making his claimant a woman whose position as claimant and subject is continually qualified by her role as object of exchange, and who becomes firstly the linchpin for the survival of the aristocratic family; then the means of both enabling a process of political transformation and of marking its limits.

This means *Lady Anna* recasts Esther Lyon's story in *Felix Holt*, as contemporary critics noted: Anna resists the legitimacy of rank in favour of her working-class childhood sweetheart, the shoemaker's son Daniel Thwaite, choosing to renounce her hereditary class position in favor of affective allegiance.[25] But again Trollope problematizes Eliot's means of ideological and fictional closure, and Anna's shifting legal and social status as both a legal claimant and a woman are equally crucial to this process, as legitimacy itself is redefined in different ideological contexts and used for varying political ends. In contrast with Ralph Newton, Anna's position

---

[24] See Rohan McWilliams, *The Tichborne Claimant* (London: Hambledon Continuum, 2007).

[25] Unsigned notice, *The Saturday Review* 9 May 1874, in Donald Smalley, *Trollope, the Critical Heritage* (London: Routledge, 1969), p. 387.

lacks the authority of paternal sanction—Trollope plays on the rhetoric of radical melodrama by making her father the old Earl a burlesque aristocratic libertine, an un-English embodiment of a Gothic *ancien régime*. Josephine and Anna's legitimacy is first taken up as a radical cause by Thomas and Daniel Thwaite, a way of opposing absolutist power, but it is then transformed into a parody of a racialized belief in rank as Josephine denies the obligations of the past and embarks on an increasingly obsessive quest to prove her daughter's legitimacy, as status hierarchy segues into rigid classificatory categories.

Anna's status, too, is continually triangulated, making her the linchpin in the formation of various kinds of national boundaries. She is ideologically sanctioned by being set against the old Earl's first wife—who is not only Italian but also seen as an impostor, and the Whiggish compromise that the Solicitor-General, Sir William Patterson, suggests—that Anna should marry the new heir and thus consolidate the aristocratic family—is complicated by Anna's own genuine attraction for the young Earl, who is himself a modern middle-class professional rather than feudal survival. Against the Solicitor-General's expediency is set the canon law concept of marriage as pre-contract, that binds Anna to Daniel as strongly as genuine affection. Here companionate rather than dynastic marriage forms the basis of civil society, and this is finally sanctioned by Sir William as the basis of a newly inclusive political nation; but is complicated, again, by Daniel's own re-creation of patriarchal power within the private sphere. "'For a man with sound views on domestic power and marital rights always choose a Radical!'" Sir William sardonically notes.[26] Through the Whig Solicitor-General the law thus forms the story's narrative framework and its internal mediation, one based on negotiation and compromise rather than principle, and resulting in a powerful investigation of how the fiction of legitimacy functions as social cement.[27]

Missing futures: *Is He Popenjoy?*

"The plan of jumping at once into the middle has often been tried ... but the writer still has to hark back and begin again from the beginning—not always very comfortably after the abnormal brightness of his few opening pages...."[28] Refusing to open *in media res*, Trollope's novel of 1878 begins with a sardonic nod towards the famous gambling scene in *Daniel Deronda*. But *Is He Popenjoy?* also returns to the future heir of Transome Court, the mixed-race infant heir of dubiously legitimate parentage, and the questions raised by Harold's "oriental"

---

[26]   Anthony Trollope, *Lady Anna* [1874] (Oxford: World's Classics, 1990), p. 483.

[27]   On the role of the Solicitor-General as emblem of the law, see also McMaster, *Trollope and the Law*, pp. 119–34. For an excellent discussion of the novel, see also Robert Tracy, *Trollope's Later Novels* (Los Angeles, University of California Press 1978).

[28]   Anthony Trollope, *Is He Popenjoy?* [1878] (Oxford, World's Classics, 1973), vol. 1, pp. 2–3.

marriage to a former slave (that are rendered irrelevant as the focus of legitimacy in *Felix Holt* moves elsewhere), are central to this novel. Both little Harry and the infant of Trollope's title are presented as dark-skinned "savage" children, but in *Is He Popenjoy?* the child's legitimacy is both the occasion of the novel's own name, and is made the subject of intense scrutiny. The novel returns to those questions of lawful ownership and moral right that *Ralph the Heir* had pushed to the point of absurdity in the two Ralph Newtons, but now the blankness of legitimacy—the name as an open totem, an empty space standing for a position and a property—is taken a stage further, to a state of almost complete absence: legitimacy is now based on projection and fantasy and is finally nothing but a (rather silly) name.

Is He Popenjoy? extends Trollope's preoccupation with the struggle for survival of the waning aristocratic family in the face of irreversible modernity, and once more the legitimacy plot is set up as a counterweight to the marriage plot and to the narrative of the younger son, in contrast to *Lady Anna*, where these elements are folded within it. Rather than being the embodiment of mobility and modernity however, George Germaine is the weak-willed, impoverished younger brother of the Marquis of Brotherton, another decadent, alienated, anachronistic aristocratic, who, like Earl Lovell in *Lady Anna*, has symbolically delegitimized himself by decamping to Italy (that resonant emblem of not-quite-otherness in the 1860s) to escape the middle-class respectability of England. Occupying the inbred, claustrophobic Manor Cross as heir presumptive, George makes an expedient marriage to Mary Lovelace, daughter of the ambitious and urbane Dean of Brotherton to consolidate his position. But George's *de facto* occupancy is disrupted by the return of the Marquis, who, in an outburst of agnatic absolutism, turns his relations into tenants on his estates and establishes himself, his Italian wife and sickly heir—the "Popenjoy" of the title. George's authority is challenged not only by this external threat, but also by the rebellion of his wife, who resists the family's collective patriarchal control, spending her time in her own separate property in London. Even the child she eventually bears is of implicitly dubious legitimacy, being born after a ten-month pregnancy![29]

Is He Popenjoy? demonstrates extraordinarily explicitly how legitimacy is always an effect of an essentially illusory symbolic power, even as it is formed by the wider concepts of kinship, race, family, and national belonging that surround that power. It is the upwardly mobile Dean who obsessively attempts to prove Popenjoy's bastardy—moving the blurring of class boundaries into the heart of the legitimacy plot—and his lawyers initially reveal that the Marquis married the Countess a year after the birth of the child, making him legitimate in Italy but both a bastard and an alien in England. But this potential conflict of laws is displaced (as it is at later stages of the Shedden case) by the revelation that the couple had undergone an earlier informal marriage, leading to a legal tangle that is only resolved by the child's untimely death. Like the case of *Shedden v Patrick* the struggle over Popenjoy's legitimacy hangs on the relative authority of different

---

[29] Thanks to Margaret Markwick for discussing this point with me.

marriage codes as well as the conflicted position of prenuptial children. Unlike the Shedden case the conflict remains within the family, but this further highlights its own internal crisis of legitimacy, as George's horror of the child as "'a blot to the family'" is temporarily overridden by the need to maintain the symbolic structures of primogeniture in the face of the Dean's ambition and the meritocratic blurring of rank that it implies (vol. 1, p.128). "'Upon my soul, I don't know whether he was legitimate or not, according to English fashions,'" the Marquis finally admits in private. "'What a rumpus there has been about a rickety brat that was bound to die!'" (vol. 2, p. 202).

So paradoxically, the baby's legitimacy is absolutely central and completely supplementary, and George's own lineage can be elevated only by a very different kind of order from the Burkean one which he upholds. In many respects the legitimacy plot, underpinned by the family as a dynastic unit, is displaced by the marriage plot that lies at the centre of *Is He Popenjoy?*, as what starts as a comedy of manners turns into a more disturbing exploration of the emotional and sexual power struggles within a notionally companionate marriage when the weak and ineffective George Germaine attempts to impose his patriarchal will. As Margaret Markwick has noted, *Is He Popenjoy?* "is one of Trollope's most subtle texts" in this respect; but what both elements of the novel "marriage" and "legitimacy" share—and what contemporary critics found most disturbing—is its relativism, its exploration, in the *Academy*'s words, of 'how very slight are the barriers which part modern civilization from ancient savagery'.[30]

"It is entirely a matter of social policy under what circumstances the issue of a man and a woman be deemed legitimate" argued the lawyer Hugh Weightman, in 1871, and Trollope's final completed novel, *Mr Scarborough's Family* (1883) pushes the idea of legitimacy as fiction to its ultimate conclusion.[31] The novel re-enacts the dispute between Brougham and Romilly in the Shedden case in the ideological contest between the ultra-pragmatist, Mr Scarborough (who alternately bastardises and re-legitimises his eldest son, Mountjoy) and the solicitor Mr Grey, who attempts to hold onto natural law principles.[32] Yet the slipperiness of legitimacy that the novel plays on also highlights the dilemma that Trollope has explored more subtly in the 1870s, and which, perhaps, forms part of the wider tension in his fiction: the friction between his detached "anthropological" investigation of the surfaces of manners and *mores* and his dramatisation of their "deeper" emotional and psychological effects. Indeed the bastard may ultimately be the *aporia* at the heart of Trollope's late fiction: a "creature of the law" that demonstrates its

---

[30]   Margaret Markwick, *Trollope and Women* (London: The Trollope Society 1997), p. 144; *The Academy*, 8 June 1878, Smalley, *Critical Heritage*, p. 440.

[31]   Hugh Weightman, *The Law of Marriage and Legitimacy, with Especial Reference to the Jurisdiction Conferred by the Legitimacy Declaration Act* (London: Henry Sweet, 1871), p. 3.

[32]   See Herbert, *Trollope and Comic Pleasure*, pp.122–9, and McMaster, *Trollope and the Law*, pp.135–54.

underlying economic interests, and a victim of a process of exclusion that Trollope can neither completely attack nor quite bring himself to defend.

Chapter 4
Out of the Closet:
Homoerotics in Trollope's Novels

Margaret Markwick

In the twenty-first century, readers turn to Trollope to critique so many aspects of Victorian cultural history. Where once Trollope was the redoubt of an old-guard, masculinist rationale, close new readings show his highly individual take on subjects as diverse as politics, commerce, empire and colonialism, class, law and, of course, gender, where his presentation of women who buck the sexual stereotypes of the age has been recognized for many years, and his equally innovative constructions of masculinity are increasingly attracting attention.[1] However, Trollope has been less frequently considered when we seek to examine men outside the parameters of heterosexual behaviour. This is a sad oversight, since when we come to examine his treatment of sexually equivocal men, we find a Trollope who challenges our perceptions of what it was to be a man attracted to other men in the times when he was writing. Michael Mason, in *The Making of Victorian Sexuality*,[2] observes that evidence about homosexuality in the period up to 1880 is extremely meager, an assertion supported by Brian Reade's earlier and originative anthology, *Sexual Heretics: Male Homosexuality in English Literature from 1850 to 1900*, which has 21 entries from the first 30 years, and 68 from the last 20.[3] And though Eve Kosofsky Sedgwick in *Between Men* examines canonical Victorian texts to challenge the assumption that homosexual existence is necessarily different from and in adversarial relation to other sorts of masculine experience, no one has yet turned to Trollope to discover a liberal and tolerant voice describing passionate love between men.

---

[1]   See, for instance, Deborah Denenholz Morse, *Women in Trollope's Palliser Novels* (Ann Arbor: UMI Research Press, 1987), Jane Nardin, *He Knew She Was Right: The Independent Woman in the Novels of Anthony Trollope* (Carbondale: Southern Illinois UP, 1989), Mark W. Turner, *Trollope and the Magazines: Gendered Issues in Mid-Victorian Britain* (Basingstoke: Macmillan, 2000), and Margaret Markwick, *New Men in Trollope's Novels: Rewriting the Victorian Male* (Aldershot: Ashgate, 2007).

[2]   Michael Mason, *The Making of Victorian Sexuality* (Oxford: Oxford University Press, 1995), p. 6.

[3]   Brian Reade, *Sexual Heretics: Male Homosexuality in English Literature from 1850 to 1900* (New York: Coward-McCann, 1970).

Sedgwick's study is a finely nuanced theory of shifting relationships between the sexes, where homophobia is an intrinsic and inevitable part of heterosexual marriage contracts, and desire between men is a part of the normal structure of gender relationships. She speaks of a "potential unbrokenness between homosocial and homosexual,"[4] and argues for a shift away from the binary opposition of homosexual/heterosexual definitions. Her analysis is critiqued by Richard Dellamora in *Masculine Desire*, which foregrounds his own writings "about texts by men from the point of view of a gay male."[5] Both Sedgwick and Dellamora examine Tennyson to support their arguments. But while Sedgwick's reading of *The Princess* explores female fantasy of male homosexual exchange,[6] Dellamora uses *In Memoriam* to enquire into the intense relationships between the Apostles at Cambridge to support his thesis of a consciously cryptic text.[7] Though this long commemoration, then as now, is regularly read as an exploration of generalized grief and loss (Queen Victoria is said to have found it particularly consoling), Reade also includes it in his anthology of homoerotic texts, because of its references to the Shakespeare of the Sonnets, Greek philosophy, and Arcady, arcadian being part of the generation's vocabulary for erotic relationships between men.[8] Dellamora argues for a much more specific reading. Using letters from Tennyson, and between other members of the Apostles (particularly Arthur Hallam and Richard Monckton-Milne), where acknowledgment of a sexual dimension to relationships is barely concealed beneath the surface, he posits that Tennyson pays tribute to a homoeroticism that is presented as a triangulation between God, the male poet, and an idealized love object, which segues between Hallam and the female.[9] This ambiguity is indeed the poem's great strength. As Dellamora says, "erotic sentiment is free continually to expand precisely because … the poem is conceived in aesthetic, not sexual-aesthetic terms."[10] This is particularly pertinent to this examination of Trollope's fiction, which, while its primary tenor promotes an ideal of the sexual and companionate union between a man and a woman, advances simultaneously a view that equally valorizes the homosocial and the homoerotic, and resonates with both Sedgwick's and Dellamora's constructions.

---

[4]   Eve Kosofsky Sedgwick, *Between Men: English Literature and Male Homosexual Desire* (New York: Columbia University Press, 1985), p. 1.

[5]   Richard Dellamora, *Masculine Desire: The Sexual Politics of Victorian Aestheticism* (Chapel Hill: University of North Carolina Press, 1990), p. 5. Since then, Dellamora has written about the marginalization of Ferdinand Lopez in *The Prime Minister* in "The Lesser Holocaust of William Gladstone and Anthony Trollope" in *Friendship's Bonds: Democracy and the Novel in Victorian England* (Philadelphia: University of Pennsylvania Press, 2004).

[6]   Sedgwick, pp. 118–33.

[7]   Dellamora, pp. 16–41.

[8]   Reade, p. 8.

[9]   Dellamora, p. 31.

[10]   Dellamora, p. 39.

As Jeffrey Weeks makes clear in his 1977 study,[11] when Trollope was writing, the prevailing ethos did not yet include the concept of homosexuality per se. Indeed, behaviors that we would describe as homosexual were at that time more likely to be seen as part of undifferentiated male lust, which, while perverse, was natural and unchangeable. Moreover, the concept of homosexuality, and the vocabulary that is used today to articulate it, did not exist in Trollope's day. The word "homosexual," coined in 1867 in a medical pamphlet by a Hungarian, Karl Maria Benkert, did not gain any currency in Britain until the mid 1890s, supporting the Foucauldian view of homosexuality as an identity as a cultural construction of the late nineteenth century.[12] This is reflected in the vocabulary of the middle years of the nineteenth century; homoerotic behavior was neutrally referred to as Arcadian, Socratic, or invert, or contrary to sexual instinct. Slang terms of disparagement such as Molly, Mary-Anne, and from the 1850s onwards, Margery and pooff did exist, but for the full range of offence and vilification, we have to wait for the twentieth century.

More recently, Harry Cocks has examined the records of criminal proceedings against men charged with sodomy and related offences through the nineteenth century. His study at times seems to imply a century-long witch-hunt of sexual aberration. However, it is clear from the Boulton and Park case that public opinion did not necessarily share the moralistic prejudices of the prosecutors.[13] And Michael Mason cites the case of the non-conformist minister John Church, who was welcomed back by his congregation after serving a two-year prison sentence for a homosexual offence.[14] Such incidents suggest a seam of liberal and tolerant attitudes in the world at large, and belie the bigotry expressed, particularly by the established Church, in Cocks's study.

In exploring relationships between men, Trollope distinguishes warm friendships between men, and relationships with a clear homoerotic element to them. His narrator is a fine articulator and analyzer of warm and lasting commitment

---

[11]   Jeffrey Weeks, *Coming Out: Homosexual Politics in Britain from the Nineteenth Century to the Present* (London: Quartet Books, 1977). This is still the primary text offering a systematic examination of the history of legal prosecution of genital sex between men, and is the reference point of all subsequent commentators, such as Graham Robb, *Strangers: Homosexual Love in the Nineteenth Century* (Basingstoke: Picador, 2003) and Harry Cocks, *Nameless Offences: Homosexual Desire in the Nineteenth Century* (London: I. B. Tauris, 2003).

[12]   Michael Foucault, *The History of Sexuality: Volume 1, an Introduction* 1976 (London: Penguin, 1990), p. 43.

[13]   See Cocks pp. 105–14 and Ronald Pearsall, *The Worm in the Bud: The World of Victorian Sexuality* 1969 (Stroud: Sutton, 2003), pp. 461–66. Both give lengthy and graphic accounts of this case of two cross-dressers and two friends, famously prosecuted in 1871 for "conspiring and inciting persons to commit an unnatural offence." The jury took less than an hour to find them not guilty.

[14]   Mason, p. 42.

in friendships such as this between Frank Fenwick and Harry Gilmour in *The Vicar of Bullhampton*:

> He loved his friend dearly. Between these two there had grown up now during a period of many years that undemonstrative, unexpressed, almost unconscious affection, which, with men, will often make the greatest charm of their lives. It may be doubted whether either of them had ever told the other of his regard. Yours always in writing was the warmest term that was ever used. These two men had never given anything, one to the other, beyond a worn-out walking stick or a cigar. They were rough to each other, caustic, and almost ill-mannered. But they thoroughly trusted each other, and the happiness, prosperity, and above all the honour of one were to the other, matters of keenest moment.[15]

The authorial voice, unafraid to call the feeling "love," in its manner of valorizing this relationship, expects his readers to recognize, and his male readers to identify with this deep and significant bond that, while it will never find expression either physical or verbal, is nevertheless of major significance—"the greatest charm of their lives." When Trollope says "Yours always in writing was the warmest term that was ever used," he makes an unapologetic affirmation of Tennyson's rather defensive back-pedaling 1870 remark "If anybody thinks I ever called him 'dearest' in his life they are much mistaken, for I never even called him 'dear.'"[16] This construction of deep but unarticulated feeling between men is reiterated but significantly qualified in the friendship between John Grey and Frank Seward in *Can You Forgive Her?* Here, John Grey asks Frank Seward, a friend from his Cambridge days, if he will stay in his house to be there when he returns from London, where he goes to see Alice, the woman he loves, who has just declared she intends to marry her reprobate cousin: "His intimacy with Seward was of that thorough kind which is engendered only out of such young and lasting friendship as had existed between them; but even to such a friend as this Mr Grey could not open his whole heart. It was only to a friend who should also be his wife that he could do that."[17] This reservation points to wider issues of appropriate expression of masculinity, and makes an important point about the significant and safe verbalization of vulnerable feelings.[18] In both these examples Trollope is making a significant point about the nature of close relationships between men, where relationships forged at university, perhaps even at school, and certainly in late adolescence, have a depth to them that transcends the heterosexual bond of

---

[15]   Anthony Trollope, *The Vicar of Bullhampton* 1870 (Oxford: Oxford University Press, 1988), p. 440.

[16]   Dellamora, p. 28.

[17]   Anthony Trollope, *Can You Forgive Her?* 1864 (Oxford: Oxford University Press, 1982), vol. 1, p. 372.

[18]   This is the subject of a much wider exploration of the issues of male emotional vulnerability in Markwick, *New Men in Trollope's Novels*.

Fig. 4.1   "The English Von Bauhr and his pupil." Millais's illustration for
Orley Farm, Chapter 18

marriage, where the expression of deep feeling is sublimated in shared activity at critical times in their growth into manhood. Relationships formed between men at public schools and the universities were, of course, fostered to bolster the hegemony of government and the professions. However, here Trollope makes emotional literacy the bedrock of a significant male bond formed in these impressionable years, and argues that this literacy is no less potent for being unarticulated. This is well illustrated in the friendship between two older men, the Earl of Brentford and Violet Effingham's father, in *Phineas Finn*: "They had been young men in the same regiment, and through life each had confided in the other. When the General's only son, then a youth of seventeen, was killed in one of our grand New Zealand wars, the bereaved father and the Earl had been together for a month in their sorrow."[19] This last sentence conveys compassion, understanding of the nature of grief, the shared bonds of the joy and pain of parenthood. And while these are examples of warm and tender friendships between men, there is no suggestion of sexual arousal.

Trollope's ventures into homoerotic territory were first explored by Mark Turner in 2000, in his decoding of *The Turkish Bath* as a soft-porn story of gay cruising. Turner's close reading of this short story, first published in *St Pauls Magazine* in 1869, under Trollope's own editorship, emphasizes Trollope's use of an oriental ambience in the location of his story. In his Turkish bath we are asked to notice the "picturesque orientalism," the "eastern tone," the "very skilful eastern boys."[20] This was followed in 2003 by Mark Forrester's examination of the links between orientalism and homoerotics in another short story, *The Banks of the Jordan*. In this essay, Forrester suggests that Trollope's choice of an oriental setting for his story offers him the opportunity more freely to explore sexual license, "these inherent ambiguities of power, identity and desire."[21] This short story had had a chequered career. It was first of all rejected by George Smith of *The Cornhill*, who asked Trollope to remove the "indelicacies," the scenes where the narrator speaks too explicitly about the chafing of the nether regions caused by a Turkish saddle, and his readiness to anoint the affected flesh of his companion with brandy. Subsequently, Trollope sold it as part of a sequence of eight short stories to *The London Review*, which published it, in 1861, without scrutiny. The proprietors were horrified by the "disapprobation" it received from their readers, and quickly pulled the series. It is clear from the letter that Lawrence Oliphant, one of the proprietors, sent to Trollope deploring the story, that the offence they charge him with was caused by the inherent impropriety of a man discovered traveling with an unmarried, unchaperoned young woman, not the undercurrents of homoeroticism.

---

[19]   Anthony Trollope, *Phineas Finn* 1869 (Ware: Wordsworth, 1996), p. 92.

[20]   Turner, p. 201.

[21]   Mark Forrester, "Redressing the Empire: Anthony Trollope and British Gender Anxiety in *The Banks of the Jordan*," in Philip Holden and Richard J Ruppel (eds), *Imperial Desire: Dissonant Sexualities and Colonial Literature* (Minneapolis: University of Minnesota Press, 2003), p. 117.

It was subsequently published in 1863 in *Tales of All Countries* (vol. 2).[22] *The Banks of the Jordan* can be entertainingly read as a tale of what Sedgwick might call "male homosexual panic."[23] A middle-aged and married man feels himself increasingly and worryingly attracted to a beautiful young man, who turns out to be a young woman. This Shakespearean narrative gambit is constructed with a great deal of comedy; we are drawn to laugh at Jones, the married man, increasingly perturbed that he finds Smith attractive. Such discomfiture being outside his habitual sexual comfort zone, there is a clear sense of relief on his part when he realizes, in the denouement, that he has been feeling attracted to a woman, and a pretty one at that. But in inviting us to identify with Jones, Trollope's authorial voice also feeds into readerly homoerotic anxieties. He beguiles us into enjoying the titillation of Jones's embarrassment, but ultimately leaves us unsure whether the relief we are cozened into feeling at the end is caused by our identification with Jones' discomfort or drawn from our own homosexual uncertainty. Both these short stories are explorations of the permissible parameters of sexual expression between men. And while there is some equivocacy in *The Banks of the Jordan*, *The Turkish Bath* has an entirely uncritical authorial voice telling of a man in his middle years, married and explicitly attracted to young women, enjoying the frisson of homosexual encounters when naked in a bath-house.

As Turner and Forrester point out, Trollope, like other men of his class and education, regularly associates the East with aberrant sexuality. This concept of racially and culturally determined sexual preferences had long been believed. As Rudi C. Bleys says in *The Geography of Perversion*: "Just as Islam had been associated with sodomy for many centuries, the Orient in its turn became almost synonymous with 'sodomitical' ... Sexuality—and sodomy in particular—thus became a major vehicle for European construction of Asian identity from an early stage."[24] In referring to a "European construction" of things eastern, Bleys is, of course, echoing Edward Said's classic work on orientalism, a concept he perceives as being entirely defined and determined by the West; the orient is "other", "not us"; orientalism the reflection of Western imperialism and superiority. "It is Europe that articulates the Orient; this articulation is the prerogative, not of a puppet master, but of a genuine creator, whose life-giving power represents, animates, constitutes the otherwise silent and dangerous space beyond familiar boundaries."[25]

---

[22]   N. John Hall, *Trollope: A Biography* (Oxford: Oxford University Press, 1991), pp. 207–9. Oliphant's letter is in *The Letters of Anthony Trollope* ed. N. John Hall (Stanford: Stanford University Press, 1983), vol. 1, pp. 140–41.

[23]   A phrase regularly used by Sedgwick—see pp. 83 and 116, and Dellamora, pp. 8 and 259.

[24]   Rudi C. Bleys, *The Geography of Perversion: Male-to-Male Sexual Behaviour Outside the West and the Ethnographic Imagination, 1750–1918* (London: Cassell, 1996), p. 31.

[25]   Edward W. Said, *Orientalism* 1978 (London: Penguin, 2003), p. 57.

This "silent and dangerous space beyond familiar boundaries" fired the imagination of so many nineteenth-century men who made their careers in Britain's ever-widening empire. Sir Richard Burton, soldier, intrepid explorer, polyglot, travel writer, diplomat, and translator of *The Arabian Nights*, spent much of his professional career from the early 1840s onwards in the Middle East. In 1845, while working under General Sir Charles Napier, having become sufficiently fluent in Hindi to pass as a native, he infiltrated the male brothels in Karachi, and wrote the report that helped Napier clamp down on pederasty. His *Terminal Essay*, published with his translation of the last volume of *The Arabian Nights* in 1888, comments on a lifetime of examination of cultural differences in all things sexual. Burton identifies what he describes as a "Sotadic zone," a region determined by geography and climate, not race, where sexual activity between men "is popular and endemic, held at the worst to be a mere pecadillo."[26] This area encompassed Mediterranean France, Iberia, Italy, and Greece, with the coastal areas of North Africa from Morocco to Egypt, and thence running eastward through Asia Minor, Persia, Afghanistan, the Punjab, and Kashmir to China and Japan. There is good literary and anecdotal evidence that such beliefs were widespread through the nineteenth century. Flaubert, for instance, sent to Cairo for his health in 1850, in his letters home speaks of his homoerotic experiences in the bath-houses with young boys. And it is certainly reflected in Trollope's experiences in his travels in the Middle East.

Trollope had spent 12 weeks from February to the end of April 1858 in Egypt and the Mediterranean on Post Office duties, and had taken a ten-day holiday in the Holy Land in the middle of March. Victoria Glendinning points out[27] that this was Trollope's first big trip abroad without his wife Rose, and that the novelty of the experience is reflected in his stories written around this time, which are full of the anxieties of traveling alone, in unfamiliar situations in foreign cultures, with a constantly changing circle of new acquaintants. This voyage may indeed have crystallized much of his thinking about ambiguous sexual orientation; three of the short stories from this period are set in the Near and Middle East, and all treat with dissonant sexualities. He began writing *The Bertrams* on 1 April , while he was still away, and packed many of his new experiences into it.

George Bertram, seriously considering entering the Church, makes a pilgrimage to the Holy Land, on something of a Cook's tour—Calvary, the Garden of Gethsemane, the Mount of Olives, the tomb of Nicodemus—and the Tabernacle of the Holy Sepulchre.

> To get into the little outside chapel, which forms, as it were, a vestibule to the cell of the Sepulchre, and from which, on Easter Sunday issue the miraculous flames, was a thing to be achieved by moderate patience. His close contiguity

---

[26]   Sir Richard Burton, "Terminal Essay, section D, "Pederasty," from *The Arabian Nights* trans. Burton, 1885, reprinted Reade, p. 159.

[27]   Victoria Glendinning, *Trollope* (London: Pimlico, 1993), p. 237.

to Candiotes and Copts, to Armenians and Abyssinians was not agreeable to our hero, for the contiguity was very close, and Christians of these nations are not very cleanly. But this was nothing to the task of entering the sanctum sanctorum. To this there is but one aperture, and that is but four feet high; men entering it go in head foremost, and those retreating come out in the other direction; and as it is impossible that two should pass, and as two or three are always trying to come out, and ten or twelve equally anxious to get in, the struggle to an Englishman is disagreeably warm, though to an Oriental it is probably a matter of interesting excitement.[28]

This is a complex passage, with an authorial voice describing the experience, the implicit voice of George, as an Englishman experiencing the situation, and that of Trollope the tourist, who has but recently experienced the tour himself. It is a passage of travel writing, aimed at an English audience, and it confirms that audience's prejudices about foreigners, and Orientals in particular. Within the novel, it is an episode building up to George's rejection of the Church as a career. It feeds into the currents of religious doubt stirred up by Strauss's account of an historical Christ.[29] In focusing on the heat, the dirt, the unseemly crush, and the uncomfortable proximity of foreign bodies, the struggle to reach the inner sanctum becomes a trope about the Roman, Greek, and Coptic veneration of relics, an affirmation of Anglican rejection of fetishism and superstition. It plays on Anglocentric prejudices, the sense of superiority that every right-thinking Briton has over Johnny Foreigner, and ends with a jesting dig at his sexual preferences. It is a piece of its time. Adult jokes about sex are commonplace in Trollope, and this one is typical.[30] Its articulation has some elegance and balance, and it is decidedly unmoralistic. It has no tinge of the "unspeakable crime" identified by Harry Cocks; and while there is clear distancing between Englishman and Oriental, there is no disparagement.

It is not the only time that Trollope makes a jocular reference to the Orient as a focus for homoerotic pleasure. In *Barchester Towers* we read:

[Bertie Stanhope] was comfortably ensconced in the ha-ha … eagerly engaged in conversation with some youngster from the further side of the county, whom he had never met before, who was also smoking under Bertie's pupillage, and listening with open ears to an account given by his companion of some of the pastimes of Eastern clime.[31]

---

[28] Anthony Trollope, *The Bertrams* 1859 (London: Penguin, 1993), p. 61.
[29] See Owen Chadwick, *The Victorian Church* (London: Black, 1966), vol. 1, pp. 487–9.
[30] See Markwick, *New Men in Trollope's Novels*, Ch. 8.
[31] Anthony Trollope, *Barchester Towers* 1857 (Oxford: Oxford University Press, 1996), vol. 2, p. 160.

Bertie's very name, Ethelbert—the yoking of Ethel and Bert—demarks his gender territory. Like the entire Stanhope family, his function in the novel is both satire and slapstick. His plasticity of creed, from Protestant to Roman Catholic to Jew and back again parodies the flexibility of Bishop Proudie, who has achieved preferment by being all things to all men.[32] His wooing of Eleanor Bold similarly parallels that of Slope, where both men are motivated by desire for her money, but where Bertie's light heart is measured against Slope's dour Evangelicanism. In his dress too, he is constructed as the antithesis of the cloth: "it was always totally opposed in every principle of colour and construction to the dress of those with whom he for the time consorted" (vol. 1, p. 81). This has particular resonance in a book where dress is the signifier of theology and creed.[33]

This predisposition magnifies the comic effect of his appearance at the Proudie's reception, where all the other men are dressed soberly in clerical black, and Bertie is in sky blue:

> Ethelbert Stanhope was dressed in light blue from head to foot. He had on the loosest possible blue coat, cut square like a shooting coat, and very short. It was lined with silk of azure blue. He had on a blue satin waistcoat, a blue neck-handkerchief which was fastened beneath his throat with a coral ring, and very loose blue trowsers which almost concealed his feet. (vol. 1, pp. 92–3)

John Harvey's full-length examination of the semiotics of men's dress[34] makes Trollope's gender-ascribing clear. Bertie's dress—its color, its cut, its shine, its softness—constructs him as other within the masculinity of the diocese. And while he explicitly takes pleasure in the company of women,[35] the air of sexual ambiguity that clings to him like a silk scarf prepares us to understand the innuendo of "pastimes of Eastern clime." Trollope is again expecting his adult audience to be amused. Its tone is light-hearted, of a piece with Bertie's unorthodox dress. "Pastimes of Eastern clime" suggests diversion, entertainment, pleasurable amusement; there is no disapprobation. Like the passage from *The Bertrams*, it has an air of live-and-let-live, of laissez-faire about Bertie's probable proclivities. It is also not an all-defining moment in Bertie's sexual orientation. In the next

---

[32] "He bore with the idolatry of Rome, tolerated even the infidelity of Socinianism, and was hand-in-glove with the Presbyterian Synods of Scotland and Ulster" (vol. 1, p. 19).

[33] For instance, Archdeacon Grantly, planning to undermine the new regime at the palace: "He would not willingly alter his own fashion of dress, but he could people Barchester with young clergymen dressed in the longest frocks, and in the highest-breasted silk waistcoats" (vol. 1, p. 46). And Mrs Arabin likes the "silken vest" of her Tractarian husband (vol. 2, p. 269).

[34] John Harvey, *Men in Black* (London: Reaktion, 1995).

[35] "He was habitually addicted to making love to ladies, and did so without any scruple of conscience, or any idea that such practice was amiss" (vol. 1, p. 81).

paragraph, his interior heart declares him capable of falling head over heels in love with a woman.

Men attracted solely to other men have a different signifier. In *The Eustace Diamonds*, Frank Greystock, after he has engaged himself to Lucy Morris, embraces his cousin Lizzie Eustace on three occasions. The detailed descriptions of each kiss belie the accompanying epithet of "brotherly." On the third occasion, Trollope attempts to excuse Frank's behavior:

> It is almost impossible for a man,—a man under forty and unmarried, and who is not a philosopher,—to have familiar and affectionate intercourse with a beautiful young woman, and carry it on, as he might do with a friend of the other sex.[36]

Trollope's disparagement-free identification of "philosopher" as a man untroubled by the charms of attractive women reiterates the catalogue of words to describe sexual relationships between men—Socratic, Arcadian, and here, philosopher. For those versed in the Classics, philosopher immediately suggested Socrates and Plato, studies of whom founded the bedrock of a public school education. By the time Trollope left school at around 18, he tells us, "We read the Greek plays, Thuridices, Pindar—if I remember rightly—Juvenal, or Perseus,—and the works of other authors which would be classed with those I have named. Herodotus and Homer we took up that we might enjoy the charm of poetry;[37] David Newsome writes in *Godliness and Good Learning*: "They knew their Plato; had certainly read the Phaedrus and the Symposium."[38] The link between Socratic and Platonic thinking, ancient Greek culture, and men-on-men sexual relationships was thus already well and widely understood when Walter Pater wrote his definitive essay on Winckelmann for the *Westminster Review* in 1867. Johann Joachim Winckelmann (1717–68) is widely credited with inspiring the Classical Revival through his studies of Greek Art and his adulation of the beauty of youths. In writing about Winckelmann's work, Pater was confident that he would have an audience who would understand his allusions.[39] When Trollope says "a man who is not a philosopher" he extends his non-judgmental vocabulary to describe men only attracted to men, knowing that this signal will be understood by all those in his audience who share his education and the belief systems of his class.

---

[36] Anthony Trollope, *The Eustace Diamonds* 1873 (Oxford: Oxford University Press, 1983), vol. 1, p. 230. Trollope uses "philosopher" in the same sense in *The American Senator* 1877 (Oxford: Oxford University Press, 1986), p. 312.

[37] Anthony Trollope, "Public Schools", *Fortnightly Review* 1 Oct 1865, p. 482; reprinted *Miscellaneous Essays and Reviews* (New York: Arno Press, 1981).

[38] David Newsome, *Godliness and Good Learning* (London: Murray, 1961), p. 84.

[39] Walter Pater, "Winckelmann," *The Westminster Review* 1867, reprinted Reade, pp. 76–104. See also Robb, pp. 91–4.

That Bertie was in the ha-ha with a "youngster," a lad on the brink of manhood, but considerably younger than himself, has reverberations of the intense sexualized relationships between older and younger boys that Trollope would have observed in his time as a boy at Harrow and Winchester. In *An Autobiography* he speaks with some heat of his humiliation at being punished while a schoolboy for some "nameless wrong-doing," of which he was entirely innocent, where the major evidence against him was that he had attended a public school, an incident widely acknowledged to be a reference to some homosexual transgression.[40] Such contact was part of the psychosexual experience of so many growing boys who endured the peculiarly British system of boarding school education, and that it might have permanent scarring consequences was acknowledged by many fathers as they contemplated sending their sons to face what they themselves had suffered. Sir James Stephen, father of Leslie Stephen (and grandfather of Virginia Woolf), moved to Windsor so that his sons could attend Eton as day-boys.[41] In Thomas Hughes' *Tom Brown's Schooldays*, Tom's father wonders enigmatically whether to advise his son about the perils of overtures from older boys.[42] Sexually charged relationships between growing youths clearly fuelled considerable anxiety for some men.

Trollope, in contrast, takes a much longer and more mature view of the undifferentiated expression of emerging sexuality amongst schoolboys and young men. As *Castle Richmond* opens, Patrick Desmond is 15, his sister Clara 17, and Owen Fitzgerald 23. Patrick, fatherless, home from Eton, seeks male company, and Owen responds, for friendship with Patrick brings contact with Clara, growing more lovely by the day. Owen's declaration of his love for Clara incurs her mother's wrath; for a year, there is no intercourse between the young people, and Patrick stays at Eton. Then Patrick is summoned home when Clara, now engaged to Herbert Fitzgerald, refuses to repudiate the alliance when Herbert is declared illegitimate and penniless. Patrick anticipates renewing the contact with his friend:

> Owen would be as tender with him as a woman, allowing the young lad's arm round his body, listening to words which the outer world would have called bosh—and have derided it as girlish. So at least thought the young earl to himself.[43]

Patrick, then, is looking forward to seeing a friend who repulses neither his physical expression of affection, nor the verbalization of tenderness, behavior that would have exposed him to some ridicule with other young men. For his

---

[40]   Anthony Trollope, *An Autobiography* 1883 (Oxford: Oxford University Press, 1980), pp. 5–6.

[41]   Pearsall, p. 454.

[42]   Thomas Hughes, *Tom Brown's Schooldays* 1857 (London: Penguin, 1994), p. 73.

[43]   Anthony Trollope, *Castle Richmond* 1860 (Oxford: Oxford University Press, 1989), p. 378.

part, Owen's open acknowledgment of the physical attraction in the relationship between himself and Clara's younger brother Patrick is equally undissimulated:

> "I can't tell you how glad I am to see you, old boy," said Owen, pressing his young friend with something almost like an embrace. "You will hardly believe how long it is since I have seen a face that I cared to look at." (p. 401)

Thus, alongside his patently heterosexual passion for Clara, Owen is also acknowledging a physical depth and attraction in his relationship with Patrick. Patrick Desmond squeezes his friend's arm "with a strong boyish love" (p. 403); later on we read: "throwing himself on Fitzgerald's breast, he burst into a passion of tears" (p. 408). Such scenes suggest a degree of homoerotic arousal between the two of them. There is a quantifiable difference between these expressions of the bond between Patrick and Owen, and between, for example, Frank Fenwick and Harry Gilmour in *The Vicar of Bullhampton*. Frank and Harry's relationship is between two men of the same age, one of whom is in a loving companionate marriage, and who may well share John Grey's view that one's deepest emotions can only find voice with a wife, and the other, in love with Mary Lowther, whom he aspires to marry. Their relationship quite explicitly does not include terms of endearment, or warmth of expression. Patrick and Owen's relationship is of a different order, constructed, in Dellamora's words, to allow erotic sentiment to be free to expand. It has space in it to read there what we will.[44]

It has more of the air of the "romantic friendships" described by Reade.[45] It has reverberations of the Socratic relationship between teacher and pupil, or older boy and fag, concepts so embedded in public school education. For the narrator of *Castle Richmond*, this is presented as a normal expression of affection between an adolescent and an older, physically handsome young man. It has overtones of a schoolboy crush, a passing phase in a lad's growth from awkward schoolboy to mature manhood, though, as we have noted, there is also some evidence that Patrick's feelings are returned by Owen; this is not a one-sided relationship. There is no suggestion that this is a relationship that either of them should shrink from acknowledging. Their love for each other is set against, though not in competition with, that other love, Owen's love for Clara, and Owen's vision of a higher chivalric code of honor, his readiness to sacrifice all things material in his quest for Clara's love. This nobility of character fuels Patrick's love for Owen, who, for his part, puts his passionate friendship for Patrick on a par with his devotion to Clara:

> "I, Owen Fitzgerald of Hap House, still love her better than all the world else can give me; indeed, there is nothing else that I do love,—except you, Desmond." (p. 407)

---

[44] This is, of course, crucial in novels targeting an audience of diverse ages and both sexes.

[45] Reade, pp. 1–2.

Patrick joins Owen traveling the world for two years before going up to Oxford. However, the novel ends with Owen Fitzgerald still searching for adventure, and the Countess Desmond still keeping alight the flame she carries for him. But no news of Patrick. Elsewhere in the book, the adolescent Patrick regularly declares that he will never marry (pp. 404, 422, 425). Did he keep to his word? Did he continue to prefer the company of men, or did he return home, with his father's ravages to the estate somewhat repaired, to settle down to be a pillar of society with a wife and family, like other survivors of the public schools?[46]

In Trollope, we find men in close caring bonds with other men, we find men that we might label effeminate expressing sexual attraction to young men and to young women, men who enjoy close physical relationships with other men, while consumed with passion for a woman, and a non-judgmental vocabulary for men only attracted to men. And while there is nothing in the text to suggest a homoerotic dimension to the relationship between Frank Fenwick and Harry Gilmour, the narrator of a sequel might well have Harry spending time in the Sotadic zones while he assuages his broken heart, and still credibly returning to Bullhampton to marry and raise a family.

It is clear from the work of Dellamora and Reade that in the times when Trollope was writing, how homoerotic behavior was perceived, presented, and portrayed was changing. That Trollope might have sought to disown any sexually ambivalent experiences of his own is implied by his hot refutation of the incident described earlier in *An Autobiography*. Nevertheless, whatever Trollope's own experience of puberty in the hothouse of a public school education, the authorial voice adopted in the novels and short stories is that of a man who grew up into a maturity at ease with his own sexuality, benignly tolerant of the orientation of other men. For when we examine his presentation of this aspect of men's sexuality, we hear the confident voice of tolerance, presenting a manhood that sits comfortably with liberal thinking today.

---

[46]   The new *Collins English Dictionary* (9th revised edition, June 2007) includes a new word, "bromance," "n. a close but non-sexual relationship between two men." Nirpal Dhaliwal (*The Guardian*, 11 June 2007) says "Bromance only really refers to a gay-straight relationship ... There is a mutual attraction in a bromance (why else would people become good friends?), but the fact that there is no sex is liberating for both involved." Future commentators could choose to define Patrick and Owen's relationship as a bromance.

PART 2
Imperial Gender

Chapter 5
"Some Girls Who Come From the Tropics": Gender, Race, and Imperialism in Anthony Trollope's *He Knew He Was Right*

Deborah Denenholz Morse

Anthony Trollope's novel *He Knew He Was Right* (1869) is a story of the imperial self run amok. In this very long narrative telling of an upper-class Englishman's marriage to a dark woman from the colonies and their subsequent violent estrangement, Trollope painstakingly shows the destructive nature of the masculine English will to power, the unrelenting efforts at dominion that he calls in his 1877 travel book *South Africa* "civilization gone mad." *He Knew He Was Right* has been praised for its powerful indictment of gender oppression since Robert Polhemus stated that "behind all the male resentment of female emancipation in the last century lies conscious or unconscious panic at the idea of equal sexual freedom for women."[1] Ruth apRoberts's germinal article "Emily and Nora and Dorothy and Priscilla and Jemima and Carry" examined Trollope's sympathies with Victorian women in detail, and first connected *He Knew He Was Right* to the parliamentary debates in which John Stuart Mill argued for women's rights.[2] Christopher Herbert, Jane Nardin, and I entered this discussion of the novel, and Margaret Markwick continued it in *Trollope and Women*.[3] Lisa Surridge contributed to the debate in

---

[1]   Robert Polhemus, *The Changing World of Anthony Trollope* (Berkeley: University of California Press, 1968), p. 164.

[2]   See Ruth apRoberts, "Emily and Nora and Dorothy and Priscilla and Jemima and Carry" in Richard A. Levine (ed.), *The Victorian Experience: The Novelists* (Athens: Ohio University Press, 1976), pp. 87–120. And to Ruth apRoberts, who died in 2006, I pay particular homage for her groundbreaking work.

[3]   See Christopher Herbert, "*He Knew He Was Right*, Mrs. Lynn Linton, and the Duplicities of Victorian Marriage," *Texas Studies in Literature and Language*, 25. 3 (1983): 448–69; Jane Nardin, *He Knew She Was Right: The Independent Woman in the Novels of Anthony Trollope* (Carbondale: Southern Illinois University Press, 1989; Deborah Denenholz Morse, "Educating Louis: Teaching the Victorian Father in *He Knew He Was Right*" in *The Erotics of Instruction*, edited by Regina Barreca and Deborah Denenholz Morse (Hanover & London: University Press of New England, 1997); and Margaret Markwick, *Trollope and Women* (London: Hambledon Press, 1997).

the "Trollope" chapter of her book *Bleak Houses*, in which she examines marital violence in Victorian novels. Kathy Psomiades's essay in this volume argues that *He Knew He Was Right*—published in the same year as Mill's *The Subjection of Women*—is a cultural site in which 1860s tensions between sexual relations and Liberalism are encoded, "one of the places where the story of the sexual contract emerges."[4]

I want to argue here that Trollope's novel is just as potent in its critique of the British Empire. The political and cultural histories of British imperialism are introduced in Trollope's narrative from its first chapter describing an Englishman's travels to the fictitious Mandarin Islands—probably the British West Indies despite their Chinese-sounding name. I will argue that the recent history of Britain's empire in Jamaica in particular informs *He Knew He Was Right*. This history is manifest from the novel's opening through its devastatingly witty chapter very late in the novel on colonial governance, in which Sir Marmaduke Rowley is exposed as a bumbling, ill-informed governor of the Mandarins. Further, British imperialism in the West Indies is coded upon a master-slave narrative that pervades Trollope's novel from beginning to end. Finally, *He Knew He Was Right* is imbued as well with the memory of European intertwinings of race, gender, and imperialism encoded in English literature from *Othello* to *Jane Eyre*.

This view of Trollope as conflicted imperialist has not been a popular one. Trollope's role as imperial traveler and travel writer has usually been seen by his critics as demonstrating his belief in England's civilizing imperial mission. Catherine Hall's influential 2002 book *Civilizing Subjects* sees Trollope as essentially jovial,

> ... safe and English; humorous as to the foibles of his own people ... a believer in the superiority of the Anglo-Saxon race ... kind, untroubling, riveted by the daily round of politics without being political, producing happy endings for his novels, believing in church, family and nation in ways which confirmed complacency rather than producing unsettled states of mind.[5]

Hall criticizes Trollope's aesthetics as well as his politics, stating that Trollope "wrote down what he saw without reflecting deeply on the judgments which he made. His writing was a craft and a livelihood to him, and he set himself a daily number of words to complete." This is the ultimate indictment of Trollope: he simply wrote too fast and was too disciplined. Anyone who is that efficient and hardworking can't be a serious—and inspired—artist! Worse yet: he confessed this

---

⁴   See Kathy Psomiades, "*He Knew He Was Right*: The Sensational Tyranny of the Sexual Contract and the Problem of Liberal Progress" in this volume, p. 31.

⁵   See Catherine Hall, *Civilising Subjects: Metropole and Subject in the English Imagination 1830–1867* (Chicago and London: University of Chicago Press, 1996), pp. 210–11.

in *An Autobiography,* and his words have dogged his reputation to this day.[6] Hall continues her lambasting of Trollope: "His mapping of empire was presented as descriptive, with no pretense at intellectual or philosophical depth."[7] Finally, Hall continues somewhat blithely that "like most middle-class men of the mid-Victorian period, he believed that familial and domestic order were at the heart of social order. A good society was one in which the classes, the races and the sexes knew their place and stayed in it."[8] Thirty years of scholarship on Trollope's originality and subversiveness, particularly in relation to gender, is simply ignored.[9] Older work on Trollope's characteristic mode of questioning received opinion, first and most brilliantly analyzed in Paul Elmer More's 1928 *The Demon of the Absolute,* is also unacknowledged.[10] This might seem all the more surprising because Hall herself, in her earlier work in *Defining the Nation,* connected the critique of marital authority to the scrutiny of imperial authority as it was exercised at Morant Bay— although she does not perceive this critique in the very limited work by Trollope upon which she bases her judgments:

> A relationship between subordination on the grounds of gender and that of race was perceived by many participants in and observers of the women's suffrage movement. Helen Taylor suggested in 1866 that the Eyre prosecution should concern women even more nearly than the franchise, for no one will suffer more than women, if arbitrary authority of any sort is to be left without any legal responsibility. [11]

Simon Gikandi is just as sure that Trollope is "English to the core," although Gikandi is more uncertain about Trollope's perspectives. In his work *Maps of Englishness*

---

[6]   Trollope scholars have tried to explain Trollope's artistic practices, in which he thought out his books completely and then wrote very quickly. See especially Walter M. Kendrick, *The Novel-Machine: The Theory and Fiction of Anthony Trollope* (Baltimore and London: Johns Hopkins Press, 1980) and Andrew Wright, *Anthony Trollope: Dream and Art* (Chicago: University of Chicago Press, 1983). See also Steve Amarnick's essay, "Trollope at Fuller Length: Lord Silverbridge and the Manuscript of *The Duke's Children*" in this volume.

[7]   See Hall, *Civilising Subjects*, p. 215.

[8]   Ibid., 219.

[9]   See Robert Polhemus, Ruth apRoberts, and Juliet McMaster through Bill Overton's *The Unofficial Trollope* and the work of Christopher Herbert, Jane Nardin, and my own writings, to more current scholarship by Mark Turner, Jeffrey Franklin, and William Cohen.

[10]   Paul Elmer More, "My Debt to Trollope" in *The Demon of the Absolute* (Princeton: Princeton University Press, 1928).

[11]   See Catherine Hall, Keith McClelland, and Jane Rendall, *Defining the Victorian Nation: Class, Race, Gender, and the Reform Act of 1867* (Cambridge: Cambridge University Press, 2000), p. 175. Hall et al. cite Helen Taylor, suffragette and youngest child of Harriet Taylor, draft letter to Clementia Taylor, 2 November 1866, Vol. XIII, f. 262, MT.

he sees Trollope as more complicated than Hall does, but he ultimately decides that "Trollope is a product of his times". Gikandi recognizes Trollope's ironical narrative stance as a destabilizing narrative technique, declaring that " ... Trollope's travel narrative derives its value from a dialectical irony that simultaneously questions and affirms Englishness," but Gikandi finally decides that ... "one has to wonder, nevertheless, how original and independent the perceptions developed in the field really are...."[12] But these representative comments from Hall and Gikandi refer, in any event, to Trollope's first travel book, *The West Indies and the Spanish Main*, published in 1859, and written in the wake of the Indian Mutiny/Sepoy Rebellion and its discursive aftermath—a full decade before *He Knew He Was Right* was published. Postcolonial critics don't seem to be much interested in exploring later Trollope.

I intend to shake up this view of Trollope as unconflicted imperialist—and I want to represent Trollope's conflicted imperialism in relation to gender. Trollope is generally accepted by now as writing a kind of novel of tolerance in which he shows sympathy for causes—let's take the "Woman Question"—upon which he has pronounced less sympathetically, or with at best less advanced views, like the famous quip from his travel book *North America*: "The best right a woman has is the right to a husband." Similarly, I would argue that although Trollope can be quoted—especially earlier on in his career—as sounding like a committed imperialist, in truth he was in the process of questioning the imperial project in complicated ways by the time he wrote the 1869 *He Knew He Was Right*. It is this sea change in Trollope's thinking—and the historical events that precipitated it—that I am interested in exploring.

There are a few exceptions to this unrelenting indictment of Trollope as complacent imperialist. A number of essays in this volume argue that Trollope undermined the conventional imperialist prerogatives to a greater or lesser degree. Mary Jean Corbett writes about Trollope's destabilizing of gender in relation to conventionally feminized Ireland in his sympathetic, respectful portrayal of the ambitious, "beautiful" young middle-class Irish Catholic Phineas Finn in *Phineas Finn* (1869) and *Phineas Redux* (1874). Lauren Goodlad's tour de force essay argues that *The Eustace Diamonds* (1871) is an exception to Trollope's usual inattention to India in his novels, and that Trollope might be responding not only to the politics of post-Mutiny India but to Collins's subversive—and successful—1868 novel, *The Moonstone*. Helen Blythe, writing about Trollope's later work in her analysis—she examines Trollope's 1878 New Zealand story "Catherine Carmichael"—also unsettles the notion of Trollope as unquestioned "Colonial Man" as she examines Trollope's vision of a more sexually egalitarian society that will counter male-generated cultural degeneration.

Perhaps most explicitly, Mark Forrester acknowledges this process of Trollope's "reappraisal" in his analysis of homoerotics in the essay "Redressing

---

[12]   Simon Gikandi, *Maps of Englishness: Writing Identity in the Culture of Colonialism* (New York; Columbia, 1996), pp. 105, 96, 108.

the Empire: Anthony Trollope and British Gender Anxiety in 'The Banks of the Jordan'" in the collection *Imperial Desire: Dissident Sexualities and Colonial Literature*.[13] Trollope published "The Banks of the Jordan" in three *London Review* installments in January of 1861.[14] The story is a Shakespearean-inflected, cross-dressing tale of an older man attracted to a much younger man (in fact a young woman) while they travel together. Forrester remarks that "during the same period that Trollope's thinking about women was growing (at least somewhat) more sympathetic and sophisticated, his 'mapping' of empire and race was likewise becoming increasingly complex." As Forrester comments, this homoerotic story completely refutes Henry James's statement that "with Trollope we are always safe." Forrester's work is chiefly contextualized by Edward Said's *Orientalism*, and thus Forrester is interested primarily in the Orient as an imaginative space in which Trollope, along with other writers, can reimagine sex, race, and gender. As Forrester declares: "At the margins of empire, on 'The Banks of the Jordan,' Trollope could more safely explore these inherent ambiguities of power, identity, and desire." Forrester's original work—evocative as it is—does not speculate about the particular historical circumstances that might have influenced Trollope's reimaginings of the nexus of gender, race, power, and empire in 1861. But I *am* going to posit a historical reason for the intensity of this reimagining after the autumn of 1865, and I intend to relate this reimagining not to that vague region of the East known as the Orient, but explicitly to the British West Indies.

I suspect that a powerful impetus for this re-thinking in the mid-to-late 1860s is what came to be known as the Governor Eyre Affair. This controversy raged in the aftermath of Governor Edward Eyre's massacre of Jamaican men, women, and children in response to the popular uprising on 11 October 1865 at Morant Bay.[15] Victorian England was deeply riven in its response to this dramatic event. Intellectuals were divided between those who condemned Eyre as a monster, a murderer of women and children, and those who saw him as a hero whose harsh reprisals and declaration of martial law had prevented another Indian Mutiny, another massacre of innocents at Cawnpore and Lucknow.[16]

---

[13] See Mark Forrester, "Redressing the Empire; Anthony Trollope and British Gender Anxiety in 'The Banks of the Jordan'" in Philip Holden and Richard J. Ruppel (eds), *Imperial Desire: Dissident Sexualities and Colonial Literature* (Minneapolis: University of Minnesota Press, 2003).

[14] Robert Polhemus discusses "The Banks of the Jordan" in his essay in this collection as well. Polhemus calls the story "A Ride Across Palestine," the story's title when it was reprinted in *Tales of All Countries* [Second Series] (1863).

[15] For a detailed history of the Rebellion, see Gad Heuman, *'The Killing Time': The Morant Bay Rebellion in Jamaica* (Knoxville: The University of Tennessee Press, 1994).

[16] There are many books on the Indian Mutiny or Sepoy Rebellion. One of the most accessible is Christopher Hibbert's *The Indian Mutiny*. See also Patrick Brantlinger, "The Well of Cawnpore" in *Rule of Darkness*. Christopher Herbert's forthcoming work,

Drawn by William Harvey.   p. 348.

ENGLAND'S WELCOME.
MAY-DAY,
ANNO DOMINI 1862.

Fig. 5.1   "England's Welcome." William Harvey's illustration for *London
                Society*, 1 May 1862.

As Ian Baucom tells us in *Out of Place: Englishness, Empire, and the Locations of Identity*: "For the marking of Morant Bay as an event *within* English history signals a crucial Victorian reimagination of the relations that obtained between England and its empire. That reconceptualization demanded, among other things, that those Black West Indians whipped, tortured, and executed by the governor's men be spoken of as English."[17] Tim Watson, in his article "Inheriting the Empire after Morant Bay," also insists upon the significance of the Governor Eyre Controversy: "The Morant Bay uprising, far more than the Sepoy Rebellion of 1857 to which it was (and is) often compared, crystallized concern on matters of governance, citizenship, and rights, both 'domestic' and 'imperial', and in so doing inaugurated the new era of 'the Empire'."[18]

So race and liberalism, race and empire, race and Englishness were being reconsidered and reconfigured during the years of the Eyre Controversy, which did not fully die out until 1872, although it was at its most intense in 1866–68. The Liberal M.P. Charles Buxton—the son of the famous abolitionist and former leader of the Anti-Slavery Society, Sir Thomas Fowell Buxton—headed up the Jamaica Committee to investigate Eyre's culpability. John Stuart Mill, recently elected M.P. for Westminster, followed Buxton as Chair of the Committee, and it was Mill who argued most forcefully for Eyre's prosecution in England after the governor was forced to resign in the face of a Royal Commission of Inquiry that ultimately found Eyre's actions unnecessarily violent and repressive. In his arguments in the House of Commons, Mill declared that "martial law is the total suspension of all law." In support of Eyre's prosecution, Mill stated that if the Governor were not held to account for his actions, "we are giving up altogether the principle of government by law, and resigning ourselves to arbitrary power."[19]

In opposition to Mill, Buxton, T. H. Huxley, Charles Darwin, Sir Charles Lyell, Thomas Hughes, John Bright, and their liberal company (including 17 members of Parliament), Thomas Carlyle and John Ruskin chaired the Governor Eyre Defence Committee, which included the social protest novelist and Anglican clergyman Charles Kingsley and Charles Dickens among its number—although, as Grace

---

War of No Pity: The Indian Mutiny and Victorian Trauma (Princeton: Princeton University Press, 2007) promises to be definitive.

[17]   Ian Baucom, *Out of Place: Englishness, Empire, and the Locations of Identity* (Princeton; Princeton University Press, 1999), p. 44.

[18]   Tim Watson's article, "Inheriting the Empire after Morant Bay" argues that the Governor Eyre controversy caused Victorian intellectuals and writers to re-think their idea of empire as the British Empire rather than Crown Colonies, Indian Empire, Colonial Empire, and other dependencies.

[19]   Quoted in Catherine Hall, Keith McClelland, and Jane Rendall, *Defining the Victorian Nation: Class, Race, Gender, and the Reform Act of 1867* (Cambridge, UK: Cambridge University Press, 2000), p. 229.

Moore states in *Dickens and Empire*, the great novelist was only a nominal member.[20] R. C. Terry tells us in *The Oxford Reader's Companion to Trollope*—confirming N. John Hall's assessment in his biography[21] that "Trollope's attitude to the Eyre Controversy was never explicit, but he was probably in Mill's camp, since his friend Charles Buxton had helped organize the Jamaica Committee."[22] Indeed, Buxton's influence over Trollope is suggested by Trollope's assertion in the *Autobiography* (p. xvi) that he entered politics and stood for the Liberals at Beverley because of Buxton's encouragement.[23] (We might guess, however, that Trollope didn't thank him for suggesting he run in the ill-starred Beverley election![24])

How does the influence of the Governor Eyre Controversy and the re-thinking of colonized subjectivity show up in *He Knew He Was Right*? This novel was written from November of 1867 through April of 1868—while the Eyre Controversy was still raging. Eyre was not tried and acquitted in court until June of 1868. In 1872, the Liberal government under Gladstone voted to defray the costs of the Governor's legal expenses, and the Conservative government granted him a pension in 1874. Trollope was therefore writing *He Knew He Was Right* just as John Stuart Mill and the Jamaica Committee were vigorously trying to get Eyre tried for using excessive force at Morant Bay, as the Royal Commission had reported.

In Trollope's heretical novel, I argue that he responds to the Eyre Affair by questioning the paradigms of imperial narrative itself. In particular, Trollope revises imperial narratives in which the dark-skinned "Other" is excessively passionate, goes mad, or is demonized—and ultimately dies. Over the course of the story, the masterful Englishman Louis Trevelyan instead enslaves and imprisons himself, exoticizing his self-starved, self-tortured body in a cruel parody of the colonized bodies of the insurrectionists at Morant Bay in Jamaica, emancipated slaves and the children of former slaves, the victims of Edward Eyre's tyranny.

---

[20]   See Grace Moore, *Dickens and Empire* (Aldershot, England: Ashgate, 2004), 157ff.

[21]   See N. John Hall, *Trollope: A Biography* (Oxford and New York: Oxford University Press, 1991): "Nor is it known what he thought of Mill's 'persecution' of Edward John Eyre, for his atrocities as Governor of Jamaica, where he put down a rebellion by indiscriminate murdering of hundreds of natives; here one suspects Trollope sided with Mill—at least in the early stages of the affair, his close friend and political sponsor Charles Buxton having been one of the original founders of the Jamaica Committee. That the opposition Eyre Defence Committee was championed by Carlyle and supported by Ruskin and Dickens would have helped tilt Trollope towards Mill" (pp. 278–9).

[22]   See *The Oxford Reader's Companion to Trollope*, edited by R. C. Terry, entries on "Eyre, Governor Edward John" and "Buxton, Charles" (Oxford: Oxford University Press, 1999, pp. 190–91 and 76.

[23]   See again *Oxford Companion*, "Buxton."

[24]   In January of 1866, Trollope wrote a review of Buxton's book *The Ideas of the Day on Policy* in *The Fortnightly Review* as well.

In the scarifying story of the Trevelyan marriage within *He Knew He Was Right*, the mediating body in the struggles of race and gender is that of the dark Englishwoman Emily Rowley Trevelyan, brought up in the colonies. Through the resistance of her rebellious spirit, and the survival of her dark-haired, "brown"-skinned body—and that "brownness" is insistently recalled in the book—the dark Englishwoman is coded as the slave who rebels against her master and usurps his authority. And this is so despite the obvious fact that Emily is the white daughter of the English colonial governor of the Mandarins.

Ultimately, the dark Englishwoman Emily Trevelyan survives her tragic oppression, although she is moved about and imprisoned or penned up at her increasingly crazy husband's will for months on end, along with her little boy and her beautiful and fiercely intelligent younger sister Nora. In the meantime, Louis Trevelyan becomes a primitive recluse and ultimately dies of his self-imposed illness—wild, feeble, crazed with his frustrated desire for mastery over his strong, dark English wife. In this depiction of the white Englishman gone mad, while his dusky, tropics-born wife stays decidedly sane, Trollope reverses the nineteenth-century stereotype that connected the racial "Other" with madness, as Sander Gilman tells us in *Difference and Pathology*.[25]

In Trevelyan's frenzied insistence on his wife's submission in intimate matters, Trollope recognizes the crucial place of carnal relations in imperial politics. The Victorian husband's obsessive tracking of his wife's body resonates with the memory of the Empire's actual control of the colonial bodies under its governance in its legislation of intimacy.[26] Ann Laura Stoler has instructed us in *Carnal Knowledge and Imperial Power* about the role that European control of sexual relations had in imperial politics in the nineteenth and early twentieth centuries. Although her study focuses primarily upon Indonesia and deals with French and Dutch imperialism, we can use her insights to illuminate the province of domestic and sexual relations within the British Empire as well.

Stoler begins her first chapter, "Genealogies of the Intimate," by quoting Georges Hardy, "one of the principal architects of French colonial educational policy" who warned a group of prospective functionaries that "A man remains a man as long as he stays under the gaze of a woman of his race." Of course, this is not what many white men did, as scholars from Stoler to Susan Morgan in *Place Matters* have documented. They had sex with women not of their race. But what if the "woman of his race" is in fact very dark, chosen because she is different from other Englishwomen—to quote the novel, like "some girls from the tropics"? What if this "woman of his race" gazes at her man and rebels against

---

[25]   See Sander Gilman, *Difference and Pathology; Stereotypes of Sexuality, Race, and Madness* (Ithaca: Cornell University Press, 1985).

[26]   See Ann Laura Stoler, *Carnal Knowledge and Imperial Power: Race and the Intimate in Colonial Rule* (Berkeley: University of California Press, 2002) for a deeply thoughtful study of the role that European control of sexual relations had in imperial politics in nineteenth and twentieth-century Indonesia.

his authority not only in the drawing room but in the bedroom? What if there is an interrogation of race and gender that includes a questioning of whiteness itself, as Anne McClintock recently suggests in relation to other Victorian writers in *Imperial Leather: Race, Gender, and Sexuality in the Colonial Context*? I want to suggest that Trollope the colonial traveler was exploring these questions of race, gender, and imperialism as he displaced them upon the Trevelyan marriage. And he explored these questions in a novel set largely in the heart of the British Empire: London.

In this tragic narrative *He Knew He Was Right*, Louis Trevelyan is, at the outset of the novel, master of his destiny, a wealthy and well-educated Cambridge man. He "had all the world before him where to choose," like Milton's Adam.[27] He travels out to the Mandarin Islands and meets a beautiful, dark English girl, Emily Rowley, with whom he falls in love. At first, he is attracted to her dark beauty, her powerful, lovely body and her independent spirit. Trollope's narrator tells us that

> Emily Rowley, when she was brought home from the Mandarin Islands to be the wife of Louis Trevelyan, was a very handsome young woman, tall, with a bust rather full for her age, with dark eyes—eyes that looked to be dark because her eye-brows and eye-lashes were nearly black…. Her brown hair was dark and very soft: and the tint of her complexion was brown also … and she was very strong, as are some girls who come from the tropics, and whom a tropical climate has suited. She could sit on her horse the whole day long, and would never be weary with dancing at the Government House balls. (pp. 6–7)

All of the Rowleys rejoice at their good fortune that Trevelyan, "such a handsome, manly fellow" (p. 3), finds their daughter at the obscure Mandarins. They hear him praised in the London world when they bring Emily there to be married:

> The Rowleys found, on reaching London, that they had lighted upon a pearl indeed. Louis Trevelyan was a man of whom all people said all good things. He might have been a fellow of his college had he not been a man of fortune. He might already,—so Sir Rowley was told,—have been in Parliament, had he not thought it to be wiser to wait awhile. Indeed, he was very wise in many things. He had gone out on his travels thus young,—not in search of excitement, to kill beasts, or to encounter he knew not what novelty or amusement, but that he might see men and know the world … And, moreover, Sir Rowley found that his son-in-law was well spoken of at the clubs by those who had known him during his university career…. (p. 3)

Trollope makes us understand Louis Trevelyan as a kind of male ideal, a man "wise in many things" who is "popular as well as wise," with "a nose divinely

---

[27]   After I brought up the allusion to *Paradise Lost* in the honors seminar, I received an insightful paper from Maggie Harvey on male fallenness in *He Knew He Was Right*.

chiseled, an Apollo's mouth, six feet high, with shoulders and legs and arms in proportion—a pearl of pearls! ... " (p. 3).[28] He is thoroughly approved by the masculine worlds of Cambridge and the clubs, and is even viewed as a future M.P.—one of the arbiters of the British Empire. Significantly, the only objection to Louis Trevelyan is voiced by a woman, Emily's mother:

> Only, as Lady Rowley was the first to find out, he liked to have his own way. 'But his way is such a good way,' said Sir Marmaduke. 'He will be such a good guide for the girls.'
>
> 'But Emily likes her way too,' said Lady Rowley.
>
> Sir Marmaduke argued the matter no further, but thought, no doubt, that such a husband as Louis Trevelyan was entitled to have his own way. He probably had not observed his daughter's temper so accurately as his wife had done. With eight of them coming up around him, how should he have observed their tempers? (p. 3)

Trollope's access to Sir Marmaduke's thoughts elucidates the father's ignorance of his own eldest daughter's character.[29] He assumes that Emily will allow herself to be governed by her sterling husband. Trollope makes the terms of this exchange of the daughter between men, between father and husband, very clear. Emily's father is relieved to have one of his many daughters married well, and he gratefully accepts Louis's statement that

> It is my idea that girls should not have fortunes. At any rate, I am quite sure that men should never look for money. A man must be more comfortable, and, I think, is likely to be more affectionate, when the money has come from himself. (p. 2)

---

[28]   Seasoned readers of Trollope may, nevertheless, be wary of any man identified as "a pearl of pearls"; the somewhat prejudiced hero Arthur Fletcher, "the pearl of the Fletcher tribe," is described similarly in the later novel *The Prime Minister* (1875). Trollope is often skeptical as well of young men who are prematurely "wise," such as Felix Graham in *Orley Farm*. More often than not, young men in Trollope who are "wise" too early in life are headed for a rude awakening, while young men who take some time to grow up— not necessarily Trollope's famous "hobbledehoys" like John Eames, but characters like Lord Silverbridge in *The Dukes's Children*, who is "gaining by degrees age and flavour," are often looked upon favorably in Trollope—and get the girl (in Silverbridge's case, the incomparable Isabel Boncassen).

[29]   Sir Marmaduke's ignorance of his daughter's firm character is akin to that of another upper-class father, the Duke of Omnium, in *The Duke's Children*. The Duke too believes that "girls must obey," and is quietly resisted by his daughter Mary Palliser—who eventually gets her way, and marries her man.

While the impecunious Sir Marmaduke "could not but admire the principles of his proposed son-in-law" (p. 2), it is evident that Emily is meant to be entirely dependent upon Louis. Her lack of a dowry makes her body and her obedience her only coin. Sir Marmaduke's belief that "such a husband as Louis Trevelyan was entitled to have his own way" echoes the narrator's statement expressing Sir Marmaduke's and the general opinion that "no man could be more independent or more justified in pleasing himself than was this lover" (p. 2). The very terms of the marriage bargain formalize Emily's entire dependence and Louis's complete independence.[30]

Despite Lady Rowley's hint of possible future tension between the lovers, no one expects the problems that ensue after only two years of marriage, when Emily refuses to allow her "lord and master" to be a god who must be worshipped. And by this time, Louis does want to be a god; he has decided that, as Trollope's narrator tells us, "he should like his own way completely" (p. 4). He is intensely jealous of the worldly old roué Colonel Osborne, an "ancient Lothario" who preens himself in being considered a rival for young wives' affections, who "was fond of intimacies with married ladies, and perhaps not averse to the excitement of marital hostility" (p. 7). When Emily—who is entirely innocent even of thinking of Colonel Osborne as anyone other than her father's old friend—resists Trevelyan's dominion, the aggrieved husband begins to reflect upon the voluptuous woman he has married as perhaps not quite the kind of pure English matron that he deserves.[31] He recalls that men have warned him that

> no man should look for a wife from among the tropics, that women educated amidst the languors of those sunny climes rarely came to possess those high ideas of conjugal duty and feminine truth which a man should regard as the first requisites of a good wife. As he thought of all this, he almost regretted that he had ever visited the Mandarins, or ever heard the name of Sir Marmaduke Rowley. (p. 25)

Like Rochester in Jean Rhys's *Wide Sargasso Sea* (and perhaps in *Jane Eyre* itself, as Gayatri Spivak, Susan Meyer, and most recently Carl Plasa have shown us),[32]

---

[30]   I want to acknowledge Charlotte Savino's lively, perceptive honors seminar paper on this subject.

[31]   Ruth apRoberts states in relation to this passage: "This seems to me to communicate a breath of a fear of Trevelyan's that Emily might be somewhat oversexed" ("Emily and Nora ... ," p. 94).

[32]   See Gayatri Spivak, "Three Women's Texts and a Critique of Imperialism," in Henry Louis Gates (ed.), *'Race', Writing, and Difference* (Chicago; Chicago University Press, 1986), pp. 252–80, first published in *Critical Inquiry* 12.1 (Autumn 1985), pp. 243–61; Susan Meyer, *Imperialism at Home: Race and Victorian Women's Fiction* (Ithaca: Cornell University Press, 1996), and Carl Plasa, *Charlotte Brontë* (London: Palgrave Critical Writers Series, 2004).

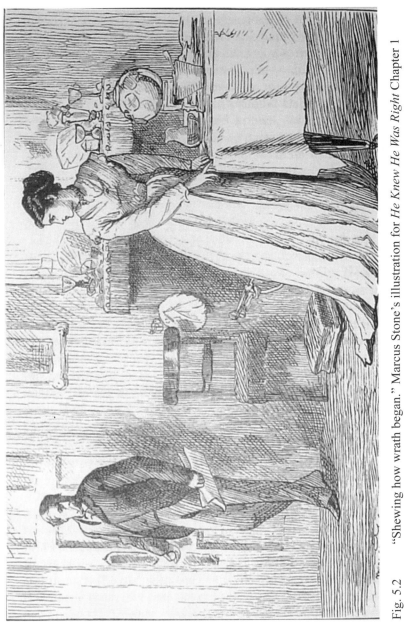

Fig. 5.2   "Shewing how wrath began." Marcus Stone's illustration for *He Knew He Was Right* Chapter 1

Louis Trevelyan begins to want the imprisonment of his wife's sexually desiring body and the quelling of her rebellious spirit. In Brontë's novel, the dark girl—daughter of the West Indian Creole planter class—goes mad. In Trollope's novel, the Anglo who imprisons his dark wife goes mad.[33] Trollope seems perhaps to have Charlotte Brontë's famous and influential novel in mind as he writes parts of *He Knew He Was Right*. There is a subtext to Louis's fear of Emily's sexual license that becomes more clear as the novel progresses, and the husband's fear becomes hysteria, in a reversal of gender expectations. When Sir Marmaduke Rowley and the kindly Charles Glascock (later Lord Peterborough) seek out and confront the madman Trevelyan in his desiccated hide-out in Italy, Casalunga, he frantically accuses his wife of deceiving him when Sir Marmaduke defends his child Emily:

> 'Your child, sir! She is my wife;—my wife;—my wife!' Trevelyan, as he spoke, advanced close up to his father-in-law; and at last hissed out his words, with his lips close to Sir Marmaduke's face. 'Your right in her is gone, sir. She is mine;–mine;–mine! And you see the way that she has treated me, Mr. Glascock. Everything I had was hers; but words of a gray-haired old sinner were sweeter to her than all my love.' (p. 736)

In the repetition of "my wife" echoed by the thrice-repeated 'mine," Trollope emphasizes that it is Trevelyan's loss of control over his possession that has unhinged him, his mastery gone awry that has caused him to become imbalanced.

Trevelyan is just as adamant that his son is his possession. He has paid his hired detective Bozzle to kidnap little Louey, and Trevelyan has taken him out of the country, to the parched Italian countryside, to live in isolation. Louey is "cowed and overcome, not only by the incidents of the moment, but by the terrible melancholy of his whole life." Louey, not yet three years old, knows

> that he was to live with his father, and that the former woman-given happinesses of his life were at an end. In this second visit from his mother he did not forget her. He recognized the luxury of her love; but it did not occur to him even to hope that she might have come to rescue him from the evil of his days. (p. 742)

Despite Louey's obvious misery, Louis responds to Mr. Glascock's statement that Emily "wants her child," by angrily declaiming:

> 'He is my child,' said Trevelyan, 'and my right to him is better than hers. Let her try it in a court of law, and she shall see. Why did she deceive me with that man? Why has she driven me to this? Look here, Mr. Glascock;—my whole life is spent in this seclusion, and it is her fault.'

---

[33]   See Morse, "Educating Louis," pp. 103–4.

Fig. 5.3   "Trevelyan at Casalunga." Marcus Stone's illustration for
              He Knew He Was Right, Chapter 84

'Your wife is innocent of all fault, Trevelyan,' said Mr. Glascock.

'Any woman can say as much as that;—and all women do say it. Yet,—what are they worth?' (p. 735)

Trevelyan's misogynist final words to Glascock lump "any woman" and "all women" together with his own wife Emily as guilty, worthless liars who hide their sexual infidelities. In Trevelyan's insistence upon Emily's sexual guilt even though he "had no such belief" (p. 743), Trollope hints that either Emily is too sexually responsive for Louis's tastes, or that Louis is at times rendered impotent by her liberated sexual desire.[34]

This explicit naming of sex is possibly the best moment to bring in Trollope's use of Shakespeare's *Othello*. P. D. Edwards first pointed out the influence of *Othello* on Trollope's novel,[35] and a few years later, Simon Gatrell fully analyzed the Shakespearean context of Trollope's novel in his essay "Jealousy, Mastery, Love, and Madness."[36] Hall thinks that "Trollope may have been prompted to write this tale of a 'modern Othello' by a review article entitled 'Madness in Literature' that appeared in the *Spectator* of 3 February of 1866." In this review, the anonymous writer "twice suggested that Trollope might be able to 'paint the morbid passion [of Othello] in its naturalistic nineteenth-century dress'."[37] David Oberhelman discusses *He Knew He Was Right* in relation to Victorian psychiatry in connecting and distinguishing Trollope's realistic novel from Shakespeare's tragedy. He concludes that "In the end, Trevelyan becomes a character who is both himself, a sane Victorian gentleman, and a mad Othello in nineteenth-century dress, and *He Knew He Was Right* becomes both a 'sane' realistic novel and a 'mad' Shakespearean tragedy."[38] Frank Kermode also discusses the Othello parallel in his *Introduction* to the Penguin edition of *He Knew He Was Right*. Kermode chiefly focuses upon what he calls Trollope's interest in "the pathology of male sexuality" or "the pathology of jealousy." Of all these critiques, only Simon Gatrell's pays some attention, oddly, to the issue of race. He mentions one of what he terms "the echoes of Othello" in stating that "the colour difference between the main characters is maintained, though the sexes are reversed. It would inconceivable that such a one as Louis Trevelyan should marry a Moorish girl, but he comes as close to it as Victorian probability would allow."[39] In Trollope's

---

[34]   Again, see Morse, "Educating Louis."

[35]   P. D. Edwards, *Trollope: His Art and Scope* (Brighton: Harvester Press, 1978).

[36]   Simon Gatrell, "Jealousy, Mastery, Love, and Madness: A Brief Reading of *He Knew He Was Right*" in *Anthony Trollope*, edited by Tony Bareham (London: Vision Press, 1980).

[37]   See N. John Hall, *Trollope: A Biography*, p. 338.

[38]   David D. Oberhelman, "Trollope's Insanity Defence: Narrative Alienation in *He Knew He Was Right*." *Studies in English Literature*, 35. 4 (1995): 789–806.

[39]   Gatrell, p. 96.

Othello-imbued tragedy, the novelist calls attention to the erotics of race as well as the mortal power of jealous mastery, as Gatrell obliquely argues—but even Gatrell does not connect these two stories of the Trevelyan marriage and the marriage of Desdemona and Othello as colonial dramas.

I argue that Trollope explicitly uses *Othello* to critique colonial racial discourse. Trollope's Desdemona revises Shakespeare's rebellious daughter and faithful wife—his white, doomed heroine—who becomes *He Knew He Was Right*'s dark, passionate Emily Trevelyan, still alive and in ruddy health at the novel's end. Unlike Desdemona, Emily has a child, a son. She is the sole surviving parent to little Louey, who—Trollope makes clear—will be raised to be a very different kind of Englishman than the father for whom he is named. Trollope's Othello is, first, a white, privileged Englishman, a gleaming "pearl of pearls." He is a man who diminishes so much in moral stature throughout the novel that Trollope clearly does not want us to think of him as a tragic hero.[40] He is, moreover, so physically as well as spiritually enervated by his self-imposed ordeal that he dies from fever and starvation, in a kind of terrible parody of the deaths of Jamaicans tortured and executed by Governor Eyre at Morant Bay—and of the suffering of their parents under British West Indian slavery until the 1 August 1834 emancipation in Jamaica following the 1833 British Abolition of Slavery Act—and their great suffering thereafter as well, even after full emancipation was granted on 1 August 1838.[41]

It is important that Trevelyan exiles and exoticizes himself in his madness. He destroys his English self as he removes himself farther and farther away from his wife, all the while fanatically insisting upon his rights as an English husband under the law. It is as if in his own body Trevelyan is finally culminating his imperial struggle, becoming the victimized "Other" as he torments himself with his lost hegemony over his dark, rebellious wife. Here is Trollope's portrayal of Trevelyan toward the end of his self-imposed ordeal, in the remarkable chapter, "Trevelyan Discourses on Life," in which his old college friend Hugh Stanbury comes to him, as Emily Trevelyan has asked, in order to convince him to come back to England and to his wife:

> He was dressed in a bright Italian dressing gown … and on his feet he had green worked slippers, and on his head a brocaded cap … His long dishevelled hair came down over his neck, and his beard covered his face. Beneath his dressing down he had a nightshirt and drawers, and was as dirty in appearance as he was gaudy in colours. (p. 868)

---

[40]   See Jane Nardin, *He Knew She Was Right*: "Ostensibly a man's tragedy, the novel is in fact the tragedy of a woman" (p. 205).

[41]   See Bob Scholnick, *Introduction* to John Bigelow, *Jamaica in 1850 or, the Effects of Sixteen Years of Freedom on a Slave Colony*, ed. Bob Scholnick (Urbana and Chicago: University of Illinois Press, 2006).

Trevelyan's adopted foreignness of appearance is reinforced by his strongly declared rejection of England and his English identity. In this *King Lear*-imbued scene, Trevelyan in his madness uses the imprisoned Lear's loving words to Cordelia only to mock Stanbury's involvement in the world in his job as newspaper reporter: "What's the news? Who's alive? Who dead? Who in? Who out?" (p. 868).[42] Even as he echoes the words of England's greatest dramatist, Trevelyan explicitly resists Stanbury's appeal to his Englishness:

> "Don't you think you would be happier at home?" he asked.
>
> "Where is my home, Sir Knight of the Midnight Pen?"
>
> "England is your home, Trevelyan."
>
> "No, sir, England was my home once; But I have taken the liberty accorded to me by my Creator of choosing a new country. Italy is now my nation, and Casalunga is my home." (p. 869)

Ironically, in Trollope's novel, when the narrator announces of Louis Trevelyan that "the maniac at last was dead" (the first line of Chapter 99), it is his long-suffering wife Emily who has just been "Acquitted"—the title of Chapter 98—by her insane husband. That Trevelyan is a completely incompetent and prejudiced judge of his wife's actions is constantly reiterated in the novel. Trevelyan himself should be in the dock—and in Trollope's novel, of course he is, figuratively. He is racked by his own obsessive need to master his wife, and the narrator's final pronouncement that Trevelyan is a "maniac" is imbued with the consequences of his "desire to achieve empire" (p. 743) at the cost of his sanity.

Against the psychic violence that Louis Trevelyan visits upon his wife and himself, Trollope relates the stories of three intelligent, sensitive Englishmen who make egalitarian marriages during the course of the novel. These men— Hugh Stanbury, a young reporter for a penny newspaper; Brooke Burgess, a 30-something clerk in a London office, with "as sweet a mouth as ever declared the excellence of a man's temper" (p. 235); and Charles Glascock, a witty, diffident, and nurturing aristocrat, just turned forty—are variously progressive in their political views, but are all united in wanting women to be equal partners in love, with the implication that they will be equal partners in the marriage bed as well. All of these men reject mastery as a mode of relating to the world, both in their

---

[42]   In her wonderful paper for the honors seminar, Sarah Vogelsong argues that Trollope consciously compared Trevelyan's history to King Lear's in order to write a modern tragedy in which there is no redeeming love. Christopher Adams too writes with sophisticated knowledge of Shakespeare about Trollopian allusiveness to *King Lear* and *Hamlet* as well as *Othello* in his honors essay on *He Knew He Was Right*.

English homes and, Trollope strongly implies, in homes that are not English.[43] In arguing the significance of this resistance to mastery on the part of the three other male lovers of the novel, I am refuting the interpretations of those who, like Christopher Herbert and Lisa Surridge, decide ultimately that there is no way to circumvent the legal structures of Victorian England, in which power is squarely in the male domain.[44] I argue that Trollope's continual emphasis on these other six lovers embodies the novelist's reimagining of alternatives to the master-slave relationship displaced upon the Trevelyan marriage.

In the chapter in which he is introduced in *He Knew He Was Right*, "Mr. Brooke Burgess," we learn right away that Brooke is not only kindly and genuine self-deprecating, but also unusually at ease in the world—the very antithesis of Louis Trevelyan:

> Brooke Burgess, or Mr. Brooke, as he came to be called very shortly by all the servants in the house, was a good-looking man, with black whiskers and black hair, which, as he said, was beginning to be thin at the top of his head, and pleasant small bright eyes. Dorothy thought that next to her brother Hugh he was the most good-natured looking man she had ever seen. (p. 293)

At his first dinner party, with mostly old people who are friends of Brooke's overbearing Aunt Jemima Stanbury, Brooke is "gay as a lark," and Dorothy wonders about how he has put everyone at his ease, and "whether anybody before had ever made those two steady old people laugh after that fashion" (pp. 294, 295).

Most writers on the novel remark upon the conventionality of Dorothy Stanbury, who is, certainly, the most self-effacing, self-sacrificing, and loving of the novel's young women. But it is important to note that Brooke is a great defender of Dorothy's sturdiness and resistance to the blandishments both of her difficult aunt and of her unloved suitor, Mr. Gibson. Here Brooke is speaking to Dorothy's brother Hugh:

> "Your aunt wanted him to marry your sister."

---

[43] See again Christopher Herbert, "Duplicities of Victorian Marriage," who disagrees with my assessment of these three relationships and stresses the essential fact of their sameness with Louis's under the law. At key moments he argues that all of the relationships follow the patriarchal model.

[44] See Christopher Herbert, "Duplicities of Victorian Marriage," who states that "the novel's final appraisal of modern marriage seems a somber one in spite of its repeated suggestions in the various subplots that humanely companionate marriage is after all a Victorian reality" (p. 466). Lisa Surridge, in *Bleak Houses*, builds upon Herbert's arguments in concluding that "the marriages of Brooke Burgess to Dorothy Stanbury and Hugh Stanbury to Nora Rowley follow a similar model, in which apparently egalitarian and companionate relationships are revealed to be underpinned by male power" (p. 167).

"So I was told."

"But your sister didn't see it," said Brooke.

"So I understand," said Stanbury ... I suppose she was right not to have him," said Hugh.

"Of course she was right," said Brooke, with a good deal of enthusiasm.

This is, of course, a comic scene, in that Brooke himself loves Dorothy and intends to propose to her, but there is a serious aspect to Brooke's approval of his beloved because she refused to be mastered, and resisted marriage without love. Later in this same conversation, when Hugh says that Dorothy is "a dear, loving, sweet-tempered creature, who is only too ready to yield in all things," Brooke reminds Hugh that Dorothy "wouldn't yield about Gibson." Hugh is convinced that his sister "wouldn't want a man to say—boo," to which Brooke replies, "I'm not so sure of that, old fellow." Brooke is, of course, right in his assessment of Dorothy, who continues to insist upon her right to determine her own fate. Her love for Brooke elicits her strongest self. Dorothy's mother remarks wonderingly to Dorothy's elder spinster sister Priscilla, "Don't you think she is very much changed?" Priscilla answers, "Not changed in the least, mother; but the sun has opened the bud, and now we see the fruit" (p. 553).

In the second of the three other love relationships in the novel, the urbane aristocrat Charles Glascock begins his courtship with the witty and fun-loving American beauty Caroline Spalding after Glascock is rejected by Nora Rowley because of her love for her newspaperman Hugh Stanbury. Glascock is attracted to Caroline, who speaks her mind and isn't above teasing the man who will soon be Lord Peterborough. He makes it clear that he doesn't want a minion, but a wife who will be his best friend. He shows that he is a good friend to women when he goes to Casalunga and argues with Trevelyan about his wife. Glascock not only takes Emily's side, but he also is the special friend of little Louey in the chapter "Mr.Glascock as Nurse." Much has been made of Glascock's teasing words about women's rights ("Can they manage that men shall have half of the babies?"), but in his actions, Glascock is a man who accepts not only the feminine, but the feminine in himself. And when we first see the young bride Caroline at Monkhams, she quells Nora's unease at the "magnificence" of Lord Peterborough's estate by reassuring Nora that "the magnificence is nothing; but the man's love is everything" (p. 903).

Finally, the most explicit statement expressing the rejection of mastery is made by Hugh Stanbury. Hugh has trained as a gentlemanly barrister, but he embraces the life of a London journalist for a penny newspaper. His democratic principles cause him to be "somewhat hot in spirit and manner ... very sage in argument, pounding down his ideas in politics, religion, or social life with his fist as well as his voice ... he possessed the sweetest temper that was ever given to a man for the blessing of a woman." As with Trollope's later description of Brook Burgess which I just quoted, Trollope uses the word "sweet" as an encomium for a man. Hugh has tried to educate his university friend Louis to allow his wife her freedom: "As far as I can see, women go straight enough nineteen times out of twenty. But they don't like being,—what I call looked after ... if I were married ... I fancy I shouldn't look after my wife at all. It seems to me that women hate to be told about their duties" (p. 148).

It is in one of the most beautiful passages of the novel that Hugh Stanbury articulates what may be taken, I think, as Trollope's antidote to the will to power, the will to mastery. In this scene, in Chapter 25, "Hugh Stanbury Smokes His Pipe," Hugh ponders his love for Nora Rowley, which seems to be facing nearly insuperable obstacles in his relative poverty and unstable employment. Here are Hugh's thoughts:

> And then he began to speculate on love, that love of which poets wrote, and of which he found that some sparkle was necessary to give light to his life. Was it not the one particle of divine breath given to man, of which he had heard since he was a boy? ... But beyond that pressing of the hand, and that kissing of the lips ... what could love do beyond that? There were children with dirty faces, and household bills, and a wife who must, perhaps, always darn the stockings,— and be sometimes cross ... Did the love of the poets lead only to that, and that only? Then, through the cloud of smoke, there came upon him some dim idea of self-abnegation,—that the mysterious valley among the mountains, the far-off prospect of which was so charming to him,—which made the poetry of his life, was, in fact, the capacity of caring more for other human beings than for himself. The beauty of it all was not so much in the thing loved, as in the loving. (p. 237)

Hugh Stanbury offers an alternative to the mastery of his friend Trevelyan. Nora Rowley, Emily's beautiful, intelligent sister, is a lucky woman. As Nora tells her friend and hostess Lady Milborough in front of her beloved fiancé Hugh, "I don't mean to submit to him at all, Lady Milborough; of course not. I am going to marry for liberty." When Lady Milborough responds that although Nora is (as Lady Milborough thinks) only joking, many young women seem to think now that after marriage, "they are to have their own way in everything. And people complain that young men won't marry. Who can wonder at it?" Nora counters: "I don't think the young men think much about the obedience" ... "Some marry for money, and some for love. But I don't think they marry to get a slave" (p. 898).

But Louis Trevelyan eventually did want a wife who was a slave. This supposedly consummate English gentleman went to the Mandarin Islands and found a dark, sultry wife. Eventually, he denied that wife liberty, and he wanted his wife's submission to his mastering will more than he desired his wife herself. But in the marriages of Trevelyan's old friend Hugh Stanbury and Hugh's own new friends Charles Glascock and Brooke Burgess, Trollope creates three liberated unions.

It is in these new Englishmen—and in their intelligent, determined wives—that Trollope constructs a new vision of Englishness in which he sees the possibility of a future in which there will be no mastery—and no slaves.

Chapter 6
Anthony Trollope's
The Eustace Diamonds and
"The Great Parliamentary Bore"

Lauren M. E. Goodlad

Why is it that Anthony Trollope, "the greatest traveler among mid-Victorian novelists"[1]—the era's archetypal "Imperial Man"[2]—neither visited nor wrote about Britain's empire in India? In 1860, the year after he published *The West Indies and the Spanish Main*, Trollope was offered £3,000 for a series of travel writings on India—more than twice what he earned for *North America* (1862) and *Australia and New Zealand* (1873), and almost four times as much as for *South Africa* (1878).[3] According to Michael Cotsell, Trollope "took no interest in India" and the author himself wrote that though it might suit him "professionally," traveling on the subcontinent would be "a bore."[4] While oblique references to South Asia crop up in his writing, Trollope was clearly as reluctant to figure India or Indians in his imaginative works as he was to encounter them in his travels. Trollope's complex racial views point to the heterogeneity of Britain's nineteenth-century expansion since they register his enthusiasm for Anglo-Saxon settlement in the world's temperate regions and his discomfort with "extended dominion over black subjects" in the global South.[5] His vision of white settler colonies as "lands in which ... the descendants of our forefathers" are "living and still speaking our language" articulated a potent "Greater British" imaginary, but placed him at odds with the New Imperialism of the 1870s.[6] Although Trollope recognized the potential geopolitical benefits of a territorial empire, and saw Anglo-Saxons

---

[1]   Michael Cotsell, "Trollope: The International Theme" in Michael Cotsell (ed.), *English Literature and The Wider World*, vol. 3, *Creditable Warriors, 1830–1876* (London: Ashfield, 1990), p. 243.

[2]   Catherine Hall, "Going a-Trolloping: Imperial Man Travels the Empire" in Clare Midgley (ed.), *Gender and Imperialism* (Manchester: Manchester University Press, 1998), pp. 180–99.

[3]   On the offer from George Smith, see R. H. Super, *The Chronicler of Barsetshire: A Life of Anthony Trollope* (Ann Arbor: University of Michigan Press, 1988), p. 125.

[4]   Cotsell, p. 249; see Trollope's July 3, 1860 letter to George Smith, in Bradford Booth (ed.), *The Letters of Anthony Trollope* (Oxford: Oxford University Press, 1951), p. 61.

[5]   Anthony Trollope, *The Tireless Traveler: Twenty Letters to the Liverpool Mercury* (Berkeley: University of California Press, 1978), p. 200.

[6]   Anthony Trollope, *South Africa*, (Cape Town: Balkema, 1973), p. 33.

as a "dominant race," he rejected both liberal and conservative arguments for an extensive imperial dominion.[7] Thus, in 1875, just a year before Victoria was proclaimed Empress of India, Trollope wrote that India was not "a colony … in any proper sense, as the English who live there are very few, and are confined to those who rule *the real people of the land*."[8] As J. H. Davidson has remarked, Trollope seems to have regarded India as an "alien, native and heathen" locale, the epitome of Southern otherness. To claim India as an imperial "keystone" was, on this Trollopian view, "preposterous."[9]

In this essay I argue that *The Eustace Diamonds* is an exception to Trollope's reticence on India. Yet, in making this case I do not suggest that Trollope wrote his third Palliser novel explicitly to weigh in on Indian policies or the emerging New Imperialism. Trollope's fictional meditation on India almost certainly sprang from a consciously literary response to a contemporary novel—Wilkie Collins's *The Moonstone* (1868).[10] Nonetheless, both works clearly attended contemporaneous debates over the governance of India, including the status of India's "princes," which have received surprisingly little critical attention. In this way, *The Eustace Diamonds* offers an illuminating window into the governmentality of a so-called liberal imperialism in the years between the Indian rebellion of 1857–58 and the Royal Titles Act of 1876—a period that included passage of the Second Reform Bill.[11] In so doing, Trollope's third Palliser novel offers a compelling example of a mid-Victorian "geopolitical aesthetic." By capturing a politico-imperial turning point at a moment when representative government was the object of intense metropolitan scrutiny, the novel visibly struggles to "figure out" the "landscapes and forces" of a global situation not yet fully accessible to individual experience.[12]

---

[7]   Anthony Trollope, *The New Zealander* (London: The Trollope Society, 1995), p. 11.

[8]   Trollope, *Tireless*, p. 93; emphasis added. Trollope's views on expansion—enthusiastic about white settler colonies but ambivalent about long-term rule over non-European people—is comparable to that of several contemporaries including Herman Merivale, Trollope's friend and author of *Lectures on Colonization and Colonies* (1841).

[9]   J. H. Davidson, "Anthony Trollope and the Colonies," *Victorian Studies*, 12.3, (March 1969): 320.

[10]   Henry James Wye Milley first made the connection in "*The Moonstone* and *The Eustace Diamonds*," *Studies in Philology*, 36 (1939): 651–63.

[11]   On the importance of imperial "others" in reconstituting the nation in 1867 see Catherine Hall, "The Nation Within and Without" in Catherine Hall, Keith McClelland and Jane Rendall (ed.), *Defining the Victorian Nation: Class, Race, Gender and The Reform Act of 1867*, (Cambridge: UK: Cambridge University Press, 2000), pp. 179–233.

[12]   Fredric Jameson, *The Geopolitical Aesthetic: Cinema and Space in the World System* (Bloomington: Indiana University Press, 1995), p. 3. Jameson's term refers to postmodern film, not nineteenth-century British realism, a genre whose aesthetic potential is sometimes underrated in ways this essay implicitly contests. My interest in reading Trollope's global-capitalist novels as richly historicist has something in common with Harry E. Shaw's arguments for an extension of Georg Lukács's approach to realism beyond the novels of

As described by George Levine, Trollope's realist fiction sustains a "myth of the ordinary." In "the solidity and complacency of its narrative movement through time it quietly resists the very radical questioning that some of its elements may seem to provoke."[13] Levine thus distinguishes Trollope from contemporaries such as Charlotte Brontë, Dickens, Eliot, and Thackeray. Whereas the latter novelists are, in effect, quasi-realists—palpably ambivalent, artistically passionate, restless and experimental—Trollope, writing in a more conventional mode, justifies the modernist complaint that realism "confirms things as they are."[14] Although Levine does not discuss *The Eustace Diamonds*, his interpretation encourages us to view the novel as naturalizing the corrupt politico-imperial order it depicts. Should we conclude that the repellent anti-Semitism of Trollope's later fiction is the only alternative it offers to "sheer plod"?[15] In what follows I suggest that such an approach underestimates the strengths of Trollope's post-Barsetshire fiction including the exceptional features of *The Eustace Diamonds*.

The years between 1855 and 1867, the period of Trollope's Barsetshire series, saw the author articulating the global outlook of a self-styled liberal power. At once the "Chronicler of Barsetshire" and "Colonial Man," Trollope alternated between English-focused novels and far-flung travel writings, creating productive play between the *heirloom sovereignty* of the nation's established institutions, and the *transportable roots* of Anglo-Saxon blood and language. Through such dialectic, Barsetshire's socio-economic limitations could be offset by the colonies while colonial expropriation was moralized by Barsetshire. To be sure, Barsetshire's rendering of an exceptional English ethico-cultural heritage was hardly innocent of presuming the supremacy of Anglo-Saxon "race." Nonetheless, as a robustly historicist and autoethnographic view, the Barsetshire imaginary could dispense with the biological and thus relatively ahistorical category of "race."[16] Thus, when "race" appears prominently in English novels such as *The Way We Live Now* (1875) and *The Prime Minister* (1876), it testifies to a devastating breach of national sovereignty—an insidious metropolitan cosmopolitanism that signals the end of Barsetshire, the collapse of an heirloom legacy, and the arrival of novels of

---

Honoré de Balzac and Walter Scott. See Lukács, *The Historical Novel*, Hannah and Stanley Mitchell, trans. (Lincoln: University of Nebraska Press, 1983) and Shaw, *Narrating Reality: Austen, Scott, and Eliot* (Ithaca: Cornell University Press, 1999).

[13]   George Levine, *The Realistic Imagination: English Fiction from Frankenstein to Lady Chatterley* (Chicago: University of Chicago Press, 1981), p. 203.

[14]   Levine, p. 202.

[15]   Ibid., p. 203.

[16]   By contrast, racial discourse was fundamental to the "Greater British" imaginary of Trollope's writings on white settler colonies; on literary "autoethnography" see James Buzard, *Disorienting Fiction: The Autoethnographic Work of Nineteenth-Century British Novels* (Princeton: Princeton University Press, 2005).

capitalist globalization.[17] Although *The Way We Live Now* is the archetype of this genre, *The Eustace Diamonds* is distinct in making the globalized metropole the site of a meditation on imperial ethics.

In *The Eustace Diamonds*, as Walter M. Kendrick has noted, a "traditional British enclosure" is "invaded by golddiggers, speculators, and Jews."[18] Kendrick's observation points to the Reverend Joseph Emilius, a "greasy" crypto-Jew, and Lizzie Eustace, the "snake-like," "harpy" whose "greedy" desire drives the main plot.[19] In Trollope's global-capitalist novels, these demonized characters function as crucial syphons, concentrating, spectacularizing, and racializing attributes of falseness and dishonesty that, in their more dispersed form, threaten to destabilize his urbane mode of realist satire. By such means, Trollope struggled, as Andrew H. Miller writes, "to define an honest understanding of ownership" in the face of pervasive capitalist—and I would add, imperialist— contradictions.[20] As the title makes clear, the focus of Trollope's third Palliser novel is not persons or places but objects—specifically, a set of family jewels—around whose ambiguous legal status much of the narrative's wrestling with ownership turns.[21] Are the jewels family heirlooms—a Burkean form of ethico-cultural property entitled to exceptional legal protection—or are they mere commodities that, like any other repositories of exchange value, may be sold on the market at the discretion of any owner? This question has invited a number of excellent analyses from feminist, Marxist, and psychoanalytic perspectives, and has begun to be considered in light of imperial questions.[22] In what follows, I supplement these readings by describing the novel's

---

[17]   These arguments are spelled out in Lauren M. E. Goodlad, "Trollopian Foreign Policy: 'Rootedness' and 'Cosmopolitanism' in the Mid-Victorian Global Imaginary," forthcoming. For a complementary historicization of Barsetshire's end in light of capitalist developments, see Elsie Michie, "Buying Brains: Trollope, Oliphant, and Vulgar Victorian Commerce," *Victorian Studies*, 44.1 (2001): pp. 77–97.

[18]   Walter M. Kendrick, "*The Eustace Diamonds:* The Truth of Trollope's Fiction," *ELH*, 46 (1979): 136–7.

[19]   Anthony Trollope, *The Eustace Diamonds* (Oxford: Oxford University Press, 1983), vol. 2, p. 241; vol. 1, p. 17, vol. 1, p. 229. Subsequent references will be abbreviated *ED* and cited parenthetically in the text. On Emilius as an example of crypto-Judaism see Michael Ragussis, *Figures of Conversion: "The Jewish Question" and English National Identity* (Durham: Duke University Press, 1995), pp. 243–6.

[20]   Andrew H. Miller, "Owning Up: Possessive Individualism in Trollope's *Autobiography* and *The Eustace Diamonds*," in *Novels Behind Glass: Commodity Culture and Victorian Narrative* (Cambridge, UK: Cambridge University Press, 1995) p. 163.

[21]   For a reading that creatively attends this object focus, see John Plotz, "Discreet Jewels: Victorian Diamond Narratives and the Problem of Sentimental Value," forthcoming.

[22]   Noteworthy readings in addition to those I have already cited include William A. Cohen, "Trollope's Trollop," *Novel: A Forum on Fiction*, 28.3 (Spring 1995): 235–56. Christoph Lindner, *Fictions of Commodity Culture: From the Victorian to the Postmodern* (Aldershot: Ashgate, 2003), ch. 4; Kathy Alexis Psomiades, "Heterosexual Exchange and Other Victorian Fictions: *The Eustace Diamonds* and Victorian Anthropology," *Novel: A*

sensitive capture of an evolving politico-imperial governmentality. Although a fuller account of Trollope's novel would also dwell on the flagrant expropriative persona of Lizzie Eustace, a figure of the New Imperialism, in this essay I focus on the surprising complexity of two "liberal" characters—Lucy Morris and Lord Fawn—and their relation to the novel's conspicuously voiceless Indian, the Sawab of Mygawb.[23]

Honest ownership

Looking back on *The Eustace Diamonds* in his autobiography, Trollope offers an oblique account of its relation to *The Moonstone*. "The plot of the diamond necklace ... produced itself without any forethought"; Wilkie Collins would have devoted "infinite labour" to such plotting (*Auto*, p. 218). Trollope thus offers an apolitical telling of his interest in Collins's novel, portraying himself as a committed realist who diverges from the sensation writer's emphasis on technique. Of course, *The Moonstone*, which begins and ends with the narration of events on the subcontinent, has become a staple of postcolonial criticism. The famous Prologue opens with the theft of the diamond from a Hindu shrine by a rapacious English officer—a primal scene that Collins deliberately embeds in an actual historical event, the 1799 storming of Seringapatam. Although *The Moonstone*'s investment in Anglo-Indian relations is plain, and the links between Trollope's novel and Collins's long-recognized, *The Eustace Diamonds* has only recently been read in light of imperialism.

To be sure, the only Indian in the novel is the Sawab of Mygawb, a minor character whose facetious name and ultra-marginalized position have led most critics to ignore or dismiss him. But as W. J. McCormack has argued, the Sawab's appearance as "a non-character" is deceptive: in fact, his claim to having "been robbed" is analogous to the theft of the Eustace diamonds and, thus, a sign of Trollope's substantive engagement with Collins's narrative of imperial ethics.[24] It is therefore worth noting that while the sensational burglary attempt on the diamonds in volume 2 was a last-minute addition to the plot (see *Auto*, p. 218), the debate over the Sawab's property is almost certainly part of the novel's original conception. Indeed, the Sawab's predicament is described even before Lizzie's dubious claim on the diamonds becomes the novel's main focus.

Forum on Fiction, 33.1 (Fall 1999): 93–118; and Suzanne Daly, "Indiscreet Jewels: *The Eustace Diamonds*," *Nineteenth Century Studies*, (2005): 69–81.

[23]   What follows is excerpted from a chapter in my current book project, tentatively entitled "The Victorian Geopolitical Aesthetic: Literature, Internationalism, and 'the South.'"

[24]   W. J. McCormack, "Introduction," in Anthony Trollope, *The Eustace Diamonds* (Oxford: Oxford University Press, 1983), p. xxiv. Subsequent references will be abbreviated as "Introduction" and cited parenthetically in the text.

The Sawab first appears in a chapter devoted to introducing Lucy Morris, governess to the sisters of Lord Fawn, who is Under-Secretary of State for India:

> There was forward just then [in Parliament] a question as to whether the Sawab of Mygawb should have twenty millions of rupees paid to him and placed upon a throne, or whether he should be kept in prison all his life. The British world generally could not be made to interest itself about the Sawab, but Lucy positively mastered the subject ... (*ED*, vol. 1, p.25).

Trollope's narrator emphasizes the gravity of the Sawab's situation only to subordinate it to the exceptional qualities of the Fawn family governess. This displacement—from an aggrieved Indian sovereign and indifferent public to the novel's most obvious foil for Lizzie Eustace—is no accident. Although Lucy is sometimes read as the closest approximation to a heroine in a novel that is explicitly said to lack one, the governess's close tie to the novel's only Indian character demands careful reading.[25]

Let us begin by considering *The Eustace Diamonds*'s account of social relations within Britain's borders, its effort to conceive honest ownership in a post-Barsetshire world. Although the diamonds are said to have originated in Golconda, Trollope's jewels, unlike Collins's Moonstone, neither point directly to any Indian character nor to particular events outside of Britain.[26] Rather, the main fascination of the Eustace diamonds, as every Trollope reader knows, is their ambiguous legal status: the question of whether they are family heirlooms—a form of property entitled to special legal protection—or mere commodities that may be sold on the market at the owner's discretion. Whereas Mr. Camperdown, the Eustace family solicitor, has assumed that the diamonds are heirlooms and, thus, bearers of the extra-economic value that Kathy Psomiades has called "Eustaceness," the law turns out to pronounce a very different view.[27]

Camperdown's mistaken assumption recalls the quasi-Burkean notion of property which Barsetshire novels such as the *The Warden* sought to privilege. As though purposely to distinguish the Eustace diamonds from the idea of inherited

---

[25] For example, Lucy is the "Una" to Lizzie's "Duessa" in Juliet McMaster's Spenserian interpretation; see *Trollope's Palliser Novels: Theme and Pattern* (New York: Oxford University Press, 1978), pp. 78–102. On the Sawab's marginality see, for example, Miller, p. 168; John Halperin, whose point is to stress the novel's underrated "political content," concludes that the Sawab's claim initiates a "silly debate," exemplary of the "ersatz issues of the day"; see *Trollope and Politics: A Study of the Pallisers and Others*, (New York: Barnes and Noble, 1977), pp. 151, 157, 156. For disagreement with Halperin, see Laurie Langbauer, *Novels of Everyday Life: The Series in English Fiction, 1850–1930* [Ithaca: Cornell University Press, 1999], p.111 and Daly, p. 75.

[26] However, for a worthwhile reading that focuses on the diamonds as a classic imperial trope, see Daly.

[27] Psomiades, p. 103.

property as an ethico-cultural legacy, the law regards them as mere "trinkets," reducible to a "dirty question of money" (*ED*, vol. 1, p. 258). In fact, according to Turtle Dove's expert opinion, diamonds are the ultimate *non*-heirlooms, incapable of signifying extra-economic value in any concrete or permanent way.[28] The novel thus creates a homology between the non-heirloom condition of the diamonds (reduced to a commodity form) and Lizzie Eustace, the non-heirloom woman ("too much the mushroom" [vol. 1, p. 190]) who trades on the residue of heirloom wealth and title. A mere pretender to the ethico-cultural value that Eustaceness may once have signified, Lizzie is rarely acknowledged as "Lady Eustace."

Of course, if anyone in this novel-without-a-hero harks back to the world of Barsetshire it is Lucy Morris. But Lucy does not exemplify the lived moral relation to an heirloom social order which Septimus Harding embodied in the Barsetshire novels. Rather, as though the governess herself were a possession, she is repeatedly likened to a litter of objects the supposed authenticity of which depend on comparison to Lizzie's spurious counterparts. Lucy is "good as gold" (vol. 1, p. 263), a bona fide "treasure" (vol. 1, pp. 22, 265), and "real stone" in contrast to Lizzie's "paste" (vol. 2, p. 230). Ironically, this objectification of her virtues leaves Lucy open to construction as the Fawn family's heirloom. Having recognized their governess as a gem, yet one too poor to attract a suitable husband, Lady Fawn and her daughter, Mrs. Hittaway, intend that Lucy be "made over to the Hittaways" like one of the loyal servants whom Lizzie is "too much of the mushroom" to cultivate (vol. 1, p. 24, cf. vol. 1, p. 22; vol. 1, p. 190). It is a fate—a loss of individual sovereignty—that Lucy actively resists.

Significantly, the novel's opening chapters suggest two ways in which Lucy's exemplary non-Lizzieness might offer a more liberal solution to the problem of honest ownership—neither of which is ultimately sustained. In the more familiar of the two, Lucy is figured as an independent, sovereign proprietor:

> What she had was her own, whether it was the old grey silk dress which she had bought with the money she had earned, or the wit which nature had given her. She coveted no man's possessions;—and no woman's; but she was minded to hold by her own" (vol. 1, p. 26).

In this fantasy of guilt-free possession, Lucy affirms the liberal individual by erasing its troubling expropriative aspects. As one who possesses without expropriating or even "coveting," Lucy is so innocuous that she neutralizes an array of ethico-cultural dangers associated with possessive individualism in the

---

[28]   Portraying diamonds as pure commodities, Trollope's novel registers the very qualities—"homogeneity," "clarity," "historylessness"—that account for the diamond's becoming, in the later nineteenth century, a new social currency; see Robert N. Proctor, "Anti-Agate: The Great Diamond Hoax and the Semiprecious Stone Scam," *Configurations*, 9 (2001): p. 398. My thanks to Jenni Lieberman for this reference.

mode of John Locke.[29] In the second idealization of the governess, Lucy figures a more sophisticated mode of liberal ethics. On this view, she is not only honest and non-expropriative but also dialogical and intersubjective—the bearer of rare communicative capacities. Lucy is "always open to familiar intercourse" (vol. 1, p. 23), able to convoke a "community of interest" (vol. 1, p. 24), and "the very best" of "listeners" (vol. 1, p. 25)—the very qualities that enable her to "take up" a subject like the Sawab's case and "make it her own" (vol. 1, p. 25). "[N]o man or woman was ever more anxious to be effective, to persuade, to obtain belief, sympathy, and co-operation" than Lucy (vol. 1, p. 26). Trollope's governess thus adumbrates a communicative subject beyond Locke's sovereign monad—perhaps even an anti-imperial ethics.

Significantly, however, this evocation of Lucy as a potential liberal exemplar is deeply gendered. Every one of her exceptional qualities—heirloomesque invaluability, non-expropriativeness, and intersubjective ethics—is expressed through the prism of an idealized femininity that, in this novel, she uniquely (if unstably) represents. Lucy's morality is likewise embedded in the gendered economy of upper-middle-class marriage. By the time the narrator introduces the Sawab, her gloomy marital prospects have been fully disclosed: she is a penniless governess who is in love with Frank Greystock, an ambitious politician who needs a rich wife. In the corrupt world of the novel, all characters acknowledge more or less openly that Frank's marriage to a governess would spell death for his professional ambitions. Thus, Lucy's honesty and Lizzie's cash value are regarded as incommensurable goods—one moral and the other economic. As against the pervasive materialism that allows Lizzie's "filthy lucre" to challenge Lucy's moral worth (vol. 1, p. 22), the narrator only occasionally insists on a tenuous idealism— a view from which Lucy's "true" good would, perforce, earn her the reward of a faithful fiancé. This shift toward depicting a "degenerate age" marks a break with earlier Trollope works in which "mercenary marriage" was portrayed as more egregious (vol. 1, pp. 219, 273).[30] But, for now, my point is simply that Lucy, the novel's principal embodiment of an ideal liberal morality, is inescapably embedded in the very "real" situation of the marriage economy. Trollope's governess might "covet no man's possessions" but she most certainly covets marriage to Frank Greystock.

---

[29]   For the classic critique of possessive individualism as found in Locke's political theory see C. B. Macpherson, *The Political Theory of Possessive Individualism: Hobbes and Locke* (Oxford: Clarendon Press, 1962). For Miller, Lucy is an exception of sorts: "her virtue represented as the proper attitude towards and behavior with possessions," p. 171; see also Psomiades, p. 95. Plotz, however, notes that Lucy's "shifting interest in the Sawab is a predictable articulation of a well-lubricated system" (p. 35).

[30]   In *Doctor Thorne* (1858), for example, Frank Gresham never wavers toward his impecunious beloved while the title hero of *Phineas Finn* (1867) ultimately remains true to his Irish sweetheart (whose early death enables a more advantageous match with Madame Max).

Over the course of the novel, as Lizzie aggressively competes with Lucy, tempting Frank to break his engagement to the governess, Lucy subtly but tenaciously, struggles to avoid the fate of a Fawn family "treasure." In *North America*, Trollope quipped that the "best right a woman has is the right to a husband."[31] In *The Eustace Diamonds*, Lady Fawn encourages Lucy to disown that right on the grounds of her poverty and to regard herself as non-marriageable. It is a view that Lucy—at once humble family retainer and Lockean proprietor— initially both accepts and rejects. Although "Lady Fawn could have no right to tell her governess not to be in love," Lucy knew "well enough" that she "was not entitled to have a lover" (vol. 1, p. 59). At various points Lucy contemplates releasing Frank from his burdensome promise (in the manner of several Trollope heroines); that she never does so reinforces her Lockean tendency "to hold by her own."[32]

Like many Trollope novels, *The Eustace Diamonds* provides numerous examples of the injury to middle-class women who lack satisfactory economic alternatives to marriage, including Miss Macnulty, Augusta Fawn, and the tragic Lucinda Roanoke. But Lucy's case stands apart in linking female adversity to a test of liberal-imperial morality. Thus, Lucy's dismal prospects concerning Frank, likened to the physical "loss of a leg or an arm," are explicitly tied to "the injured prince," with her maimed condition corresponding to the Indian's jeopardized sovereignty (vol. 1, pp. 25–6). Although Lucy is a potential double for the Sawab—like him, the victim of social injustice—she is instead depicted as his advocate. Lucy not only "masters" the Sawab's case, she also nearly persuades Fawn to "stand up against his chief," the Secretary of State for India, on the prince's behalf (vol. 1, p. 25). Lucy's arguments in favor of the voiceless royal are never described. What takes the place of such elaboration is the unmistakable fact that Lucy's supposed empathy and advocacy fuel a fantasy about Frank's heroism. In a detail that cannot be accidental, Lucy is contemplating her lamentable romance when "Lord Fawn suddenly put into her hands a cruelly long printed document respecting the Sawab," the reading of which prompts her to think, "*how wonderfully Frank Greystock would plead the cause of the Indian prince*" (vol. 1, pp. 26–7; emphasis added).

And that is only the beginning. In a chapter entitled "Mr. Burke's Speeches," Lucy's fantasy, after a fashion, comes true. For unspecified reasons, Fawn's chief has found it politically necessary to oppose the Sawab's claim, providing Frank, a Tory, with an opportunity to attack him and Fawn in Parliament:

> We all know the meaning of such speeches. Had not Frank belonged to the party
> that was out, and had not the resistance to the Sawab's claim come from the
> party that was in, Frank would not probably have cared much about the prince

---

[31] Anthony Trollope, *North America* (New York: Harper, 1862), p. 262.

[32] As McMaster notes, Lucy is thus unlike "self-abnegating" Barsetshire heroines such as Mary Thorne and Grace Crawley, p. 83.

> ... It is thus the war is waged. Frank Greystock took up the Sawab's case, and
> would have drawn mingled tears and indignation from his hearers, had not his
> hearers all known the conditions of the contest. On neither side did the hearers
> care much for the Sawab's *claims*. (vol. 1, p. 61; emphasis added).

Thus, though Frank is motivated purely by the desire to get "his lance within the
joints of his enemies' harness" and though Fawn, in fact, is more desirous than
his attacker "to favour the ill-used chieftain," Lucy's amorous fantasy of Frank's
pleading the Sawab's cause is realized (vol. 1, pp. 61–2).

The plot thickens when Fawn takes Greystock's political tactics personally and
accuses him, in Lucy's hearing, of ungentlemanly behavior. Now it is Lucy's turn
to engage in *realpolitik*: "it seemed to her that she could rush into the battle, giving
a side blow at his lordship on behalf of his absent antagonist, *but appearing to
fight for the Sawab*" (vol. 1, p. 64; emphasis added). When Lucy reveals her actual
motive, calling Frank's speech "the very best" she has ever read, the thin-skinned
Fawn pompously quizzes her on parliamentary oratory. This amusing scuffle
between overbearing Under-Secretary and feisty governess explains the title of the
chapter, since in flaunting his superior knowledge of Parliament, Fawn alludes to
Edmund Burke's "opening address on the trial of Warren Hastings" (vol. 1, p. 66).
A few chapters later, Lucy, now Frank's fiancée, quarrels again with Fawn. When
Fawn accuses Frank of bearing a personal grudge "because he was so ridiculously
wrong about the Sawab," Lucy declares that Frank is incapable of "bearing malice
about a thing like that wild Indian" (vol. 1, pp. 245–6; emphasis added). It is in
this way that the voiceless Sawab exposes Lucy's ethical limitations: "English
blood is thicker than Indian justice" (McCormack, "Introduction," p. xxv). Yet, it
is also in this way that Lucy increases her odds in the uphill battle for "the right to
a husband." Her argument with Fawn provides a reason for her to remove herself
from the Fawn family's patronage while tenaciously clinging to her "property" in
Frank's tendered proposal of marriage (vol. 1, p. 132).

As McCormack avers, Trollope's allusion to the prosecution of the infamous
imperial administrator Warren Hastings and his debt to *The Moonstone* are
"integral parts of a larger pattern" ("Introduction" xxiv).[33] I propose that they are
even more integral than his excellent reading suggests. In the late 1860s, when
Trollope began writing *The Eustace Diamonds*, the subject of Indian sovereigns
was very far from an "ersatz" issue.[34] Whereas Trollope, the inveterate traveler,
pronounces India "a bore," the author of the Palliser series places a dispossessed

---

[33]   Hastings' trial for high crimes and misdemeanors reflected an increasing metropolitan
awareness that Britain's empire in India required greater legitimacy and stability; see, for
example, Mithi Mukherjee, "Justice, War, and the Imperium: India and Britain in Edmund
Burke's Prosecutorial Speeches in the Impeachment Trial of Warren Hastings," *Law and
History Review*, 23.3 (2005): electronic.

[34]   Halperin, p. 156.

Indian prince at the fore of his tale of metropolitan politics—only to deprive him of voice or character.

The great parliamentary bore

In an 1866 article in *The Fortnightly Review*, John Morley, a rising figure in liberal circles, wrote that a "very remarkable and important episode in the history of English rule in India [was] occurring at the present moment."[35] Like Collins's *The Moonstone*, Morley's story begins with the 1799 siege of Seringapatam, after which Mysore fell "by right of conquest" to the East India Company ("England," p. 260). Yet, what many present-day Collins readers may not realize is that the Company did not opt for direct rule of Mysore in the wake of its 1799 victory but, rather, signed a treaty conferring sovereignty for the region upon an old line of Rajahs. The state of Mysore was thus part of the large fraction of Britain's empire on the subcontinent—about one third—which was not governed directly by British officials either before or after 1857.[36] Moreover, the loyalty of these sovereigns, including the Rajah of Mysore, was widely believed to have been critical in containing the rebellion. Hence, in 1858, when the East India Company was abolished and the Crown assumed direct responsibility for governing the empire, the Queen's Proclamation explicitly assured these crucial allies that "We shall respect the rights, dignity, and honour of the native princes as our own."[37] Surprisingly, then, less than a decade later, the crisis reported by Morley concerned the British government's apparent intention to annex Mysore upon the death of the same Rajah who had been installed after Seringapatam.[38]

---

[35] John Morley, "England and the Annexation of Mysore," *The Fortnightly Review*, 33 (September 1866): 259. See also "Dangers in India," *Macmillan's Magazine* (April 1867): 412. As co-founder of *The Fortnightly*, in which *The Eustace Diamonds* was published, Trollope almost certainly knew Morley's article.

[36] The actual terms of "indirect" rule varied greatly from case to case, since the so-called princely states were "semi-sovereign political entities whose varying shades of internal sovereignty" depended on the terms of existing treaties and customs; see Adrian Sever (ed.), *Documents and Speeches on the Indian Princely States* (Delhi: B. R. Publishing, 1985), vol 1, p. 37.

[37] "Proclamation by Queen Victoria (1 November 1858)," in Sever (ed.), p. 233.

[38] Under the doctrine of "lapse," the British could refuse to recognize the adopted heir of a childless sovereign and, thus, claim (supposedly) legitimate grounds for annexation. In my forthcoming chapter, I discuss the importance of the Mysore controversy in light of tensions in imperial sovereignty. From the metropolitan standpoint of Trollope's Palliser novels, the Mysore debate, coinciding with debates over parliamentary reform, reflected on Britain's vaunted political institutions—their claim to being "liberal" in any meaningful sense. For another reading of *The Eustace Diamonds* in light of the debate over Mysore, see Daly.

Although the debate over Mysore marked a much-discussed turning point in imperial policy—an official embrace of "indirect" rule—Indian royals like Trollope's fictional Sawab were in various ways becoming common features of mid-Victorian metropolitan culture. Throughout this period, questions of "honest ownership" extended to Indian sovereignty in multiple ways. In the 1860s, after Prince Gholam Mohammed (the son of Tipu Sultan) traveled to Britain twice to increase his family's stipend, direct "princely appeals" to Parliament and the press became common—much to the chagrin of Secretaries of State for India such as Sir Charles Wood and Lord Salisbury.[39] In some ways the Sawab's predicament—either to "have twenty millions of rupees paid to him and placed upon a throne," or to "be kept in prison all his life"—is, though deliberately facetious, reminiscent of the situation of Prince Azeem Jah. Described at length in *The Great Parliamentary Bore* (1869), one of several books on India by the British writer T. Evans Bell, Jah sought to succeed his nephew as titular sovereign of the Carnatic.[40] It was Jah's claim that prompted Bell, a vocal supporter of indirect rule, to allege that India was "by common consent of all political parties," "a great Parliamentary bore."[41]

If Trollope read Bell's book in 1869 he knew that yet another deposed prince, the heir of the Rajah of Sattara, a territory annexed in 1848, "is, or was lately, a state prisoner" near Bombay, suspected of treason during the rebellion.[42] Bell's book may thus have inspired Trollope's vision of an Indian royal teetering between enthronement and incarceration. What is certain is that in the 1860s the Indian "prince" became a familiar metropolitan figure: a signifier of feudal loyalty and an occasional rallying cry for imperial justice. In 1863, Duleep Singh, titular Maharaja of the Punjab and friend of the Queen, purchased Elveden Hall in Norfolk.[43] In April 1870, as Trollope resumed writing *The Eustace Diamonds* after a brief pause spent on a non-fictional project, *Vanity Fair* published a sympathetic account of Syud Munsoor Ullee, the Nawab Nazim of Bengal. Ullee had arrived

---

[39]   Knight, p. 503

[40]   Jah's case was brought before the Commons six times between 1860 and 1865, but without any result. I use the term "titular" to refer to the wholly nominal mode of sovereignty that was sometimes preserved after annexation. When the Carnatic was annexed in 1801, a royal stipend was conferred by treaty for the deposed Nawab and his heirs. Prince Azeem Jah was thus attempting to be recognized as the heir to the title under these terms. For more on Bell, a writer whose "inspiration was an ardent belief in the material and moral importance of indirect imperialism," see Knight, p. 503.

[41]   Major [T.] Evans Bell, *The Great Parliamentary Bore* (London: Trübner, 1869), p. iii.

[42]   Bell, *The Great Parliamentary Bore*, p. 158.

[43]   Nicknamed the "Black Prince," Singh could name the Prince of Wales among his hunting guests. As the infant Maharaja of the Punjab, Singh had not yet begun to govern when, in 1849, he was forced to renounce his rule and to hand over the famous Koh-i-noor diamond as a "gift" to Queen Victoria; see Rozina Visram, *Ayahs, Lascars and Princes: The Story of Indians in Britain, 1700–1947* (London: Pluto, 1986), pp. 71–3.

VANITY FAIR.   April 16, 1870.

No. 76.   SOVEREIGNS No. 8.

"A living monument of English injustice."

Fig. 6.1   "A living monument to English injustice." *Vanity Fair*, 16 April 1870

in London to protest a series of reductions in the stipend promised to his family according to the eighteenth-century treaty in which they surrendered their rule to British authority. The caption described Ullee, a titular sovereign, as "A living monument to British injustice".[44]

Though Bell may have popularized the idea of Parliament's apathy toward India, he did not invent it. An 1860 article in *Fraser's* began, "India, which is forgotten when Parliament is sitting, rises into importance when the vacation gives us time to think how we are to govern a hundred millions of Orientals."[45] According to Walter Bagehot, "the greatest defect of the House of Commons" was the "distracting routine" of attending the empire.[46] Trollope himself returned to the topic in *Phineas Redux* and *The Prime Minister*.[47] Addressing Parliament in 1867, Lord Salisbury, Secretary of State for India, enhanced the impression of a boring India, describing Indian administration as "routine," "listless," "elaborate," and characterized by "extreme centralization."[48]

Herman Merivale, the real-life Permanent Under-Secretary of State for India during the Mysore debate, and an old friend of Trollope's, declared himself positively flummoxed by Indian matters. A lawyer and political economist who had spent 13 years in the Colonial Office before transferring to Indian administration in 1860, Merivale "admitted to his friends"—including Trollope, perhaps—that "the more detailed questions of Indian affairs amused him in their randomness and sometimes impenetrability."[49] Like Trollope, whose views on the topic Merivale had influenced,[50] the Under-Secretary of State for India was an enthusiast of white settler colonies that, by 1860, were semi-autonomous and did not require "minute" supervision from London. A respected authority on emigration and settler colonialism, Merivale, like Trollope, identified himself with "the great

---

[44]   See *Vanity Fair*, "Sovereigns No. 8" (16 April 1870): no page.

[45]   "Chronicle of Current History," *Fraser's* (October 1860): 543.

[46]   *The English Constitution*, Ithaca: Cornell, 1966, p. 135.

[47]   In *Phineas Redux*, the narrator notes "any allusion to our Eastern Empire will certainly empty [the House of Comons]," Oxford: Oxford University Press, 1973, p. 322. Wryly describing the intense public interest in Glencora Palliser's conduct, the narrator of *The Prime Minister* notes that if "the welfare of the Indian Empire [had] occupied the House, the House would have been empty" (Harmondsworth: Penguin, 1996), p. 492.

[48]   Salisbury (then Viscount Cranborne), quoted in Williams, p. 235.

[49]   Edward Beasley, *Mid-Victorian Imperialists: British Gentlemen and the Empire of the Mind* (London: Routledge, 2005), p. 40. Note that Merivale's civil service position as Permanent Under-Secretary of State for India is distinct from the politically appointed position, Parliamentary Under-Secretary, that Fawn holds in *The Eustace Diamonds*. Williams describes the increasing importance of the permanent position relative to the parliamentary position during the 1860s when the latter office was held by ten different occupants between 1858 and 1869, p. 120. Trollope's longstanding friendship with the Merivale family, including Herman, is described in his autobiography (*Auto*, p. 40).

[50]   See Catherine Hall, *Civilising Subjects: Metropole and Colony in the English Imagination* (Chicago: University of Chicago Press, 2002), pp. 212–13.

general thrust forward of ... English-speaking civilization."[51] Just as the transfer from Colonial to India Office left Merivale feeling like "a fish out of water,"[52] so the idea of "extended dominion" over non-Europeans seemed to both worry and alienate Trollope.[53]

As a novelist eager neither for a liberal civilizing mission nor a conservative romanticization of neo-feudal ties, Trollope was not so much strongly opposed to the Indian empire as uninspired by the vision of Britain's future to which it gave rise. At various moments his suspicion of imperial dishonesty is unmistakable. Moreover, as a writer completing his transition from Barsetshire's chronicler to the author of the Palliser series, Trollope doubtless heeded the political discussions generated by the Mysore debate and the claims of sundry titular royals.

The most resonant imperial focus for *The Eustace Diamonds* is, thus, not India itself or even the Sawab but the Parliament that decides his case: a metropolitan institution enmeshed in the moral fog of a territorial empire. As late as 1864, the narrator of *Can You Forgive Her?* had eulogized Parliament, describing "that more than royal staircase" that leads to "those passages and halls which require the hallowing breath of centuries to give them the glory in British eyes which they shall one day possess" (*Can*, vol. 2, p. 44). Trollope here renders the House of Commons, physically rebuilt in 1834, as an heirloom establishment whose historical legacy is as yet ongoing—a political institution from which "flow[s] ... the world's progress" and an "advancing civilization" (vol. 2, p. 45). Throughout the series, Plantagenet Palliser, even when cast as an ineffective leader, maintains his reputation as a dignified "legislator who served his country with the utmost assiduity" (vol. 1, p. 191; cf. *Auto*, p. 118). *The Eustace Diamonds* thus stands out as the Palliser novel in which earnest political struggle is least in evidence and parliamentary affairs almost wholly reduced to the kind of party politics occasioned by the Sawab's case.

We have seen how the Sawab enters the novel as an adjunct to Lucy's marriage plot. The governess's readiness to make use of the "injured prince" in the "game" of husband-hunting (*ED* vol. 2, p. 28) tarnishes the sterling morality that Lucy would otherwise uniquely exemplify. We can by now appreciate that the "cruelly long printed document" that Lucy "masters" (vol. 2, pp. 27, 25) concerns the technical legalities of the Sawab's claim. Lucy's interpretation of the case—that the prince is being "kept out of his rights" and "used very ill" (vol. 2, p. 65)—is one that Fawn initially finds persuasive; but, like the real-life Merivale, who served under Wood in the early stages of the Mysore debate, Fawn feels obligated to bow to the needs of his chief. According to Donovan Williams, Merivale probably took the annexationist position on Mysore not from conviction but "from a sense of duty towards" Wood who "was perpetually anxious about Indian affairs being

---

[51]   Beasley, pp. 38, 39.

[52]   Ibid., p. 38.

[53]   See Trollope, *Tireless*, p. 200.

aired in Parliament."[54] Yet if Merivale was quietly ambivalent about the Rajah of Mysore, he felt strongly enough about Azeem Jah, future subject of *The Great Parliamentary Bore*, to pen a private memorandum. A close look at the relevant documents, Merivale told Wood, had "left on [his] mind the strongest impressions" that Jah is "entitled to what he asks for, that great wrong has been done him by withholding it." "It may seem easy, in theory," he wrote, "to separate the question of right from that of expediency," but "in practice it would be found extremely difficult indeed."[55]

Did Merivale discuss such ethical quandaries with his old friend Trollope, providing inspiration for *The Eustace Diamonds*? Although it is entirely possible, the point is not so much to identify Trollope's sources as to capture the liberal-imperial aesthetic his novel maps. I suggest that the absence of concrete details about the Sawab's case is integral to a novel that is precisely *not* concerned to parse the fine points of any one imperial dispute. What *The Eustace Diamonds* evokes is not a particular disagreement about a claim or treaty, but an entire category of debate over right and expediency—a full-blown governmentality—that a so-called liberal imperialism has introduced into public life. There is, as a defensive Fawn tells Lucy, "a great deal to be said on both sides" about the Sawab's case (*ED*, vol. 1, p. 65). If the "British world could not be made to interest itself" in such affairs (vol. 1, p. 25), it was because the "details of Indian administration" were, as Morley wrote, "repulsive … from their technicality"—"random" and "impenetrable" according to Merivale; "routine" and "elaborate" according to Salisbury; and "very dull and long" according to *The Eustace Diamonds* (vol. 1, p. 61). Yet what the novel thus shows is that India's position as the "great Parliamentary bore" is no isolated or even purely imperial feature of the metropolitan political condition. It is the signpost of a governmental malaise quite unlike the glorious parliamentary future limned in *Can You Forgive Her?* Boredom is the sign of a pervasive conflation between right and expediency, a technocratization of ethics so abstruse it produces boredom as the answer to what would otherwise stand out as dishonest ownership and illegitimate sovereignty.

Lord Fawn, a respectable man made interesting according to *The Times* and *The Spectator*,[56] is the novel's chief embodiment of this liberal-imperial lifeworld: a thoroughly conventional man "gifted with but little of that insight into things which teaches men to know what is right and what is wrong" (*ED*, vol. 2, p. 139). Personifying the technocratic governmentality that came to prevail in an

---

[54]   Williams, pp. 220, 126.

[55]   Merivale, quoted in Williams, p.126.

[56]   According to *The Times*'s reviewer, "Lord Fawn is interesting in spite of his small ideas, his slow perceptions, and, above all, his eminent respectability," in Donald Smalley (ed.), *Anthony Trollope: The Critical Heritage* (London: Routledge, 1969), p. 374. *The Spectator* described "the picture of Lord Fawn's official and personal weakness, and upright moral cowardice," as "one of the most striking of Mr. Trollope's innumerable striking studies of modern life," Smalley, p. 373.

era of expedient policy and mass politics, Fawn is, according to Lizzie, "a load of Government waste-paper" whose very marriage proposals are spun out "like an Act of Parliament" (vol. 2, pp. 253–4). Yet, if the ultra-realist Fawn is, on one reading of the novel, a likely example of Levine's Trollopian "plod," the Under-Secretary's interrelation with the Sawab—who is a clear mutation of the realist form—points to the geopolitical aesthetic at work. Less "character" than figural marker of a politico-imperial map, the Sawab of Mygawb recurs uncannily in narratives about marriage, party politics, empire, the nation's coinage, and, of course, the Eustace diamonds.

First introduced in light of Lucy's marital worries, the Sawab's later appearances haunt the amatory woes of her employer, Lord Fawn. The disappointed suitor of Madame Max and Violet Effingham, Fawn is accepted by Lizzie early on but then insists that she return the Eustace diamonds. Pressured by Frank to renew his pledge, Fawn is pictured at the India Office bemoaning his bad luck in love: "*As he read some special letter in which instructions were conveyed as to the insufficiency of the Sawab's claims,* he thought of Frank Greystock's attack upon him, and of Frank Greystock's cousin" (*ED* vol. 1, p. 103; emphasis added). As in the earlier entwinement between Lucy and the Sawab, Fawn's reflection on the Indian's case is displaced by thoughts about personal romantic misfortune, occluding the reader's knowledge of claims that the Under-Secretary had initially found compelling.

As the Conservatives transform from defenders of the Sawab to avowed "Lizzieites," exposing Fawn to gossip and ridicule, the Under-Secretary is "hardly as true to the affairs of India as he … wished" (vol. 1, p. 143). A "whipped dog" on account of Lizzie's Tory champions (vol. 1, p. 147), Fawn is soon assailed within his own party by Lady Glencora who, in quasi-feminist admiration of Lizzie's pluck, takes the young widow's part. A Liberal social event at which ministers gather to advise Palliser on his five-farthing bill includes Fawn so that Glencora may "flatter" him "*as to the manner in which he had finally arranged the affair of the Sawab*" (vol. 2, p. 141; emphasis added). In this oblique fashion, wedged between Planty's penny and Glencora's marital maneuvers, Trollope reveals that the prince's case has been decided. When we next hear of the Sawab, the still beleaguered Fawn is explaining to his brother-in-law that there is no support to be had against Lizzie from Camperdown, who was mistaken about heirlooms and has withdrawn his bill in Chancery. "As far as I can see," Fawn tells Hittaway, "lawyers always are wrong": the Eustace family solicitor as wrong about heirlooms as the government's lawyer, Finlay, had been wrong about "*those nine lacs of rupees for the Sawab*" (vol. 2, p. 149; emphasis added). The precise fate of the Indian royal—enthronement? incarceration? some Fawnian compromise between the two?—is never divulged.

To be sure, such rendering of a South Asian sovereign as a voiceless subaltern seems to extend the racial hierarchism of Trollope's colonial writings. Throughout his massive oeuvre, Trollope's vision of encounter between "races," though always premised on the presumed superiority of Anglo-Saxons, varies according to the relevant geopolitical aim. Thus, whereas racial intermixture is described as a progressive outcome in the West Indies, in works such as *Australia and New Zealand*, Trollope foresees the extinction of indigenous people in climates suitable to British settlement. Then again, in Ireland, where Trollope spent the early part of his career, he advocates paternalistic kinship between colonizer and colonized—precisely the relation he *rejects* in India and other non-European locales.[57] Clearly, Trollope was enough of a racial absolutist to disdain the idea of a "liberal" civilizing mission bent on anglicizing Indians, but enough of a liberal to dislike the premise of territorial domination without justifiable cause. Thus, the Sawab of Mygawb is a non-raced figure—a blank screen who marks the novel's geopolitical unconscious—not because Trollope resisted the notion of "Oriental" essence, but because the novel captures a guise of imperial justice that takes "Oriental" essence for its alibi. As the Sawab who does not speak, the prince figures an entire discourse over the Indian sovereign: from the loyal feudatories of the Queen's Proclamation, to the Rajah of Mysore, to *Vanity Fair*'s "living monument to British injustice."

Thus, in *The Eustace Diamonds*, "the great Parliamentary bore" extends beyond the claim of a single Indian royal (a more stimulating topic, as it happens, than the hours-long Palliser penny speech which leaves Mr. Gresham "fast asleep" [*ED* vol. 2, p. 133]). Nor is boredom limited to the "repulsive" technicalities that a so-called liberal imperialism invents to obscure what Salisbury described as "the nakedness of the sword on which [the British empire] really relies."[58] The bore the novel captures is the politico-imperial governmentality that prompted Herman Merivale to observe that questions of "right" and "expediency" were, in practice, inseparable. It is the cover for an imperial theft more demoralizing even than the mercenary culture that prompts "an honest" aristocrat to propose to a wealthy widow "he knew nothing about" (vol. 1, pp. 76, 78). Both quasi-sociological in the mode of a sophisticated mid-Victorian realism, and formally inventive in the ways I have described, *The Eustace Diamonds* is among those works of the 1870s to capture the world-historical processes of imperial expansion and their uncanny metropolitan returns.[59] Realism of this kind, neither naïve nor self-naturalizing, aspires to that historical grasp that defines the geopolitical aesthetic at work.

---

[57]   See Hall, "Going," for a helpful introduction to Trollope on race; in Goodlad, "Trollopian," I describe Trollope's view that the work of white Europeans in the West Indies is nearly done. On Trollope and Ireland see, for example, Mary Jean Corbett, *Allegories of Union in Irish and English Writing: 1790–1870* (Cambridge: Cambridge University Press, 2000), ch. 4, and Patrick Longeran, "The Representation of Phineas Finn: Anthony Trollope's Palliser Series and Victorian Ireland," *Victorian Literature and Culture*, 32.1 (Spring 2004): 147–58.

[58]   Salisbury's remarks to Viceroy Lytton are quoted in Knight, p. 500.

[59]   Once again, a fuller reading of *The Eustace Diamonds* would describe the ways in which Lizzie's hyper-romantic performativity and hardcore acquisitiveness capture the emerging New Imperialism as it aligned with a Bagehotian era of mass politics.

Chapter 7
"Two Identities":
Gender, Ethnicity, and Phineas Finn

Mary Jean Corbett

Reviewing two decades of Trollope scholarship, Mark W. Turner remarks that "Trollope's work is clearly significant to Irish questions," citing a special issue of *Victorian Literature and Culture* (2004) and the several essays therein that attend to gender in his Irish novels as representative of a broader critical interest in "the way in which identity is formed in mid-Victorian Britain."[1] In earlier work, I have pursued the relationship between Trollope and Ireland from a point of view that inverts Turner's formulation, asking how and why "Irish questions" are significant to Trollope's fiction, hoping to problematize the distinction between English and Irish questions as it is still imagined not only within Trollope studies, but on the broader terrain of postcolonial approaches to nineteenth-century literatures in English.[2] Even though numerous critics have explored the hybridity within both English and Irish identities, the status of the author at hand as the quintessential representative of an Englishness untroubled by its heterogeneous relations to "others" still maintains considerable sway. "Irish questions"—even "*the* Irish Question"—should be fundamental both to how we read Trollope and to how we understand the complex formation of identities at mid-century, identities in which norms of gender, class, race, and ethnicity intersect with one another. In this essay, I argue that Irish questions do matter to Trollope and, moreover, that the question of Phineas Finn's Irishness—which has mattered as much or more to Trollope's critics as it ever did to Trollope—provides an especially good site for understanding this.

In representing gender and ethnicity in a cross-cultural context, the *Phineas* novels disturb the polarity between a masculine Englishness and a feminine Irishness. Critics have identified this binary as fundamental to Trollope's very first novel, *The Macdermots of Ballycloran* (1847), in which a gendered plot of seduction allegorically represents the inequities of colonial rule; I have analyzed a similar pattern in the late novella *An Eye for an Eye* (1879), which both deploys

---

[1] Mark W. Turner, "Trollope Studies: 1987–2004," *Dickens Studies Annual*, 37 (2006): 235.

[2] For my reading of "Trollope's Ireland," see *Allegories of Union in Irish and English Writing, 1790–1870: Politics, History, and the Family from Edgeworth to Arnold* (Cambridge, UK: Cambridge University Press, 2000), pp. 114–47.

and critiques allegory as a narrative form for representing Irish-English "union."[3] Rather than assume a stable gendered opposition throughout Trollope's writing, however, we might notice instances where it is interrupted or challenged. The construction of ineffectual Irish conspirators in *The Macdermots* or improvident Irish landlords in *Castle Richmond* (1860) may illustrate the native incapacity for political action that Trollope sometimes associates with femininity, but it may also register a gap within Irish manhood itself. In reading the *Phineas* novels for what they say about (gentle)manliness, we can also explore the interactions between norms of gender and ethnicity by analyzing how Trollope reveals and manages the tensions within constructions and performances of (gentle)manly identity through the figure of "the Irish member."

Phineas finally secures a place in government upon the death of Lord Bosanquet, as detailed in a letter that does not quite deliver on all his hopes:

> "as [Mr. Mottram] was Under-Secretary for the Colonies, and as the Under-Secretary must be in the Lower House, the vacancy must be filled up." The heart of Phineas Finn at this moment was almost in his mouth ... But his great triumph soon received a check. "Mr. Mildmay has spoken to me on the subject," continued the letter, "and informs me that he has offered the place at the colonies to his old supporter, Mr. Laurence Fitzgibbon." Laurence Fitzgibbon! "I am inclined to think that he could not have done better, as Mr. Fitzgibbon has shown great zeal for his party. This will vacate the Irish seat at the Treasury Board, and I am commissioned by Mr. Mildmay to offer it to you."[4]

The narrator continues: "Phineas was himself surprised to find that his first feeling on reading this letter was one of dissatisfaction ... Had the new Under-Secretary been a man whom he had not known, whom he had not learned to look down upon as inferior to himself, he would not have minded it ... But Laurence Fitzgibbon was such a poor creature, that the idea of filling a place from which Laurence had risen was distasteful to him" (vol. 2, p. 44). Fitzgibbon rises from "'favour and convenience ... without any reference to the service'" (vol. 2, p. 44) and without a shilling to his name. While Finn's own "mastery of standard English forms" may be an asset to his career, Fitzgibbon's brogue does not prohibit his advancing to a salaried post of £2000 a year.[5] Most of all, Fitzgibbon rises owing to his "'great

---

[3]   See Michael Cotsell, "Trollope: The International Theme," in Michael Cotsell (ed.), *English Literature and the Wider World, Volume III: Creditable Warriors, 1830–1876* (London: The Ashfield Press, 1990), pp. 243–56; Conor Johnston, "*The Macdermots of Ballycloran*: Trollope as Conservative Liberal," *Éire-Ireland*, 16 (1981): 71–92; Corbett, pp. 182–5.

[4]   Anthony Trollope, *Phineas Finn: The Irish Member*, ed. Jacques Berthoud (Oxford: Oxford University Press, 1982), vol. 2, pp. 43–4. Hereafter referred to as *PF*.

[5]   John McCourt, "Domesticating the Other: Phineas Finn, Trollope's Patriotic Irishman," *Rivista di Studi Vittoriani*, 6 (2001): 53.

zeal for his party,'" but falls four short chapters later because he will not do his work. "'Nothing on earth would induce him to look at a paper during all those weeks he was at the Colonial Office'" (vol. 2, p. 100), Barrington Erle tells Finn, who becomes an Under-Secretary for the Colonies after all.

Phineas attacks his new job with the "great zeal" Fitzgibbon reserves for politicking. Although "his back was broken" from Violet Effingham's refusal, he prepares for a meeting with Lord Cantrip and Mr Gresham, determined that "as long as he took the public pay, he would earn it" (vol. 2, p. 143). And his efforts meet with praise of a particular kind: "'He's about the first Irishman we've had that has been worth his salt,' said Mr. Gresham to his colleague afterwards. 'That other Irishman was a terrible fellow,' said Lord Cantrip, shaking his head" (vol. 2, p. 144). Like Phineas, Gresham and Cantrip have "learned to look down upon" Fitzgibbon "as inferior to [Finn] himself," to see one Irishman as better than another, with their favorite preferred for his superior industry, his devotion to his work, his willingness not just to collect but to earn "the public pay." And Fitzgibbon also characterizes Finn's value in these terms. When the party men gather at the opening of *Phineas Redux* (1874) to choose candidates who will help them to take back the "Whitehall cake" from Daubeny and the Conservatives, some of the men he left behind on his return to Ireland are still singing his praises:

> "He's the best Irishman we ever got hold of," said Barrington Erle—"present company always excepted, Laurence."

> "Bedad, you needn't except me, Barrington. I know what a man's made of, and what a man can do. And I know what he can't do. I'm not bad at the outside skirmishing. I'm worth me salt. I say that with a just reliance on me own powers. But Phinny is a different sort of man. Phinny can stick to a desk from twelve to seven, and wish to come back again after dinner."[6]

Whereas Barrington Erle pronounces the ethnic superlative, Fitzgibbon neither surrenders his own claims to efficacy nor makes the ethnic distinction that all the Englishmen make. "'A different sort of man,'" he says, not necessarily a better or worse man, but different from himself in his possession of different "powers"— close application, industry, commitment.

The opposition between these two figures of Irish manhood belies Nicholas Dames's claim that "Phineas's career sequence obscures ... any element of ethnic or class conflict" in the novel.[7] I am sympathetic to Dames's approach to "the career," and particularly to his point that "'the colonies,' as an avenue of professional advancement, signifies in Trollope a necessary *specialization*," like

---

[6] Anthony Trollope, *Phineas Redux* (London: Penguin Books, 2003), pp. 10, 12–13. Hereafter referred to as *PR*.

[7] Nicholas Dames, "Trollope and the Career: Vocational Trajectories and the Management of Ambition," *Victorian Studies*, 45 (2003): 260.

Plantagenet Palliser's passion for the decimal coinage, "that mitigates against any more all-encompassing ambition."[8] But it's not quite right to say that class and ethnicity are "washed out" in *Phineas Finn*. Clearly, Trollope makes some strategic choices, and one of them lies in departing from explicit stereotypes of Irishness in his central character and his plot(s) while projecting them on other characters.[9] In contrast to the striving Phineas, Fitzgibbon is the classic improvident "youngest son" (vol. 1, p. 3) of an Irish lord, an example of what the Irish historian R. F. Foster calls "micks on the make"; his very name both puns on the popular simian stereotype of the day and calls into question his legitimacy to rule as a member of the Protestant Ascendancy.[10] Once Finn arrives on the English scene, Fitzgibbon takes on the dubious title of that "other Irishman," "a terrible fellow" from the administrative point of view, so that our hero need not be tarred with that brush.

To begin to understand the "class and ethnic trajectories" in play thus requires an initial recognition that neither these Irishmen nor their Parliamentary masters, nor even Trollope himself, constructs Irishness exclusively in opposition to Englishness. As both John McCourt and Jane Elizabeth Dougherty have established, Phineas's Irishness is not signified, as Fitzgibbon's is, through the stereotyped conventions of Irish speech, phenotype, or conduct. The son of a professional and not a landlord, associated with the Catholic middlings rather than the Anglo-Irish gentry, Phineas belongs to the class stratum to which Trollope, in the years after the famine, assigned some of the modernizing powers of progress.[11] The differences between the backgrounds and careers of the two Irishmen are thus given ideological weight. Like Fitzgibbon, Finn gets his start by filling "the Irish seat at the Treasury Board," for which their national origins alone presumably qualify them both. Having "achieved his declared object in getting into place," however, he "felt that he was almost constrained to adopt the views of others, let them be what they might" (vol. 2, p. 163)—a conscientious qualm to which Fitzgibbon is never apparently subject. Phineas ultimately resigns his position as Under-Secretary for the Colonies so as to support the legislation for Irish tenant right to which he commits himself on his Irish tour with Mr. Monk, legislation that would (and did, in 1870) give Irish tenants security for improvements they made to their land holdings. Here Trollope makes Finn's Irishness matter, as he gives up his post and thus his seat on the basis of nationalist and patriotic principle: "his Irish birth and Irish connection had brought this misfortune of his country so closely home to him that he had found the task of extricating himself from it to

---

8   Dames, p. 268.
9   On this point, see Jane Elizabeth Dougherty, "An Angel in the House: The Act of Union and Anthony Trollope's Irish Hero," *Victorian Literature and Culture*, 32 (2004): 140.
10   R. F. Foster, "Marginal Men and Micks on the Make: The Uses of Irish Exile, *c.* 1840–1922," *Paddy & Mr Punch: Connections in Irish and English History* (London: Penguin Books, 1995), pp. 281–305. Thanks to Margaret Markwick for reminding me that the prefix "Fitz" denotes illegitimacy of birth.
11   See Corbett, pp. 128–37.

be impossible" (vol. 2, p. 330). Having failed to accept that "he must abandon all idea of independent action" (vol. 2, p. 179), he chooses to leave English public life rather than follow a career that his fiery friend Mr. Low calls "'slavery and degradation'" (vol. 1, p. 46).

Visibly differentiated from other male figures in the novel, English and Irish alike, Phineas thus enacts a crucial element of the ideology of manliness. John Tosh defines this Victorian gender and class ideal as an internal state made evident in outward display: "Sometimes there was an implied claim to natural endowment; more often a manly bearing was taken to be the outcome of self-improvement and self-discipline. This aspect was explicit in what was for the Victorians the key attribute of manliness—independence" of thought, speech, and conduct.[12] "The manly man," Tosh writes, "paid more attention to the promptings of his inner self than to the dictates of social expectation," with the opposition between the two, which I will problematize below, something that Tosh and his sources take almost as a given.[13] In politics, attention to said promptings would lead to "a rejection of all forms of patronage," which vitiated "autonomy of action and opinion"; "manly independence" constituted "a vital prerequisite" for, rather than being an effect of, "responsible political agency."[14] Such a construction not only divides independent men from dependent women, sustaining the power of a Robert Kennedy over his wife; it also distinguishes between and among men.[15] While all women were

---

[12] John Tosh, *A Man's Place: Masculinity and the Middle-Class Home in Victorian England* (New Haven and London: Yale University Press, 1999), p. 111.

[13] Tosh, "Gentlemanly Politeness and Manly Simplicity in Victorian England," in *Manliness and Masculinities in Nineteenth-Century Britain: Essays on Gender, Family and Empire* (Harlow: Pearson Longman, 2005), p. 87.

[14] Tosh, "Middle-Class Masculinities in the Era of the Women's Suffrage Movement, 1860–1914," in *Manliness and Masculinities*, p. 111; Tosh, "Gentlemanly Politeness," p. 96.

[15] In recurrent references to Lady Laura as "'bone of my bone, and flesh of my flesh'" (e.g., *PR*, p. 86), Kennedy represents womanly dependence through the biblical figure enshrined in the doctrine of "one flesh," which legitimated coverture even after the liberalization of divorce in 1857; this figure is, not coincidentally, one that the narrator uses to describe England's conjugal relation to Ireland (see Corbett, pp. 148–51, and Dougherty, pp. 133–6, for recent discussions of the metaphor). While Trollope becomes increasingly fascinated with the figure of the independent woman over the course of his career, he frequently treats her as a contradiction in terms, effectively maintaining independence as a male preserve. Thus by comparison with Lady Laura, "who from her earliest years of girlish womanhood had resolved that she would use the world as men use it, and not as women do" (*PF*, vol. 2, pp. 10–11), and lives to regret the only meaningful choice she had the opportunity to make, Phineas possesses a good deal of autonomy. For groundbreaking feminist studies of Trollope that pursue related questions in much more detail than I can do here, see Deborah Denenholz Morse, *Women in Trollope's Palliser Novels* (Ann Arbor: UMI Research Press, 1987); Jane Nardin, *He Knew She Was Right: The Independent Woman in the Novels of Anthony Trollope* (Carbondale: Southern Illinois University Press, 1989); and Margaret Markwick, *Trollope and Women* (London: Hambledon Press, 1997).

Fig. 7.1   "I wish to regard you as a dear friend,—both of my own and of my husband." Millais's illustration for *Phineas Finn*, Chapter 15

(ideologically if not actually) excluded from political life, many men, too, were debarred from full participation in civil society on the basis of class, race, religion, and ethnicity, even if accidents of "birth, breeding and education" were deemed "secondary" to "the moral qualities [that] marked the truly manly character."[16] To be sure, the dominant ideological construction of Catholic Irishmen in England during the 1860s was predicated on their perceived incapacity for exercising political autonomy, as registered in the conventional associations of Catholics with secrecy and duplicity and their attendant implications of "vast foreign conspiracies" in which these plotting people were perpetually engaged.[17] I believe that Trollope aims in part to counter such associations by situating Phineas firmly within the manly paradigm. While Fitzgibbon embodies one aspect of an Irish stereotype, which is thereby detached from the hero, Trollope makes Phineas a Catholic, in an ironic gesture, so as to counter another: "the Irish member"— potentially feminized by his colonial status, his religious background, and even his potential for dissimulation—epitomizes "manly independence," at least in the first of the *Phineas* novels.

As opposed, then, to both the place-seeking of his peers and the insurrectionary activism of his Fenian contemporaries, Phineas's adherence to "independent action" outwardly displays his inner convictions in a thoroughly manly way. What's yet more important to remember here is precisely the relational character of both manliness and independence. So in England, Phineas looks autonomous in supporting Mr. Monk in the debate over tenant right by contrast not just with his countryman Fitzgibbon, but also with the whole pack of English functionaries for whom the concept of voting against the party is anathema because keeping power and place is the supreme goal. (It's the possibility that Phineas will *not* side with them that elicits feminizing rhetoric: as Bonteen says to Ratler, "'I'll bet you a sovereign Finn votes with us yet. There's nothing like being a little coy to set off a girl's charms'" [vol. 2, p. 296]). Trollope indeed supports an ideal of "manly independence," against which he measures Finn and other characters (including such female ones as Lady Laura and Madame Max), but he persistently figures that ideal within the contexts of class and gender privilege, ethnic origin and national context. Thus McCourt's observation that "Phineas has neither the political nor financial resources to be independent of the men who put him into parliament" is sound, but his claim that Phineas's position "is surely metonymic of

---

[16]   Tosh, "Gentlemanly Politeness," p. 86.

[17]   James Eli Adams, *Dandies and Desert Saints: Styles of Victorian Masculinity* (Ithaca and London: Cornell University Press, 1995), p. 87. Both Adams and Tosh confine their studies to English men, which may further indicate the marginal status of non-native-born, non-Protestant men within the ideological construct of (gentle)manliness. I suggest that taking notice of a persistently feminized and racialized Catholic Irishness within the gendered imaginary of "English" culture would deepen our understanding of the discourse.

Ireland's more general dependency on English favours" is debatable.[18] If Phineas is "dependent" in some contexts, and thus represented or understood as "effeminate" or "feminized," then he is very much the manly man in the specifically political dimension of his identity, rejecting the patronage that got him his place because it impedes his "autonomy of action and opinion." He is freer as an individual than the nation whose collective interests he indirectly represents, and Trollope emphasizes this in scripting the course of action that takes him back to Ireland at the conclusion of *Phineas Finn*.

But if Phineas's manliness is not really in question at the very end of this novel, his gentlemanliness may be. While the manly ideal was represented as democratically open, the gentlemanly one, in being associated with "exclusiveness and affluence," depended explicitly on limiting potential aspirants to that status.[19] As James Eli Adams argues, gentlemanliness was "the subject of protracted contention throughout Victorian culture, because the concept served so effectively to regulate social mobility and its attendant privileges."[20] Much more so than Tosh, Adams emphasizes the performative dimension of gentlemanly identity and its susceptibility to appropriation by indiscriminate others: "as the ideal of the gentleman broadened—at least in theory—it also gave new moral urgency to the seemingly banal task of distinguishing between sincerity and performance."[21] Contemporary examples warning of the dangers of inauthenticity abound: even as John Henry Newman praises the gentlemanly ideal in *The Idea of a University* (1852), for example, he deems it both incomplete and vulnerable to misappropriation. Robin Gilmour describes the famous passages near the end of Discourse V (where "Liberal Education" is said to make "not the Christian, not the Catholic, but the gentleman") and Discourse VIII (where Newman claims that "the *beau-ideal* of the world ... partly assist[s] and partly distort[s] the development of the Catholic") as a critique of gentlemanliness, which is only "a simulacrum of Christian virtue" rather than the thing itself.[22] Newman emphasizes the continuity between internal discipline and external display as the index of true gentlemanliness, yet he also worries that "the man of the world" can feign the appearance of gentility, "decked out in" a suit of garments not his own.[23]

As with Ferdinand Lopez in *The Prime Minister* (1876), who manipulates the performative conventions of gentlemanliness to his own ends yet is also rendered suspect from the beginning by his associations with Jewishness, the dual ability to simulate and to dissimulate may enable even a man of no apparent means and

---

[18]   McCourt, p. 55.

[19]   Tosh, "Gentlemanly Politeness," p. 96.

[20]   Adams, p. 6.

[21]   Adams, p. 53.

[22]   John Henry Cardinal Newman, *The Idea of a University*, ed. Martin J. Svaglic (San Francisco: Rinehart Press, 1960), pp. 91, 161; Robin Gilmour, *The Idea of the Gentleman in the Victorian Novel* (London: George Allen and Unwin, 1981), p. 90.

[23]   Newman, p. 91.

questionable origins to secure a share of English political and economic power. Moreover, because both Jews and (Irish) Catholics had long figured in the English Protestant imaginary as practitioners of disguise, even after religious disabilities that had, in some instances, demanded a degree of dissimulation were abolished, their ability to feign or, more neutrally, perform conformity was always already assumed. Although he absolves Phineas of being an adventurer or a deceiver in the political realm, Trollope's narrator does test his claims to (gentle)manly status in two other arenas: the marriage plots that dominate *Phineas Finn*, intersecting as they do with the plots of political ambition, and Phineas's breakdown in the aftermath of the murder trial in *Phineas Redux*. Turning briefly to these examples, I will show that shifts in location and material circumstance, precipitated by the dual national context in which Finn circulates, provide an occasion for Trollope to affirm his character's manly integrity in *Phineas Finn*. But in sounding the more troubled waters of *Redux*, Trollope's narrator more fully problematizes the performative aspect of gendered ideals and ideologies and, in the process, redefines manliness even as he breaks with the polarities that underwrite a fixed concept of sexual difference.

Issues of "manly independence" and gentlemanly integrity shape all of Phineas's romantic entanglements, especially his relationship to his girl back home, which waxes and wanes according to his English fortunes. From the outset, Finn exploits the distance between Ireland and England in pursuing marital possibilities. Each time he returns to Ireland in *Phineas Finn*, he does so having spent a good part of the previous six or nine months wooing an Englishwoman. Rejected by Lady Laura, he nonetheless tells Mary Flood Jones "'how often'" he's thought of her, committing one of those "perjuries" that "can hardly be avoided altogether in the difficult circumstances of a successful gentleman's life. Phineas was a traitor, of course, but he was almost forced to be a traitor, by the simple fact that Lady Laura Standish was in London, and Mary Flood Jones in Killaloe" (vol. 1, p. 145). Refused for the first time by Violet Effingham after the end of the next parliamentary session, he goes home only to find that Mary and her mother have decamped "because it was thought that he had ill-treated the lady" (vol. 1, pp. 328–9). Instead of pouring mild irony on the nature of a "gentleman's life," the narrator gives us Finn's point of view without comment: "He felt that he had two identities,—that he was, as it were, two separate persons,—and that he could, without any real faithlessness, be very much in love with Violet Effingham in his position of man of fashion and member of Parliament in England, and also warmly attached to dear little Mary Flood Jones as an Irishman of Killaloe" (vol. 1, p. 330).

Through the conceit of the "two identities," Phineas revises the allegation of "faithlessness" as a matter of the distance between there and here, his public career in London and his private position as "Irishman of Killaloe." At this point in the novel, it is the first of the two that he most wants to maintain. Being "constant to Miss Effingham" (vol. 1, p. 145) would mean achieving the "politico-social success" (vol. 1, p. 143) in England that an alliance with her would guarantee: he would gain "Violet's hand for his own comfort, and Violet's fortune to support his position" (vol. 2, p. 131). What begins as comedy, however, takes a more serious turn. When Finn goes back to Ireland to stand for the Loughshane seat, the narrator remarks on the danger to his character: "Perhaps there is no position more perilous to a man's honesty than that in which Phineas now found himself;—that, namely of knowing himself to be quite loved by a girl whom he almost loves himself ... Phineas was not in love with Mary Flood Jones," but "he would have liked to have an episode,—and did, at the moment, think that it might be possible to have one life in London and another life altogether different at Killaloe" (vol. 2, p. 107). The gap between the two locations widens, as potential success with Violet enables the fiction of "two identities" to persist, even while Phineas puts his integrity in peril. On his next visit to Killaloe, however, when he knows for certain "that all hope was over" of ever marrying Violet, "Mary had kept aloof from him": and "as a natural consequence of this, Phineas was more in love with her than ever" (vol. 2, p. 261). When he returns from the tour with Monk, having "pledged himself" (vol. 2, p. 263) to tenant-right and thus knowing that they "must give up the places which they held under the Crown" (vol. 2, p. 264), he pledges himself to Mary as well.

For Phineas at this juncture, independence in political matters means loss of independence in financial ones: when Mary tells her future mother-in-law "it was quite possible that Phineas would be called upon to resign" so "'that he may maintain his independence,'" "'Fiddlestick!' said Mrs. Finn. 'How is he to maintain you, or himself either, if he goes on in that way?'" (vol. 2, p. 276). With the narrative focus of this chapter moving from Killaloe to a London drawing-room in the space of a single paragraph, thus collapsing the narrative distance between islands and identities, Madame Max tells Phineas that "'a poor fellow need not be a poor fellow unless he likes'" (vol. 2, p. 276), holding out another hand and another fortune that would make him financially and thus politically independent. The terms in which Phineas contemplates her offer suggests the mix of materialist and psychic motivations that underpin his fantasy of total success:

> Immediately after this Phineas left her, and as he went along the street he began to question himself whether the prospects of his own darling Mary were at all endangered by his visits to Park Lane; and to reflect what sort of a blackguard he would be,—a blackguard of how deep a dye,—were he to desert Mary and marry Madame Max Goesler. Then he also asked himself as to the nature and quality of his own political honesty if he were to abandon Mary in order that he might maintain his parliamentary independence. After all, if it should ever come to pass that his biography should be written, his biographer would say very much more about the manner in which he kept his seat in Parliament than of the manner in which he kept his engagement with Miss Mary Flood Jones. Half a dozen people who knew him and her might think ill of him for his conduct to Mary, but the world would not condemn him! And when he thundered forth his Liberal eloquence from below the gangway as an independent member, having

the fortune of his charming wife to back him, giving excellent dinners at the same time in Park Lane, would not the world praise him very loudly? (vol. 2, pp. 276–7)

Phineas imagines a biographer who, like Trollope himself in *An Autobiography* (1883), will subordinate "the little details of my private life" and write instead of "what I, and perhaps others round me, have done in" public and professional matters, "of my failures and successes."[24] Because the distance between London and Killaloe has enabled Phineas not just to think of his engagement to Mary as "a thing quite apart and separate from his life in England" (vol. 2, p. 271), but to keep it entirely out of London view, the fiction of "two identities" proves to have some currency after all, for "the world" certainly could "not condemn him" for his "faithlessness" if "the world" effectively knew nothing about it. To break his vow to Mary would be bad, very bad, certainly an un(gentle)manly thing to do, but a thing that, like the engagement itself, could be kept hidden; if he could do it, and by marrying Madame Max "maintain his parliamentary independence," Phineas could "[thunder] forth his Liberal eloquence" without stint.

Associated not only with Turnbull/Bright and Daubeny/Disraeli, but also with the most important Irish M.P. of the previous generation, Daniel O'Connell, the dicey term "eloquence" should give us pause. As part of a rhetoric of display—what one puts on for "the world," like "excellent dinners"—fine words are opposed to (gentle)manly speech and raise the specter of dissimulation. Ultimately, Trollope frames the desire to look well and to have a reputation, to be a public figure constituted for (or even by) others, as the end to be avoided—not only for Phineas, but also for Madame Max, who turns down the Duke of Omnium's proposal just a few chapters before Phineas turns down hers. Here authenticity, for both gentleman and lady, means resisting the lure of display. Standing in Madame Max's elegantly appointed drawing room, Phineas thinks, "What would such a life as his want, if graced by such a companion,—such a life as his might be, if the means which were hers were at his command? It would want one thing, he thought,—the self-respect that he would lose if he were false to the girl who was trusting him with such sweet trust at home in Ireland" (vol. 2, p. 314). "The promptings of his inner self," to recall Tosh's terms, trump "the dictates of social expectation." In disavowing English publicity in favor of a private, non-narratable Irish life, however, Phineas's faithful return home to his bride does not so much suture the gap between "two identities" as simply cast one of them aside.

The relationship between public performance and private integrity also structures the definition of manliness that Trollope's narrator offers late in *Phineas Redux*, but this passage from the novel, which similarly thematizes the temptations of display, makes a far more searching analysis of the gender dichotomy that putatively distinguishes manly men from womanly women. Acquitted of Bonteen's

---

[24] Anthony Trollope, *An Autobiography*, ed. Michael Sadleir and Frederick Page (Oxford: Oxford University Press, 1980), p. 10.

murder, the experience of the public trial has "'unmanned'" Phineas, as he puts it in a note to Madame Max, whom he refuses to see for fear that he "'should only weep in your presence like a school-girl'" (*PR*, p. 539). Counseling him "to return to his usual mode of life," "Lord Chiltern told him plainly that he was weak and womanly—or rather that he would be were he to continue to dread the faces of his fellow-creatures" (p. 540). "'I am womanly,' said Phineas. 'I begin to feel it. But I can't alter my nature'" (p. 541). To be at once "unmanned," "not manly," and "womanly"—which might all mean slightly different things, to be sure—appears to Phineas himself to be not just a temporary state, an aftereffect of his ordeal, but a constitutive part of his "nature."[25] Here Phineas represents his womanliness, brought out by his trial, not only as a way of naming the collapse of his ability to perform a manly part, but also as an intrinsic aspect of his character. Outward display still corresponds with his inward state, as "he could not pretend to be other than he was" (p. 543), so there is no feigning or inauthenticity in his stance. But Phineas's desire for privacy and obscurity, his wish to retire from public life, and his emotional lability—that last not only a stereotypically feminine, but also a stereotypically Celtic attribute in the nineteenth-century ethnic imaginary— indicate a further iteration of "two identities" along gendered lines, one that in this particular instance the narrator is eager to contest.[26]

Defending his hero from the charge of unmanliness, the narrator ascribes a false and superficial understanding of manliness-as-performance primarily to women, who are said to "look for a certain outward magnificence of demeanour, a pretended indifference to stings and little torments, a would-be superiority to the bread-and-butter side of life, an unreal assumption of personal grandeur" (pp. 541–2):

> But a robe of State such as this—however well the garment may be worn with practice—can never be the raiment natural to a man; and men, dressing themselves in women's eyes, have consented to walk about in buckram. A composure of the eye, which has been studied, a reticence as to the little things of life, a certain slowness of speech unless the occasion call for passion, an indifference to small surroundings, these—joined, of course, with personal bravery—are supposed to constitute manliness ... But the first requirement of all must be described by a negative. Manliness is not compatible with affectation ... An affected man ... may be honest, may be generous, may be pious—but surely he cannot be manly ... Before the man can be manly, the gifts which make him so must be there, collected by him slowly, unconsciously, as are his bones, his flesh, and his blood. They cannot be put on like a garment for the nonce—as may a little learning.

---

[25]   For further discussion on this point, see both the fine essay by Christopher S. Noble in this volume and "Sex and the Single Man," chapter five of Margaret Markwick's *New Men in Trollope's Novels: Rewriting the Victorian Male* (Aldershot: Ashgate Publishing, 2007).

[26]   See Corbett, pp. 159–65, for an analysis of the feminized Celt in Matthew Arnold's *On the Study of Celtic Literature* (1867), published during the height of Fenian unrest in England.

A man cannot become faithful to his friends, unsuspicious before the world, gentle with women, loving with children, considerate to his inferiors, kindly with servants, tender-hearted with all—and at the same time be frank, of open speech, with springing eager energies—simply because he desires it. (*PR*, p. 542)

The narrator recuperates Phineas's threatened manliness by distinguishing it from "affectation" or false display and casting the "inner self"—conceived physically, as "his bones, his flesh, and his blood"—in opposition to the "garment" the affected man wears to constitute himself as manly "in women's eyes." Closely echoing Newman in his use of the dress metaphor, as in much of the other content of the passage, he argues that the absence of affectation or a performative aspect to Phineas's behavior after the trial confirms that Finn acts naturally; and "the natural man will probably be manly"—even while he is being "womanly," it would seem—while "the affected man cannot be so" (p. 542). Having assigned responsibility for determining "the dictates of social expectation" to women, who are said to enforce an "unreal" standard of manliness, Trollope's narrator aims to suggest instead that Phineas's "womanly" susceptibility is not incompatible with being "manly": the problem lies not in Phineas, but in the falsely polarized gender norms that the world's wife, Phineas's friends, and even the narrator himself, at other moments, enforce and reinscribe.

While Trollope thus shares the broader cultural concern over the possible duplicities of a performed and performative self, he also calls into question the naturalness of the ethnic and gendered norms that shape the representation of a "natural" one. If inauthenticity is a danger, then so, too, is the demand for conformity to polarized scripts for ethnicity and gender. Read for its progressive potential, the discourse on (gentle)manliness in the *Phineas* novels establishes that what is understood as English or Irish, masculine or feminine, is both context-dependent and subject to change. While this may not seem so radical a position now, I believe that in the 1860s and 70s, Trollope's anxious questioning as to what comes naturally—to men or to women, to the Irish or to the English—represents a genuine effort to come to terms with the shifting political climate of the times. Even as English workers (and some women) agitated for the extension of the franchise in the face of élite anxiety about their ability properly to use it, while revolutionary Fenian activism was construed as demonstrating the native Irish inability for exercising responsible political autonomy, the *Phineas* novels challenge dominant assumptions about gender, ethnicity, and the intersection of the two. Famously undercut by his subsequent claim that "to take [Phineas] from Ireland" was "a blunder," the characterization signifies a crucial moment in the broader literary history of Trollope's relationship to Ireland.[27] For in what became an increasingly polarized debate on English-Irish relations after 1870, he would never again take such a progressive view of an Irish member.

---

[27]   Trollope, *An Autobiography*, p. 318.

Fig. 8.1   "The New Zealander." Gustave Doré's illustration for *London, a Pilgrimage*, Chapter 21

Chapter 8

The Rough and the Beautiful in "Catherine Carmichael": Class and Gender in Trollope's Colonial Aesthetic

Helen Lucy Blythe

> Aesthetic intolerance can be terribly violent.... The most intolerable thing for those who regard themselves as possessors of legitimate culture is the sacrilegious reuniting of tastes which taste dictates shall be separated.[1]

Almost 20 years before Anthony Trollope travelled to New Zealand, he composed a cultural critique of England entitled *The New Zealander*. Trollope's prose work was named after "Macaulay's New Zealander," a famous rhetorical figure of a future tourist on London Bridge contemplating his cultural heritage before the ruined dome of St. Paul's Cathedral.[2] Trollope's New Zealanders are a sophisticated honeymoon couple and exquisite objects of wealth and culture. The groom is an "ornate man of art" with a jeweled cane; and the bride wears a crystal eyeglass "cut from a pure diamond," and "a thousand golden beads ... glitter through her auburn hair."[3] The figures seem to be polished jewels from the goldfields making the fortunes of antipodean settlers as Trollope was writing his book.[4] The pair represents cultural as well as economic value; in embellishing their forms and appreciating the beautiful, they possess what Pierre Bourdieu calls "an elaborated taste for the most refined objects," exhibiting the "cultural competence" to find pleasure and meaning "in a work of art or any other kind of beauty," including their bodies.[5] Bourdieu analyzes how aesthetic tastes function as "markers of class,"

---

[1]   Pierre Bourdieu, *Distinction. A Social Critique of the Judgement of Taste,* trans. Richard Nice (Cambridge, MA: Harvard University Press, 1984), pp. 56–7.

[2]   *Thomas Babington Macaulay, the Modern British Essayists* (Philadelphia: Carey & Hart, 1846), p. 401. The historian Thomas Babington Macaulay popularized the figure after the annexation of New Zealand in 1840.

[3]   Anthony Trollope, *The New Zealander*, ed. N. John Hall (Oxford: Clarendon Press, 1972), p. 5.

[4]   Gold rushes occurred in New Zealand in 1851 and 1852. See A. H. Reed, *The Story of Early Dunedin* (Wellington: A. H. and A. W. Reed, 1956), p. 52.

[5]   Bourdieu, p. 2.

which distinctions Trollope was acutely aware of a century before, analyzing in his 1878 Christmas story "Catherine Carmichael" the transformations engendered by the colony's more fluid relations of gender and divisions of labor.[6]

Trollope visited New Zealand in the early 1870s, writing a travel account and meeting the New Zealanders he dreamed of in the 1850s, but only in "Catherine Carmichael" are they represented in fiction. *Australia and New Zealand* (1873) mentions that New Zealand is too rough for gentlemen and ladies but is helpful for industrious workers. I frame my study with these comments on class, the early description of New Zealanders, and the portrayal of Australian gold miners in *John Caldigate* (1879), composed almost alongside "Catherine Carmichael," to show that, while Trollope imagined a highly-evolved future England in New Zealand, after visiting the colony he saw it inhabited only by working-class people open to middle-class tastes and ways of living. "Catherine Carmichael" specifies that New Zealanders of the future will be youthful naturally attractive people who not only make money but also use it to nurture each other and beautify their lives.

The story's heroine Catherine has Scottish gentry origins but was raised roughly in the colonial gold-diggings. Orphaned and in undeclared love with a handsome miner, John Carmichael, she is married off summarily to his relative, an old mining associate of her father's, now a wealthy sheep-farmer. Lacking aesthetic and romantic desires, Peter Carmichael's only pleasure is viewing his money in the bank. Catherine's silent beloved disappears, and she endures an intolerable married life on an isolated sheep station. After delineating marital disharmony as a divergence in aesthetic taste, Trollope drowns the husband and reunites the lovers, expunging from the colony the rich but rough man who retains the habits of a poor man surviving in scarcity.

Trollope could not have written the story without visiting the colony, but he interpreted what he saw through the lens of metropolitan middle-class taste and debates on gender and male suffrage surrounding the 1867 Reform Act, together with popular discourses of emigration and masculinity. Opportunities were increasing in the settler colonies for new versions of "Anglo-Saxon manliness to flourish"[7]; and even in the 1830s, colonial reformers like Edward Gibbon Wakefield claimed that equality of the sexes would be more possible there.[8] Wakefield saw New Zealand as a place of bourgeois and professional settlement and wanted his colonists to have an "interest in the arts of civilised existence," so he encouraged literary men, men of science, and philosophers to emigrate, believing that they

---

[6]   Anthony Trollope, "Catherine Carmichael," *The Complete Shorter Fiction*, ed. Julian Thompson (New York: Carroll & Graf Publishers Inc., 1992).

[7]   Catherine Hall, Keith McClelland, and Jane Rendall, *Defining the Victorian Nation; Class, Race, Gender, and the British Reform Act of 1867* (Cambridge, UK: Cambridge University Press, 2000), p. 55.

[8]   Edward Gibbon Wakefield, *England and America; A Comparison of the Social and Political State of Both Nations* [1834] (New York: A. M. Kelley, 1967), pp. 205–14.

would do so only if an educated colonial society admired their accomplishments.[9] New Zealand "excited a special feeling" in idealists like Thomas Carlyle and Thomas Arnold who thought it a place "where such a better society had its best hopes." [10] Arnold bought land from Wakefield, contemplating emigrating to rear a "hopeful form of society." By 1850, emigration manuals were claiming that the bourgeois settler could enjoy in New Zealand "emancipation from the thralldom of convention, immunity from the compulsion to keep up appearances, and to seem to be what he is not." [11]

While the men of gentility encouraged by Wakefield had the right taste for Trollope's future antipodean England, Trollope's fictions imply that colonial experiences harmed them, and so he banished the gentry along with rough men. He writes idealistically of emigration as "God's ordained means of populating the world"[12]; but advised "no young lady to go out to any colony either to get a husband, or to be a governess, or to win her bread after any so-called ladylike fashion," because, like Catherine Carmichael's gentry mother, "she may suffer much before she can succeed."[13]

Catherine's father, John Baird, is a "Scotchman of good birth ... once possessed of fair means" (p. 885), who took his family to New Zealand after "the world had gone against him" (p. 885). For years he failed in the goldfields, forcing the family into an increasingly rougher existence. His genteel wife suffered much, but "decent in language, in manners, and in morals" (p. 884), she taught her children to "have some taste" for reading and writing (p. 884), before succumbing to the harsh life. Her husband then drank himself to death having degenerated into a rough miner. The simple adjective "rough" describes Catherine's childhood: "Everything around the young Bairds was rough" (p. 884). They lived in a "rough shanty" (p. 884), and were forced to move as Baird "became more and more hardened to the rough usages of a digger's life" (p. 888). The last shanty was always "the roughest" (p. 884); they ate "food of the roughest" (p. 884); they lived in a "rough household" (p. 887), alongside "rough miners" (p. 887), "rough men" (p. 888), and "the roughest of the rough" (p. 888). Nothing could be further from the world of Catherine's metropolitan counterpart, nor more remote to the young gentleman.

---

[9] Donald Winch, *Classical Political Economy and Colonies* (Cambridge, UK: Cambridge University Press, 1965), p. 153; and Fred Hitchins, *Colonial Land and Emigration Commission 1840–78* (Cambridge, MA: Harvard University Press, 1931), pp. 7–8.

[10] Michael Cotsell, *1830–1876 Creditable Warriors. English Literature and the Wider World* (London: The Ashfield Press, 1990), p. 43.

[11] Sidney Smith, *The Settler's New Home or Whether to Go, and Whither, A Guide to Emigrants* (London, 1849), p. 1.

[12] Anthony Trollope, 'Mrs. Sewell's "The Rose of Cheriton"' *Fortnightly Review* (London, 1 February 1867).

[13] Anthony Trollope, *Australia and New Zealand* (London: Chapman and Hall, 1873), p. 495.

Trollope's travel account affirms that the gentleman degenerated in the gold-diggings: "He loses his gentility, his love of cleanliness, his ease of words, his grace of bearing, his preference for good economy, and his social exigencies."[14] Trollope records meeting in Australia, a gentleman miner who had visited his sons:

> He had been softly nurtured, well educated, and was a handsome fellow to boot; and there he was eating a nauseous lump of beef out of a greasy frying-pan with his pocket-knife, just in front of the contiguous blankets stretched on the ground, which constituted the beds of himself and his companion. (pp. 134–5)

After ruining his prospects at home, the gentleman hero in Trollope's novel *John Caldigate* likewise reels from the rough dirty Australian gold-diggings; and his friend calls one "the beastliest hole I ever put my foot in."[15] The "grub" is "rough" (p. 80), though Trollope substitutes "dirty" for the "rough" of "Catherine Carmichael." The hotel has "dirty-looking beds" (p. 80); a "dirty table" (p. 80); "dirty knives and forks" (p. 81); and a "dirty old woman" (p. 81) serves them.

Trollope juxtaposes the rough colonial miner with the New Zealand gentleman possessing cultural capital and gazing on his English heritage by contrasting their definitions of manliness, foregrounding how gender shores up divisions of social class. A gold miner mocks Caldigate for his clothes and luxurious straw mattress, finding these and even John's name "womanish" (pp. 97; 100–101). In exclaiming, "It's unmanly having all them togs" (p. 96), the miner rejects gendered material markers of middle-class comfort because they represent a refinement he associates with a womanly pleasure in form and beautifying the body. His utilitarian approach springs from his value as manual labor manifested in physical strength, as Bourdieu points out: "the working class depends on labour power which the laws of the market reduce to muscle power."[16] Trollope also prefigures Bourdieu's idea that the laboring man fears a "dual repudiation of virility" in surrendering "to demands perceived as simultaneously feminine and bourgeois."[17] In presenting manliness as class-bound in *John Caldigate* and "Catherine Carmichael," Trollope implies that colonial workers themselves enforce the distinctions, seeing them as vital to social identity.

John Caldigate contrasts miners and gentlemen through the former's roughness and the latter's softness and physical grace. Though dressed as a miner on the emigrant ship, Caldigate remains visibly upper-class, as Mrs. Smith states: "You are making a delightful experiment in roughing it" (p. 51). Once a seasoned gold digger, Caldigate almost but not quite dissolves the opposition:

---

[14]　Anthony Trollope, *New South Wales and Queensland* (London: Chapman and Hall, 1874), p. 132.

[15]　Anthony Trollope, *John Caldigate* 1879 (Oxford: Oxford University Press, 1993), p. 79.

[16]　Bourdieu, p. 384.

[17]　Ibid., p. 382.

dressed as a miner might be dressed who was off work and out for a holiday;—clean, rough, and arranged with a studied intention to look as little like a gentleman as possible. The main figure and manner were so completely those of a gentleman that the disguise was not perfect; but yet he was rough. (p. 112)

The passage implies that one becomes a gentleman through education in form, and through manners and deportment together with nurturing, not using the body. Caldigate's privileged origins are inscribed on his body, and the miner prides himself on resisting these cultural markers privileging form over function or beauty over utility in what Bourdieu would call a working-class "anti-Kantian aesthetic."[18]

Symbols of working-class strength and identity, bodily marks of manual labor signal inferiority to Trollope's middle-class English as Karen Volland Waters points out: "if a man could appear to attain prosperity without resorting to manual labor, he might be considered a gentleman."[19] And while Caldigate's disguise is imperfect to fellow miners, the more he physically labors the less his English class considers him still a gentleman. The novel focuses on his alienation after returning to England, for though his gold-mining fortune enables him to regain his property, the colonial work taints him nonetheless, producing a mistrust that foregrounds the destabilizing threat of imperial labor to the metropolitan capitalist and moralist. Caldigate's fortune raises the suspicions of the bank manager, for instance, who dislikes all sudden acquisitions of wealth, believing that money should be earned "in a gradual, industrious manner, and in accordance with recognised forms" (pp. 122–3). Not only does imperial treasure dissolve the economic hierarchy, it weakens the connection between goodness and prosperity anxiously protected by the Victorian middle classes. It raises the possibility that the lazy, reckless, or lawless person could deceive honest Victorians by pretending to be a gentleman, hiding behind trappings of respectability acquired by an indecently hasty acquisition of wealth.

In particular, thinks Mr. Bolton the bank manager, such a man will not be a dutiful and reliable "family man" suitable to marry England's daughters, especially his own. He doubts "whether a successful gold-digger will settle down quietly as an English country gentleman" (p. 121). Much worse, his wife insists that

young men who went out to the colonies because they were ruined, were, to her thinking, the worst among the bad.... And to her thinking, among men none were so rough as miners,— and among miners, none were so godless, so unrestrained, so wild as the seekers after gold. (p. 161)

---

[18]   Ibid., pp. 41–2.

[19]   Karen Volland Waters, *The Perfect Gentleman; Masculine Control in Victorian Men's Fiction, 1870–1901*, (New York: Peter Lang, 1997), p. 17.

Despite the opposition, Caldigate marries their daughter Hester, but then is imprisoned for bigamy after his unscrupulous mistress in Australia comes to England claiming to be his wife. Moreover fortunes so acquired disappear with equal rapidity, and Caldigate concedes 20,000 of his 60,000 pounds to a mining associate, now his mistress's new partner. Ultimately justice prevails and the Caldigates resume married life after John's pardon, but the devastating disruption to their marriage justifies the Boltons' fear of their daughter's suitor for his antipodean labors.

The metropolitan lack of trust in an antipodean miner's integrity demonstrates that while colonial money elevated a man economically to the position of gentleman, his moral contamination from imperial wildness and physical work undercut ideas about gentlemanliness increasingly preoccupying Victorians. Earlier in the century, "literary representations of the gentleman are less ambiguous than they are later when the definitions get murkier,"[20] as the industrial revolution and growth of market society created a more fluid class structure. By 1884, *The Standard* could state: "In an age in which no one knows exactly what a 'gentleman' is, the anxiety to be one has become curiously, not to say grotesquely morbid."[21] Between 1870 and 1901, the middle-class Victorian had an increasingly "large number of conduct, etiquette, and self help books to assist him"[22] in finding out what a gentleman was supposed to be. Most manuals agree with the qualities in *Self Help* by Samuel Smiles: "honest, truthful, upright, polite, temperate, courageous, self-respecting, and self-helping."[23]

Trollope affirms these features in novels set in England, as Shirley Robin Letwin explains,[24] but those with antipodean settings need something more for the settler to become the ancestor of his elite couple on London Bridge. There must be a visible admiration of forms, and more than a utilitarian appreciation of the working body. In "Catherine Carmichael," Trollope adds the adjectives "youthful" and "comely" (p. 892) to the future New Zealander's ancestor, suggesting that he must be young and handsome. Moreover, he must exhibit an instinctual taste for pleasure and appreciate the decencies of bourgeois life, or at least be amenable to learning them. "Catherine Carmichael" implies that the new society will emerge through fusing the working and middle classes, but the fusion must include cultural capital or a taste for the beautiful, which neither money nor respectable labor can buy. Only with the right cultivated taste will descendents of the colony's working-class settlers eventually produce the beautiful tourist with golden beads in her hair

[20]   Waters, p. 27.

[21]   Ibid., p. 28. See also Robin Gilmour, *The Idea of the Gentleman in the Victorian Novel* (London: Allen and Unwin, 1981).

[22]   Waters, p. 19.

[23]   Martin Danahay, *Gender at Work in Victorian Culture; Literature, Art, and Masculinity* (Aldershot: Ashgate Press, 2005), p. 31.

[24]   Shirley Robin Letwin, *The Gentleman in Trollope, Individuality and Moral Conduct* (Cambridge, MA: Harvard University Press, 1982).

and the ornate man of art standing on London Bridge. These opinions created a problem for Trollope encountering rough penniless men transformed into wealthy settlers by gold digging or sheep farming.

Trollope believed that New Zealand life lowered the gentry, but offered new possibilities for the working classes. Any well-behaved young woman," he observes in *Australia and New Zealand*, "who now earns sixteen pounds as a housekeeper in England would find in New Zealand a much happier home" (p. 378). He calls the colony a paradise for all the working classes; they will earn more money, and transform their "whole condition of life" (pp. 499–500). The cultural transformation results from the absence of traditional class markers; so manual labor, for instance, is no longer inferior as in England:

> The slight estimation in which labour is held here will be changed for a general respect. The humbleness, the hat-touching, the servility which is still incidental to such work as theirs in the old country, and which is hardly compatible with exalted manhood, has found no footing there. (pp. 499–500)

Trollope associates colonial labor now with self-help and self-respect, characteristics of the gentleman in *Self Help*. The reference to exalted manhood also reveals the central role of gender in Trollope's idea of how colonies advanced society, and a non-monetary element such as manliness even becomes the symbol of fortune: "I regard such manhood among the masses of the people as the highest sign of prosperity which a country can give" (p. 500).

In analyzing the nineteenth-century British working-man's entry into the political nation via the vote, historian Keith McLelland describes the manhood that reformers thought worthy of "having a fair share in the representation of the country."[25] Until 1848, the basis of masculine political identity for the independent working man was his labor as his property. By the 1860s, however, as "moral considerations were increasingly subordinated to market ones,"[26] reformers increasingly excluded the "poor and 'rough,'" and included the less impoverished and more domesticated working classes: "They overlaid the idea of property in labour with cultural distinctions which differentiated between forms of working-class masculinity—between sober, respectable and independent manhood and those 'rough' men."[27]

McClelland sees in this shift the absorption and reformulation of the working man "within the elaboration of a commercial and industrial-based middle class,"[28] which created a polarity between "'the regularly employed, rate-paying working man (possessed of a house, a wife, children, furniture, and the habit of obeying the

---

[25]   Keith McClelland, "England's greatness, the working man," in Hall, McClelland, and Rendall, p. 101.

[26]   Ibid., p. 107.

[27]   Ibid., p. 101.

[28]   Ibid., p. 100.

law) [who] was the heir of the Anglo-Saxon freeman,' and a residuum which was 'intemperate,' 'profligate,' and 'naturally incapable'"[29] or "rough" in short. Who fitted these categories and what constituted a family were much debated, especially in parliamentary discussions about household and manhood suffrage in 1866–67. A decade later Trollope extended the discussion to the colonies, imagining the future culture developing there through his generation's tastes, actions, and laws. "Catherine Carmichael" thus supports the metropolitan debate on the rough, the respectable, and the refined, exemplifying its contradictory articulations of manliness and the family structure.

Earlier in the decade, novelist Wilkie Collins provides compelling evidence that the term "rough" entered public discussion of what constituted an acceptable working-class man. In the preface to *Man and Wife* (1870), Collins attacks the bourgeois fascination with muscular cultivation that Herbert Sussman calls a "form of class-bound muscle envy that runs throughout the century."[30] Collins asserts that the current vogue for physical cultivation has spread "grossness and brutality among certain classes of the English population" and labels the term "roughs" similarly fashionable. [31] He remarks of the violent members of society that "we recognise them as a necessary ingredient in our social system, and class our savages as a representative part of our population, under the newly invented name of 'Roughs.'"[32] Unconcerned with the working-class "dirty Rough," Collins's novel focuses on his own class's "washed Rough in broadcloth,"[33] but in the preface nonetheless demonstrates the invention and popularity of the term.

As McClelland shows in his study of the working man, family life is a sign of middle-class status as opposed to the world of Trollope's single men in the antipodes, and "Catherine Carmichael" advocates a future society for respectable working-class families free from single male roughness. Although Catherine's gentry mother instilled ideas in her daughter "of things better than those around her" (p. 887), and a "gentry" desire to "do something for others, and then, if possible to do something for herself" (p. 887), Catherine lives as a poor mining girl toiling for a "rough household" (p. 887) from morning to night in a world of labor and scarcity. Though "hard," her work is performed out of familial love (p. 887). She is a middle-class "angel of the house" in the midst of roughness, a familiar model of self-sacrificing Victorian womanhood.

Despite her "gentle blood" (p. 887), Catherine has never known "the amusements, or the lightness and pleasures" of a lady's life; and "To sit vacant for an hour dreaming over a book had never come to her" (p. 887). Denied access

---

[29]   Ibid., p. 98.

[30]   Herbert Sussman, *Victorian Masculinities, Manhood and Masculine Poetics in Early Victorian Literature and Art* (Cambridge, UK: Cambridge University Press, 1995), p. 41.

[31]   Wilkie Collins, *Man and Wife* [1870] (Oxford: Oxford University Press, 1995), p. 6.

[32]   Ibid., p. 6.

[33]   Ibid., p. 7.

to leisure and the aesthetic necessities of her class origins, Catherine nevertheless appreciates beautiful forms; in her world of roughness and scarcity, only the youthful male body becomes an object of beauty. She concentrates her aesthetic desires on John Carmichael, a "comely" (p. 892) young man with "soft brown hair and broad open brow" (p. 892), who gives "grace to her days," and helps with her siblings. Representing a manliness receptive to feminine influence, unlike the rough men around them, John is a potential husband figure that liberals would have applauded in the 1860s. His willingness to accept moral improvement makes him a sober, respectable working-class man permitted entry into the political nation and the middle classes in the Second Reform Act.

But Trollope's tale turns not on their marriage but its prevention by the rough single man with new money. After Catherine's father dies, Peter Carmichael comes "to settle things as only a man with money can" (p. 887). His fortune grants him authority over the diffident young lovers because "Only he could cause aught to be done" (p. 887). Generated by gender, money, and age, his authority causes Catherine to lose "all sense of independence" (p. 887). Money silences her and John's desire; speechless and stupefied, she submits to marrying Peter. Trollope's description of the journey to Peter's sheep-station foregrounds his lack of aesthetic sensibility. Nothing is "to be seen on either way but the long everlasting plain of grey, stunted, stony grass" (p. 896), and the rivers are "bridgeless, and pathless" (p. 888).

Catherine soon loathes her husband, superficially exhibiting a feminine resistance to masculine authority, but Trollope illuminates that her violent revulsion stems also from their conflicting tastes. Of her husband's origins, the reader learns that Peter was a miner and then a "squatter" (occupying land without purchasing it), so he probably emigrated to the colony with nothing. Now possessing 15,000 sheep worth 15,000 pounds, he is considerably wealthy. Decades older than Catherine and John, Peter is hard, rough, and mannerless, and has never wanted a wife. He is the reverse of the gentility defined in Trollope's *New South Wales & Queensland* as "the combination of soft words, soft manners, and soft hands with manly bearing, and high courage, and intellectual pursuits" (p. 132). Just as the word "rough" describes the gold miner, similarly monosyllabic adjectives present Carmichael as "coarse and altogether without sentiment" (p. 886); "hard working"; "dry, hard, middle-aged" (p. 887); "hard of hand"; "hard of heart"; a "hard dry man" (p. 888); "stern, stubborn"; "ungenial"; and "harsh in his ways with her, sometimes almost violent" (p. 891). These characteristics and his history link him to the rough, independent, single laborers rejected by the Reform League.

In Peter's value system, the body is functional, an object of labor in goldfields, sheep stations, and households, and so he says nothing to Catherine of "love making" (p. 886). He does not wish to create the bourgeois family by loving his wife, producing children, and adorning his property and self. For years, only a Maori man and old working-class woman have helped him. Catherine likes the former for his soft words and manners, but views the latter with disgust. On noticing Catherine's pleasure in the gentlemanly Maori, Carmichael expels his rival from the station. He uses Catherine around the house, and her frequent references to "leers" (pp. 892, 894), and "foul" (p. 894) treatment imply that she functions as a sexual body, since Carmichael could have treated her as a daughter. Her fierce hatred for husband and home surfaces in short, repetitive phrases: "She was the man's wife, and she hated him" (888); "She had never known before what it was to hate a human being" (p. 888); and "she hated a man with all the strength of her heart and he was her husband" (p. 888). She calls her husband a "wretch," "meaner than a crawling worm" (p. 890); "so suspicious; so *unmanly*; so inhuman" [my emphasis] (p. 892).

Along with Catherine's buried desire for John and revulsion for Peter, the narrator's allusions to her "gentle" ancestry suggest that the disgust for her husband and his way of life stems from an aesthetic intolerance of the working-class taste inflecting his masculinity. Trollope explores the class-bound nature of the gender distinctions preventing their marital harmony through their antithetical tastes in food and domestic forms, which Bourdieu claims are fundamental to social critiques of the judgment of taste, arguing that we "cannot fully understand cultural practices, unless ... the elaborated taste for the most refined objects is reconnected with the elementary taste for the flavours of food."[34] Bourdieu and Trollope both base the working-class meal on function and the immediate appeasement of appetite: "Plain speaking, plain eating: the working-class meal is characterized by plenty," writes Bourdieu.[35] Likewise Trollope's narrator records that Carmichael "offers a plentiful supply of meat (p. 889), and had Catherine enjoyed "mutton she might have lived a blessed life" (p. 889).

But with her more refined origins, Catherine values manner over function and wants, as Bourdieu remarks of the bourgeoisie, "to eat with all due form."[36] She hates her husband's denial of the manners and refinements due to the wife of a man with his means, loathing him for "the way in which it [food] was doled out to her" (p. 889), and for treating her like a station hand, weighing every ounce of food: "So much tea for the week, so much sugar, so much flour, and so much salt" (p. 889). Carmichael sells delicacies including "jam, pickles and sardines" to his shepherds, but gives her no access to them because "there would be no profit from sending them into the house" (p. 889). Even worse, he does not increase the rations on her arrival, showing how Trollope anticipates Bourdieu's theory that food quantity and variety represent social distinctions. In the working-class value system, the abundance of food available for the men is "often balanced ... by restrictions which generally apply to the women, who will share one portion between two, or eat the left-overs of the previous day; a girl's accession to womanhood is marked by doing without. It is part of men's status to eat and to eat well."[37] Carmichael's plentiful supply of mutton indicates a working-class sensibility that infuriates Catherine, who associates money with variety, manners, and an increase in objects

---

34   Bourdieu, p. 1.
35   Ibid., p. 194.
36   Ibid., p. 196.
37   Ibid., pp. 194–5.

of pleasure. By keeping her deprived unnecessarily, Carmichael makes her "hate him worse and worse,—to hate and despise him" (p. 890).

In this respect, Trollope departs from contemporary theorists of political economy like W. Stanley Jevons, who claimed that humans "labour to produce with the sole object of consuming,"[38] and Nassau Senior, who argued that increased wealth produces an insatiable desire for variety, creation, and adornment:

> The necessaries of life are so few and simple, that a man is soon satisfied in regard to these and desires to extend his range of enjoyment. His first object is to vary his food; but there soon arises the desire of variety and elegance in dress; and to this succeeds the desire to build, to ornament, and to furnish—tastes which, where they exist, are absolutely insatiable and seem to increase with every improvement.[39]

In "Catherine Carmichael," Trollope presents a wealthy man lacking any taste for this consumption. Without cultural capital acquired through education and habit, he has no desire to build, ornament, or furnish for pleasure.

Though the third-person narrator presents Catherine's point of view, the narrative structure exhibits a formal and thematic bareness more representative of her husband's scarcity of taste; after all, his thoughts and lifestyle form and control her existence. Events are stripped of detail, extrapolation, or ornament, and nothing surfaces of material and linguistic variety or cultivated form. Moreover, Carmichael's "list of domestic goods" (p. 889) in the homestead reads like a "condition of England" novel depicting the interior rooms of half-starved factory workers. Not ruinous itself, the house contains "a few chairs"; "a table or two"; "a bedstead with an old featherbed"; "a washing basin with a broken jug"; "four or five boxes in lieu of presses"; "an iron pot or two"; "a frying pan"; and "ill-matched broken crockery" (p. 889), nothing more.

Form and content thus merge to illuminate Carmichael's inability to enjoy pleasures usually considered necessary to a man of his means. He is not W. Stanley Jevons's "untutored savage ... wholly occupied with the pleasures and the troubles of the moment"; and only at first glance could he be Jevons's civilized man, whose "vague though powerful feeling of the future is the main incentive to industry and saving."[40] For Jevons quotes T. E. Banfield to insist that along with industry and saving, money generates an insatiable desire to consume increasingly refined objects of art:

> The first proposition of the theory of consumption is that the satisfaction of every lower want in the scale creates a desire of a higher character. ... The

---

[38]   W. Stanley Jevons, *The Theory of Political Economy*, 1871 (New York: Kelley and Millman, 1957), p. 39.

[39]   Nassau Senior, quoted by Jevons, pp. 39–40.

[40]   Ibid., p 35.

highest grade in the scale of wants, that of pleasure derived from the beauties of nature and art, is usually confined to men who are exempted from all the lower privations.[41]

Trollope displays a very different notion of pleasure, privation, and aesthetics consistent with Bourdieu's idea that a "taste for necessity"[42] arises in people when poverty blocks their access to "necessary goods,"[43] and which lives on after "the disappearance of the condition which produced it."[44] He mentions parvenus so entrenched in scarcity, they cannot spend their new money: "Having a million does not in itself make one able to live like a millionaire; and parvenus generally take a long time to learn that what they see as culpable prodigality is, in their new condition, expenditure of basic necessity."[45] Carmichael merely looks at his money in the bank; and like the parvenu, he avoids consumption not as the civilized man saving for delayed gratification, but because he has no cultural competence to find pleasure and meaning in Senior's "beauties of art and nature."[46]

Furthermore, Carmichael's inability to fulfill his wife's bourgeois aesthetic desires results from a "submission to necessity" that Bourdieu declares, "inclines working-class people to a pragmatic, functionalist 'aesthetic,' refusing the gratuity and futility of formal exercises and of every form of art for art's sake" and leading them to "reject specifically aesthetic intentions as aberrations."[47] Bourdieu helps us to see that Trollope recognizes a logic of taste underlying his character, one based on manliness as physical strength, utility, and the economic pressure to repudiate disinterested pleasures as unnecessary luxuries. Readers thus cannot dismiss Carmichael outright; moreover, we assume that his fortune was acquired through industry

I began with Bourdieu's statement that those who claim possession of "legitimate culture" cannot bear the "sacrilegious" reuniting of tastes that they find distasteful.[48] Trollope's heroine is disgusted by the mingling of her and her husband's disparate tastes; but lacking a voice, she performs her wifely duties miserably while daydreaming about the John who brought her grace and waiting for death. Violent disgust is common in matters of taste, claims Bourdieu, because tastes are "perhaps first and foremost distastes, disgust provoked by horror or visceral intolerance ('sick-making') of the tastes of others."[49] Carmichael offends his wife for daily imposing on her his abhorrent taste and ways of living, which

---

[41]   Ibid., pp. 42–3.
[42]   Bourdieu, p. 374.
[43]   Ibid., p. 372.
[44]   Ibid., p. 374.
[45]   Ibid.
[46]   Nassau Senior quoted in Jevons, pp. 42–3.
[47]   Bourdieu, p. 376.
[48]   Ibid., p. 57.
[49]   Ibid., pp. 56–7.

also objectify her as his property and deny her a subjectivity requiring his care. If the working-class utilitarian taste in food appeases an appetite that the higher class transcends through form, then a similar hunger leads Carmichael to marry a woman who should be his daughter. Their merging is sick-making to the abject melancholy Catherine; it obliterates her entire self, not just her desire for John.

Catherine's revulsion was not unusual for settlers of gentility. Consider a letter by Thomas Arnold's son who emigrated to New Zealand in the 1840s, inspired by dreams of laboring alongside the industrious poor to build the new society on his father's land. After staying at the sheep station of a "shrewd Scotsman," who emigrated with nothing but became one of the richest men in the colony like Trollope's Carmichael, Tom Arnold writes of being sickened by the emphasis on money and avoidance of the beautiful:

> Yet, as I asked myself while walking round the farm the next morning, and observing the untidiness, and squalor.... no garden, no orchard, an ugly house, and a filthy homestead— everything else sacrificed to the one end of making money, what does such success as this really amount to? What is the use of money, if it does not tend to make its possessor, and those who live about him, and the place of his dwelling, more beautiful or more happy? What folly to attribute a sort of magical power to gold and bank-notes.[50]

Trollope has been criticized for his commercial attitude towards writing, for seeing himself as a "manufacturer" of material goods for the marketplace.[51] But "Catherine Carmichael" endorses Arnold's sense that money alone cannot bridge the gap between the classes; it requires also a cultivated cultural competence to distinguish between the ugly and the beautiful.

Trollope finally resolves his story through the young lover John coming to live with the couple at the station. In tenderly uttering her name, "Kate," John resurrects Catherine as an individual subject; for as Julian Wolfrey explains of *Phineas Finn*: "something is always at stake, ideologically, in the proper name and its uses, in the proper name's propriety, and in the property that the name gathers to it."[52] In terms of gender relations, John's recognition of Catherine's subjectivity empowers her to contemplate fleeing with him, inwardly railing against being "trammelled by the laws which the world had laid down for her sex" (p. 894). But Trollope forces us to note the imprisoning effect of gentility in the colonies, for what prevents Catherine's escape is her bourgeois view of marriage as sacred:

---

[50] Tom Arnold, *Letters of Thomas Arnold the Younger 1850–1900*, ed. James Bertram (Auckland: Oxford University Press, Auckland University Press, 1981), p. 52.

[51] Andrew Dowling, *Manliness and the Male Novelist in Victorian Literature* (Aldershot: Ashgate Press, 2001), p. 88.

[52] Julian Wolfrey, *Being English; Narratives, Idioms, and Performances of National Identity from Coleridge to Trollope* (Albany: State University of New York, 1994), p. 154.

"Then the word wife crept into her ears, and she remembered words that she had read as to woman's virtue" (p. 894).

Trollope sympathizes too much with his young heroine to abandon her, finding a solution that anticipates the freer sexual and discursive power of women in the *fin de siècle* manifested most powerfully in New Zealand by women's enfranchisement in 1893, though the New Zealand parliament was fighting over suffrage bills in the 1870s when Trollope was composing his story. In a performative move, Catherine tells her husband about her desires, demanding John's departure to avoid temptation. Her utterance simultaneously renounces sexual desire in an act of bourgeois self regulation that transcends animal passion by privileging form as wifehood. The speech instantly crushes the rough working-class man with money; he cowers in despairing submission before the bourgeois female word, leaving readers to conclude that Catherine needed only to speak to escape her thralldom. A newly despairing Peter obediently drives John away from the station; and then Trollope abruptly drowns the former in a swollen river. Now a useless "object" (p. 898) without any function, Carmichael's body is buried to guard it from rats with a "rough palisade" (p. 898). John and Catherine reunite lovingly and inherit the property. Trollope removes all trace of Peter since as John Carmichael's wife, Catherine Carmichael need not even change her name.

Trollope first wrote of the New Zealanders during the 1850s gold rushes, and gold subsequently flowed into England as capital, not as the gloating, beautiful couple introduced in his early text. But if John and Catherine Carmichael are the antecedents of Trollope's honeymoon pair, then his ideal English civilization will evolve from merging middle-class feminine taste with working-class male beauty, industry, and receptiveness to moral improvement, qualities common enough in Victorian writing. Not so familiar to readers are Trollope's subtle juxtaposition of the rough and the genteel, and his elision of the working-class necessity of taste that laid the foundations of his future ideal society, and from which labors Victorian England reaped such reward.

PART 3
Genderized Economics

Chapter 9
Mister Trollope, Lady Credit, and *The Way We Live Now*

Nathan K. Hensley[1]

"The spirit of speculative commerce"

A self-consciously literary man who was also self-consciously obsessed with money, Anthony Trollope has long earned attention from readers interested in the connections between economics and fiction. Since the mid-1990s especially, critics have decoded Trollope's obsession with markets, showing not just how his own novels behaved like commodities, but also how the characters in them speculate, invest, and go bust in such interdependent ways that Trollope's fictional worlds themselves seem to follow economic laws.[2] At the same time that "The New Economic Criticism" began this renewed engagement with Trollope's money matters, work by Kathy Psomiades and Lauren Goodlad, among others, sought to explore Trollope's varied investments in the legacies of political liberalism, using gender, in Psomiades's case, as a central category to do so.[3] This essay looks to supplement these important discussions of money, liberalism, and gender in Trollope by introducing a fourth term, one not usually taken account of in these arguments: empire.

By taking seriously the relationship *The Way We Live Now* (1875) draws between speculation and imperial global investment, this essay looks to show

[1]   I thank Deborah Morse and Margaret Markwick for their helpful suggestions on this essay, and Kathy Psomiades for guidance on each of its many iterations.

[2]   See, for example, Elsie Michie, "Buying Brains: Trollope, Oliphant, and Vulgar Victorian Commerce," *Victorian Studies*, 44.1 (2001): 77–91; Audrey Jaffe, "Trollope in the Stock Market: Irrational Exuberance and *The Prime Minister*." *Victorian Studies*, 45.1 (2002): 43–64; and J. Jeffrey Franklin, "Anthony Trollope Meets Pierre Bourdieu: The Conversion of Capital as Plot in the Mid-Victorian British Novel," *Victorian Literature and Culture*, 31.2 (2003): 501–21. The most important methodological statement for this avenue of investigation is Regenia Gagnier's, *The Insatiability of Human Wants: Economic and Aesthetics in Market Society* (Chicago: University of Chicago Press, 2000).

[3]   Lauren Goodlad, *Victorian Literature and the Victorian State: Character and Governance in a Liberal Society* (Baltimore: Johns Hopkins University Press, 2003), pp. 118–58, and Kathy Alexis Psomiades, "Heterosexual Exchange and Other Victorian Fictions: *The Eustace Diamonds* and Victorian Anthropology," *NOVEL: A Forum on Fiction*, 33.1 (1999): 93–118.

how the novel's very conservatism in gender matters might open up more broadly feminist possibilities; in this way, I want to suggest, it may push us to reconsider the yardsticks we use to judge "good" and "bad" feminist politics in the first place. In my first two sections, I chart a more or less familiar story about how Trollope's indictment of England's deteriorating social world uses a gendered dichotomy, borrowed from its critique of speculative capital, to structure each of its intertwined critiques—of finance, fiction, politics, and marriage. In each of these areas of potentially "real" or "false" representation, Trollope's novel advocates for the manly half: here fake money is like the worst women, and landed gentlemen are the manliest men. Trollope's gendered assault on the abstraction of speculative commerce in this way redeploys a history of commentary on "ungrounded" finance capital, one that reaches from eighteenth century invocations of "Lady Credit" to discussions of global finance of our own day. But I also want to suggest that placing Trollope's misogynist program in a broader geopolitical context— that of the imperial globalization it also criticizes—might complicate the apparent "badness" of what seems like Trollope's anti-feminist imaginary.

Trollope's "conservative" tone in this late novel may be keyed to his move rightwards in the latter part of his career, but it also addresses a very specific moment in the history of imperial high finance, when an England immersed in a newly abstracted world economy, one unprecedented in world history until our own day, found itself on the cusp of what seemed an entirely new way of living. "Nothing was wrong in the country," we are told in *Phineas Finn* (1869), "but the over-dominant spirit of speculative commerce."[4] Begun four years after this judgment (in 1873) and published in book form in 1875, *The Way We Live Now* was even better positioned to speak to this supposed commercial decline. As P. J. Cain and A. G. Hopkins show in their history of the Victorian empire's balance sheets, the fading of the railroad and mercantile booms of the 1840s and 50s led to an increased dependence on speculative foreign investment: in the 20-plus years between 1850 and the mid 1870s, the amount of investment capital circulating in the British imperial economy increased 2,000 percent.[5] Although this post-1870 phase of financial globalization has received relatively little attention from cultural critics, transactions in what Cain and Hopkins call "invisible income" (often targeting what is now known as the developing world) defined wealth-making in this period more than any previous decade of England's history. Like today's neoliberal globalization, the British Empire's impressive scheme of abstraction, so antithetical to Trollope's nostalgic fantasies of gentlemanliness, disproportionately affected women. Trollope's novel, therefore, presents us with two countervailing feminist readings: on the one hand, it unfolds a misogynist symbolic system; on

    [4]   Anthony Trollope, *Phineas Finn* [1869] (2 vols., New York: Oxford University Press, 1973), vol. 1, p. 333.
    [5]   P. J. Cain and A. G. Hopkins, *British Imperialism: 1688–2000*. (London: Longman, 2000), pp. 107–34. See also Giovanni Arrighi, *The Long Twentieth Century: Money, Power, and the Origins of our Times* (London: Verso, 1994), pp. 363, 159–74.

the other, it offers a "misogynist" criticism of the very global structures whose outcomes, then as now, are materially harmful to women. In light of this double-valence, it may be that among *The Way We Live Now*'s greatest accomplishments is that it stages a profound and very current political tension, one that may open up a new way for Trollope's famously enigmatic "advanced, but still ... conservative Liberal[ism]" to be read productively.[6]

"The *chief matter of Property*"

In critiquing what it understands as England's already-declined social condition, *The Way We Live Now* equates "the commercial profligacy of the age" with the world's pernicious new distaste for the real, describing both in the symbolic language of gender.[7] Financial and social matters intertwine, and in scenes and dialogue, plotlines and satiric asides, readers learn repeatedly that while in the old days men had substance, money was earned by hard work, and women behaved with due modesty, "[t]hings are changed, Georgiana."[8] To Trollope's eye, the new trade in abstraction is an apt metaphor for a host of unseemly returns at home: false women, unmanly men, poor writing, even shabby dress. "In these days," we learn in a moment of Thackaray-esque editorializing:

> men regard the form and outward lines of a woman's face and figure more than either the colour or the expression.... With padding and false hair without limit a figure may be constructed of almost any dimensions. The sculptors who construct them, male and female, hairdressers and milliners, are very skilful, and figures are constructed of noble dimensions, sometimes with voluptuous expansion, sometimes with classic reticence.... Colours indeed are added, but not the colours which we used to love. The taste for flesh and blood has for the day given place to an appetite for horsehair and pearl powder. (p. 212)

In every sphere of the novel's social world, that is, the "flesh and blood" realism of former times (p. 212) has given way to an artifice here coded as female, and to improper relationships between sign and thing (also feminine).[9] As this and corresponding passages in *The Prime Minister* (1876) suggest, for the Trollope of the mid 1870s, finance, writing, and marriage have all degenerated into the realm

---

[6]   Anthony Trollope, *An Autobiography* [1883] (New York: World's Classics, 1999), p. 291.

[7]   *An Autobiography*, p. 353.

[8]   As the Longstaffe debutante's mother says. Anthony Trollope, *The Way We Live Now* [1875] (New York: Modern Library, 2001), p. 179.

[9]   Although cagy as ever, Trollope here leaves ambiguous whether he's *documenting* a social fact or endorsing it: "*men regard* the form ... ," is how this passage begins. On this crucial aspect of Trollope's style, see David Skilton's introduction to *The Prime Minister*, (New York: Penguin, 1994), pp. xxiii–xxiv.

of suspicious fiction, a defectively masculine or "improper" state of deracination. "Things are changed," Paul Montague repeats (p. 211). Melmotte's elaborate speculations have replaced Roger Carbury's hard work; meaningless Beargarden IOU's have replaced "ready money" (p. 368); and love has become speculation too, though it is fey men who gamble and women who either return an investment or don't. "Look here, mother," says the rascally Felix Carbury of what he calls his "scheme" to marry Melmotte's daughter (p. 237), "this is a risky sort of game, I grant, but I am playing it by your advice" (p. 22).

Trollope's wide-angle satire in other words charts the rise of speculative commerce as a disruption in proper gender roles, and in this way participates in a story that has its ideological origins in seventeenth and eighteenth century political theory. For John Locke, who defined Victorian political assumptions more than any other early English thinker, property was the very wellspring of gentlemanly *propriety*, in both of that word's senses of "owned things" and "personal identity," what is *proper* to one's (masculine) self.[10] As C. B. MacPherson and others have shown, Locke held that both gentlemanly identity and value were created at a mythic, original moment when land in a state of nature was combined with human labor; all "propriety" could thus be understood as a combination of land and work. In the *Second Treatise* (1690), Locke explains that man's character is formed in a kind of primal scene, one where work gets "mixed" with land:

> The *Labour* of his Body, and the *Work* of his hands, we may say, are properly his. Whatsoever he removes out of the State that Nature hath provided, and left it in, he hath mixed his *Labour* with, and joined to it something that is his own, and thereby makes it his *Property*.

Locke specifies that this newly acquired propriety inheres in physical terrain: "the *chief matter of Property*," he writes, is "the *Earth it self*."[11] For this central text of the liberal political tradition, then, land acts as the very anchor of proper masculine identity, its "roots" (as a related Trollopian figure has it) in "ground."

Trollope was no great reader of Locke—the theorist is not mentioned in his letters once—but by the 1870s he would replicate the father of private property's ideological formula nearly perfectly, in the person of Arthur Fletcher (in *The Prime Minister*) and in *The Way We Live Now*'s Roger Carbury. A case study in

---

[10]   J. G. A. Pocock, *Virtue, Commerce, and History: Essays on Political Thought and History, Chiefly in the Eighteenth Century* (New York: Cambridge University Press, 1985). See also the multiple, linked usages listed in *Oxford English Dictionary*'s entry on the word "proper."

[11]   *Sic*; italics original. John Locke, *The Second Treatise of Government*, in *Two Treatises of Government* (New York: Cambridge University Press, 1988), pp. 287–8, 290. For the most influential critique of Locke's theory of property, see C. B. Macpherson, *The Political Theory of Possessive Individualism: Hobbes to Locke* (New York: Oxford University Press, 1964), pp. 194–262.

Trollopian masculinity, Carbury is offered up as the precise negation of Melmotte the fraud, more solid than Sir Felix and more consistent even than the sympathetic Paul Montague (who is "half true," "half false" [p. 214]). Roger is someone who can be "believed altogether" (p. 163), we are told—"a rock of strength" (p. 316). "If one did whatever he said," Hetta Carbury tells Montague,

> one would never get wrong. Whenever he thinks anything he says it;—or at least, he never says anything that he doesn't think. If he spent a thousand pounds, everybody would know that he's got it to spend; but other people are not like that."
>
> "You're thinking of Mr. Melmotte," [Montague said].
>
> "I'm thinking of everybody, Mr. Montague; —of everybody except Roger."
> (p. 316)

In the same way that Arthur Fletcher derives his good character from a long history ("he has a decent father and mother," Mr. Wharton says [p. 88]), Roger's hyperbolic honesty, linked here to his behavior with money, is tied elsewhere in *The Way We Live Now* to his attachment to the family seat at Carbury Hall, where for generation after generation his family had "been true to their acres and their acres true to them" (p. 44). The novel's property-based or "conservative" fantasy of value is well-documented, of course, in Trollope criticism: Paul Delany calls it Trollope's "myth of the land."[12] What I want to emphasize here is that Trollope's 1875 critique draws on political theory's founding myth to valorize proper manliness, offering its gendered plea at a moment when the center of world speculation, London, was working harder than ever to spread its ungrounded capital across the globe.

"If you court her, you lose her"

Land has long been seen to act, in Patrick Brantlinger's words, as Trollope's "ultimate 'real'"[13]—that is, as the grounding that makes for manly character. But it is less remarked upon that in *The Way We Live Now's* symbolic system, the "improper" practice of credit-based speculation has a gender valence too, one that

---

[12]   Paul Delaney, "Land, Money, and the Jews in the Later Trollope," *Studies in English Literature*, 32.4 (1992): 765. For an earlier discussion, see Paul Elmer More, "My Debt to Trollope," in *The Demon of the Absolute* (Princeton: Princeton University Press, 1928). David Skilton similarly notices, of *The Prime Minister*, that "finally the novel comes to rest in a nostalgic picture of landed society" (p. xxvi).

[13]   Patrick Brantlinger, *Fictions of State: Culture and Credit in Britain, 1694–1994*. (Ithaca: Cornell University Press, 1996), p. 171.

is itself inherited from a long history of writing about money. The *Oxford English Dictionary*[14] defines speculation as any "transaction of a venturesome or risky nature," then goes further, calling it "[t]he action or practice of buying and selling goods, land, stocks and shares, etc., in order to profit by the rise or fall in the market value, *as distinct from regular trading or investment*."[15] For the earliest commentators on this type of "irregular" trading—Daniel Defoe and David Hume—the proliferation of speculation was linked directly to the appearance of paper money and public debt in the early eighteenth century, both innovations devised to fund overseas imperial war.

Defoe, Hume, and, as I am suggesting, Trollope all understand speculation as an issue of deracination: in credit-based economies, the initial abstraction of the money form is, through monetary instruments, bills of exchange, and credit, removed further and further away from its material referent, until the process of capital accumulation becomes unmoored from production in any traditional sense at all. Cut off from its "proper" foundations, money begins to make more money—"fructifying," as Trollope calls it in *The Prime Minister* (p. 401). Wealth without substance, this capital form derives profit, in other words, not from land rents, manufacturing outputs, or "hard work"—Trollope's favorite—but from a managed combination of speed, public opinion, and risk. In *The Way We Live Now*, Melmotte describes the vexing abstraction of this form in terms borrowed from meteorology, referring to "the nature of credit, how strong it is,—as the air,—to buoy you up; [and] how slight it is,—as a mere vapour,—when roughly touched" (p. 332). Like vapor, air, or a perverse kind of self-generating fruit, speculative capital stands as the most complex and (for these writers) problematically abstract stage of monetary acquisition. As Fredric Jameson writes in his own aerial metaphor, "Now, like the butterfly stirring within the chrysalis, [money] separates itself off from [its] concrete breeding ground and prepares to take flight."[16]

What I want to emphasize is the way women figure in this shared vocabulary for describing economies dependent on what Defoe called "Lady Credit." Surveying eighteenth century political theory, J. G. A. Pocock has charted how images of credit and financial speculation (typically feminized), and criticisms of those images (often anti-feminine), circulated at multiple levels of British political discourse. In his *Review* (1720), Defoe himself argued *in favor* of the eighteenth century's new monetary abstraction, but even his descriptions of Lady

---

[14]   Hereafter referred to as *OED*.

[15]   My emphasis. In its pejorative Victorian usage, the term "speculation" was ambiguous, as Audrey Jaffe has noted, and one effect of anti-speculation literature may have been to demonstrate what "bad" investing looked like, so as to encourage the "good" kind. See Jaffe, "Trollope in the Stock Market: Irrational Exuberance and *The Prime Minister*," p. 54.

[16]   Fredric Jameson, "Culture and Finance Capital" (1997), in *The Cultural Turn: Selected Writings on the Postmodern* (London: Verso, 1998), p. 142.

Fig. 9.1   "Mr Melmotte speculates." Lionel Grimshaw Fawkes's illustration
for *The Way We Live Now*

Credit's fickle power —"if you court her, you lose her," he wrote[17]—show how, as Pocock writes in reference to Defoe, "masculine minds constantly symbolize the changeable, the unpredictable, and the imaginative as feminine."[18] Indeed it may be that Defoe's changeful lady, Trollope's decorated women (sporting "padding and false hair without limit"), and even the diamond dust shoes that grace the cover of Jameson's *Postmodernism* (1994) all equally suggest that in the minds of male social critics, speculative economies old and new tend to find themselves draped in the garb of the feminine.[19]

For Trollope, Lady Carbury's hack literary efforts further confirm the novel's heavy symbolic association between falsehood and the feminine qualities of failed character. His graspy, scribbling woman is a writer of sham histories and bad novels: she "schemed," we are told, "and lied, and lived a life of manoeuvres" (*sic*, p. 13); she was (on the same page) "sharp, incredulous, and untrustworthy"; and in a telling phrase that underscores Trollope's sense that Lady Carbury's only character is a lack of one, we learn that "lying had become her nature" (p. 250). (Trollope would later admit that *The Way We Live Now*'s "accusations are exaggerated."[20]) It comes as little surprise, then, that Lady Carbury's fake history, *Criminal Queens*, is about false women and written by one: this text stands as the very paradigm of good writing gone bad, the foil, we can only assume, to the giant work of male realism we hold in our hands. (Her other title is *The Wheel of Fortune*, which also makes a quiet connection between bad fiction and the turning, feminized lotteries of financial speculation.[21]) "[S]he was essentially worldly," Roger comments of this "Lady,"

> believing that good could come out of evil, that falsehood might in certain conditions be better than truth, that shams and pretences might do the work of true service, that a strong house might be built on a foundation of sand! (p. 11)

---

[17]   Defoe, *Review* (facsimile book 6), vol. III, no. 5, pp. 17–18, quoted in Pocock, *The Machiavellian Moment: Florentine Political Thought and the Atlantic Republican Tradition* (Princeton: Princeton University Press, 1975), p. 463.

[18]   Pocock, *Virtue, Commerce, History*, p. 99.

[19]   For Jameson, Warhol's dangling women's shoes are the emblem of the distance postmodernity's investments interpose between cultural object and a more authentic lived experience. See *Postmodernism; or, The Cultural Logic of Late Capitalism* (Durham: Duke University Press, 1991), p. 9. For an analysis of how women figure across contemporary globalization discourse, see John Marx, "The Feminization of Globalization," *Cultural Critique* 63 (2006): 1–32.

[20]   *An Autobiography*, p. 355.

[21]   Carbury's work, in other words, well attests to what in reference to Defoe Sandra Sherman calls "the credit-fiction homology," or what Patrick Brantlinger identifies as *The Way We Live Now*'s "underlying identity, based on credit, between the commodity forms of fiction and money." See Sherman, *Finance and Fictionality in the Early Eighteenth Century: Accounting for Defoe* (New York: Cambridge University Press, 1996), p. 14, *et passim*, and Brantlinger, *Fictions of State*, p. 165.

Trollope uses a biblical trope to underscore his moral outrage here, invoking the houses and sand of, for example, Matthew 7:26.[22] But importantly it is *land* that is again invoked to diagnose the problem, and land that is called upon for the values that would correct it. The beautiful but most unladylike Winifred Hurtle, too, lacks a history grounded in property (she's from America), further suggesting the way women register this novel's critique of what Pocock calls the "epistemology of the investing society."[23]

Of course, *The Way We Live Now's* critique of London's linked genres of speculation borrow the logics and language of its discussion of actual finance capital, and trace a similarly gendered moralizing trajectory—though this time it is not femininity but masculinity that's at issue. The grandest speculative venture in the novel (and its controlling metaphor) promises to conjure its earnings out of the air, not the ground: as all investors know, the point of what advertisements call "The Great Railway to Vera Cruz" is "not to make a railway to Vera Cruz, but to float a company" (p. 70). Fisker's slyly feminized marketing materials—those "gorgeous" and "beautiful" "little" "programmes" (p. 70)—may accomplish this floating for a time, but not even those overly pretty picture books can mask the moral-economic lack Trollope so relentlessly savages. "[F]ortunes were to be made out of the concern," he writes with thick irony, "before a spadeful of earth had been moved" (p. 70). The fact that no "*earth*" would be "*moved*," provides the Lockean undercurrent to the sense of scandal here, confirming the scheme as the precise inversion of proper, character-building labor.

With an unknown pedigree based somewhere outside England and with a rap sheet that may or may not include financial crimes in capitals across Europe, Melmotte is a cipher of literally transcontinental proportions, in this sense completing the novel's polemic on proper masculinity. Replicated in even more force in *The Prime Minister*, where Trollope withholds from Lopez even the grudging respect he cedes to Melmotte, *The Way We Live Now's* complicated anti-Semitic gesture is capped off when the cosmopolitan history of its famous swindler is laid bare. Having "made his wealth in France," built railways in Russia, had dealings in America, "supplied Austria with arms," and lived in Vienna, New York, and Paris (p. 29), Melmotte is now, outrageously, set up in the very heart of English society. The speculator's heavily marked (but never confirmed) Jewishness is important here, for the relationship of perceived Jewish "statelessness" was closely related to the expansion of globalizing finance in the late Victorian period. With images of the Rothschilds and other denationalized banking families circulating in the cultural air, the symbolic figure of "the Jew" could, for the Trollope of the 1870s, efficiently stand in for the newly visible figure of the "improperly" international man—subject to no nation, beholden to

---

[22]   The verse reads: "Everyone who hears these words of Mine and does not act on them, will be like a foolish man who built his house on the sand." Melmotte's reputation is also said to be "built upon the sands" (p. 76).

[23]   Pocock, *The Machiavellian Moment*, p. 440.

no forces but the borderless interests of money capital. (George Eliot would inflect this "postnational" trope more positively, and with less emphasis on finance, in *Daniel Deronda*, of 1876.[24]) Even *The Way We Live Now*'s falsest "necromancer" (p. 102), however, knows how honest masculine identity is tied up with earth: the speculator explains to Dolly Longstaffe that "property could not be created by the waving of any wand or the boiling of any cauldron" (p. 102). And as if in response to this necromancer's paradoxical status—ungrounded but temporarily productive, fake but passing for real—Trollope grants Melmotte, with important reserve, "a certain manliness" (p. 668).

"Opening new worlds"

So far I have outlined *The Way We Live Now*'s figurative or symbolic system to underscore how the novel critiques the related problems of finance capital—the distance between sign and thing, between material wealth and its abstracted forms—across its social fields, using gender as one register on which this polemic is made visible. And if painted ladies, sham fiction, and feminized international men work as the ideal metaphors for the novel's critique of speculation's logic, it would appear that Trollope's moral-economic analysis here understands landed men to have proper identity, while most women, feminized men, and finance capital are problematically ungrounded. Whether women in this order can possess "character," in other words, is far from clear. (Even Hetta Carbury, virtuous as she is, merely facilitates this logic, settling down with Paul Montague to produce a male heir for the Carbury Manor.) Following this line, there is much to support a reading of *The Way We Live Now*'s "bad" or "anti-feminist" symbolic politics. Trollope himself assists in such a reading, writing in *An Autobiography*, for example, that "inequality is the work of God" (p. 292). Fuller engagements with Trollope's long career—including those in this volume— show him to be more complex than this, but in focusing on one novel, and on one moment in the history of Victorian imperial finance, I have emphasized the neo-romantic, or structurally conservative logic of the landed realism this 1875 novel articulates as its fantasy.[25]

---

[24]   There is much to say on *The Way We Live Now's* sometimes startling anti-Semitism (or "anti-anti-Semitism," as David Brooks optimistically calls it in his introduction to the novel [p. xx]). Paul Delany writes that "Trollope bases his anti-Semitism on the long association between Jews and finance capital…. For Trollope, the Jews are embodied symbol of such power, unencumbered as they are by land, national loyalty, or custom." Delany, "Land, Money, and the Jews in the Later Trollope," p. 774. For a discussion of Eliot and Trollope's very different comportments toward "the Jew," see Michael Ragussis, *Figures of Conversion: "The Jewish Question" and English National Identity* (Durham: Duke University Press, 1995), pp. 234–90.

[25]   Trollope's well-documented tendency toward "postmodern" or superficial characterization could be seen to countervail my claims here, as would the fact that Trollope

Nevertheless, I want to suggest that following even this conservative symbolism might provide terms for imagining a progressive feminist reading, albeit one cast in a different, more global register.

In an appraisal of Trollope's financial politics in *Fictions of State: Culture and Credit in Britain, 1694–1994*, Patrick Brantlinger notices that the author's understanding of landed property as "the ultimate form of wealth" is linked directly to his nationalism, suggesting, as well, that those two positions imply a more generally unsavory politics, one that Brantlinger calls "intensely patriotic and conservative."[26] It is axiomatic, in Brantlinger's analysis, that a "bad" romantic nationalism would imply equally unappealing positions in other areas, an extrapolation that extends to imperialism itself, where Trollope's novels portray, for Brantlinger, "the unified, taken-for-granted nation-state with its almost equally taken for granted empire."[27] Whatever may be expressed in his travel writings and elsewhere,[28] we have seen that in *The Way We Live Now*, Trollope's moral-symbolic system understands legitimacy to spring from masculine ties to land and history, and indeed from the "family values" that make nations.

Uncomfortably, then, this logic places its emphasis on the importance of *staying home*; its injunction is to avoid engaging in foreign development schemes, and to refuse peripheral investment projects like Lopez's adventure to Guatemala or Melmotte's foray into Vera Cruz. In this way, the same landlocked nationalism Brantlinger criticizes as patriotic and conservative—we might also add anti-feminist—places Trollope's late novel in direct *opposition* to the worldwide financial expansion that we could follow recent economic historians in calling Victorian globalization. Indeed the novel's hostility to the cosmopolitan operations of "soft" imperial trade is made explicit when Roger Carbury recommends what he calls "elbow grease" at home instead of expansion abroad, refusing a request by a Dr. Palmoil to "open the interior of Africa a little further" (p. 318). Melmotte and his capital, on the other hand, have the ability to "open new worlds" (p. 359), and look to do just that in the peripheral zone of Mexico. His cosmopolitan schemes of uplift reach further than this, extending, we are told, to plans in China, South Africa, and in "the lately annexed country on the African lakes" (p. 360). Rumored, too, is Melmotte's "philanthropic scheme for buying the liberty

---

himself was no landed aristocrat but a "rising man"— as well as a speculator in an art whose own serialized form bet both on its ability to conjure belief and on the future interest of readers.

[26] Brantlinger, *Fictions of State*, pp. 171, 172.

[27] Ibid.

[28] Trollope's comments about savage races are notorious. In *Australia and New Zealand* (1873), for example—written directly before *The Way We Live Now*—Trollope tells us that "the Australian black man" is "ineradicably savage": "That he should perish without unnecessary suffering should be the aim of all who are concerned in the matter." *Australia and New Zealand* (1873), ed. P. D. Edwards and R. B. Joyce (St. Lucia, Queensland, Australia: U of Queensland Press, 1967), pp. 175, 113.

of the Arabian fellahs from the Khedive of Egypt for thirty millions sterling"
(p. 360). (Ferdinand Lopez's shady trade in Latin American guano and African
alcohol announce a similarly worldwide reach.) Arguing *against* these schemes
for spreading civilization, ironizing their ability to "afford relief to … oppressed
nationalities" (p. 360), *The Way We Live Now*'s return to the land calls attention
to the hypocrisy attending British finance capital's wide-angled, "philanthropic"
flights —those same abstract transactions that defined the British global project in
the 1870s more than in any other decade.

In this way, the novel offers a slanted critique of the tenets at the heart of what
was, in the 1870s, a fully fledged, worldwide imperial economy, one that, like
ours, was centered in metropolitan banking houses and managed by the class of
men that Cain and Hopkins call "gentlemanly capitalists."[29] Then as now, when
wealth migrates along circuits of abstract trade to the metropoles of the global
North, it is women far more than men who are affected.[30] Indeed if we recall the
fact that globalization's bleakest outcomes fall excessively on the fairer sex, we
begin to appreciate another level of Trollope's apparently misogynist intervention.
On the one hand, his novel inveighs against lady credit in favor of what seems like
a natural inequality and a masculinist fantasy of land. On the other, however, when
this representational system is viewed from a more global perspective—that is, in
light of its opposition to a particular phase of imperial globalization—it becomes
apparent that this symbolic system's very "badness" might paradoxically articulate
positions that could have "good" or materially feminist consequences.

To see how, we can put Trollope's advanced, but still conservative liberalism
in the context of Victorian liberalism itself. Nostalgically arguing for the value
of property over un-placed, ahistorical, endlessly transferable finance capital,
The Way We Live Now agitates for what the Victorian legal anthropologist Henry
Maine called the state of patriarchal "status" over the more modern state of liberal
"contract." It argues, that is, for the value of an authority understood to be *natural*,
a male or "gentlemanly" right vested in land and in history ("status"), over and
against the formal equalities and general human equivalence that nineteenth-century
liberal theory was so effective in naturalizing ("contract").[31] In *The Subjection of
Women*, John Stuart Mill framed this distinction as one between the old way of
fathers—"a social relation grounded on force"—and the new law of exchange, one
characterized by "institutions grounded on equal justice."[32] Status against contract,
patriarchalism versus equality, old custom against new liberty: from within the

[29]   Cain and Hopkins, *British Imperialism*, pp. 7–10.

[30]   For the tip of the iceberg on this vast and contested topic in our contemporary
era, see the data in the U.N. Human Development Report's "Gender-Related Development
Index," 2005, available at http://hdr.undp.org/reports/global/2005, accessed 13 June 2007.

[31]   Henry Sumner Maine, *Ancient Law: Its Connection with the Family History of
Society, and its Relation to Modern Ideas*, 1861 (New York: Henry Holt, 1873).

[32]   John Stuart Mill, "The Subjection of Women," in *On Liberty and Other Writings*.
Stefan Collini, ed. (New York: Cambridge University Press, 1989), pp. 124–5.

terms made available by this nineteenth century dichotomy (one still operative now), Trollope's return to the land would seem to be bad news for women, and from a certain perspective it certainly is. But here disturbing questions present themselves, since it was precisely this idiom of anachronism and rights that, in the nineteenth century, provided justification for campaigns abroad that we would have to also call bad for women. (The importance of Indian "suttee" to rationales for civilizing India provides one well-known example.) Today, too, a language of rights and modernity provides cover for international actions whose outcomes for women (and men) across the globe are doubtful at best. Now as in the Victorian day, armed intervention prefers to arrive under the banner of equality, and the "barbaric" or "prehistoric" treatment of women sits among the most effective justifications for international war.[33]

The troubling, possibly hypocritical connection between the rhetoric of liberal feminism and anti-feminist geopolitical outcomes is not the only way Trollope might speak to us now. We know that it was not "the despotism of custom"—as Mill called this allegedly prehistoric, patriarchal form of society[34]—that proved itself to be exportable across the globe. Rather it was *the contract form* that emerged as the universally valid formula for establishing what was already, by the late 1870s, an expanding, intertwining global marketplace. It was, in other words, the very regime of "modern" liberal exchange—one whose formally equal agents could seem, like elements of an economic matrix, calculable, regular, and interchangeable—that by the 1870s had already come to structure the Victorian empire's world-making project. It continues to structure ours.[35] In this way, *The Way We Live Now*'s deep, blithely misogynist criticism of foreign investment can be seen to attack the logics of exchange at the heart of what was, in the 1870s, a fully functional imperial

---

[33]   A White House document from 2004 explains that "[t]he advance of freedom in the greater Middle East has given new rights and new hopes to women. And America will do its part to continue the spread of liberty." "President, Mrs. Bush Mark Progress in Global Women's Human Rights," 12 March 2004. Available at http://www.whitehouse.gov/news/releases/2004/03/20040312-5.html, accessed 15 June 2007. I cannot hope, here, to come close to outlining the complex issues this quote raises. As a beginning, see Wendy Brown, *Regulating Aversion: Tolerance in the Age of Identity and Empire* (Princeton: Princeton University Press, 2006) and Katherine Viner, "Feminism as Imperialism," *Guardian*, 21 September, 2002, reposted at http://www.commondreams.org/views02/0923-07.htm, accessed 9 July 2007.

[34]   John Stuart Mill, "On Liberty," p. 70.

[35]   Ian Baucom has recently argued that global capitalism works to "refashion" women of the global South, looking "to move them from alterity to likeness, to shift them from a regime of difference ... to a regime of identity.... [T]he normalizing project of the colonial state has been taken over, largely intact, as the civilizing mission of multinational capital[.]" *Specters of the Atlantic: Finance Capital, Slavery, and the Philosophy of History*. (Durham: Duke University Press, 2006), p. 148. See also Gayatri Spivak , *A Critique of Postcolonial Reason: Toward a History of the Vanishing Present* (Cambridge: Harvard University Press, 1999), p. 399.

democracy, one that operated according to the political-economic principles of universal equivalence ("equality"). I want to be clear that because a return to a romanticized era of patriarchalism might oppose imperial globalization does not make that patriarchalism desirable, and a rescue of Trollope's politics is not what I intend. Rather I want to suggest that part of Trollope's achievement in *The Way We Live Now* is to usefully scramble our assumptions about what might count as "good" and "bad" feminist politics, especially in a moment, like ours, when "liberal" assumptions, perhaps even more than "conservative" ones, provide the motor for an imperial order unparalleled since the days when Trollope took pen to paper.

In this sense the novel's polemic is extremely current. As David Harvey and others have shown, twenty-first century doctrines of free trade and global uplift rely heavily, indeed structurally, on the logics and profit-making powers of high finance.[36] Our neoliberal era *depends* on finance capital, and in this very literal way, speculation can be said to underwrite contemporary life as we know it. Large numbers bear this out. As economists Edward Li Puma and Benjamin Lee point out, worldwide transactions in financial derivatives—or purely monetary, speculative exchanges—accounted for less than $50 million in 1970. By 2000, capital traded in this form reached $100 trillion. This amount is a one followed by fourteen zeroes. It is also equal to the total manufacturing output of the entire globe for the past one thousand years.[37] "Finance capital," Jameson concludes in his own analysis, "underpins and sustains postmodernity as such."[38] Jameson means "late capitalism" when he says postmodernity, emphasizing the material foundations of an abstract culture. If my own reading has followed this argumentative strategy, contrasting the "concrete" conditions of global financial rule with what I have charted as Trollope's "abstract" gender symbolism, I do not want to endorse this privileging of one term in a dichotomy between the real and the ineffable—a strategy similar, in its way, to Trollope's own. Rather I want to use these terms to suggest that Trollope's novel about its "new aera in money matters" (*sic* p. 369), reread at the height of our own "new era" of finance and empire, can productively complicate the categories we use to evaluate feminist politics. In this way, I think, it challenges us to imagine new ways of thinking about gender now.

---

[36]   See David Harvey, *A Brief History of Neoliberalism* (New York: Oxford University Press, 2005).

[37]   Edward Li Puma and Benjamin Lee, *Financial Derivatives and the Globalization of Risk* (Durham: Duke University Press, 2004), p. 47.

[38]   Jameson, "Culture and Finance Capital," p. 149.

Chapter 10
A Woman of Money:
Miss Dunstable, Thomas Holloway,
and Victorian Commercial Wealth

Elsie B. Michie

The novels of Anthony Trollope [are] . . . just as real as if some giant had hewn a great lump out of the earth, and put it under a glass case, with all the inhabitants going about their daily business, and not suspecting that they were being made a show of.

Nathaniel Hawthorne, Letter to Joseph M. Field[1]

The deepest affiliation of *Doctor Thorne* with latter day theories of culture lies . . . in its strand of meditation on how a certain social and psychological environment is bound together, in ways of which its inhabitants are largely unconscious.

Christopher Herbert[2]

The passages quoted above show how easy it is to experience Anthony Trollope as offering self-enclosed worlds peopled by inhabitants largely unconscious of the rules that govern their surroundings. Such perceptions arise in part because Trollope rarely takes the position of omniscient commentator, who, like the giant in Hawthorne's image or the anthropologist implicit in Herbert's, looks down at social interactions from a distance, explaining their significance. Trollope refuses, as Henry James notes, "to take the so-called scientific view," choosing instead to describe, "the life that lay nearest to him."[3] His narratives focus on individuals in the midst of events, caught up in negotiating a world of everyday objects, partly grasping and partly avoiding a full understanding of the material forces that were impacting their culture, forces that, most often and most infamously, in terms of Trollope's later reputation, involved money. In the reading that follows, I argue that this "near" view allowed Trollope to be surprisingly astute about the contradictory psychological motivations, both spoken and unspoken, that shaped late Victorian society's conceptions of its own material practices. Trollope links his characters' individual psychological reactions to Victorian social history through the practice of referencing actual historical figures. We know that in the

---

[1]   Quoted in Donald Smalley (ed.), *Anthony Trollope: The Critical Heritage* (London: Routledge and Kegan Paul, 1969), p. 110.

[2]   Christopher Herbert, *Culture and Anarchy: Ethnographic Imagination in the Nineteenth Century* (Chicago: The University of Chicago Press, 1991), p. 269.

[3]   Quoted in Smalley, p. 529.

Palliser novels, Gresham stands for Gladstone, Daubeny for Disraeli. I explore here a connection less obvious to us than it would have been to the Victorians, the similarities between the ointment heiress Miss Dunstable, who appears in three of the Barsetshire novels,[4] and the patent medicine magnate, Thomas Holloway.[5] Tracing the resonances between Trollope's fictional representation and depictions of a contemporary historical figure, I find a similar set of rhetorical and psychological images governing both, images that allow us to map out the complexity of nineteenth-century reactions to economic changes that were experienced as transforming the terrain of English society.

These were the changes that meant that, "for the first time in history, non-landed incomes and wealth had begun to overtake land alone as the main source of economic power."[6] Through Miss Dunstable, Trollope references the form non-landed wealth typically took in the latter half of the nineteenth century when England's financial success was marked by the advent of commercial fortunes. This was the "age of millionaires,"[7] a period dominated financially by "the new shopocracy,"[8] whose money came not from the railways, steel, and manufacturing but from the sale of commodities like soap, beer, tea, patent medicines, and diamonds. It was a time when the enormous wealth amassed by entrepreneurs like Thomas Lipton or Lord Leverhulme and merchant bankers like Baron Meyer de Rothschild was spectacularly visible and enabled the exercise of extraordinary power at the level of both individual and national interchanges. Indeed one could have said of many of these millionaires what a modern biographer wrote of the man contemporary readers would have recognized as a shadow presence behind Trollope's Miss Dunstable. The famously successful pill and ointment magnate

---

[4]   *Doctor Thorne* (London: Penguin, 1991), *Framley Parsonage* (London: Penguin, 1986), (hereafter cited in the text as *DT* and *FP*), and *The Last Chronicle of Barset* (Oxford: Oxford University Press, 1980).

[5]   One contemporary review noted that readers, "may think they recognize traits in … the great heiress Miss Dunstable" (quoted in Smalley, p. 73). Holloway was so famous that, by 1876 (when Trollope's *The Prime Minister* was appearing), "Gladstone, then in opposition, made a speech … in which he compared the efficacy of his politics to the purifying powers of the famous pills" (Anthony Harrison-Barbet, *Thomas Holloway: Victorian Philanthropist* (London: Royal Holloway, 1994), p. 76).

[6]   Harold Perkin, *The Rise of Professional Society: England Since 1880* (London: Routledge, 1989), p. 64.

[7]   Perkin, p. 69.

[8]   Martin Wiener, *English Culture and the Decline of the Industrial Spirit, 1850-1980* (Cambridge: Cambridge University Press, 1981), p. 64. For further discussions of these figures, see Peter Mathias, *The First Industrial Nation: An Economic History of Britain 1700–1914* (Methuen: London, 1969), W. D. Rubinstein, *Men of Property: The Very Wealthy in Britain Since the Industrial Revolution* (New Brunswick: Rutgers University Press, 1981), and F. M. L. Thompson, "Business and Landed Elites," in F. M. L. Thompson (ed.), *Landowners, Capitalists, and Entrepreneurs: Essays for Sir John Habakkuk* (Oxford: Clarendon, 1996).

Sir Thomas Holloway was described as "epitomiz[ing] the finest qualities of his age—an age of which it may be fairly said he was as much an architect as a product."[9] But if men like Holloway were the "architects" of the late Victorian age that produced them, if what they produced made England great, then the country's renown had come to be identified chiefly with the sale of commodities and possession of money.

This is the dilemma that Trollope addresses with particular clarity in the opening chapters of *Doctor Thorne* where the novel's story stops as the narrator exclaims:

> England a commercial country! Yes; as Venice was. She may excel other countries in commerce, but yet it is not that in which she most prides herself, in which she most excels. Merchants as such are not the first men among us; though it may perhaps be open, barely open, to a merchant to become one of them. Buying and selling is good and necessary; it is very necessary, and may, possibly be very good; but it cannot be the noblest work of man; and let us hope that it may not in your time be esteemed the noblest work of any Englishman. (*DT*, p. 15)

As it stretches through time and space, comparing England to Venice, this passage seems to provide the overview I argue Trollope's novels typically avoid. Yet, even here, the writing works less to convey a distanced critical analysis of the problems of the age than to immerse readers in the ambivalent feelings triggered by them. What is most effective about the passage is not the content of the sentences, which invoke an image commonly referenced in Victorian discussions of commerce,[10] but their structure, the movement that starts with a yes then shifts to a but. This movement conveys the mental ebb and flow that psychologists since Freud have associated with fetishism[11] and prepares readers for a novel in which Miss Dunstable reveals Victorian culture's awareness of its own propensity to fetishize wealth.

---

[9]   Harrison-Barbet, p. 9.

[10]   For Victorian allusions to Venice see Ronald Thomas, "Spectacle and Speculation: the Victorian Economy of Vision in *Little Dorrit*," in Anny Sadrin (ed.) *Dickens, Europe and the New Worlds,* (London: Macmillan, 1999), pp. 34–46.

[11]   Slavoj Zizek identifies this back and forth movement of acceptance and denial with the phrase "'I know very well, but still'" and links it to practical fetishism, whose practitioners "know very well how things really are, but still they are doing it as if they did not know" (*The Sublime Object of Ideology* (London: Verso, 1989), pp. 18, 32). Patrick Brantlinger uses Zizek's model to discuss nineteenth-century ideas about debt in *Fictions of State: Culture and Credit in Britain, 1694–1994* (Ithaca: Cornell University Press, 1996), pp. 4–5. Christopher Linder uses it to discuss fetishism in *The Eustace Diamonds* in "Trollope's Material Girls," *Yearbook of English Studies* 32 (2002): 36–51.

The view Trollope presents here is broader than that of modern critics who have tended to dwell not on the movement between two contradictory reactions but on the rhetoric of denial that infuses the second half of Trollope's sentences. They have explored at length the ways in which nineteenth-century culture sought to empty out the power of commerce it saw so visibly enhancing the country's status. Such denials are powerfully catalogued in Martin Wiener's *English Culture and the Decline of the Industrial Spirit*, which shows the ways in which England resurrected an idyllic image of its pre-commercial past which it sought to superimpose over its commercial present. Wiener cites the passage quoted above from *Doctor Thorne* to place Trollope among a series of critics, including Ruskin, Arnold, and Dickens, whose writings extolled their distaste for the entrepreneurial spirit and advocated instead a whole other set of values associated with the gentry and the possession of land. But the logic of Trollope's passage invites us to see this reading of nineteenth-century culture as presenting only half the picture, the half that involves the need to disavow change. The series of non-commercial values and images that Wiener traces were part of an attempt to deny what everyone knew, that the new commercial wealth was enormously powerful and successful and that it was transforming the face of English society in ways that could never be reversed.

In his Barsetshire novels, Trollope solves the problem of representing his culture's "yes, but" response to its own financial success by incarnating the "yes" part of the equation in a female figure who possesses the wealth that made historical figures like Holloway powerful. In Trollope's fictions Miss Dunstable stands in for economic developments that could not be named directly without the author and his works becoming too vulgarly associated with commerce.[12] Using a female figure to evoke such financial forces makes sense because of women's traditional symbolic positioning as being closer to material practices than men are. As Henry James explains, in identifying Trollope's flair for the everyday as feminine, "women ... hold their noses close, as it were to the texture of life."[13] The closeness of this feminine position means that female characters can function as what Laura Brown calls proxies; they can represent and evoke a culture's uneasy relationship to its own commercial successes.[14] Trollope's novels make it clear that

---

[12]   Trollope was repeatedly characterized as being able "to give characteristic touches, yet escape vulgarity"; he is "a novelist who can paint vulgarity of this sort, while he manages to inspire a constant conviction that he himself is not the least vulgar" (quoted in Smalley, pp. 47, 184).

[13]   Smalley, p. 527.

[14]   Brown argues that figures like Belinda in Pope's "The Rape of the Lock," "become the proxies for men, object and agent of accumulation are reversed, and thus the female figure is made to bear responsibility for empire" (*The Ends of Empire: Women and Ideology in Early Eighteenth-Century Literature* [Ithaca: Cornell University Press, 1993], p. 16). In Trollope's novels, the female figure that represents wealth is used less as a scapegoat than as an emblem of "the tabooed pleasures" that were "part of the tangle of new affects that

he saw such successes as an integral part of the social make-up of his period. He could not accurately depict that small world under glass that Hawthorne describes without referencing them. In the Barsetshire novels, Miss Dunstable allows him to explore his society's awareness of its own propensity to make a fetish of commercial wealth. But we can only grasp the complexity of the psychological reactions to Miss Dunstable within Trollope's novels by first understanding the impact of the historical figure that lies behind his fictional portrait of her.

A real ointment magnate

What Miss Dunstable says about herself in *Framley Parsonage*, that she possesses "half a dozen millions of money—as I believe some people think" (*FP*, p. 447) was said of Thomas Holloway, the pill and ointment manufacturer who was described at his death in 1883 as having, "left an enormous property valued, perhaps with some exaggeration, at some five million pounds sterling."[15] Holloway himself commented that, "As regards my business I have certainly done very well, but it is ridiculous to see what the papers say about my wealth."[16] These exaggerated images of his wealth came into being because of his extraordinary success. The son of a baker and publican in Penzance, Holloway began making pills and ointments in his kitchen in 1837. Realizing that the key to his success would be promoting his product, Holloway committed himself to producing a series of advertisements that, as we will see, became icons of Victorian commercial culture[17]; his "annual advertising expenditure rose from £5,000 in 1842, to £10,000 in 1845, £20,000 in 1851, and £40,000 in 1863."[18] "In 1883, the year of his death, he invested a staggering £50,000, which resulted in the return of an equal sum as clear profit. This

---

the transition to a mature market economy brings with it" (Jonathan Freedman, *The Temple of Culture: Assimilation and Anti-Semitism in Literary Anglo-America* [New York: Oxford University Press, 2000], p. 60).

[15]   Quoted in "The Victorians and the Pill," *Sunday Times Magazine*, (18 February 1968): 43.

[16]   Quoted in Harrison-Barbet, p. 74.

[17]   Since these endorsements were written by Holloway and his product was designed largely to have nothing harmful in it, Holloway's business would have been an instance of what John Ruskin calls, "'lying label, title, pretence, or advertisement'" (*Unto This Last and Other Writings* [London: Penguin, 1985], p. 190). For an overview of nineteenth-century attitudes toward advertising see Regenia Gagnier, *Idylls of the Marketplace: Oscar Wilde and the Victorian Public* (Stanford: Stanford University Press, 1986), pp. 52–6.

[18]   John Elliot, *Palaces, Patronage and Pills: Thomas Holloway: His Sanatorium, College and Picture Gallery* (London: Royal Holloway, 1996), p. 3. Trollope cites Holloway's advertising expenditure as £30,000 p.a. in *The Struggles of Brown, Jones and Robinson* (Oxford: OUP, 1992) p. 185.

would be equivalent to over a million pounds today."[19] This process generated an amount of wealth so enormous that it seemed as if Holloway was virtually minting money, which he literally did in 1857 (the year before Trollope's ointment heiress made her first appearance in *Doctor Thorne*), issuing currency tokens the size of old penny and halfpenny pieces that bore his profile and the legend "Professor Holloway, London."[20] He was, as the writer of his obituary in *The Times* put it, "one of that remarkable class who seemed destined to become rich, who roll wealth together in a way which ordinary men fail either to follow or understand."[21]

Holloway's career showed quite clearly how, as John Henry Newman put it in his sermon on the danger of riches, "Money is a sort of creation and gives the acquirer, even more than the possessor, an imagination of his power."[22] Holloway himself consciously realized this power in global terms, explaining, of the early part of his career, that, "in the end [I] succeeded in creating for my preparations a limited reputation throughout the British Isles. This might have satisfied me at one time, but as our desires increase with our success, I made up my mind to be content with nothing less than the girdling of the Globe with depots of my remedies."[23] In Trollope's novels, the restless ambitions that drove Holloway are triggered by the wealth of the ointment heiress which elicits desire in suitors because, as the narrator comments, "we all know, from the lessons of our early youth, how the love of money increases and gains strength by its own success" (*DT*, p. 218). In Holloway's case, that restless desire led him to paper the world with advertisements for his product,[24] translating its description into "a multitude of languages, including Arabic, Chinese, Armenian, Turkish, Sanskrit, and 'most of the vernaculars of India.'"[25] Depicting Chinese emperors and Arabian chieftains enjoying

---

[19]   Harrison-Barbet, p. 28. For a list of the fortunes made from the sale of nostrums in the nineteenth century see W.D. Rubinstein, pp. 80–81. For a discussion of patent medicine advertising in the period following Holloway's success see Thomas Richards, "The Patent Medicine System" in *The Commodity Culture of Victorian England: Advertising and Spectacle, 1851–1914* (Stanford: Stanford University Press, 1990), pp. 168–204.

[20]   Caroline Bingham, *The History of Royal Holloway College 1886–1986* (London: Constable, 1987), p. 27.

[21]   Quoted in 'The Victorians and the Pill," p. 43.

[22]   John Henry Newman, "The Danger of Riches," in *The Works of Cardinal Newman in Eight Volumes, Parochial and Plain Sermons*, vol. 2 (London: Longman, Green and Co., 1902), p. 335.

[23]   Quoted in Bingham, p. 20.

[24]   Posters for Holloway's Pills and Ointments were plastered beside the Great Pyramids of Egypt and Niagara Falls; "It was reported … that when a young lieutenant was asked what had struck him most about on first arriving in the Fiji islands he replied, 'Why, the placard posted on a pile of stones at the entrance to the harbor announcing the arrival of a hogshead of Holloway's Pills'" (Harrison-Barbet, p. 31).

[25]   Ibid.

the benefits of his pills and ointments,[26] Holloway created images that engendered the admiring relation between foreigner and English product they evoked. As he proudly explained, "'Among my correspondents I number Kings and Princes equally with other distinguished foreigners of all nations'. Indeed, King Mongkut of Siam (of 'The King and I' fame) was so pleased with 'the man who had been as it were the saviour of his country' that when an Embassy was sent to Queen Victoria Holloway was presented with an autographed letter from the King as a token of his esteem."[27]

His contemporaries understood Holloway's advertisements to be inviting consumers to worship not just his product as the one thing needful for their happiness, but also the man himself, the author of that product, as someone whose success gives him an almost godlike power. He was, in the words of the *Stockport Advertiser*, "Mr. Thomas Holloway, whose pills and ointments are household words in every civilized age, and uncivilized country in the world. In the Wilds of Tartary, the Siberian Desert, the celestial empire, yea the very mountains of the moon, are the praises of the great pilular deity Holloway sung, and his name blessed in every known and unknown tongue as the 'mighty healer.'"[28] The mocking tone of this characterization is reiterated in other reactions to the great millionaires of the period, as when Beatrice Webb describes the social reception of the South African diamond millionaire, Julius Wehner by insisting that, "there might just as well have been a Goddess of Gold erected for overt worship—the impression of worship in thought, feeling, and action could hardly have been stronger."[29] Both these passages tell us that the Victorian public did not need Matthew Arnold to tell them that the economic changes in the latter half of the century had led to "the honouring of a false ideal ... of wealth and station, pleasure and ease," a practice he describes as "worshipping ... Hebraistically, as a kind of fetish."[30] It was abundantly clear to Trollope's contemporaries that the financial successes of the period elicited a vexed admiration that they conceived of as fetishism that, as we will see, followed the patterns both of anthropological and psychological thinking.

In the case of Thomas Holloway, the uneasy link between commercial success and fetishism was made explicit in the African explorer Winwood Reade's story "Hollowayphobia."[31] The tale opens in language that might remind us of a Freudian

---

[26]   These representations were not limited to non-English-speaking peoples; "during the Civil War in the United States wounded Union soldiers could be seen on posters stretching out imploring hands for Holloway's Ointment" ("The Victorians and the Pill," 43).

[27]   Harrison-Barbet, p. 31.

[28]   Quoted in Harrison-Barbet, p. 75.

[29]   Quoted in F. M. L. Thompson, *English Landed Society in the Nineteenth Century* (London: Routledge, 1963), p. 300.

[30]   Matthew Arnold, *Culture and Anarchy* (New Haven: Yale University Press, 1994), pp. 118, 123.

[31]   Felix Driver discusses Reade's career, the short story, and Holloway's success in *Geography Militant: Cultures of Exploration and Empire* (Oxford: Blackwell, 2001),

Fig. 10.1   Cigarette card advertising the merits of Holloway's Pills (n.d.) side 1

2. ELEPHANT.

The largest quadruped now existing. It is found in India and Africa. It has a naked thick and wrinkled skin, of a dirty grey or blackish color, and is peculiar in having a long "trunk," which answers the same purpose as a man's hand and arm. It possesses marvellous intelligence, and, when tamed and trained, it is very useful in moving and carrying great weights.

EVERY GOOD NURSE

USES AND

RECOMMENDS

HOLLOWAY'S

Pills and Ointment.

Thousands of written Testimonials—from all quarters of the world—bear testimony to their

UNFAILING AND MARVELLOUS EFFICACY.

Manufactured only at 78, New Oxford Street, London; sold by all Chemists and Medicine Vendors.

Fig. 10.2   Cigarette card advertising the merits of Holloway's Pills (n.d.) side 2

case history with an Englishman, Archibald Potter, who suffers from excessive sensitivity; "it made him wretched to see certain sights or hear certain sounds, and instead of struggling against these peculiar feelings, he indulged them and nourished them, and finally they became his masters."[32] Tormented by men with their hats on sidewise, women in discordant colors, barking dogs, whistling boys, creeping plants, and men with purple noses, Potter concentrates his aversions in the advertisements for Holloway's pills that he sees displayed everywhere around him. Seeking to escape the omnipresent signs of a commercial culture that has made England great, Potter travels to Africa, settles in a pastorally reclusive village, and uses his wealth to enact the role of benevolent father. All goes well until his boots wear out and he needs to order replacements that come from England. Predictably, given both Reade's audience's knowledge of the enormous extent of Holloway's success and the psychic logic that says that everything you hold in aversion will automatically come back to haunt you, the boots arrive wrapped in an advertisement for Holloway's pills. After fainting dead away, Potter recovers to find the advertisement has vanished. Though he wonders whether he imagined it, he cannot remain in the village because it too is now permeated with what he abhors; "all it had contained, became an abomination in his eyes: the murmuring of the brook, which could be plainly heard at his house, and the crowing of the cocks sounded always like *Holloway's Pills! Holloway's Pills!*"[33] The signs of their material success threatened to mark everything that surrounded the Victorians.

Traveling deeper into Africa, Potter arrives at an even more remote location where the people have never had any contact with a European. Approaching the village, he sees on its purlieus a great tree, whose "branches [are] hung with human skulls and with streamers of white cloth," which he identifies as "a Fetish."[34] Here Reade brings what the Victorians understood to be the "primitive" practice of fetishism together with modern commercial practices as Potter discovers, when he approaches the tree, that what the Africans are worshipping is the advertisement for Holloway's pills that had wrapped his boots.[35] (It turns out that Potter's African

---

pp. 90–116, 209. Driver's book also contains images of Holloway's more imperial advertisements, p. 210.

32   Winwood Reade, "Hollowayphobia," in *The African Sketch-Book* (London: Smith, Elder, and Co., 1873), p. 172.

33   Reade, p. 181.

34   Reade, p. 184.

35   In *The Devil and Commodity Fetishism in South America* (Chapel Hill: University of North Carolina Press, 1980), Michael Taussig finds a self-conscious linking of fetishism to capitalistic practices in those oppressed by and resistant to capitalism. Reade's story suggests that those who derive their success from capitalist practices are also conscious of its interconnection with fetishism. For another discussion of Africa, Victorian advertising, and the practice of fetishism, see Anne McClintock, *Imperial Leather: Race, Gender and Sexuality in the Colonial Context* (New York: Routledge, 1995), pp. 181–9. She notes that "[t]he fetish emerged in the inhabited intercultural spaces created among the West African

guide, impressed by the intensity of Potter's reaction to the paper, had secreted it and sold it to the village elders, averring it was a powerful conduit to the gods.) Enraged at the ubiquitous power of the thing he seeks most to escape, Potter rips the offending paper from the tree and tears it to bits. At this juncture he is almost killed not so much because he has destroyed a sacred object as because its worship has brought wealth to an isolated and impoverished region. The Africans themselves understand the practice of fetishism to be a form of advertisement. After a series of negotiations in which it is unclear who is more credulous, the Africans or the European, Potter is ransomed and returns home where he finally takes the pills whose advertisements he has traveled halfway round the globe to escape. Swallowing the thing that threatened to swallow him, he finds, with the inverted logic of a psychological case history, that doing what you fear at last cures you of your phobia (think of Jimmy Stewart climbing the bell tower at the end of *Vertigo*). The pills finally relieve Potter of his excessive sensitivity after which he becomes a walking advertisement for Holloway's products, tirelessly testifying to their miraculous curative power.

Trollope and fetishism

Rather than alluding specifically to Holloway, as Reade does, Trollope introduces, in the novels in which the ointment heiress Miss Dunstable appears, a character contemporary readers would inevitably have linked with that visible public figure. In making this more general gesture, Trollope is able to invoke both the admiration and fears associated with the drives that enabled extraordinary economic achievements like Holloway's, the admiration that we see in descriptions of his life and the fear that is articulated in Reade's fictional response to that life. In Trollope's Barsetshire novels, Miss Dunstable functions as a medium through which others read the world of late Victorian commerce and their position in it, a position they know but do not necessarily wish to acknowledge. Trollope insistently invites readers to enjoy Miss Dunstable's irrepressible energy, to see her as "cramped for space in an inadequate role,"[36] and to "feel the vitality and appeal of her fast paced life."[37] Here he makes us feel the drive that enabled Holloway to create an enterprise that could be read as "a permanent embodiment of his vision, energy and genuine concern for his fellow men."[38] Miss Dunstable represents the powers

---

coast by new trade relations between cultures so radically different as to seem almost incomprehensible to each other" (p. 186). This is the region Reade describes in his story.

[36]   Elizabeth Bowen, "Suspense Without Mystery," in T. Bareham (ed.), *Trollope: The Barsetshire Novels* (London: Macmillan, 1983), p. 173.

[37]   John Kucich, *The Power of Lies: Transgression in Victorian Fiction* (Ithaca: Cornell University Press, 1994), p. 72.

[38]   Harrison-Barbet, p. 9. Holloway's modern biographer is describing the institutions Holloway founded in his will, a college for women and a sanatorium "'for the treatment of

and pleasures of commerce that Trollope's friend the economist Walter Bagehot praised when he argued that England contained "no sluggish capital." In it, "the whole machine of industry is stimulated to the maximum of energy"; "no country of great hereditary trade, no European country at least, was ever so little 'sleepy' to use the only fit word as England."[39] Miss Dunstable makes her first appearance in a Trollope novel insisting that, "'I am not to be fatigued.... Why, in May we came through all the way from Rome to Paris without sleeping," a rush, that, as she explains later, depended on "something about money matters.... Something to do with the ointment. I was selling the business just then'" (*DT*, p. 187). She epitomizes the restlessness that drove Holloway to expand his business until it became a world-recognized commercial enterprise.

Such energy was, however, also problematic because, as the writer for *The Times* put it in Holloway's obituary; it "demands the devotion of the whole man. Sleeping or waking, his thoughts must be absolutely surrendered to it. Every event must be looked at from the one single point of view of the money value which must be found in it."[40] It requires, in John Henry Newman's words, "the concentration of a mind upon some worldly object, which admits of being constantly pursued."[41] This is the concentration evoked in the Reade story not as a pursuit but as an experience of being pursued. Even Bagehot, though generally a whole-hearted advocate of English commerce, worried that this single-mindedness meant that England was beginning to be governed by, "the rule of wealth—the religion of gold. This is the obvious and natural idol of the Anglo-Saxon. He is always trying to make money."[42] In the Barsetshire novels Miss Dunstable is specifically associated with the worship of wealth. Shortly after she makes her first appearance in *Doctor Thorne*, Mrs. Proudie, the Bishop's wife, exclaims, "Idolatry is, I believe, more rampant than ever in Rome" (*DT*, p. 187). Because that statement is made immediately after Trollope's narrator has insisted, of Miss Dunstable, that, "mammon, in her person was receiving worship from the temporalities and spiritualities of the land" (*DT*, p. 186), we know that we are to identify such behavior with idolatry of the kind that so troubled critics of capitalism like John Ruskin. In the lecture on "Traffic" (1864) he excoriates his audience for worshipping "this idol of yours; this golden

---

the less prosperous middle classes'" (quoted in "The Victorians and the Pill," p. 43).

[39]   Walter Bagehot, *Lombard Street: A Description of the Money Market* (New York: John Wiley and Sons, 1999), pp. 125, 128, 10.

[40]   Quoted in "The Victorians and the Pill," p. 43.

[41]   Newman, p. 353.

[42]   Walter Bagehot, *The English Constitution* (Cambridge: Cambridge University Press, 2001), p. 69. While Bagehot praised commerce, he was also anxious because the new economic man was "never limited in his craving for wealth by any countervailing impulses, and this craving is by definition perpetually unappeased and unappeasable. He seeks not just wealth but infinite wealth. He will never have enough no matter how much he gets" (Christopher Herbert, *Culture and Anomie: Ethnographic Imagination in the Nineteenth Century* [Chicago: University of Chicago Press, 1991], p. 133).

image, high by measureless cubits, set up where your green fields of England are furnace-burnt into the likeness of the plain of Dura: this idol, forbidden to us, first of all idols, by our own Master and faith."[43]

Though Miss Dunstable is shown articulating the Ruskinian position when she insists that, "I would not sell one jot of liberty for mountains of gold" (*DT*, p. 240), and marries a man who "never worshipped wealth on his own behalf" (*DT*, p. 96), she is also shown evoking the desire to worship wealth that is captured in Ruskin's reference to the golden image that Nebuchadnezzar erected. Such images were typical of the way the worship of wealth was invoked in the period. One has only to think of Beatrice Webb's association of the diamond merchant Julius Wehner with a goddess of gold. The imagery Trollope's narrator uses to describe Barsetshire society as eager to be "seized" in the "golden embrace" of "this daughter of Plutus" (*DT* , pp. 162, 214) is thus echoed in a memoir of the period where Lady Dorothy Nevill describes contemporary reactions to the new commercial fortunes. She writes that in the 1860s and 70s English society realized that, "unless it swallowed the new millionaires, the millionaires, keen-witted, pushing, clever and energetic, would engulf it in their capacious maw. So everywhere doors were flung open for Croesus to enter."[44] Here we have the language of embrace that has become engulfment, and, in a reversal that might remind us of Reade's story, society is made to swallow something in fear of being swallowed by it. It is in the uneasy moment in which Nevill describes the social acceptance of the new millionaires that she shifts to referencing them in mythical terms. They are no longer men of money, but Croesus, as Miss Dunstable, when she is sought for her wealth, becomes no longer a woman of money but the daughter of Plutus. But Trollope also understands that language like this disavows the power of wealth by associating its worship with pre-Christian cultures and by identifying it with gold.

He uncovers the willed denial encapsulated in such classical images by having Miss Dunstable insistently remind her audience of the material presence and the social importance of money in late nineteenth-century society. Her name refers to the long straight road from London to Dunstable and means "direct, straightforward, plain, downright" (*OED*), also "plain speaking or language" (*OED*). In the space between the description of her being worshipped as mammon and Mrs. Proudie's comment about idolatry, Miss Dunstable speaks the first line she utters in any of Trollope's novels, telling its hero that her unfashionable curls will "'always pass muster ... when they are done up with bank-notes'" (*DT*, p. 187). Throughout the novels in which she appears she speaks directly about the wealth that her more socially elevated Victorian counterparts refuse to mention. She tells Mark Robarts, the vicar hero of *Framley Parsonage*, "'you clergymen are so proud—aristocratic would be the genteel word, I know—that you won't take the money of common ordinary people. You must be paid from land and endowments'" (*FP*, p. 60). As one of her interlocutors

---

43   John Ruskin, p. 249.
44   Quoted in Perkin, p. 69.

later tells her, "'You make one speak in such a bald, naked way.'" (*FP*, p, 297) Miss Dunstable makes her society aware of its fascination with and revulsion towards what Max Weber calls "naked economic power still bearing the stigma of its extra-status origin."[45] Though Asa Briggs has asserted that, "for Trollope the world of wealth was associated not with the creation of valuable real capital, but with senseless speculation, dangerous bubbles and 'the infamous trade of stock-jobbing,'"[46] Trollope's representation of Miss Dunstable, with its echoes of the real history life of Thomas Holloway, suggests how intensely the novelist was concerned to depict the impact "real capital" was having on Victorian society.

Briggs presumably came to the conclusion he did because the representations of the failures of commerce are so prominent in Trollope's novels, vividly captured in figures like Augustus Melmotte in *The Way We Live Now* and Ferdinand Lopez in *The Prime Minister.*[47] To focus solely on the male speculator figures in considering Trollope's representations of commerce is, however, implicitly to participate in the logic of denial that Trollope himself has depicted as characteristic of his culture. It is to insist that the commercial sector of society never really had power, that it was a place of loss and absence where wealth was just a fetish, as empty as the speculative projects that both Lopez and Melmotte offer their willing audiences. Yet the career of Thomas Holloway reveals that those projects that seem empty bubbles when they are proposed in Trollope's novels, could, in the late Victorian era, be fully realized. The whole process by which Holloway invented and sold his pills and ointments is perfectly captured in Lopez's descriptions of his plans for the product Bios, which, he argues, will be made into an enormous financial success,

> "By telling [people] that they ought to drink it. Advertise it. It has become a certainty now that if you will only advertise sufficiently you may make a fortune by selling anything. Only the interest on the money expended increases in so large a ratio in accordance with the magnitude of the operation! If you spend a few hundreds in advertising you throw them away. A hundred thousand pounds well laid out makes a certainty of anything."[48]

---

[45]   Max Weber, "Class, Status, Party," in *From Max Weber: Essays in Sociology* (New York: Oxford University Press, 1958), p. 193.

[46]   Asa Briggs, "Trollope, Bagehot and the English Constitution," *Cambridge Journal*, (1951–52): 331.

[47]   Wiener refers to Melmotte as an emblem of the "commercial values [that] were infecting and corrupting an older, quasi-feudal society" (p. 31). For a reading of Lopez see Audrey Jaffe, "Trollope in the Stock Market: Irrational Exuberance and *The Prime Minister*," *Victorian Studies*, 45/1 (Autumn 2002): 43–64. For discussions of both see Paul Delany, *Literature, Money and the Market: From Trollope to Amis* (Houndsmills: Palgrave, 2002), pp. 23–31.

[48]   Anthony Trollope. *The Prime Minister* (Oxford: Oxford University Press, 1983), vol. 2, p. 134.

Though Trollope's novel invites readers to dismiss these ideas as idle fantasies, he knows, and his Victorian audience knew, that there were instances where such strategies were made real.

By creating a Miss Dunstable as well as a Lopez and a Melmotte, Trollope evokes England's Janus-like reaction to the economic changes of the latter half of the nineteenth century, changes that involved fears and fantasies not just about the absence of wealth, but about its presence, as well. Trollope's representations might make us pause to rethink our general tendency, as critics writing about Victorian literature and economics, to focus on issues of debt and credit, of speculation and bankruptcy. In doing so we are, I would argue, concentrating on a gesture of fetishistic disavowal that denies the impact of commerce. Trollope's novels insist that that gesture was initially made to counter anxieties about the massive and visible material presence of non-landed wealth in late Victorian society. To return to the image from Hawthorne with which I began, I would suggest that readings of novels that emphasize the movement of debt and loss are, in some sense, the readings you get if you approach fictional representations of Victorian commerce from outside the glass case that Hawthorne describes. These readings are epitomized in the title of Andrew Miller's book *Novels Behind Glass*. But Trollope's novels invite us also to take into account the perspective of those who are in the midst of events, going busily to and fro, amassing goods and transacting financial exchanges. Using those figures to evoke the complexly ambivalent awareness that is experienced at the level of everyday life, Trollope's novels invite us to complement our distanced overview of the specters of Victorian capitalism with a close look at its practitioners' conscious understanding of their own material practices.

Chapter 11
Otherwise Occupied:
Masculine Widows in Trollope's Novels

Christopher S. Noble

> Widow: that great, vacant estate!
>
> Sylvia Plath[1]

> All true manhood consists in the defiance of circumstances.
>
> Charles Kingsley, *Historical Lectures and Essays*[2]

In an October 1857 *Westminster Review* article, George Meredith recommended *Barchester Towers*, praising its "masculine delineations of modern life" and approving it as "a novel that men can enjoy."[3] Much of this enjoyment, Meredith explains, derives from the intrigue of Eleanor Bold's widowhood:

> The plot is as simple as the siege of Troy. We are sure that Mr. Slope cannot succeed, or that if he is allowed to, another three volumes will confound him. We are equally convinced that the Widow Bold will never surrender to him, or that if she should, he will have to repent it equally. Nevertheless, our appetite for the closing chapters does not languish. We are anxious for the widow, and long to get her havened out of her perilous widowhood in fast wedlock ....[4]

Why does Meredith find widows so delectable and widowhood so perilous? His "appetite" cannot be fully explained by the tantalizing effects of narrative deferral found in traditional courtship plots, for he explicitly affirms the text's simplicity and transparency. Indeed, his self-assurance is authorized by an infamous intrusion in *Barchester Towers* itself, an intrusion which sabotages the suspense commonly relied upon to whet readerly appetite: "But let the gentle-hearted reader be under no apprehension whatsoever. It is not destined that Eleanor shall marry Mr. Slope

---

[1]   Sylvia Plath, "Widow," *The Collected Poems*, ed. Ted Hughes (Cutchogue, New York: Buccaneer Books, 1981), pp. 164–5.

[2]   Charles Kingsley, *Historical Lectures and Essays* (London: Macmillan, 1902), p. 203.

[3]   George Meredith, "Belles Lettres and Art," *The Westminster Review*, 68 (1857): 326–7. Originally an unsigned review. On Meredith's authorship, see R. C. Terry, *Oxford Reader's Companion to Trollope* (Oxford: Oxford University Press, 1999), p. 363.

[4]   Ibid., p. 327. Meredith himself married the widowed Mary Ellen Nicolls in 1849. She left him a year after the publication of this review.

or Bertie Stanhope."[5] Given all this open and easy confidence, what can explain Meredith's rapacious anxiety?

The apparent contradiction can, I believe, best be resolved by analyzing what Sylvia Plath called the "vacancy" of widowhood. To be vacant is not merely to be empty, but to have been previously occupied. Cultural representations of widowhood—far more so in Trollope's nineteenth century than in Plath's twentieth—construe the death of a husband not as a past event but as an active and ongoing loss. For Victorian widows vacancy was a vocation, requiring bodily entombment in crape and prolonged social seclusion.[6] In cultural (though not legal) terms the Victorian widow continued to be married to her husband long after his demise, her identity subsumed in his absence; loss was her occupation.

In *Barchester Towers*, then, the allure of marrying a widow despite these cultural obstacles compensates for the abandonment of ordinary narrative suspense, and this explains why Meredith's response to the novel is at once blasé and eager. As a reader, Meredith shares a chummy confidence with Trollope's narrator: he knows Eleanor will not marry either of the "wrong" men. Because Eleanor is a widow, however, it is impossible to guarantee that she will marry the "right" man. In this way, her vacancy helps to account for what Meredith sees as the "masculine" tenor of Trollope's text. As scholars such as James Eli Adams and John Tosh have shown, mid-Victorian constructions of manliness demanded frankness in speech and action, studied self-possession, a willingness to overcome adversity and an ability to—in Charles Kingsley's words—"defy the circumstances."[7] *Barchester Towers* is, for Meredith, "a novel that men can enjoy" because Arabin's precarious masculinity is tested and validated not by overcoming the relatively insignificant obstacles of unworthy rivals, but by surmounting the far more daunting barricade of widowhood. Eleanor's vacancy seems designed, first, to promote narrative appetite and, second, to bolster the manly prowess of the successful suitor.

In this essay, however, I would like to propose that vacancy assumes a third, less visible, function: it evokes masculine[8] performances not only from the suitors,

---

[5]   Anthony Trollope, *Barchester Towers*, eds. Michael Sadleir and Frederick Page (Oxford: Oxford University Press, 1996), vol. 1, p. 143.

[6]   For an excellent resource on Victorian mourning rituals, see John Morley, *Death, Heaven, and the Victorians* (Pittsburgh: University of Pittsburgh Press, 1977).

[7]   See James Eli Adams, *Dandies and Desert Saints: Styles of Victorian Manhood* (Ithaca: Cornell University Press, 1995), p. 95. See also John Tosh, *Manliness and Masculinities in Nineteenth-Century Britain* (Harlow, England: Pearson Longman, 2005), pp. 94–6.

[8]   Tosh asserts that the terms "masculine" and "masculinity" did not begin to denote the "interiority of being, or feeling a man" until the end of the nineteenth century, arguing that the word "manliness" served that function in the mid-Victorian period (see *Manliness and Masculinities*, pp. 24–5). "Masculinity," Tosh believes, "had a much more restricted meaning, denoting the legal prerogatives of the male sex (such as primogeniture)." However, Meredith's use of the word "masculine" in 1857 to describe the quality of Trollope's prose

but from the widows as well. Unlike maids and spinsters, Trollope's widows are culturally authorized to exhibit what the Victorians would have recognized as "manliness." With grief as her official occupation, and assuming that she had the money to support her position, a widow's self-possession and her will to "defy the circumstances" could equal or surpass her suitor's.[9] Writing in 1884, the American Mrs. John Sherwood remarked on the peculiar independence and agency conferred by widow's weeds: "A mourning dress does protect a woman while in deepest grief against the untimely gayety of a passing stranger. It is a wall, a cell of refuge. Behind a black veil she can hide herself as she goes out for business or recreation, fearless of any intrusion."[10] John Harvey, in his analysis of nineteenth-century men's clothing, suggests that the ubiquitous use of the color black constituted masculine power-dressing, carrying associations not just of "wealth and financial authority" but also of "spirituality and spiritual power," culminating in a "politics … of the spirit."[11] It is little wonder then that some Victorian widows persevered in their mourning, using it to appropriate male privilege and authority. In narrative terms, this unusual authority introduces a disruptive alternative into traditional courtship plots. It raises the specter of an unmarried, sexually experienced, legally independent woman who, far from laboring under a social obligation to marry, is authorized to assert exactly the opposite: the "duty" to remain faithful to a corpse. In Victorian society, upper-class widowhood was the closest approximation of male privilege available to women, a fact that helps to explain Queen Victoria's own celebrated refusal to lay aside her weeds.

At the same time, however, the strenuous demands of deep mourning etiquette aimed to disarm this nascent masculinity by removing widows from society altogether. As Sophie Gilmartin has shown, Victorians exhibited profound anxiety over the cultural implications of such strict mourning regulations.[12] In 1837, for instance, an early number of *Bentley's Miscellany* published a satirical "Chapter on Widows," which intimated that, "it is very well known, that, though maids

---

would seem to blur Tosh's proposed distinction between the terms. Nevertheless, in this essay I prefer to use the terms "masculine" / "masculinity" when referring to my twenty-first century analysis of Trollope's texts and "manly" / "manliness" when referring to the way Victorians described their own gender constructions.

[9]   This importance of class must not be overlooked here. The gendered masculinity I am describing was available only to upper-class widows. For middle and lower-class widows, "manly self-possession" was nearly impossible, because they lacked the financial wherewithal to assert their independence from close male relatives. See Cynthia Curran, *When I First Began My Life Anew: Middle-Class Widows in Nineteenth-Century Britain* (Bristol: Wyndam Hall Press, 2000).

[10]   Mary Elizabeth Sherwood, *Manners and Social Usages* (New York: Harper and Brothers, 1884), pp. 188–9.

[11]   John Harvey, *Men in Black* (Chicago: University of Chicago Press, 1995), pp. 14–15.

[12]   Sophie Gilmartin, "The Sati, the Bride, and the Widow: Sacrificial Women in the Nineteenth Century," *Victorian Literature and Culture*, 25.1 (1997): 141–58.

are wooed, widows are not. The first time a woman marries is very frequently to please another; the second time, invariably herself.... "[13] As the essay proceeds to consider unmarried widows, however, the satire merges violent misogyny with a scathing lampoon of Victorian attitudes:

> We do occasionally encounter some "*rara avis in terris*"—a middle-aged widow who thinks nothing of further matrimony; and so convinced are we of the "dangerous tendency" of such characters, that we would at once consign them to perpetual imprisonment. If they declared their resolution in time, we would undoubtedly try it, by burying them with their first lover, or burning them Hindoo fashion; for, supposing them to have no children, to what possible good end can they propose to live? It is our firm belief that they know too much to be at perfect liberty, with safety to society; and they must of necessity be so thoroughly idle, beyond knitting purses and reading novels, as to make mischief the end and aim of their existence.[14]

The "dangerous tendency" remarked on by the *Bentley's* writer recalls the "perilous widowhood" of Meredith's essay in the *Westminster Review*. Like the hypothetical specimen of the unmarrying widow, Eleanor Bold's widowhood is "perilous" because her vacancy puts her "at perfect liberty"; because of her sexual experience, she presumably "knows too much" for a male reader's comfort. Her widowhood effectively makes her a bachelor. The masculine potential of her widowhood therefore threatens, however briefly, to destabilize the comfortable predictability of the courtship plot. In order for men to enjoy Trollope's novel, then, wedlock should indeed be "fast"—immediate and ironclad. Indeed, since the seventeenth century, folk wisdom had declared that widows should be wooed quickly and brazenly precisely because of their sexual experience, a logic which derives from medical opinions that young widows who "lye fallow ... feele within themselves a frequent titillation, their seed being hot and prurient"[15] and which features prominently in Jacobean stage comedies. Trollope, however, does not merely recycle this longstanding imperative to redeploy the supercharged sexuality of widowhood. Rather, he exploits it as a comic principle throughout *Barchester Towers*, employing it to ruffle complacent Victorian attitudes about gender roles. Christopher Herbert, in his study of Trollope's adaptation of Jacobean stage comedy, has suggested that "the most anachronistic-seeming element of his fiction turns out to be basic to its most riskily modern lines of thought and its most inventive artistic experimentation."[16] Trollope's improvisations on the

---

[13]   "A Chapter on Widows," *Bentley's Miscellany*, 2 (1837), pp. 485–94.

[14]   Ibid., pp. 490–91.

[15]   Quoted in Jennifer Panek, *Widows and Suitors in Early Modern English Comedy* (Cambridge, UK: Cambridge University Press, 2004), p. 6.

[16]   Christopher Herbert, *Trollope and Comic Pleasure* (Chicago: University of Chicago Press, 1987), p. 9.

clichés of merry widowhood constitute just such an experiment, one which draws on the comic masculinity of stock characters, but which gradually transforms that masculinity into a version of Victorian manliness, especially manliness struggling to purge itself of melancholy. In order to map that transformation in the remainder of this essay, I propose first to examine a crucial scene in the widow-hunt subplot of *Barchester Towers*[17] more closely, and then to compare the representation of Eleanor to that of three major widow characters in the Palliser novels: Mrs. Greenow, Emily Lopez, and Madame Max Goesler.

Though her adherence to conventional Victorian mourning makes her an extremely unlikely candidate for merry widowhood, Eleanor nevertheless becomes identified with that figure in the narrative intrusion following the scene in which she strikes Slope across the face for proposing to her. The narrator's defense of Eleanor functions by anticipating and then only partially contradicting suspicions that she has been a closeted merry widow from the start:

> And now it is to be feared that every well-bred reader of these pages will lay down the book with disgust, feeling that, after all, the heroine is unworthy of sympathy. She is a hoyden, one will say. At any rate she is not a lady, another will exclaim. I have suspected her all through, a third will declare; and she has no idea of the dignity of a matron; or of the peculiar propriety which her position demands. At one moment she is romping with young Stanhope; then she is making eyes at Mr. Arabin; anon she comes to fisty-cuffs with a third lover; and all before she is yet a widow of two years' standing. … She cannot altogether be defended; and yet it may be averred that she is not a hoyden, not given to romping, nor prone to boxing. … Had she lived longer under the rule of a husband she might, perhaps, have saved herself from this great fault. (*BT*, vol. 2, p. 144–5)

But few readers are likely to regard Eleanor's "miniature thunder-clap" as a serious fault, least of all Meredith, who quips that Slope "cannot move without inspiring nausea even in the female bosom (for it is notorious how much that sex can bear.)"[18] Her physical rebuke of Slope, steeped though it is in farce, constitutes a masculine posture. The narrator is therefore quick to douse the threat of Eleanor's "little hand" in a wash of sensual femininity: "Ladies' hands so soft, so sweet, so delicious to the touch, so grateful to the eye, so gracious in their gentle doings, were not made to belabour men's faces" (*BT*, vol. 2, p. 146). Yet, by mounting a formal and conspicuous, but patently exaggerated and overweening defense of Eleanor's femininity, the narrator's intrusion calls into question not the propriety of her behavior, but the defensibility of the conventions that forbid it. In this passage, Eleanor plays the literally slapstick role of the lusty widow rejecting an unworthy suitor, and this stock figure of stage comedy clashes with

---

[17]   *Barchester Towers* will hereafter be referred to in citations as *BT*.

[18]   Meredith, p. 327.

the morbid, dignified, matronly widow of Victorian expectations, a woman who remains sexually dormant until miraculously regenerated years after her husband's death. Trollope implicitly asks us to consider which fiction is more ridiculous, all the while relying on the difference between them to sustain the interest of his own narrative.

Jane Nardin has argued that *Barchester Towers* constitutes a "conservative comedy," and that it stands as the last bastion of Trollope's faith in conventional Victorian gender roles prior to his adopting a more progressive attitude in the novels following *The Belton Estate* (1865). According to Nardin, "the pattern of Eleanor's story reinforces the conventional terms in which, all along, the narrator has analyzed it; there seems no reason to read its conclusion ironically."[19] Without question, the logic of the plot is designed to chasten Eleanor, to teach her how not to be a man. When Charlotte Stanhope confirms the depth of her folly and self-deception, Eleanor determines "that she would never again take any man's part" (*BT*, vol. 2, p. 152), a wonderfully theatrical turn of phrase that indicates both that she intends to refrain from further participation in men's debates and that she will strive to tailor her performance to more closely reflect Victorian norms. She will, we presume, now take the part of a woman. Indeed, the narrator confirms as much when, after her engagement, he proclaims that she will "once more assume the position of a woman" (*BT*, vol. 2, p. 240), implying that the assertiveness displayed during her widowhood had been an abortive detour into masculinity.

I believe it is a mistake, however, to conclude that the novel therefore endorses a wholesale embrace of convention. Rather, Trollope achieves his literary effect by playing one form of conservatism against another. *Barchester Towers* may indeed be conservative comedy, but it is not a comedy that straightforwardly *reinforces* conservatism; it is a comedy *of* conservatisms. In the particular case I have been exploring, the patriarchal seventeenth-century convention that seeks to justify the immediate reincorporation of widows into marriage conflicts with the patriarchal nineteenth-century convention that seeks to delay their remarriage indefinitely. One conservatism demands that widows remarry as quickly as possible; the other insists that they share their husband's death, rendering remarriage unthinkable. The contradictory conventions emerge from a shared cultural drive to defuse the masculine potential of moneyed widows, and Trollope employs both to create his comedy, without attempting a synthesis between them, and without offering a third alternative. The resulting gender ambivalence—Eleanor's "masculinity" and the "femininity" of Bertie, Slope, and Arabin—can hardly be termed progressive, but neither is it complacent. D. A. Miller offers a powerful analysis of these gender dynamics when he points out that

> the gentleman-woman and the lady-man in Trollope are not symptoms of a
> patriarchy in disarray; nor do they imply a critique of the established gender

---

[19]   Jane Nardin, *He Knew She Was Right: The Independent Woman in the Novels of Anthony Trollope* (Carbondale: South Illinois University Press, 1989), p. 39.

code or an invitation to transsexual experimentation. Rather, they are the raw material for that massive stereotyping which, turning them into remainders of the gender norms they seem to transgress, makes radical transgression impossible. The virago, the siren, the "independent" woman … are roles in the patriarchal image-repertory as stock as the ladies' man, the henpecked husband, the feckless father.… Trollope develops these with an easy confidence—as though it were not an emergency measure, but the routine task of liberal patriarchy to contain therein the dynamic that might otherwise issue in female "feminism" and male "homosexuality."[20]

For Miller, then, masculine performances by women in *Barchester Towers*, widows or otherwise, are to be understood as patriarchal safety valves that allow anxieties to be performed as fantasies so that they need never be acknowledged as opportunities for genuine revolt. But Miller, it seems to me, both underestimates the complexity underlying Trollope's "easy confidence" and overestimates the threshold of transgression. In faulting *Barchester Towers* for balking at the prospects of radicalism, Miller asserts the same liberal pastorship over novels that Trollope applied to characters. If only *Barchester Towers* had produced a suffragette Eleanor and an unequivocally gay Arabin, then we could have been proud of it, Miller implies—as if those hypothetical characters would not have been stereotypes too. Radical transgression is an elusive standard, for limits cease to be radical the moment they are transgressed. Although it operates within conventional limits, Trollope's "easy confidence" arises not simply from the orderly replication of stock types, but additionally, as we have seen, from the juxtaposition of *incompatible* patriarchal stock types in the same character (merry widow vs. matronly widow, neither of which is properly "feminine"). Trollope's portrait of Eleanor contemplates patriarchy's tendency to parody itself. Miller is surely correct that the mere presence of masculine women or feminine men in Trollope's fiction does not constitute a *de facto* critique of Victorian gender ideology. We find in Eleanor's widowhood, however, an impasse of "masculine women" stock types. While this no doubt falls short of a "radical transgression," it does generate the kind of shady, second-rate transgression that parody entails: a nagging inability to determine which version of liberal patriarchy is ultimately in charge. Trollope does not produce stereotypes in *Barchester Towers*; he overproduces them. Consequently, the critical desire to determine whether Trollope's novel reinforces or erodes patriarchal attitudes is actually an effect of the very novel being analyzed, and indeed this helps to explain why readers continue to find it appetizing, even when their tastes differ so markedly from those of the *Westminster Review*.

The blend of "masculine women" types, the negotiation between merry and morbid, between widows who assert the power to pursue men and widows who assert the right to ignore them, can be seen operating in much more sophisticated

---

[20]   D. A. Miller, *The Novel and the Police* (Berkeley: University of California Press, 1988), pp. 140–41.

ways in the major widow characters of the Palliser series. Unlike in *Barchester Towers*, however, the internal contradictions of the merry widow type are increasingly somber, even tragic. As the series progresses, the exaggerated aggression of merry widows—their frank sexuality, their tendency to consume husbands with serial efficiency, their mercenary scheming, their lack of grief for the husbands left in their wake—that is, all the qualities which made them appear comic because "unwomanly," come gradually to be transformed by Trollope into a form of pragmatic manliness, opposed to the affectations of Victorian custom: an openness, directness, and a freedom from melancholy which men themselves would do well to adopt. In the Palliser novels Trollope contemplates widowhood as a credible, though certainly not a foolproof, model for transforming loss into social power and, as such, it becomes an idealized strategy for overcoming obstacles that many of the male characters themselves attempt but fail to surmount. Widows are thus the "men" that gentlemen only wish they could be.

Even in the case of Trollope's merriest widow, Mrs. Greenow, conventional comedic themes are leveraged into a bid for socially meaningful agency. Although she does attempt to accelerate her mourning, Mrs. Greenow nonetheless luxuriates in her widow's weeds and even imbues them with bourgeois sexuality:

> Kate was surprised to see that real tears—one or two on each side—were making their way down her aunt's cheeks. But they were soon checked with a handkerchief of the broadest hem and of the finest cambric. ... The charm of the woman was in this,—that she was not in the least ashamed of anything that she did. She turned over all her wardrobe of mourning, showing the richness of each article, the stiffness of the crape, the fineness of the cambric, the breadth of the frills,—telling the price of each to a shilling, while she explained how the whole had been amassed without any consideration of expense. This she did with the pride of a young bride when she shows the glories of her trousseau to the friend of her bosom.[21]

It is tempting to dismiss Mrs. Greenow, whose handkerchief is always at the ready, as a figure of serious social commentary. She is, after all, the main character of the comic subplot. Trollope himself seems to harbor this casual opinion of her, writing of her in the *Autobiography* merely as "very good fun."[22] She is that, certainly, but she is also one of the most independent characters in the Palliser novels, male or female. She is comic, but the joke is never finally on her. Her tears are "real," but their predictability and relative scarcity show that they are carefully controlled. She submits to traditional mourning weeds, but transforms them into commodities. Ultimately, she is not a widow but a "bride": she is married not to

---

[21]   Anthony Trollope, *Can You Forgive Her?*, ed. Stephen Wall (London: Penguin, 1972), pp. 102–3. Hereafter abbreviated in citations as *CYFH*.

[22]   Anthony Trollope, *An Autobiography*, eds. Michael Sadleir and Frederick Page (Oxford: Oxford University Press, 1999), p. 180.

any man, but to herself, to the identity of widowhood, a fact which changes little when she determines to marry Bellfield, whose eventual death always remains in view. Even after her engagement, we read that "Mrs. Greenow … put her handkerchief to her eyes, and Alice observed that that which she held still bore the deepest hem of widowhood. They would be used, no doubt, till the last day, and then put by in lavender for future possible occasions" (*CYFH*, p. 804). As we saw with *Barchester Towers*, Trollope's experimentation with merry widowhood, his technique of drawing one kind of patriarchal cliché into conflict with another, functions as a parodic overproduction of the courtship plot. There are too many husbands and only one true bride, who is also her own groom. Over 30 years ago, George Levine argued that the impetus behind *Can You Forgive Her?* directs its readers inexorably toward an acceptance of the status quo. For Levine, Trollope's "myth of realism" seeks always to convince us that "wisdom resides in learning the rules of society and acquiescing in them."[23] In Mrs. Greenow's case, this judgment appears only half right, for while she learns the rules perfectly, she surely does not acquiesce. The narrator's assurance that she "was quite a pattern wife" (*CYFH*, p. 99) while married to Mr. Greenow accrues much greater complexity in the later chapters, since it is her mastery of patriarchal "patterns" that allows her to manipulate them:

> I believe that she had not sinned in her dress against any of those canons which the semi-ecclesiastical authorities on widowhood have laid down as to the outward garments fitted for gentlemen's relicts. … But there was that of genius about Mrs. Greenow, that she had turned every seeming disadvantage to some special profit, and had so dressed herself that though she had obeyed the law to the letter, she had thrown the spirit of it to the winds. (*CYFH*, p. 426)

In Judith Butler's terms, Mrs. Greenow wears her mourning as drag.[24]

If Mrs. Greenow's performance of widowhood has an antipode in the Palliser novels, it is surely Emily Lopez, whose character and narrative retain no comic traces. Instead of accelerating her mourning, she refuses to leave it until cajoled and bullied into accepting Arthur Fletcher. Her words of "acceptance" are, "I should disgrace you,"[25] which Arthur takes as formal consent. Emily Lopez's widowhood makes audible the silent dissent implied in many of Trollope's proposal scenes,

---

[23]   George Levine, "Can You Forgive Him?: Trollope's *Can You Forgive Her?* and the Myth of Realism," *Victorian Studies*, 18 (1974): 6.

[24]   According to Butler, "drag … effectively mocks both the expressive model of gender and the notion of a true gender identity." My suggestion is that Mrs. Greenow's weeds are similarly parodic, denaturalizing the conventions of mourning by exploiting them to their logical extreme. See Judith Butler, *Gender Trouble: Feminism and the Subversion of Identity*, 10th Anniversary Edition, (New York: Routledge, 1999), p. 174.

[25]   Anthony Trollope, *The Prime Minister*, ed. David Skilton (London: Penguin, 1994), p. 685. Hereafter cited as *PM*.

enacting a defiance that connects her to similar but less obvious resistance exhibited by other unmarried female characters. Emily's widowhood allows her to "defy the circumstances" of courtship far more openly, for instance, than Alice Vavasor. While Mrs. Greenow's story shows that the courtship pattern can be troubled by an exaggerated performance of the merry widow type, Emily's shows that the same result can be achieved by overacting morbid propriety. Whereas Greenow infuses her widow's weeds with sexual charm, Emily becomes a gothic figure, a "black shade—something like a dark ghost" (*PM*, p. 589); indeed, her dress absorbs her body: "her very face and limbs had so adapted themselves to her crape, that she looked like a monument of bereaved woe" (*PM*, p. 594). And yet, the very excessiveness of her mourning has the effect of elevating her self-possession. Because Ferdinand Lopez is so hated by her family, everyone refuses to call her "Mrs. Lopez," and of course she is no longer "Miss Wharton," so she can only be called "Emily"—neither her husband's nor her father's name can endure. While her brother can suggest that she reduce the severity of her mourning, he cannot force her to do so. Her physical appearance cows other women, like Mrs. Parker, into submission. In response to one of Arthur's unsuccessful marriage proposals, she rebuffs him with a direct challenge to his own manliness as well as an implied promise of her own, "Be a man and conquer your love,—as I will" (*PM*, p. 643).

Between these two extremes—Mrs. Greenow exemplifying the comic masculinity of widowhood and Emily the tragic—stands Madame Max Goesler. From the moment Trollope introduces her at one of Glencora's "semi-political dinners," she is described, both by the narrator and by other women, in masculine terms: "She seemed to intend that you should know that she employed [her eyes] to conquer you, looking as a knight may have looked in olden days who entered a chamber with his sword drawn from the scabbard and in his hand."[26] Her clothing is "unlike the dress of other women," and although it is fashionably black, it conforms neither to the merry exactitude of Mrs. Greenow nor to the morbid entombment of Emily, but instead produces the effect of color, in erotically untraceable threads:

> In colour she was abundant, and yet the fabric of her garment was always black. My pen may not dare to describe the traceries of yellow and ruby silk which went in and out through the black lace, across her bosom, and round her neck, and over her shoulders, and along her arms, and down to the very ground at her feet, robbing the black stuff of all its somber solemnity, and producing a brightness in which there was nothing gaudy. (*PF*, vol. 2, p. 26)

During her first encounter with Phineas Finn, she proposes all the topics of conversation, and asserts a desire to "out-Turnbull Mr. Turnbull, to vote for everything that could be voted for ... " (*PF*, vol. 2, pp. 26–7). On the question of marriage, she refuses the Duke of Omnium and then herself proposes to Phineas, an

---

26   Anthony Trollope, *Phineas Finn*, ed. Jacques Berthoud (Oxford: Oxford University Press, 1982), vol. 2, p. 25. Hereafter cited as *PF*.

Fig. 11.1   "You must come." Millais's illustration for *Phineas Finn*, Chapter 57

overture which, as Deborah Denenholz Morse has argued, places her "on the verge of enacting her equality with men by assuming the masculine role in a traditional sexual ritual…. "[27] Indeed, Shirley Letwin's assessment of Madame Max as "the most perfect gentleman in Trollope's novels"[28] is easy to confirm, though it is complicated by the xenophobic ways in which Trollope allows other characters to describe her. Even those descriptions, however, seem to enhance her physically masculine features, if not her gentlemanliness. For instance, at an early stage in their relationship, Glencora sees in Madame Max a "black-browed, yellow-visaged woman with ringlets and devil's eyes, and with a beard on her upper lip" (*PF*, vol. 2, p. 216). Similarly, in *Phineas Redux*, Laura Kennedy, stung by the ruin of her own marriage, describes Madame Max as "this strange female, this Moabitish woman…this unfeminine upstart."[29] Against such accusations, however, the narrator consistently exerts counterbalancing moral correctives: "poor Lady Laura wronged her rival foully…" (*PR*, vol. 2, p. 225). Even if Madame Max is not a perfect gentleman—she sports a "wicked smile" when rebuffing Mr. Maule (*PR*, vol. 2, p. 265)—she embodies the Victorian manliness ideal more completely than most of Trollope's male characters.

Although Madame Max's masculinity has long been recognized, the relationship between her widowhood and this gendered characterization has not. In Madame Max Trollope creates a main plot female character who blends contradictory widow types: she is merry and proper, foreign and domestic, light and dark, open and opaque. The masculine implications of this equilibrium, however, are fully realized only when they are thrown into sharp relief by Phineas Finn's psychological imbalance and self-proclaimed "unmanning" following his acquittal in *Phineas Redux*.[30] In this episode, it is Phineas who acts the part expected of a widow, waxing melancholic and withdrawing from society. Emotionally drained, Phineas himself joins a chorus of other voices who view his behavior as feminine, flatly stating, "I am womanly" (*PR*, vol. 2, p. 250).

---

[27]   Deborah Denenholz Morse, *Women in Trollope's Palliser Novels* (Ann Arbor: UMI Research Press, 1987), p. 79.

[28]   Shirley Letwin, *The Gentleman in Trollope: Individuality and Moral Conduct* (Cambridge,Massachusetts: Harvard University Press, 1982), p. 74.

[29]   Anthony Trollope, *Phineas Redux*, ed. John C. Whale (Oxford: Oxford University Press, 2000), vol. 2, p. 225. Hereafter cited as *PR*. "Moabitish" refers not only to Madame Max's vaguely Semitic identity but also to her remarkable agency as a woman. The term connects her to Lot's oldest daughter, who arranges incest with her father and subsequently gives birth to Moab in Genesis 19. More distantly, "Moabitish" may allude to the biblical Ruth who lived in the land of Moab. Like Madame Max, Ruth becomes a widow who pursues a new husband in a foreign country. The King James Version styles Ruth as "the Moabitish damsel" (Ruth 2:6).

[30]   It should be noted that Trollope's construction of Phineas's manliness is further linked to questions of Irish identity, much as Madame Max's seems connected to her foreignness. For a full consideration of this issue, see Mary Jean Corbett's essay, "'Two Identities': Gender, Ethnicity, and Phineas Finn," in this volume.

In order to defend Phineas from these feminizing accusations, however, Trollope interrupts the narrative with an extended discourse on the definition of manliness, concluding that "manliness is not compatible with affectation," and defining affectation as "the self-conscious assumption of any outward manner" (*PR*, vol. 2, pp. 252). Such affectations, Trollope argues, destroy the qualities essential to manly subjectivity, an imagined balance between social relations on the one hand— "faithful to friends, unsuspicious before the world, gentle with women, loving with children, considerate to his inferiors, kindly with servants, tender-hearted with all"—and disruptive individuality on the other: "frank, of open speech, with springing eager energies" (vol. 2, pp. 252). Crucially, by dissociating manliness from the cavalier values of physical strength and stoic reserve, and by aligning it with the middle-class liberal values of self-improvement and self-expression, Trollope rewrites manliness as a largely androgynous ideal, theoretically available to both men and women.

Furthermore—and here is a crucial point—Madame Max gains special access to this redefined manliness not merely because she is a woman of property, but also because she is a widow, and thus *formally* vacant, occupied by loss rather than by a husband. That is to say, her widowed status authorizes her to appropriate male social roles (such as the detective role she plays in Prague) and to inhabit the idealized manly subjectivity championed by Trollope (she is "faithful to friends" and "springing with eager energy"). By contrast, Glencora, who possesses greater financial resources than Madame Max, looks impotent. Confronted with the possibility of Phineas's execution, Glencora merely threatens to go into mourning for him: "If,—if,—if this ends badly for Mr. Finn I'll wear mourning to the day of my death. I'll go to the Drawing Room in mourning, to show what I think of it" (*PR*, vol. 2, p. 189). Thus, while Glencora craves the symbolic power that widowhood conveys, Madame Max practices it. Investigating Mr. Bonteen's murder in Northumberland Street, she "deal[s] out sovereigns—womanfully" (vol. 2, p. 144), a fascinating adverb suggesting equivalence with "manfully," a word used elsewhere in the novel to describe work and consumption: "Sir Gregory, with his two assistants, went through his work manfully" (vol. 2, p. 32). When the search for evidence leads to Prague, Madame Max remarks on her own superior independence: "You would do as much, Duchess, if you were as free as I am" (vol. 2, p. 150). By the same token, Laura Kennedy—though a widow by the time of Phineas's trial—is a widow too late. Because her husband has died recently, she is still encumbered by the full weight of her widow's weeds, and is therefore unable to mobilize the advantages of her new status. She can only listen to the news of Madame Max "spending her wealth, employing her wits, bearing fatigue," much as a "manly man" might do for a woman he loved. (vol. 2, p. 224) By contrast, Lady Laura visits Phineas in prison, wearing such deep mourning that he cannot even recognize her at first: "womanlike, she had gone to him in her trouble" (vol. 2, p. 225). For Trollope, it would seem, there is a world of difference between "womanlike" and "womanfully." Indeed, this difference between Madame Max and Lady Laura dramatizes the Victorian ambivalence about widowhood: it could empower or suffocate.

Although Madame Max represents the pinnacle of widowhood's masculine potential in Trollope's novels, many other of his widowed characters seem masculine, I think, because Trollope positions them in opposition to the "affectation" he identifies as the one quality manliness cannot abide. He approves of widows who can, like manly men, assert their self-possession without resorting to affectation. It is remarkable that, despite their diverse characterizations, and despite the rigorous mourning conventions widows were forced to observe, Mrs. Greenow and Emily Lopez are both noted for their lack of affectation. Kate Vavasor, repenting of her first impressions of Mrs. Greenow, remarks in a letter to Alice, "With all her absurdities I like her. Her faults are terrible faults, but she has not the fault of hiding them by falsehood" (*CYFH*, p. 169). Everett Wharton's patronizing evaluation of Emily is similar: "Women are generally superficial,—but some are honestly superficial and some dishonestly. Emily is at any rate honest" (*PM*, p. 22).

Trollope's tendency to create masculine widows is motivated, finally, by an impulse to champion liberal agency against the demands of social affectation, to uphold self-possession against imposed fictions of mourning. In the *Autobiography*, Trollope reports taking terrible vengeance on a volume of Samuel Johnson's *Lives of the Poets*, throwing it out of his apartment window and into the back door of the Marylebone Workhouse "because [Johnson] spoke sneeringly of *Lycidas*" (p. 53). Johnson had complained that Milton's elegy was rife with affectation, that its overt and self-conscious mourning belied its authenticity: "Where there is leisure for fiction there is little grief."[31] Though Trollope surely concurs that fiction is incompatible with grief, he apparently could not abide the accusation that the mourning of *Lycidas*—one of his favorite poems—was mere rhetorical posturing. This aversion to affectation forges a link between mourning and manliness, both of which, in Trollope's thinking, are invalidated by posturing. Trollope's widows are thus at their most manly when they master their weeds, when they defy the circumstances of enforced affectation in which they found themselves every day.

---

[31]   Samuel Johnson, *Lives of the English Poets* (London: J. M. Dent and Sons, 1925), pp. 95–6.

PART 4

The Gender of Narrative Construction

Chapter 12
Trollope at Fuller Length:
Lord Silverbridge and the Manuscript of
The Duke's Children[1]

Steven Amarnick

Few fictional babies—and perhaps few real ones, either—emerge to the kind of fanfare and relief that greet the son of Plantagenet and Glencora Palliser at the end of *Can You Forgive Her?* That he is a son, of course, and not a mere child, is hardly incidental. "Yes, my bonny boy,—you have made it all right for me;—have you not?" Glencora tells "the small, purple-born one" not long after his birth.[2] Though for an alarmingly long time, Glencora had shown no signs of even being able to become pregnant, she well knows that producing a healthy baby is not nearly enough to make things "all right." Her tiny "mannikin" (vol. 2, p. 415) may not act much different from any other infant, of whatever sex, but that he is the healthy male heir to the future Duke of Omnium means the pressure is off. "I shall dare to assert myself, now" (vol. 2, p. 416), Glencora declares. And indeed she does, or tries to—with enormous vivacity—through the next four books of the Palliser series.[3]

[1]   I am indebted to the PSC-CUNY Research Foundation for a grant that allowed me to research this article, and to the staff of the Beinecke Library for making it a pleasure to study not only the manuscript of *The Duke's Children* but the many other Trollope manuscripts in its possession. My title is taken from Gordon Ray's important 1968 article, "Trollope at Full Length," *Huntington Library Quarterly*, 31 (1968): 313–40, which argues that Trollope's greatest works are his longest, and also that it is only by looking at the full breadth of Trollope's career—including the excellent work of his final years—that Trollope's achievement as a master of the English novel can be appreciated.

[2]   Anthony Trollope, *Can You Forgive Her?* 1864 (Oxford: Oxford University Press, 1982), vol. 2, p. 415. See Deborah Denenholz Morse, *Women in Trollope's Palliser Novels* (Ann Arbor: UMI Research Press, 1987), pp. 21–2, for a discussion of both this passage and the telling illustration—reprinted here—that accompanied it.

[3]   Though Trollope did not consider *The Eustace Diamonds* to be part of the series, Glencora and Plantagenet play a small role in the novel, and it has long been recognized as the third Palliser novel, after *Can You Forgive Her?* and *Phineas Finn,* and before *Phineas Redux*, *The Prime Minister*, and *The Duke's Children.*

Fig. 12.1   "Yes, my bonny boy, – you have made it all right for me." E. Taylor's
                   illustration for *Can You Forgive Her?*, Chapter 80

In a stunning move at the beginning of *The Duke's Children*, the sixth and final Palliser novel, Trollope announces Glencora's sudden death.[4] Throughout the series, we have seen plenty of the Pallisers, but almost nothing of them as parents. It is Plantagenet, now the Duke of the book's title, who will fumble along trying to deal with the grown-up heir and his two siblings, the youngest of whom is 19.[5] And while these two youngest, Mary and Gerald, do not change appreciably through the course of the novel, the bonny baby now known as Lord Silverbridge goes through many subtle transformations as he becomes more of his father's son. In the way his character is shaped and re-shaped, Silverbridge dominates the story—at least as much as the Duke himself—resulting in Trollope's most vibrant, nuanced, and fully realized portrait of what he regards as a new masculine ideal. Biological maleness is all that matters for Silverbridge at the beginning of the series; at the end, it is the kind of man he becomes that is given a full-scale exploration.

No doubt, what I have described above sounds like a puzzling account of *The Duke's Children* to those who know the novel well. For I am referring to the never-published original manuscript, written between May and October of 1876, and housed at the Beinecke Rare Book and Manuscript Library, Yale University.[6] Trollope himself cut this manuscript in April and May of 1878, and in some ways succeeded brilliantly in the task. With a mandate from Charles Dickens Jr., editor of the periodical *All the Year Round*, to reduce the length of the novel by about a quarter, Trollope kept all 80 chapters intact, making no structural changes. Instead, he looked for extraneous language—cutting a word or two wherever he could, a sentence, a paragraph, occasionally a page; occasionally, several pages. What was to have been a book published in long monthly installments for 20 months was transformed into a novel that would appear weekly between October 1879 and July 1880, after which it was published by Chapman & Hall in three volumes rather than the originally planned four.[7]

Trollope's final version of *The Duke's Children* flows smoothly from start to end, with no gaping holes causing us to suspect the hand of an awkward novice editor, and with far tighter, leaner prose than we might expect from him. Yet the novel as a whole suffers. Subtleties of characterization are lost, many references to earlier parts of the Palliser saga disappear, and Trollope's unique genial narrator forges a less distinctive relationship with the reader. The book becomes more depoliticized, and crucial matters of pacing are altered. And while neither version of *The Duke's Children* has nearly the same elegiac tone as *The Last Chronicle of Barset*, Trollope's finale to his other major series, the original manuscript conveys

---

[4]   Anthony Trollope, *The Duke's Children* 1879 (Oxford: Oxford University Press, 1999), p. 1.

[5]   Three siblings at first, as the early pages of the original manuscript show, but he quickly decided that two would be enough.

[6]   This can be found in the Chauncey Brewster Tinker Papers, General Collection.

[7]   See N. John Hall, *Trollope: A Biography* (Oxford: Clarendon Press, 1991), pp. 418–19.

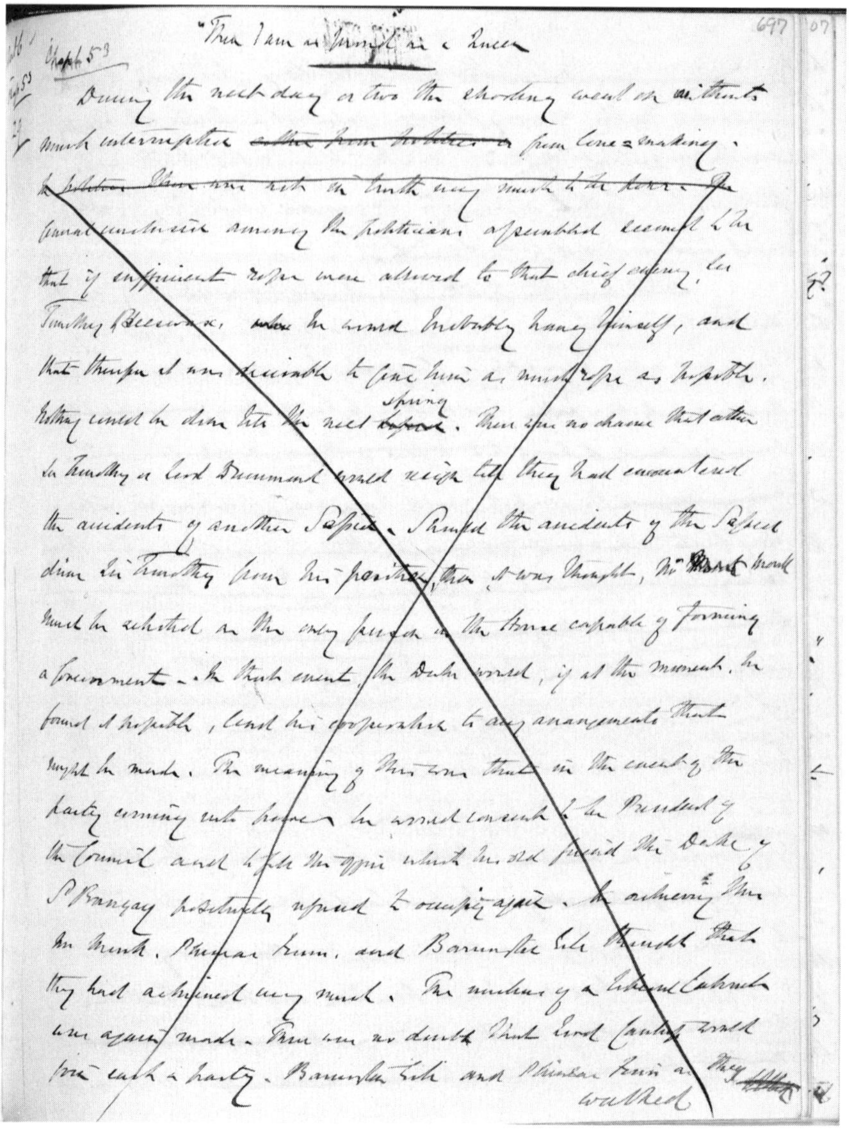

Fig. 12.2   Trollope's manuscript of *The Duke's Children*, first page of Chapter 53

a far greater sense of monumentality than the published version, more befitting the conclusion of such an ambitious group of works.[8]

Far from being an early version of a novel that was always meant to be revised, the original manuscript is more representative of Trollope's painstakingly developed practices. I will begin by looking at some of the important ways the edited manuscript suffers, and then turn my attention more fully to what is perhaps the most significant loss in the published novel: the diminished presence of Lord Silverbridge.

My first point might seem superficial, yet appearances do matter. Even before we open one page of the final novel of Trollope's other series, that book announces its importance by its sheer massiveness. The title helps too, *The Last Chronicle of Barset* being the final weighty tome in a series filled with many other chronicles. By contrast, the slimmed-down *Duke's Children* seems to offer less promise of monumentality, of epic grandeur.

Moreover, a bulkier *Duke's Children* makes a certain thematic sense. For the book is in part about the Duke resisting various truths—most notably, that he will have to give his blessing to the marriages of his children, or earlier in the novel, that he will have to admit to Mrs. Finn how shabbily he has treated her. But he also resists reckoning with other not inconsequential matters: his past deficiencies as a father, and, most particularly, the deficiencies of his marriage. When his acceptance of these truths is delayed, his plight becomes even more poignant. He is a man who knows he must adapt but who does not want to. As he forestalls the inevitable, there is great power in seeing the novel (and the Palliser series) itself resisting inevitable closure through a couple of hundred additional pages.

To be sure, whatever gains there are in a delayed climax or the appearance of monumentality would be overshadowed if the novel were simply dragged out with mindless filler or numbing repetition. But that is not the case. Some of the cut passages, while not deeply significant, are hugely entertaining, such as the comments the narrator makes in Chapter 70 about dining.[9] It may be that the more we are reminded of the narrator, the more we are reminded of Trollope, so that

---

[8] Though scholars have from time to time taken a look at the original *Duke's Children* manuscript, the prevailing view has been to praise Trollope's editing and to bemoan the loss of only a very few passages. One exception is J. W. Bailey's "*The Duke's Children*: Rediscovering a Trollope Manuscript," *Yale University Library Gazette* 57.1–2 (October 1982): 34–8, which states: "One has the sense that the manuscript is like a balloon from which some air has been released: the overall shape remains, but the size and density are diminished" (p. 36). The most extensive discussion of Trollope's cuts appears in Andrew Wright's "Trollope Revises Trollope," in *Trollope Centenary Essays* (New York: St. Martin's, 1982), pp. 109–33, an article that examines a number of Trollope manuscripts. See also note 13 below.

[9] The narrator begins: "There can I think be no doubt that, as an opportunity for social gatherings, lunches are a mistake. It may be that nature requires that such a meal should be made; and if so, it is of course convenient that the inhabitants of one and the same house should eat it in company. But it should never become a convivial gathering and should

his own reluctant need to say goodbye to the Pallisers and to move on has greater resonance. In *The Last Chronicle of Barset*, the connection between the narrator and the author is made explicit in the emotional leave-taking of the final pages. In *The Duke's Children* there is no such farewell at the end, even in the original manuscript, but there are perhaps greater echoes of a farewell when the narrator's presence is more noticeable throughout the novel.[10]

Overall, Trollope did not cut a huge number of passages featuring remarks from the friendly intrusive narrator. Where there *are* extensive cuts is in the political dimension of the novel. This can be seen starting with the very first paragraph, which originally contained a passage about the Duke's own tenure as Prime Minister and about what happened after his coalition was broken up. Perhaps the most obvious place to see the cumulative depoliticizing effect of Trollope's cuts is in Chapter 53, which originally began, "During the next day or two the shooting went on without much interruption either from politics or from love-making," but which appears without the reference to politics in the revised version, and without the account of just where those politics stood. The result of such cuts is a less sweeping canvas in the novel as a whole and an unfortunate shift in the balance between public and private.[11]

In addition, while the published version retains many references to previous occurrences in the Palliser series, there are far more such references in the original version. Often, these passages do not merely remind us of something that happened previously but also contribute to the novel's, and the series', psychological richness.[12] For instance, in the first chapter Trollope deleted a passage in which the grieving Duke thinks first of calling upon Alice Grey, known more familiarly to us as Alice Vavasor from *Can You Forgive Her?*. This raises immediate questions

---

be partaken only by those who use it as the simple mode of obtaining the nourishment necessary to them."

[10] This lack of a finale has caused some readers to wonder if Trollope even intended *The Duke's Children* to be his last Palliser novel. I would speculate, though, that popularity is the key factor in this matter. That is, in the late 1860s, Trollope's many readers were more than glad for him to keep churning out Barsetshire novels. To resist this temptation—and the artistic stultification that he feared—Trollope gave the series an elaborate send-off; after such a farewell, he knew it would be embarrassing to attempt another Barsetshire novel, even if he somehow changed his mind eventually. On the other hand, a decade later there was no such clamoring for another Palliser novel, and Trollope might have found it presumptuous, and unnecessary, to deliver a lofty farewell.

[11] All who have written on *The Duke's Children* in the last half-century are indebted to John H. Hagan's "*The Duke's Children*: Trollope's Psychological Masterpiece," *Nineteenth-Century Fiction*, 13 (1958): 1–21. It is worth noting, however, that Hagan begins the article by talking about the "perfunctory" political element in the novel—a claim that is impossible to make when reading the original manuscript.

[12] See Lowry Pei, "*The Duke's Children*: Reflection and Reconciliation," *Modern Language Quarterly*, 39 (1978): 284–302, who writes that "the novel has a gigantic fictive past" (p. 284).

about why the Duke's first choice was not Mrs. Finn, the former Madame Max, who after all had become Glencora's closest friend and confidante, and whose husband is one of the Duke's closest political allies. We can suspect then quite soon—earlier than in the published manuscript—that the Duke has a vague, lingering distrust of Mrs. Finn. In an omitted passage from Chapter 13, when his anger at Mrs. Finn is still at its height, the Duke returns to the key events depicted in *Phineas Finn*, wondering "what else he had a right to expect from the mysterious widow of an unheard of old husband." That he demonstrates his continued awareness of her previous noble actions makes his thorough rejection of her all the more fascinating; years of accumulated knowledge count for nothing, as he so readily reverts to his initial prejudices.[13] In another deleted passage, from Chapter 26, the Duke thinks back to so many nights in his marriage when Glencora would go off alone after dinner while he would be "satisfied with blue books, newspapers, and speculations on political economy." This is not exactly news to those who have read the entire series; what is so powerful here is the narrator's comment that one is comforted, on a long trip, by knowing that one has packed a book to read, even when one never reads it—and in the same way the Duke had been comforted knowing that his wife was there. For though he "had never crossed the threshold of his wife's drawing room ..., now, when there was no longer a threshold that he could cross, he felt himself to be deserted." We are left to wonder just how much the Duke consciously regrets those lost opportunities on those many, many nights.

With all the many cuts, the most significant ones may well be those that affect the characterization and prominence of Lord Silverbridge. When Trollope was first writing the novel, he toyed with several different titles before settling on *The Duke's Children*. One of those discarded titles, *Lord Silverbridge*, would seem to make little sense ... until we review the original manuscript. In a novel filled with rich characters, only the Duke and his eldest son can be said to change significantly through the course of the story, in both versions.[14] The Duke's changes, however, are less dramatic. He is a fully grown man, set in his ways, who must learn to budge because of the new situation he faces as a widower and because of the demands his children make. Silverbridge, on the other hand, is presented to us early in the novel as having, according to Lady Mabel (who at first appears likely to marry him), the

---

[13] In the footnotes of her chapter on *The Duke's Children* in *Trollope's Palliser Novels: Theme and Pattern* (London: Macmillan, 1978), Juliet McMaster mentions the uncut manuscript several times, pointing out, among other things, both Alice Grey's greater visibility in that manuscript and the stronger evidence of the Duke's buried prejudice.

[14] I differ slightly here from McMaster, who argues that Frank changes too (pp. 149–51). More significantly, McMaster writes that the Duke's changes make a far greater impact on the reader, to the point where the novel becomes a "bildungsroman [in which] the hero who receives the education is a middle-aged man" (p. 141). I believe that McMaster is correct about the way the Duke dominates the text—but only insofar as the published manuscript is concerned.

potential "of being made into a man—in the process of time" (p. 128); he becomes wholly a man only at the end, when he switches his political allegiances from the Conservatives to the Liberals and marries the American, Isabel Boncassen. Too much of that maturation process is rushed or minimized or lost in the edited version because of the cuts that Trollope made.[15]

And it is not only scenes in which Silverbridge appears that matter, as cuts made with other characters play an important role in how we perceive him, too. For instance, Major Tifto in the original, while maintaining the same flaws that ultimately lead him to drive a nail into the foot of Silverbridge's racehorse, is seen in a more positive light, so much so that his story originally ends with him accepting an annual stipend from Silverbridge but then marrying the daughter of a publican; when his father-in-law dies, Tifto inherits the business, makes a good living, and is able to tell Silverbridge that he no longer needs the money from him. Such a gesture on Tifto's part would not fit the edited manuscript, where he comes across as more sniveling, and indeed the last we hear of him is that Silverbridge will give him the stipend forever. What is lost is a richer understanding of why Silverbridge was drawn to him in the first place. It is far easier to see, in the original version, how Silverbridge might be lured by someone like Tifto; because he has so minimal a relationship with his own father, he is in need of some kind of father figure.

Silverbridge's friend Frank is, if not a father figure, an elder brother figure, and though Trollope withholds his affection for Frank—which I will say more about later—it becomes clear fairly early in the narrative that he will not be a terrible match for the Duke's daughter, that he is not another Burgo Fitzgerald— Glencora's true love before she was forced to marry Plantagenet—as the Duke fears. In the original manuscript, though, it takes longer for us to see that Frank is a safe husband for Mary, that he is far more strong and sober-minded than the feckless Burgo, who almost surely would have ruined Glencora's life had the two been allowed to marry. One struck passage shows Mrs. Finn deciding, after a first meeting, that he is utterly unworthy of Mary—and since Mrs. Finn is never wrong, we too are led to believe at first that Frank might be a scamp. We still are told, at the end of Chapter 4, about the "chilling note" (p. 33) that he has sent Mrs. Finn, but the chapter no longer ends dramatically with her damning assessment of him. Another cut shows that Frank did far better than expected at school—which would ordinarily be to his credit, except that yet another deleted passage shows him to

---

[15]   In his article "Trollope and the Fixity of the Self," *PMLA*, 93 (March 1978): 228–39, Christopher Herbert argues, I think rightly, that the Duke makes "adjustments" rather than fundamental changes, whereas Silverbridge demonstrates "a capacity for supple growth and change." Herbert continues: "To show how Trollope renders Silverbridge's acquisition of 'age and flavour' page by page … would require masses of long quotation, for the whole effect lies in fine nuances" (p. 238). I agree that those nuances exist in the published version, even if many have been eliminated; however, the impression Silverbridge makes on the reader is severely diminished, for reasons that I discuss in the following pages.

be not only lacking in direction but also unwilling to put in much effort to get anywhere. Frank's mindset is akin to that of a wealthy aristocrat, and we suspect that the only way that he will live up to his image of himself will be to marry a wealthy girl.

As we wonder for a longer time about Frank, we wonder much more about Silverbridge too, about why he would befriend such a man. The longer Frank remains a mystery, then, the more unsettled Silverbridge's character is to us. This is a young man, after all, who was thrown out of Oxford for painting a dean's house scarlet. When we look at him early in the novel, is Silverbridge simply immature, or too irredeemably stupid not to recognize how unworthy his companions are? Ultimately, we see that he is not stupid at all; that even as an immature youth he chose well in befriending Frank, and that his choice of Tifto was not as thoroughly ridiculous as it may seem in the edited version. And so as our process of discovery regarding Silverbridge unfolds more gradually, his character takes up more of our thoughts.

The depoliticizing effect of Trollope's cuts in the manuscript, and the extent to which they reduce the richness of Silverbridge's characterization, come together in the unfolding of Silverbridge's political maturation. For Silverbridge's growing sense that he has made a mistake in abandoning the Liberal politics of the Pallisers runs parallel with his growing maturity. It also runs parallel with his father's growing sense that he must no longer hide away and instead must return to play an active role in the party. Whereas in the published version it is possible to see Silverbridge's switch to the Liberals as mainly a private matter, a peace offering made to his suffering father, the original version allows us to see him developing more as a political creature as well. As an example, while in the edited version we continue to be told how odious Sir Timothy Beeswax, the leader of the Conservatives, is, we are barely shown how this is so. Trollope cut one passage where Sir Timothy flaunts Silverbridge as a prize while ushering him into Parliament, and another passage where Sir Timothy claims that the Duke has basically written Silverbridge's letter declining the opportunity of speaking in Parliament. In the former example, we see Sir Timothy's crudeness; in the latter, we recognize his sneering inability to notice that Silverbridge is developing a mind of his own and that the Duke is too principled to interfere in such a manner. The more Sir Timothy, then, emerges as a real character and not just a stock figure, the more we see, in Silverbridge's rejection of him, a young man who for the first time is truly starting to think for himself. Of course, Trollope would never wish to write a novel in which all political virtue resided with one party and all vice with another; indeed, in another cut passage, Silverbridge comments privately on the phoniness of his Liberal opponent. However there is no question that, by the end of *The Duke's Children*, Trollope intended Silverbridge to have grown into a genuine Liberal like his father and like Trollope himself—an *advanced conservative* Liberal, to be sure, but a Liberal nonetheless.

As Trollope makes abundantly clear, in both his autobiography and *The Prime Minister*, both Liberals and Conservatives are necessary for the political process to work smoothly; it would be too dangerous if Liberals had all the power. Yet Liberals and Conservatives do differ, particularly in the matter of inequality between rich and poor; whereas Liberals believe in change and progress, Conservatives see 'the diminution of that inequality ... as an evil, the consummation of which it is his duty to retard.'[16] If Lady Mabel is a bit worn and stale and not quite right for Silverbridge, her staunch ties to the Conservatives are another part of the problem. With the intricate connection, in *The Duke's Children*, between the political world and the private world, it is understandable that Silverbridge takes his time to muddle through, to figure out who he is. We can regret, then, not only all the cuts that diminish the political dimension of the novel, but cuts that diminish the subtle process by which he works his way out of this muddle.

After all, Silverbridge has reason to be confused. Isabel Boncassen emerges as a perfect mate for him, but that does not mean Mabel would have necessarily been a disastrous alternative, only a vastly inferior one. Early in the book, we are made to believe that if Mabel were to marry Silverbridge, she would act as another of his mentors. In a passage from the published version, Silverbridge reflects on how she "would be his superior, and in some degree his master. Though not older she was wiser than he,—and not only wiser but more powerful also" (p. 148). What Trollope cut from the passage, however, is the notion that Silverbridge senses this problem without being able to put it into words; the "drawback" to Mabel is something "he had never as yet succeeded in defining." As a result, after the cut he comes across as more mature and thoughtful than he should be at this point in the narrative. A later struck passage from Chapter 27, while he still courts Mabel, shows him trying to convince himself that he does love her—and for the moment, he succeeds in persuading himself.[17] What remains in this part of the published version is his awareness that he must marry Mabel as a way of getting rid of Tifto; there is little thought of love. This occurs immediately before Silverbridge meets Isabel Boncassen for the first time—a meeting that is far more powerful if we feel that Silverbridge has as yet no *conscious* awareness that a marriage to Mabel will be one mainly of convenience, not love. For with Isabel the difference is palpable; only when he experiences a true connection with a woman can he understand what was missing beforehand. Had he married Mabel, Silverbridge might have been tolerably content—but he would not have discovered that best self which Isabel draws out of him.

For in each succeeding encounter with Isabel, we see Silverbridge growing more confident and mature; she brings out the best in him by treating him as an equal, not someone who under her tutelage will be molded. The first time they

---

[16] Anthony Trollope, *An Autobiography*, 1883 (Oxford: Oxford University Press, 1980), p. 293.

[17] "He had told the Duke that he had quite made up his mind, and the thing would be done. He was glad that it was so because he was sure that he loved her. Nothing ever was so pretty, so nice, so sweet as Mabel Grex,—or nobody ever so clever! And then he himself felt that he was a young man who ought to marry."

meet, in Chapter 28, almost all of the sparkling dialogue comes from her.[18] But gradually, he begins to hold his own, such as when he talks about a Lady Clanfiddle, and the "most melancholy catastrophe" that ensued when '[a] great spout of rain had come upon her daughter's hat' (p. 269). This sort of witty repartee would have been beyond his capabilities earlier in the novel, but now it seems natural as his self-confidence has blossomed. We miss, then, some of the repartee that Trollope deleted—and not only because of the omitted details but also because of the way the pacing is altered. Isabel and Silverbridge get together a little too quickly in the published version, and Silverbridge's road to full maturity is a bit too smooth. Moreover, the narrative develops more elegantly when Silverbridge's reluctance to give up so quickly on the wrong woman echoes more fully the greater struggle his father makes in reluctantly giving up his own wrong decisions.

Silverbridge's *process* of discovery and of change is emphasized, in the original manuscript, up to the final page, when we are told that "since his marriage [he] seemed even to his father to be much more of a man than he had been before." Also omitted are the final words of the novel, when the younger son, Gerald, says to Silverbridge, "It will be my turn next.... After what you and Mary have done, I think he must let me have my own way whatever it is." This original ending reminds us that while the maturation process may be nearly complete for Silverbridge, it has barely begun for his brother. The original ending also leaves us with the focus on the Pallisers—as is surely fitting for the Palliser series—and not, as it is in the edited version, on Frank and his supposed courage; those last words in the published edition are the Duke's, saying of his new son-in-law, "But now I will accept that as courage which I before regarded as arrogance" (p. 633).

Another important omitted passage near the end emphasizes just how tenderhearted Silverbridge is, as even amidst his celebrations he feels extraordinary compassion for Mabel, the woman left behind with bleak prospects ahead.[19] The comparison to Frank is glaring, as Frank simply does not have the same sort of sensitivity. And so too while Silverbridge has slowly come to understand his father's suffering, Frank has no such appreciation for the Duke; in the weeks leading up to his wedding, Frank peevishly dwells on how he has still not been fully embraced. Frank is not a bad man, and he does muster some pity for Mabel, but by the end of the novel he has been thoroughly outshone by Silverbridge, his former underling—a transformation that is vastly more dramatic and powerful in the original manuscript. Even if one wants to credit Frank with courage

---

[18]   This includes a deleted section in which Isabel makes teasing reference to her father's erudite connections, culminating with her comment that "[w]e always go to learned places;—never anywhere else. On the next evening there's a grand meeting of vivisectors. You won't be there I dare say."

[19]   For a fine extensive discussion of Mabel as a "tragic figure," see Morse, pp. 125–32. I would add that the more sensitive we are to Mabel's plight, the more Silverbridge's stature grows as well, as we admire his perspicacity and compassion.

and other manly qualities, his is a masculinity that is clearly devalued next to Silverbridge's.

For by the end of the original novel, Silverbridge has come to represent a new ideal—a soft-hearted, virile man, who can be both playful *and* serious, who relishes his enjoyments but who is also eager and ready to do good work in the world; who as an advanced conservative Liberal is comfortable with tradition and traditional roles but also open to genuine change; who in his marriage of equals with an American, the granddaughter of a common laborer, exemplifies the cosmopolitan spirit that is present in the Phineas novels as well, when the Irish Catholic male and the reputedly Jewish, foreign-looking female also make a union of equals while establishing a place for themselves at the center of English society. In his lengthy reflections on manliness in *Phineas Redux*, Trollope's narrator argues that the ideal man must be "faithful to his friends, unsuspicious before the world, gentle with women, loving with children, considerate to his inferiors, kindly with servants, tender-hearted with all,—and at the same time be frank, of open speech, with springing eager energies.'[20] Says Phineas after the murder trial that has nearly destroyed him, "I am womanly....I begin to feel it. But I can't alter my nature' (vol. 2, p. 250). Nor should he alter his nature. If such softness is labeled womanly, then the genuine man is womanly too.

It takes the trauma of the trial for Phineas to achieve his full growth and to become a mate fully worthy of Marie, but there is a sense that as successful as his marriage is, Phineas will always carry around some of the bitterness he felt when so many people thought him capable of not only murdering a man but then lying about it, too. Indeed, Marie's careful decision not to tell her husband about the Duke's casting her out, after the Duke has displaced blame onto her from his deceased wife for withholding information about Mary and Frank's courtship, makes it clear that Phineas is still capable of overreacting, of letting his anger overcome his better judgment. By the end of *The Duke's Children,* Silverbridge becomes as worthily masculine as Phineas is, but without the trauma; all of Silverbridge's "springing eager energies" are ready to help create a different world.[21]

With all that is lost in the shrunken manuscript, it is worth emphasizing, finally, just how settled Trollope's writing and editing practices were, and how the original *Duke's Children*, the one that he put aside after he first completed the book in 1876, represents the "real" Trollope—or at least the Trollope we know from his other published novels. In *An Autobiography* he talks about his rapid writing—250 words every 15 minutes, after 30 minutes spent looking over what he had done

---

[20]		Anthony Trollope, *Phineas Redux* 1873 (Oxford: Oxford University Press, 1983), vol. 2, p. 252.

[21]		For detailed discussions of Phineas's masculinity, see Morse, ch. 2; Robert Polhemus, *Erotic Faith: Being in Love from Jane Austen to D.H. Lawrence* (Chicago: Univeristy of Chicago Press, 1990), ch. 8; Margaret Markwick, *New Men in Trollope's Novels: Rewriting the Victorian Male* (Aldershot: Ashgate, 2007), ch. 6; and Mary Jean Corbett's article in this collection.

the previous day, for a total of three hours every morning. But he also defends his speed of composition, saying, "I believe that the work which has been done quickest has been done the best" (p. 174). Trollope admits that rapid writing can lead to many "errors," and that as a result he would "read everything four times at least—thrice in manuscript and once in print" (p. 178). But he is talking here about a very circumscribed kind of proofreading, not full-scale editing. In the autobiography, he refers mainly to fixing grammar mistakes. Though in practice he did more than that, it was only a bit more. He might delete or add (much more commonly the latter) a few words to clarify something, to bring out a character's essence, or to alter some other minor detail. He might change a few words for the sake of sentence rhythm or flow. And occasionally he might play with the dramatic effect of his chapter endings, either changing where a chapter would end, moving the previous ending to the beginning of a new chapter, or briefly adding something.[22]

Given how well Trollope's methods had worked for him, and given how long he had been putting these methods into practice, it seems astonishing that he would go along with anyone's insistence that he cut the manuscript significantly. Yet in 1878 when Charles Dickens Jr. requested that he do so for publication in *All the Year Round,* he acceded. We do not have Trollope's own explanation, for *The Duke's Children* was begun after *An Autobiography*, and despite returning to the manuscript of the latter several years later, he did not update the book to include accounts of what he had written since. But unlike *An Autobiography*, the reason for putting the novel into a drawer had nothing to do with plans for posthumous publication. The fifth Palliser book, *The Prime Minister*, had appeared while he was writing *The Duke's Children* and had received harsh reviews. Trollope might well have preferred to wait a few years before publishing *The Duke's Children* in the hope that there would be some kind of demand for another Palliser novel. When that demand showed no sign of emerging, he evidently felt that the offer by Dickens Jr. was good enough.

Yet Trollope's decision is still puzzling, for in *An Autobiography* he had proudly recounted the story of how, despite being relatively unknown, he stood up to his publisher. Though "Mr. W. Longman" wanted the three-volume *Barchester Towers* cut to two volumes, Trollope resisted, "declaring at last that no consideration should induce me to put out a third of my work." He then explains: "I am at a loss to know how such a task could be performed. I could burn the MS, no doubt, and write another book on the same story; but how two words out of every six are to be withdrawn from a written novel, I cannot conceive. I believe such tasks have been attempted—perhaps performed; but I refused to make even the attempt" (pp. 103–4). If Trollope can write so proudly in claiming to resist a publisher at a time in his career when he was still making his name, it is hard to imagine that he wouldn't

---

[22] I base these observations primarily on the manuscripts of *The Last Chronicle of Barset, Can You Forgive Her?*, *Phineas Finn*, and *Phineas Redux*, all in the Beinecke Library.

put up more of a fight with a novel that was such a major part of his legacy—even with the decline in his readership and hence his bargaining power.

Let me close, then, with this speculation. A still insufficiently appreciated aspect of Trollope's career is his carefully considered plan to stay fresh, to avoid having his late work become dull and mechanical. I think that Trollope was always looking for sensible opportunities to shake himself up, to do something very different,[23] and thus he decided to rise to the initially unwelcome challenge of significantly cutting a novel on a scale that he had never before attempted.[24] The fact that he was several years removed from having written *The Duke's Children* allowed him some emotional distance, too—enough to chip away at the kind of fierce attachment that would have made him as stubborn as he says he was when asked to cut *Barchester Towers*. And so he decided to *not* fight the battle of publishing *The Duke's Children* intact, thus bequeathing to us the extraordinary achievement that the well-edited *Duke's Children* is—and nonetheless leaving behind the even more extraordinary achievement of his original manuscript.

---

[23]   I write about one such moment—his leaving his full-time position at the post office—in "Why He Left the Post Office: Trollope, Dickens, and the Farewell Banquets of 1867," *Trollopiana*, 54 (August 2001): 18–23.

[24]   Trollope did make lesser cuts in two other novels: *The Three Clerks* for the 1859 edition, and *The Macdermots of Ballycloran* for the 1860 edition. As he wrote to his publisher Richard Bentley, "When you were about to bring out your 5/- edition of *The Three Clerks*, I reduced the book by about 60 pages, and I fear I should find it impossible to put out 100 more. It gives more trouble to strike out pages, than to write new ones, as the whole sequence of a story, hangs page on page—There is an episode—a story of some 40 pages in the three vol. edit., which I would put out if that would suit you— But even that wd. require some care as it is alluded to in different places." N. John Hall, ed., *The Letters of Anthony Trollope*, vol. 1, 1835–70 (Stanford: Stanford University Press, 1983), pp. 85–6. And for the later edition of *The Macdermots of Ballycloran*, Trollope's first novel, which was originally published in 1847, he removed three entire chapters.

Chapter 13
"Depth of Portraiture": What Should Distinguish a Victorian Man from a Victorian Woman?

David Skilton

Forty years ago, when I was writing about how Trollope's contemporary critics received his fiction, I sought to discover not principally which books they liked and which they disliked (a preoccupation that reveals remarkably little about the works in question), but rather something about how they read, and what assumptions they brought to the act of reading fiction, regardless of whether the value judgments they then passed on the basis of these assumptions were favorable or unfavorable to the author's sales prospects or self-esteem. One of the assumptions that I found shared by a good number of critics concerned the portrayal of fictional personages in works that they characterized as displaying what was then called "truth to life." The test that was applied was whether authors presented an "inside" to their characters as well as a social, visible "outside." The question had been largely unremarked by twentieth-century commentators, I discovered, because up to that date they largely shared the standards that these Victorian critics had handed down, and I found parallel assumptions not only among twentieth-century writers on Trollope, most notably David Cecil and Bradford A. Booth, but also in reviews of current fiction in the *Times Literary Supplement*.

Briefly put, the lack of "inward portraiture" (as it was often called) was held in the mid-Victorian period to preclude the presentation of the fundamentals of religious belief, and of certain emotions that, it was believed, could only be expressed in something analogous to lyric poetry. Later writers were more explicitly looking for evidence of a another ineffable, the subconscious, guessed at more or less poetically, and not indicated through action, conscious thought or behaviour. To some extent the critics I shall be quoting can be seen testing the relevance of Romantic theories of creativity to realistic prose fiction, and it is hardly surprising to find Carlyle early among those voicing these concerns. Writing in a pre-Victorian notebook, he worries about Scott's characterization:

> Is [the "poorest pauper"] not an INDIVIDUAL; and who shall explain all the significance of that word?—not one of Scott's Fairservices of Deanses &c. is alive. As far as prose could go, he has gone; and we have fair outsides; but within all is rather hollow, nicht wahr?—Alas! I do not see into this, and must

talk rather falsely of it, or 'altogether hold my peace,' which perhaps were better— .[1]

Carlyle's use of biblical phrasing (surely one senses an echo of Matthew 23:27)[2] suggests that what is missing is an indication of a soul or religious sense. Elsewhere Carlyle voices another aspect of the question of "depth" and "surface", this time in terms of what Lancelot Whyte influentially dubbed "the unconscious before Freud":[3]

> Of our Thinking, we might say, it is but the mere upper surface that we shape into articulate thoughts;—underneath the region of argument and conscious discourse, lies the region of meditation; here in its quiet, mysterious depths, dwells what vital force is in us; here, if aught is to be created, and not merely manufactured and communicated, must the work go on. Manufacture is intelligible, but trivial; Creation is great, and cannot be understood. Thus if the Debater and Demonstrator, whom we may rank as the lowest of true thinkers, knows what he has done, and how he did it, the Artist, whom we rank as the highest, knows not; must speak of Inspiration, and in one or the other dialect, call his work the gift of a divinity.

And then again:

> [T]hroughout the whole world of man, in all manifestations and performances of his nature, outward and inward, personal and social, the Perfect, the Great is a mystery to itself, knows not itself; whatsoever does know itself is already little, and more or less imperfect. Or otherwise we may say, Unconsciousness belongs to pure unmixed life; Consciousness to a diseased mixture and conflict of life and death; Unconsciousness is the sign of creation; Consciousness, at best, that of manufacture.[4]

The association of a lack of "inwardness" with "manufacture" is significant in that another strand in Trollope's early reception involves the supposition that as an author he undertakes a mechanical "copying," as distinct from an inspired creativity. Here again the culprit may be Scott, whose authority was held by some to sanction bad practice in rapid composition, and the clearest statement of this

---

[1]   Charles Eliot Norton (ed.), *Two Notebooks of Thomas Carlyle. From 23rd March 1822 to 16th May 1832,* (Mamaroneck, NY: Paul P. Appel, 1972), pp. 126–7.

[2]   "Woe unto you, scribes and Pharisees, hypocrites! for ye are like unto whited sepulchres, which indeed appear beautiful outward, but are within full of dead men's bones, and of all uncleanness" (Matthew 23:27).

[3]   Lancelot Law Whyte, *The Unconscious before Freud* (New York: Basic Books, 1960).

[4]   Thomas Carlyle, "Characteristics" (1831), in *Critical and Miscellaneous Essays,* (7 vols, London: Chapman and Hall, 1872), vol. 4, pp. 4 and 14.

position is found in *Main Currents in Nineteenth Century Literature* by the great Danish critic, Georg Brandes, who regrets that Scott bequeathed his practice of "rapid scribbling" to the rest of the nineteenth century, so that Victorian novelists, "with immense payments before their eyes, drove authorship forward like a manufacturing industry."[5] The implication in Brandes's statement, as in many of the reviews of Trollope's fiction, is that skilled writers were writing too much and of too low a quality, for the sake of earnings—a conclusion plausibly derived from Lockhart's account of Scott's efforts following his financial crash in 1826,[6] and easily generalized in such judgments as the following from the *Saturday Review*: "Of course, if Mr. Trollope only looks upon his art as manufacture, there can be no reason why he should not take as just a pride in turning so many novels out of his brain in the twelvemonth as a machine-maker takes in turning so many locomotives or looms out of his shed."[7] How such pronouncements have determined persistent misreadings of *An Autobiography* is too large a subject to take up here, but is part of a large complex of assumptions whereby Trollope was once disparaged for qualities that we now value, in the present instance, his characterization of women

Before developing my argument further, I wish to acknowledge that Trollope, in common with many Victorians, showed an unsystematic awareness of unconscious motivation, which hardly qualifies him as a Freudian precursor, but still, with our knowledge of what was to come, startles us with its clarity. In Chapter 43 of *Castle Richmond* (1860), for example, he has Lady Desmond write to her daughter, Clara, some time after she has renounced any hope of Owen Fitzgerald's love so that Clara may have him:

> My anxiety has been only for your welfare, to further which I have been willing to make any possible sacrifice." Clara when she read this did not know what sacrifice had been made, nor had the countess thought as she wrote the words what had been the sacrifice to which she had thus alluded, though her heart was ever conscious of it, unconsciously."[8]

My aim when I first worked on these questions in the 1960s was historical enlightenment, since I felt that we might gain new insights into Victorian fiction if we knew more about how readers as well as practitioners approached the act

---

[5] George Brandes, *Samlede Skrifter* (18 vols, Copenhagen: Gyldendal, 1899–1910), vol. 5, pp. 381–2: "[D]er var fra først af en stor Mislighed ved disse Romaners Frembringelsesmaade, en Mislighed, som i den følgende Tid gik i Arv til en hel Klasse af talentfulde Romanforfattere: det unkunstneriske Hurtigskriveri, der med umaadelige Honorarer før Øje drev Digtningen fabriksmæssigt som en Industri" (my translation).

[6] J. G. Lockhart, *Memoirs of the Life of Sir Walter Scott*, (7 vols, Edinburgh: Cadell, 1837–38).

[7] Review of *The Belton Estate*, *Saturday Review*, 21 (3 February 1866): 140–42.

[8] Anthony Trollope, *Castle Richmond*, (Oxford: Oxford University Press, 1989), p. 478.

of reading, and if we interrogated reviewers—professional readers who had read more of the fiction of the period than we could ever hope to do.[9]

Finding resistance to my approach, I did not then think of applying the ideas I had generated to problems that might face us in our reading today, even though it had originally been my project to do so. Recently, however, I found myself confronting yet again one of the oft-asked questions in Trollope studies: "How does it happen that an author who mocks systematic feminists and repeatedly has his narrator assert that marriage and child-rearing is the best career for a woman, is also thought by both non-academic women readers and by feminist commentators of the late twentieth century to present his female characters in a very acceptable way, which allows sympathy or identification without embarrassment, after the passage of well over a hundred years?"[10] Having heard this position supported by more than one practising woman novelist, I feel it appropriate to quote Joanna Trollope:

> Anthony Trollope was unquestionably in favour of marriage. He had two robust reasons for this, the first being that his own marriage—about which he was so maddeningly and stuffily reticent in his Autobiography—was a safe haven for him after the storms and tempests of his childhood. The second reason was a Victorian one; he knew that marriage was the best career open to the vast majority of nineteenth-century girls. He was not at all unusual in this, nor for being opposed to women's suffrage and professional opportunities, but he was unusual in his perception of, and admiration for, female independence of spirit.[11]

The explanation for the approval many modern women extend to Trollope's women seems to be that he in no way diminishes the mental processes of his women characters, however much, as a man of his age, he restricted their socio-economic activity not to mention their sexual activities. It is worth noting, too,

---

[9]   I found I could not share the belief current 40 years ago that one would discover all one wanted to know by concentrating on works and authors that were sanctioned for study by tradition or authority, and by the pronouncements of critics who were approved at whichever university one happened to attend. Finding in 1969–71 that my PhD examiners did not approve my approach, I launched my failed thesis on the world as a book, leaving it to mercy of such readers as it might attract, but not attempting to build on its ideas, which had appeared too petty or too unfamiliar in Cambridge. I must acknowledge the generous encouragement I received from Tony Tanner, Raymond Williams, and J. Hillis Miller, to the last of whom I owe a great debt of gratitude.

[10]   See, for instance, Deborah Denenholz Morse, *Women in Trollope's Palliser Novels* (Ann Arbor: UMI Research Press, 1987) and Jane Nardin, *He Knew She Was Right* (Carbondale: Southern Illinios University Press, 1989).

[11]   Joanna Trollope, "Foreword," in Anthony Trollope, *The Complete Short Stories*, (5 vols, London: The Trollope Society, [nd]), vol. 4, p. v.

that he did not object in principle to women earning a living. Obviously the family trade of authorship was a permitted occupation, to which he only objected when dishonestly conducted, as he would have objected equally to dishonest shoe-making. To judge from "The Telegraph Girl" (1878), and the note of pride which enters into his description of the fairly liberal working conditions in the telegraph office in St. Martin's-le-Grand, he even seems to have welcomed the availability of work for otherwise unsupported single women.

If one wants to assess his attitudes in terms of those of his contemporaries, a passage from a letter of 1874 by the artist, Charles Fairfax Murray, will be revealing. Murray is writing to his friend, William Spanton, who was at one time his fellow lodger in London, concerning their landlady's teenaged daughters: "I have never got over the interest that Clara & afterwards Emma excited in me some years ago—Clara especially I used to think a very nice girl until she went out to work ... She changed entirely afterwards, but doubtless still retains her prettiness."[12] The ability to negotiate the world beyond the domestic sphere makes the girl an unsuitable object of "interest," or perhaps too threatening to be an object of sentimental-cum-sexual desire. One wonders what the nature of Murray's "interest" was, and whether he understood it as we might. My point, however, is how distant this is from anything we know about Trollope in real life or in his presentation of women characters in his books. In "The Telegraph Girl", for example, the heroine, Lucy Graham, is not diminished as an attractive young woman by working and (more important in the story and for my thesis) by becoming self-reliant and living successfully in lodgings in London while having no support from any man. Indeed, as an admirably strong-minded young woman, she even turns down repeated offers of help from the man she later loves and marries, and moreover gains in attractiveness in the process. In a different social sphere in the fiction, we also remember that Madame Max conducts business on her own behalf without forfeiting her eligibility as wife to Phineas Finn, and that Shirley Letwin goes so far as to nominate her as the ideal "gentleman" in the Trollopian canon.[13] Besides, as Morse in her study of the Palliser novels makes clear,[14] Trollope was sensitive to the aspirations of his women, and his fiction is full of women who long for a place in public life, and who would clearly fill it better than their menfolk do theirs. When it comes to marriage as a career, many of his women, and not just the eponymous parson's daughter of Oxney Colne or Lucy Robarts, the vicar's sister of Framley, have a very clear measure of their own

---

[12]   Letter of 30 May 1874, quoted in *I Giardini delle Regine. Of Queens' Gardens: the Myth of Florence in the Pre-Raphaelite Milieu and in American Culture (19th – 20th Centuries)*, (Livorno: Sillabe, 2004), p. 175.

[13]   See Shirley Letwin, *The Gentleman in Trollope: Individuality and Moral Conduct*, (London: Macmillan, 1982).

[14]   Morse, *Women in Trollope's Palliser Novels*. See also Victoria Glendinning, *Trollope*, (London: Hutchinson, 1992) for an imaginatively realized account of his friendships with women of advanced opinions.

worth, and will not consent to be defined by the evaluations of their lovers and their lovers' families. Charles Fairfax Murray would certainly not do for them.

Trollope usually makes it clear that when it comes to real working relationships between the sexes, either partner may dominate, and that the Victorian ideal of womanly submission is a myth, and a potentially dangerous one at that:

> The theory of man and wife—that special theory in accordance with which the wife is to bend herself in loving submission before her husband — is very beautiful; and would be good altogether if it could only be arranged that the husband should be the stronger and the greater of the two. The theory is based upon that hypothesis;—and the hypothesis sometimes fails of confirmation. In ordinary marriages the vessel rights itself, and the stronger and greater takes the lead, whether clothed in petticoats, or in coat, waistcoat, and trousers; but there sometimes comes a terrible shipwreck, when the woman before marriage has filled herself full of ideas of submission, and then finds that her golden-headed god has got an iron body and feet of clay.[15]

It is no coincidence that he develops this idea most clearly in *The Belton Estate* (1865–66), a novel he wrote for the newly founded *Fortnightly Review*. He had been one of a group who late in 1864 had put up the money to launch a new periodical devoted to freedom of speech and opinion, "something on the plan of the Revue des Deux Mondes." This was to be "an organ for the unbiassed expression of many and various minds on topics of general interest in Politics, Literature, Philosophy, Science, and Arts," and unlike its competitors, it was to carry only signed articles and never allow opinion to shelter behind anonymity.[16] Its first editor was George Henry Lewes, who wrote for it a series of papers on literary realism, under the title *The Principles of Success in Literature*.

The Principles of Success in Literature is Lewes's most extended contribution to literary theory, and makes the most coherent case in the mid-Victorian period for realism as intellectually respectable, imaginative art. Lewes protests that the "imaginative power" of a work is "too frequently estimated according to the extent of *departure* from ordinary experience in the images selected." After all, he argues, it is a "psychological fact that fairies and demons, remote as they are from experience, are not created by a more vigorous effort of imagination than milkmaids and poachers."[17] On the contrary, he claims, "artistic power" is displayed in "the *selection of the characteristic details*" which make up the work of art, as materials from the artist's memory store undergo "a transformation" whereby

---

[15]   Anthony Trollope, *The Belton Estate*, (Oxford: Oxford University Press, 1986), p. 132.

[16]   N. John Hall (ed.),*The Letters of Anthony Trollope*, (Stanford: Stanford University Press, 1986), p. 298.

[17]   George Henry Lewes, *The Principles of Success in Literature*, ed. T. S. Knowlson, (London: W. Scott, [1898]), p. 58.

multifarious "kaleidoscopic fragments are recomposed into images that seem to have a corresponding reality of their own."[18] Thus it is greatly to a novelist's credit when a fictional world seems "real", and not the sign of the supposedly facile "copyism" that critics of the day regularly deplored. It must have been a deliberate tactical decision that made Trollope write a novel that would come out alongside Lewes's theoretical work and would demonstrate his principles in action: and the result was *The Belton Estate*, which was the first fiction in the new journal.

In a broad sense of the word Trollope was always a "realist"—a portrayer of recognizable English daily life with little violent sensation and less moonshine about it. One of the contrasts was the sensationalism of Braddon and Wilkie Collins. The other was "idealism". Idealism was held to be a pointing towards something that could not literally be seen, the recognition of a "beyond," or the depiction of characters who were clearly motivated by a belief in eternal or transcendent values. The contrast is between "life as it is actually and historically" on the one hand and "characters of ideal perfection and beauty" and "situation and scenery ... beyond the margin of everyday life" on the other.[19] Bulwer-Lytton wrote eloquently on the "ideal" in the Preface to the 1845 edition of his *Night and Morning*, where he proposed that the office of the novelist should not be to present the actual, but

> to take man from the low passions, and the miserable troubles of life, into a higher region, to beguile weary and selfish pain, to excite a generous sorrow at vicissitudes not his own, to raise the passions into sympathy with heroic struggles—and to admit the soul into that serener atmosphere from which it rarely returns to ordinary existence, without some memory or association which ought to enlarge the domain of thought and exalt the motives of action ...[20]

The Belton Estate is realistic in a far more exacting sense than that of being a novel of contemporary life written in a down-to-earth way. It adheres to the principles of minimal plot interest and of avoidance of that comedy that was held to elevate characters into types, while the characters' motivations are psychologically plausible in worldly terms, and without noble-sounding sentiment. Right from the start of *The Belton Estate* Trollope makes it clear that he refuses to "idealize" his characters and their motivations. As a quite run-of-the-mill example take some of the human reactions surrounding the death of Bernard Amedroz's only son and heir. These, for example, are the reactions of the two characters concerned when

---

[18]   *Principles*, pp. 15 and 78.

[19]   David Masson on the "real" and "ideal" art of Thackeray and Dickens, in his *British Novelists and Their Styles; being a Critical Sketch of the History of British Prose Fiction*, (Cambridge, UK: Macmillan, 1859), pp. 248–9.

[20]   Edward G. E. L. Bulwer, Preface, *Night and Morning*, (3 vols, London: Saunders and Otley, 1841).

the Amedroz family lawyer communicates with Will Belton, now heir in tail to Belton Castle:

> Belton had acknowledged the letter with the ordinary expressions of regret. The lawyer had alluded to the entail, saying that it was improbable that Mr. Amedroz would have another son. To this Belton had replied that for his cousin Clara's sake he hoped that the squire's life might be long spared. The lawyer smiled as he read the wish, thinking to himself that luckily no wish on the part of Will Belton could influence his old client either for good or evil. What man, let alone what lawyer, will ever believe in the sincerity of such a wish as that expressed by the heir to a property? And yet where is the man who will not declare to himself that such, under such circumstances, would be his own wish? (p. 9).

It is not only the characters but the reader as well who is shown in an unideal light.

In this novel nothing is done for a self-consciously elevated or religious motive. Despite the depiction of an Evangelical old lady, there is no recognition of "the indissoluble relation in which earthly life must for ever stand to both Heaven and Hell" that Richard Holt Hutton maintained was essential for religious fiction.[21] Indeed *The Belton Estate* is practically a rationalist work, with religion relegated to the utilitarian role of regulating people's social habits. For the reader of the time, religious doubt can be detected everywhere in the novel, almost confirming the Dean of Canterbury's impression that Trollope was "evidently more at home among phenomena of unbelief, than among those of undoubting faith and obedience."[22] Will Belton's crippled sister, Mary, is said to be "one of those whose lot in life drives us ... to inquire within ourselves whether future compensation is to be given" (p. 156). As befits a future founder member of the Cremation Society of England, Trollope takes a rational view of the observances decreed for the bereaved when he remarks of Clara

> I do not know that she quite succeeded in recognizing it as a truth that sorrow should be allowed to bar out no joy that it does not bar out ... by its own weight, without reference to conventional ideas; that sorrow should never, under any circumstances, be nursed into activity, as though it were a thing in itself divine or praiseworthy (p. 131).

Although such remarks are the commonplace stuff of intellectual debate at the time, and are often met with in private letters or journals, we give inadequate credit to Trollope's modernity if we fail to notice them as relatively "advanced" in the

[21]   Richard Holt Hutton (anon.), 'The Hard Church Novel', *National Review*, 3 (July 1856): 134.

[22]   Henry Alford (anon.), review of *Clerical Sketches*, *Contemporary Review*, 2 (June 1866): 364.

context of a novel. The common theme is obedience or submission to convention, and Trollope is at his best when recording the hypocrisy that Victorian ideology tries to impose on women. When Mr Possitt, the curate, asks Clara to kneel and pray with him after her aunt's death, "the struggle within her bosom was hard, and ... she doubted for a moment between rebellion and hypocrisy. But she had determined to be meek, and so hypocrisy carried the hour" (p. 109).

It is now possible to view divergent Victorian views on the presentation of the mental workings of female characters in a broader cultural context, to hint, in fact, at some of what was at stake for those who held inherited views on the subject at the time. Reviewing *Sir Harry Hotspur of Humblethwaite* the *Spectator* finds the novel only partially successful, because, while the character of Sir Harry is very fine, that of Emily is a failure:

> Mr. Trollope's picture of the irresolution of the haughty and usually absolute old baronet, and the see-saw of policy into which this irresolution plunges him ... is as good of its kind as any moral picture he has ever yet drawn for us. No subject ever suited Mr. Trollope better. He is, before all things, a man of the world, and as a man of the world he understands to the core every passion involved in this conflict ... [23]

Trollope "delineates" the external effects of Sir Harry's passion "with the most accurate and sure artistic touch". On the other hand the novelist "can tell you what a girl of Emily Hotspur's passion of nature would *do*, and how she would do it, but he cannot tell you what she feels". He does not attempt the necessary "intensiveness of style," and lacks Thackeray's power of condensing passion into words":

> He has drawn a nature which needed portraiture by the expression of feeling as much as by action, and has failed to portray the intensity of feeling of which he has given the sign ... He needed the command of a "lyrical cry" in addition to the ordinary resource of a great novelist, and he had it not at his disposal.

As Richard Holt Hutton, the literary editor of the *Spectator*, explains elsewhere, a great poet, such as Shakespeare or Goethe, "works ... by intense sympathy from within, leaving the final outline to crystallise as it may, according to the internal law and nature of the life thus germinating in his imagination."[24] Hutton explains that this faculty, necessary in depicting a female character, is not necessary in presenting male characters:

---

[23]   *Spectator*, 43 (26 November 1870): 1415.

[24]   Richard Holt Hutton, *Essays Theological and Literary*, (2 vols, London: Strahan and Co., 1871), vol. 2, p. 205.

"There was sorrow in her heart, and deep thought in her mind."

Fig. 13.1   "There was sorrow in her heart, and deep thought in her mind."
Millais's illustration for *Orley Farm*, Chapter 5

Educated *men's* characters are naturally *in position*, and most vigorous masculine characters of any kind have a defined bearing on the rest of the world, a characteristic attitude, a personal latitude and longitude on the map of human affairs, which an intellectual eye can seize and mark out at once. But it is not so usually with women's characters. They are best expressed not by attitude and outline, but by essence and indefinite tone. As an odour expresses and characterises a flower even better than its shape and colour, as the note of a bird is in some sense a more personal expression of it than its form and feathers; so there is something of vital essence in a great poet's delineations of women which is far more expressive than any outline or colour (pp. 204–5)

In one of his reviews of *An Autobiography* Hutton sums up what he sees as a principal weakness in Trollope's œuvre: "The feminine essence is beyond the reach of men unless they be true poets, and never was there a man of great creative power who had less of the poet in him than Mr. Trollope."[25] As E. S. Dallas puts the dilemma facing the novelist: "The first object of the novelist is to get personages in whom we can be interested; the next is to put them in action. But when women are the chief characters, how are you to set them in motion? The life of women cannot well be described as a life of action."[26]

In a review of unknown authorship, which stylistically resembles those known to be by Hutton, the *Spectator* elaborates on this view:

Mr. Trollope's imagination is not one that ever seems, to the critic's observation, at least, to brood long over visions that task its full power. ... There is nothing, apparently, of the agony of meditative travail about his mind. We know how Miss Brontë used to brood for months before she could satisfy herself about the life of her imaginative offspring, when all at once the mist drew up before her mind and she saw how to strike out a great scene or reach a new passion. No true critic, we think, who read Miss Brontë's novels, could have failed to gather this impression long before it was confirmed from her own pen. No one would gather it ... from Mr. Trollope's tales. There is an easy, sliding manner about Mr. Trollope's imaginative delineations that, at least, disguises, if it does not disprove, the birth-throes which ushered them into the world of art.[27]

---

[25]   Richard Holt Hutton (anon.), "Mr. Trollope as Critic," *Spectator*, 56 (27 October 1883): 1373–4. Attribution from the *Spectator* editorial records, described in R. H. Tener, "The *Spectator* Records 1874–1897," *Victorian Newsletter*, 17 (Spring 1960): 33–6. I am grateful to the editor and proprietors of the *Spectator* for access to these records.

[26]   Eneas Sweetland Dallas, *The Gay Science*, (2 vols, London: Chapman and Hall, 1866), vol. 2, p. 293.

[27]   *Spectator*, 35 (11 October 1862): 1136–8. Attributed to Hutton on satisfying stylistic grounds by R. H. Tener, "A Clue for some R. H. Hutton Attributions", *Notes and Queries*, (ns) 14 (October 1967): 382–3.

To Hutton, Trollope's characterization therefore lacks those things that cannot be described intellectually. "A thousand skilful outlines of character based on mere individualities of taste and talent and temper, are not near as moving to us as one vivid picture of a massive nature, stirred to the very depths of its commonplace instinct and commonplace faith."[28]

The different creative approaches involved are based on a pseudo-Romantic division between thought and feeling. Poetry—or "true" poetry, in any case—derives from the faculty of feeling, while imitation of appearances or "surfaces" is a matter of observation. In other words, this is a matter of Carlyle's distinction between creation and manufacture. The difference between Hutton the post-Romantic religious thinker and Lewes the theorist of literary realism is well worth examining for its own sake, but the relevance here is to Trollope's women's characters. For Lewes it is no reproach, for Hutton it is, that Trollope's women are presented as he does, and indeed should, as "a man of the world," present his men. For us it makes Trollope the most refreshing of male novelists in the mid-Victorian period in his presentation of the mental life of women. "Inward portraiture" of a religious or "poetic" kind there may not be, but mental life there is a-plenty.

One thing that is striking about Trollope's women is that they think about almost the same things as his men: how to conduct life honestly with respect to self and others, and how to make decisions on the great occasions of existence that shall lead to a moral and satisfying life. Of course, given Trollope's acceptance of the social gender constructions of his age, the men think of these things in terms of their professions and of estate and financial management; the women think of them most often in terms of the career of marriage. Yet to Trollope these are closely similar: both are dominated by the choice of a career or profession, and, far more important, the choice of whether or not to pursue that career honestly. These are also the dominant concerns of *An Autobiography*, and it would not be too much to assert that career choices are Trollope's main subject, and carry with them the major concerns of the construction of gender roles for the individual, in the family and in the wider world. As the narrator tells us in chapter eleven of *Can You Forgive Her?*

> A woman's life is important to her,—as is that of a man to him,—not chiefly in regard to that which she shall do with it. The chief thing for her to look to is the manner in which that something shall be done. It is of moment to a young man when entering life to decide whether he shall make hats or shoes; but not of half the moment that will be that other decision, whether he shall make good shoes or bad. And so with a woman;—if she shall have recognized the necessity of truth and honesty for the purposes of her life, I do not know that she need ask herself many questions as to what she will do with it.[29]

---

[28]   R. H. Hutton, *Essays Theological and Literary*, vol. 2, pp. 294–367, 304.

[29]   Anthony Trollope, *Can You Forgive Her?* (London: Dent, 1994), pp. 95–6.

Like one of Trollope's young men who think they want to apply chemistry to farming, or go in for Civil Engineering on the Metropolitan Railway, Alice Vavasor has not yet learned to prioritise these questions, and was constantly asking herself "what she would do with" her life,

> and had by degrees filled herself with a vague idea that there was a something to be done; a something over and beyond, or perhaps altogether beside that of marrying and having two children if she only knew what it was. ... When she told herself that she would have no scope for action in that life in Cambridgeshire which Mr Grey was preparing for her, she did not herself know what she meant by action. ... She was not so far advanced as to think that women should be lawyers and doctors, or to wish that she might have the privilege of the franchise for herself; but she had undoubtedly a hankering after some second-hand political manoeuvring. She would have liked, I think, to have been the wife of a leader of a Radical opposition, in the time when such men were put in prison, and to have kept up for him his seditious correspondence while he lay in the Tower. She would have carried the answers to him inside her stays,—and would have made long journeys down into Northern parts without any money, if the cause required it. She would have liked to have around her ardent spirits, male or female, who would have talked of "the cause," and have kept alive in her some flame of political fire. As it was, she had no cause (p. 96).

Even when these thoughts are fantasy or daydream, they are about interaction (real or imaginary) between the subject and the world and not about passive states of being— part of the presentation of a fictional person "in position" in respect of a world. In this case, as in so many others, the thoughts are part of the process that can be generalized as the choice of a career.

In *The Claverings*, when Julia Brabazon declines to face financial hardship with Harry, and jilts him for a wealthy, dissipated, and decrepit nobleman, Lord Ongar, we are given her thoughts:

> She had chosen her profession, as Harry Clavering had chosen his; and having so far succeeded, she would do her best to make her success perfect. Mercenary! Of course she had been mercenary. Were not all men and women mercenary upon whom devolved the necessity of earning their bread?[30]

The equation between women's and men's careers could not be clearer, though the final question represents Julia's special pleading, which fails to conceal that she has behaved dishonestly in her chosen profession, trading her integrity for gain, rather as a corrupt lawyer might sell his, and just as criminally. "Whatever price she might have paid," the narrators tells us, "she had at any rate got the thing

---

[30]   Anthony Trollope, *The Claverings* (Oxford: Oxford University Press, 1986), p. 32.

which she had intended to buy" (p. 32). Two years later, she is a rich widow, and it is Harry's turn to have to decide whether to exchange his honour for wealth.

However restricted the career opportunities for women compared to men, the mental processes associated with them are more similar in Trollope than many of his critics could approve. These women cannot be characterised by a passive quality like exuding a perfume, any more than their men folk can. It is possible that Trollope's interest in more mature women like Lady Mason, Mrs Woodward or Lady Carbury is based on his fundamental preoccupation with character "in position." Of course, one of these three is a criminal, and one a writer of worthless books, but how good Trollope is at engaging the minds of his characters, male and female, with the world, and enabling the reader to engage with the thoughts of the guilty as much as the innocent! Those of his critics who considered him limited by a lack of "inward portraiture" were objecting in part to women engaged with the world around them. They also objected to the absence of religious thoughts, and (though this is beyond the scope of the present chapter) to the secularization of the conscience. It is arguably one of Trollope's most original features as a male novelist that he tried to break down the separation between methods of characterization of men and women, and in the process to expose the falseness of many Victorian pieties, while evolving a secular account of human life and thought. This distances him from his conservative contemporaries, and places him firmly among mid-Victorian radicals, where, to the surprise of many, he deserves to be.

Chapter 14
The Weight of Religion and History: Women Dying of Virtue in Trollope's Later Short Fiction[1]

Anca Vlasopolos

In "*Mary Gresley*" and *Sir Harry Hotspur*, Trollope creates female protagonists who internalize the Law of the Father to a fanatical degree. Such strict adherence to Victorian duty leads to young women's deaths—in the short story the death of a promising novelist (as well as charming potential wife and mother) and in the novella of an accomplished, beautiful, and right-minded potential wife and mother. Trollope exposes in "Mary Gresley" the role that provincial, unexamined religious tenets play in shaping womanly duty into sterile sacrifice, and in *Sir Harry Hotspur* he savages the pernicious influence of class and gender historiography on mate selection. From a perspective informed by 30-some years of the latest wave of feminist thinking, we conclude that Trollope means to show the dire effects of strict Victorian propriety on the best of young womanhood. If *Sir Harry Hotspur* and "Mary Gresley" may be taken as representative of Trollope's later short works, we can be justified in asserting that Trollope in and around 1870 delivers a radical critique of the great machines of History and Religion, both of which grind up promising women. The argument, however, becomes complicated; in regard to the fates of young women intent on offering themselves up as sacrifices, Trollope both emphasizes the young women's resistance to the uses made of them by men and appears to condemn them along with the cultural apparati that destroy them, at the same time that he presents them as rebelling into death to escape their burden of obedience.

When Nardin writes that

> Among those who think that Trollope's later novels express sympathy with dissatisfied women … there does seem to be a consensus that the shift did not occur before the mid-1860s.… This deep interest and open sympathy, however, did not appear out of nowhere,[2]

---

[1] I am indebted for the frame of this essay to Deborah Denenholz Morse's comments and suggestions.

[2] Jane Nardin, *He Knew She Was Right: the Independent Woman in the Novels of Anthony Trollope* (Carbondale: Southern Illinois UP, 1989), p. xvii.

Fig. 14.1   "When the letter was completed, she found it to be one which she
could not send." Millais's single illustration for *Kept in the Dark*

an unseasoned Trollope reader may be led to expect that deep interest and sympathy in the latter works to be salient. A number of other critics ably argue for Trollope's unusual sympathy for women, even those regarded as marginal in their choices and/or virtue, or at least for his awareness and recognition of their suffering.[3] Morse's claims accord more with my argument here: "if Trollope's perception of Woman's role was limited, it was much more elastic than that of most of his contemporaries."[4] The elasticity of Trollope's views depends on a comparison with his contemporaries; in the shorter works, where Trollope does not give himself the chance to expand development of character over generations or a large expanse of time, his views are, if not limited, certainly limiting. However, those views as readily apply to the strictures of his society as they do to what Trollope himself perceives to be the duties of women. As Polhemus speculates in regard to *The Small House at Allington*, Trollope indicts a society that promotes "a perverted atmosphere of infertility,"[5] an atmosphere that pervades both the short story and the novella under analysis.

There is always the tendency for special pleading in the case of an author we admire. Because we do not have the textual evidence to "prove" Trollope's position in absolute terms, we tend to perceive sly critiques in his less flexible portrayals of women, even when his own pronouncements in his *Autobiography* generally indicate a straightforward identification with the narrative personae. In my examination of these two shorter works (and for whom other than the Victorians would a 246-page novel count as a novella?), *Sir Harry Hotspur* and "Mary Gresley," both of 1870 vintage, I find that Trollope's sympathies with women's fates and perceptions of their roles arise from the author's disturbed viewpoint about his own culture's demands regarding gentlemen's daughters' virtues. Perhaps this tortuous sentence signals my own unease with the apparent conventionality of Trollope's heroines Emily Hotspur and Mary Gresley (who are rather typical in their obstinacy of women in his fiction, except in their march toward self-destruction), as well as with Trollope's seeming endorsement of at least Mary's choice, and certainly of both heroines' goodness.

Female sacrifice, the cornerstone (literally, in folk tales) of empire, nation, religion, and domestic felicity, appears in Trollope with great frequency, except that in his novels the sacrifice, perhaps because so bloodless, seems sterile and wasteful. While operating under the approval of an overt discourse devoted to

[3]   Margaret Markwick, *Trollope and Women* (London and Rio Grande: Hambledon, 1997); Joanna Trollope, "The Lady in Trollope," 13th Annual Lecture (http://www. trollopesociety.org/themag.htm#50); Daniel Wiseman, "The Broken Basilisk—Madeline Neroni & Barchester Towers," The Trollope Prize, 2000 (http://www.fas.harvard.edu/~trollope/results.html).

[4]   Deborah Denenholz Morse, *Women in Trollope's Palliser Novels* (Ann Arbor: UMI Research Press, 1987), p. 6.

[5]   Robert M. Polhemus, *The Changing World of Anthony Trollope* (Berkeley and Los Angeles: University of California Press, 1968), p. 98.

Victorian verities about Virtue and Duty, the trope of young female bodies vanishing from excessive virtue becomes troubling and painful, leading the reader to melancholy or to regrets about wasted potential. The emotions generated by these texts in turn make us question if the home, the nation, religion, and empire can long endure death after death of promising young women.

The story and the novella analyzed here represent contrasting ways in which Trollope adapts the medium to his ends. In the story, Mary Gresley is seen entirely from the outside, her inner life pieced together by her editor and admirer. At the end, we are left with the question of the justness of such an appraisal of a young woman by an older man when that man is not the authorial persona. Turner has analyzed the editorial first-person-plural viewpoint as both a locus of power and a diffusion of responsibility that makes the reader complicit with the editor in the soft-porn seduction of the child/daughter.[6] The "we" pretends to a distanced look at the destruction of a young woman's talent and, not long after, life, although the narrator uses his authority to manipulate the young woman respecting her talent and therefore contributes to male-power apparatus that destroys Mary's professional hopes. Mary's flaw is that she places too much faith in both her elder mentor and her priggish dying fiancé, as well as in the religion that has left her nearly destitute and that sends her to her untimely death. The approving tone that tells us of her sacrifice is the voice of the Father, different from yet nodding to the "Godly" authority that drives Mary to the choices leading to her death.

In *Sir Harry Hotspur*, Trollope provides glimpses of the inner workings of Emily Hotspur's mind, as well as the way in which she is viewed by her family, would-be lovers, and the social circle in which she moves. Emily's inner life is an echo chamber for the historical law of inheritance and contains a magnifying mirror of the Duty that grinds her down and finally kills her. As Tracy notes, father and daughter in the novel are united in the goal of preserving "aristocracy,"[7] but while Tracy calls Emily's "devotion to George and to the Hotspur family ... suicidal,"[8] he does not see her drive to self-destruction as resistance to the marriage market precisely through a mimicry of paternal concerns that attempt to erase her personhood. By echoing her father's fetishizing of the aristocratic title, Emily demonstrates just how lethal her father's plans for her are. Trollope develops a narrative richness of viewpoints that gives a nuanced insight into Victorian gender politics and historiography as they fashion the marriageable woman as commodity. In embracing to a fervent and perverse degree her role as commodity, Emily manages to "devalue" herself so as to take herself out of the market, but only by driving herself to an early death.

---

[6]   Mark W. Turner, *Trollope and the Magazines* (London: Macmillan, 2000), pp. 196–212.

[7]   Robert Tracy, *Trollope's Later Novels* (Berkeley and Los Angeles: University of California Press, 1978), p. 111.

[8]   Tracy, p. 113.

In "Mary Gresley" (1869) the issue of "redundant" women, examined in detail by Durey in her *Trollope and the Church of England*,[9] becomes a central feature of the story. It is, however, only glancingly addressed, mostly through the widow Gresley and her other daughter, referred to only as "poor Fanny,[10] whose redundancy is made manifest by her being only a shadow in the margin of the text, left behind in Cornboro with some local family as the mother and Mary come to London, and never mentioned again in the story. Yet clearly because of the family's economic condition following the death of the breadwinner, Mary's choice of mates is nearly annihilated, despite her personal charms. At the mere age of 17, Mary engages herself to a very young curate boarding with the family, a man who has no income to support a household but who imprudently pairs with her as the "birds" do (p. 29), not as a rational and religious man should. In London, Mary and her mother subsist on nearly nothing.

That Mary is a young woman ideally suited for the career of wife and mother is clear from the 50-some-year-old editor's infatuation with her charms and seductive but correct behavior. The editor goes to great lengths to defend his infatuation as within the bounds of propriety, yet his description of his reaction to Mary makes her the perfect object of the male gaze: "We loved her, in short, as we should not have loved her, but that she was young and gentle, and could smile,—and, above all, but that she looked at us with those bright, beseeching tear-laden eyes" (p. 27). He compares himself to Sterne, Goethe, and Johnson; like them, he feels the attraction of the young, but does not come to ridicule and misbehavior like Sterne, nor just to misbehavior like Goethe, but like Johnson prevails over his attraction by insisting that he sees Mary as a child (pp. 27–8). The supposed distancing does not prevent the editor from frequently commenting on Mary's womanly charms and on assessing her fiancé, Arthur Donne, more sharply than he might have otherwise. While Arthur's name may seem typically English and allude to the poet, I would argue that Trollope is punning on both "dun" as a drab color and on his being "done" in or with, as the plot shows. The editor reports that Arthur Donne should not have become engaged to be married, for as the vicar's wife put it, on 100 pounds a year, "there would come … children, and destitution, and ruin" (p. 29).

The girl-child affianced, however, is more than a charming young woman who respectably eschews trading on her charms. She has literary ambitions that precede her engagement to the impoverished curate, and when the engagement appears to be doomed to indefinite extensions because of Donne's lack of wherewithal, Mary takes it upon herself to augment the couple's income by her writerly endeavors, even in the teeth of her fiancé's disapproval of novel writing (p. 31). She energetically persuades her mother to rent their house to the new, married curate, and to come to London for a trial period in which Mary might test her talents and

---

⁹   Jill Felicity Durey, *Trollope and the Church of England* (Basingstoke: Palgrave Macmillan, 2002), pp. 120–24.

¹⁰   Anthony Trollope, "Mary Gresley," *The Complete Short Stories*, ed. Betty Jane Slemp Breyer (Fort Worth: Texan Christian University Press, 1979), vol. 2, pp. 25–49, 28.

their marketability, with the object of shortening the engagement period (p. 30). At this early point in Mary's love affair, she is still independent enough to make decisions that go against her lover's judgment, but since the purpose is pure, the enterprise must be acceptable; she is not overtly seeking literary fame, after all, but merely the money to conclude an indeterminate engagement. Arthur Donne, moreover, has little power to alter Mary's plans since he has been forced by ill health to find a post in Dorsetshire, so the couple is separated when Mary puts her plan into motion.

Besieged by aspiring authors, especially "female literary aspirants" who, unlike Mary, are not "'modest-like,'" the editor hesitates to receive yet another woman with a manuscript. Once he meets her, however, he takes upon himself the role of mentor and elder friend. He places two of her stories, which earn Mary 12 guineas—a princely sum to the mother and daughter who live so marginally as to be prevented from the pretence of the "elegant" economies practiced by the Cranford ladies. He nurtures Mary's talent, teaching her the basics of what we now call creative writing; he has her undergo an apprenticeship, whereby she learns to outline a plot, sketch characters and dialogue, before attempting the full-fledged novel. His assessment of Mary's abilities as an author is indistinguishable from his view of her as a woman: "There was a grace and delicacy in her work which were charming" (p. 37), he tells us about her novel, a veiled autobiographical account of her nearly hopeless engagement, ending, prophetically, in tragedy. Of her, he iterates that she was "a dear, well-bred, modest, clever little girl" (p. 42). Is it not his desire to keep her near that leads the editor to tell Mary that, "even presuming she were entitled to hope for ultimate success, she must go through an apprenticeship of ten years before she could reach it" (p. 42)? The narrator's motives are in question since he later gainsays his own editorial wisdom: in retrospect, he doubts "whether the old, sad, simple story was not the better of the two" (p. 40), preferring Mary's original to the much revised version she produces under his tutelage. When the danger of her returning to Cornboro is imminent, he suddenly sees far more promise in her abilities: "there did spring up within our mind a feeling, greatly opposed to the conviction which formerly we had endeavored to impress upon herself,—that she was destined to make for herself a successful career" (p. 47). The young woman's response to the idea of a ten-year apprenticeship is, again, prophetic—she sees herself as dead in that time, a prediction that makes the reader wonder why such a lively girl, with a good sense of humor, with ambition, natural talent, and love in her life, sees her future in such bleak terms, different to be sure from the vicar's wife's foretelling of "destitution, and ruin," but if anything more bleak. Is it her resistance to the thrall that the editor is attempting to practice upon her? Perhaps being caught between the curate's narrow-minded interdictions and the editor's self-serving assessment of the meagerness of her talent gives Mary insight into how she might end up.

The trajectory follows Mary's prophecy rather than the editor's. When her fiancé on his deathbed prohibits her from writing novels, she immediately burns her manuscripts and notes. Regardless of Mary's talents, ambition, and her absolute lack of funds, which Donne's death will do nothing to relieve, the curate finds it morally just to cut off her only avenue of supporting herself slightly above poverty level. She, as a good Victorian heroine, retreats without a protest from the field in which, the editor admits belatedly, she may have had access long before his requisite 10 years. When the editor tries to make Mary reconsider, she silences him with the Trollopian heroine's self-abasement: "Is he not one of God's ordained priests? In all the world is there one so bound to obey him as I?" (p. 47). That in the editor's view Donne was a self-centered prig, not the voice of God, is clear from his comments on Donne's letters to Mary, in which "he spoke ever of himself and not of her," and in which he categorizes Donne as "a simple, pious, commonplace young man" (pp. 44, 29). Yet is the editor any less selfish when he tells the young woman that before any hope of making money she must submit to a ten-year trial? His own change of mind, after Donne's death, about Mary being able to make a career in writing makes his earlier pronouncement both unreliable and cruel. His desire to be Mary's sole male guide, as Turner has observed, is an elaborate seduction scheme.[11]

Yet the editor, and implicitly the reader, is obligated to honor Mary's sentiments and see her go back to Cornboro: "As far as we knew her, she never moved a single point from what was right" (p. 48). The immolation of self practiced by Mary Gresley upon her fiancé's death makes her into an automaton of faith and virtue. She becomes a "female Scripture reader," who strangles her writerly ambitions by producing "wonderful little dialogues between Tom the Saint and Bob the Sinner," through which, despite her "restless piety inspired by the curate" (p. 30), her talent breaks through: "though that mode of religious teaching is most distasteful to us, the literary merit shown even in such works as these was very manifest" (pp. 48–9). Trollope has Mary name Currer Bell as a predecessor in the literary field, and the editor shows his resentment about Charlotte Brontë's spectacular success by snidely commenting on the "injury done by Currer Bell" in encouraging literary ambitions in young girls (p. 38). Trollope himself, however, pays homage to Charlotte Brontë by alluding to the plot of *Jane Eyre*. Mary falls into the religious trap that weighs heavily upon Jane and is only removed by Jane's uncanny ability to hear the true voice of passion, Rochester's call for her from the depths of Ferndean. But no Rochester sighs for Mary. She remains an impoverished young woman who allows herself to be bullied into retreating from an independent life by a dying curate who does not care how she will survive and by an older man who designs to keep her coming to his office for tête-à-têtes that rejuvenate him. Eight years after Donne's death she remarries another, more energetic Donne, a St. John type, who puts himself and his notions of religion above cherishing her—"a missionary who was going to some forlorn country on the confines of African colonization"—, and thereupon she promptly dies without issue (pp. 48 9), a sterile female sacrifice to Victorian religious duty.

---

[11] Turner, p. 212.

Whereas Mary Gresley represents the genteel class of women suffering from malnutrition, inadequate clothing, and other privations that severely limit the scope of their ambitions and marriageability, Emily Hotspur, the heroine of *Sir Harry Hotspur*, stands at the other end of the socioeconomic scale. Trollope undisguisedly attacks Sir Harry's national, class, and genetic allegiances. Sir Harry's very name, Hotspur, recalls national historiography memorialized in such shrines as Shakespeare's *Henry IV*, Part One. By choosing the fateful surname given to Henry Percy, Hotspur, Trollope alludes to the wayward prince whose allegiance to the monarchic succession leads to his death. Significantly, he insists on Sir Harry's wrong-headed pride in the name, which consists of the desire to keep property and title together, on Sir Harry and Lady Elizabeth initially encouraging relations with the man who will be "the head of the family" no matter what the man's character, and on Sir Harry's belief that "blood"—that is. aristocratic descent—is "gold" and will eventually shine through the dross.

The novella opens to the untimely death of Sir Harry's son and heir. After her only sibling's death, Emily Hotspur becomes heiress to Sir Harry's fortune and ancestral lands, on that score alone a most eligible match. In addition, she is handsome, bright, and imbued with as much a sense of the "family" as an entity to be safeguarded and perpetuated as is Sir Harry himself. Yet, like Mary Gresley, Emily dies without issue, and more tragically than Mary she never lives to enjoy reciprocal love, let alone sexual satisfaction. For an author who is quite aware of women's sexual desires and the kind of disquiet that an unsatisfactory sex life brings, Trollope condemns Emily more thoroughly than he does even Lily in *The Small House at Allington*. Is Emily yet another of Trollope's female prigs? Is a more expansive critique intended in the novella than the novel? After all, in the novel at least one of the Dales, Bell, is a strong-minded young woman who marries a man worthy of her and contributes to the progeny that will sustain the nation.

Trollope names his novella after the father, not the daughter, and this decision may sway the reader to consider whether the blame for the end of the house of Hotspur falls on Sir Harry or on Emily, or whether it is shared by the two, who are seen as alike by several characters in the novella, including Lady Elizabeth, who ought to know and in Trollope's view does. The Hotspur estate, unlike Longbourn in *Pride and Prejudice*, is not entailed, so after the death of Sir Harry's son, the father must decide how to dispose of his property and his daughter, the two becoming synonymous at crucial points. The one thing Sir Harry has no control over is the title, which is to go to the next male heir, the troublesome cousin George. The one thing that Emily thinks her father has no control over is her heart; in this surmise she is both magnificently right and tragically wrong. In order for Emily to inherit the entire estate, Sir Harry stipulates that she must marry a man who will take the surname Hotspur upon marriage, since "to leave a Hotspur behind [Sir Harry] living at Humblethwaite, and Hotspurs who should follow that Hotspur, was all in all to him."[12] The prenuptial condition about the surname already narrows the field of suitors for Emily's hand; Sir Harry is fully aware that a first son from the kind of family with which he wants to ally himself will hardly forego his own surname, so that Sir Harry is in effect attempting to buy posterity for his name by selling his property via Emily. Yet even that concession from Emily's putative future husband will not satisfy Sir Harry's emotional cravings for a male descendant because he believes in "blood" being transmitted through primogeniture, not the female line:

> By certain courtesies of the law of descent his future heirs would be Hotspurs were his daughter married to Lord Alfred or the like; but the children of such a marriage would not be Hotspurs *in very truth*, nor by any courtesy of law, or even by any kindness of the Minister or Sovereign, could the child of such a union become the baronet, the Sir Harry of the day, the head of the family. (p. 38) [emphasis mine]

The incoherence of the sentence replicates the inchoate state of Sir Harry's mind regarding descent. Sir Harry believes that his daughter cannot give him true Hotspurs, even if so in name, thereby opening himself up to the wishful thinking of uniting the title, i.e. George, with the property—in other words, Emily—even after he suspects George of being deficient: "if the worst came to the worst, the title and property would be kept together" (p. 75). Later, when he has found enough about George to know that the match would make Emily's life miserable, Sir Harry still defends the privileges of his gender and class through his implicit belief in George's breeding, even if the interests of the "family" are pitted directly against Emily's welfare, as if in this instance the family and the daughter who stands for the property were different entities: "Was his higher duty due to his daughter, or to his family,—and through his family to his country, which, as he believed, owed its security and glory to the maintenance of its aristocracy?" (p. 195). In the defense of aristocracy as national duty, Sir Harry's cogitations are represented satirically, for how can we take seriously the proposition that "the family" excludes the only progeny? In the same chapter (20– "Cousin George's Success"), the omniscient voice ceases to be distant and becomes engaged and condemnatory. Sir Harry, who trusts his lawyer's probity, nevertheless resents Mr. Boltby's presumption in characterizing George, the future baronet, in terms of opprobrium: Sir Harry cogitates, "It is astonishing what blood will do in bringing in a horse through mud at the end of the day. Mr. Boltby probably did not understand how much, at the very last, might be expected from breeding" (p. 158). The breach of class hierarchy committed by Mr. Boltby in advising his client as to how to dispose of his daughter makes Sir Harry recoil, and he ends up as much a dupe to George's eugenic glamour as is Emily:

---

[12]   Anthony Trollope, *Sir Harry Hotspur*, ed. Geoffrey Cumberlege, 1870 (London: Oxford University Press, 1928), p. 36.

[I]n that matter of blood, as to which Sir Harry's ideas were so strong, and indeed so noble, he entertained but a muddled theory. Noblesse oblige. High position will demand, and will often exact, high work. But that rule holds as good, with a Buonaparte as with a Bourbon, with a Cromwell as with a Stewart; and succeeds as often and fails as often with the low born as with the high. And good blood too will have its effect,—physical for the most part,—and will produce bottom, lasting courage, that capacity of carrying on through the mud to which Sir Harry was wont to allude; but good blood will bring no man back to honesty. (p. 197)

Having exposed Sir Harry's notions of "family," "blood," the duty to country and its perpetuity as both wrong-headed and ethically wrong, Trollope ensures that the readers get the point through the inexorable movement of the novel toward the demise of the House of Hotspur.

Yet the only way in which Sir Harry's delusions can take their destructive path is through Emily's participation in them. Tracy argues that "their [Sir Harry's and Emily's] virtues bring about their doom,"[13] but Trollope shows Sir Harry as unable to accept the lot of humankind in the death of his only son, and it is this obsession, not virtue, that destroys him. The same mystique about the "head of the family" and the union of property and title operates on Emily. Her arguments about cleaving to Cousin George despite all his failings are that "he has our name and he must some day be at the head of the family" (p. 170) and thus worthy of being rescued and rehabilitated. Given that the "family" consists, insofar as Trollope shows it, of father, mother, and daughter, the notion of "head of the family" strikes us as both an empty signifier and an anachronistic clinging to a past that cannot co-exist without damage to the present. Tracy hints at the Freudian motives behind Emily's infatuation, namely George's similarity to her father, and her desire to replace her mother as Lady (Hotspur).[14] But the more relevant motives in Emily's behavior are not her desire for the father as much as her complete identification of her desire with his, for ends that prove antiquated, stagnant, and ultimately deadly. The contrast, for instance, between Emily Hotspur and Austen's Anne Elliot as daughters of baronets obsessed with the family line could not be clearer: Anne moves into the future by throwing in her lot with a new class of people who advance through meritocracy and by rejecting the seductive image of herself in her mother's place if she married her cousin Walter, who will inherit the title *and* the property; Emily ties herself to a dying past by binding herself to a "double obedience …—the obedience of a child added to that which was now required from her as the future transmitter of honours of the house" (p. 12).

From the first encounters, Emily has made a "god" of Cousin George because after her brother's death George is the inheritor to the title, so that she finds all other suitors mere men by comparison, even Lord Alfred, whose attributes far exceed George's: "the man must have enough in her eyes of that godlike glory

---

[13]   Tracy, p. 115.

[14]   Tracy, p. 113.

to satisfy her that she had found in him one who would be almost a divinity.... Could he speak as that other man [George] spoke? Could he look as that other one looked? Would there be in his eye such a depth of colour, in his voice such a sound of music, in his gait as divine a grace?" (p. 15). Despite Emily's conviction that her heart is free, by the time she is thrown on the market she is already beyond the reach of any man but George, whom she has endowed with a "divinity" (p. 15) that she herself hardly understands, since "she was one in whom intentional deceit was impossible" (p. 12), but in whom unconscious deceit and self-deceit have already taken root: "Of her preference for that other man she never told herself anything. She was not aware that it existed" (p. 16). Such self-deception of course serves to take Emily out of the market and preempts her father's disposal of her.

As Emily is being offered to various suitors, Trollope's language regarding the economics of marriage is coarse in its directness: "Emily Hotspur was taken up to London, in order that she might be suited with a husband" (p. 31); "So he had brought her up to London, and thrown her as it were upon the market" (p. 34). Emily is the bait by which at least name and property can be wedded. During the season, George remains nearly as seductive to the parents as he is to Emily, so that following Emily's discussion with her mother about "black sheep," the young woman feels entitled to indulge in her exclusive passion for her cousin. Like Lily Dale and unlike Trollope's pluckier heroines, Emily becomes a one-man woman—her explicit resistance to the way she is being used:

> Emily ... felt that she had a possession of her own with which neither father nor mother might be allowed to interfere. It was for them, or rather for him, to say that a hand so weighted as was hers should not be given here or there; but it was not for them, not even for him, to say that her heart was to be given here, or to be given there. Let them put upon her what weight they might of family honours, and of family responsibility, that was her own property;—if not, perhaps, to be bestowed at her own pleasure, because of the pressure of the weight, still her own, and absolutely beyond the bestowal of any other. (p. 13)

This spark of independence, however, proves to be the same straitjacket of aristocratic prejudice and conventional prizing of virginity that deliver Emily into the maw of Duty and tradition.

As revelations about George's moral depravity surface, as does his utter inability to change, no matter what plans for reform and great advantages are dangled before him, Emily persists in her loyalty to him, convinced of her moral purity because she was sanctioned by her parents in entertaining George's attentions in the first place: "It was herself that she had given, and there was no retracting the offering" (p. 137). Emily even has the audacity to compare herself to Christ in her self-immolation upon the altar of her love (p. 222). Yet she remains unwilling to take the smallest step toward her own satisfaction in a union with the man who represents the only sweetness in life to her. This perversity Emily labels duty to her parents and especially to class-bound norms of proper femininity:

> She had read and heard of girls who would correspond with their lovers clandestinely, would run away with their lovers, would marry their lovers as it were behind their fathers' backs. No act of this kind would she do.... She would do nothing that could be thrown in her teeth; nothing that could be called unfeminine, indelicate, or undutiful.... She had her own rights and her own privileges, with which grievous and cruel interference would be made, should her father, because he was her father, rob her of the only thing which was sweet to her taste or desirable in her esteem. Because she was his heiress he had no right to make her his slave.... Because she would cling to her duty and keep the promise which she had made to him, it would be in his power to prevent the marriage upon which she had set her heart; but it was not within his power, or within his privilege as a father, to force upon her any other marriage. (pp. 162–3)

Emily's resistance to the "market," her delusion that in giving her heart to George she is going against paternal desires, becomes the means by which she escapes in the only way she sees open to her, by an obstinate devotion to duty and female virtue.

When she experiences the last straw—George's letter, written by Mrs. Morton, George's mistress, asserting that he does not love her—Emily finds life itself unendurable, a position that is hardly Christian and that even lacks the aristocratic "pluck" that George, too, is sadly missing. Emily's language of love, like Lily's, is so charged that it hints of sexual misdeeds. There are many women in Trollope whose "heart" functions as a metonymy of the body and who consequently feel as if they have given themselves to the man to whom they are betrothed, even when there has been no opportunity for sexual relations. Like Lily, who did have the chance for premarital relations with Crosbie,[15] Emily speaks of having given herself: "She had given herself up to one utterly worthless, and she knew it. But yet she had given herself, and could not revoke the gift" (p. 243). However, the only time she and George were physically together was on a bridge within sight of a tourist party; later, when they take a walk together, Emily forbids him any physical contact since she expects him to earn her by redeeming himself first. Regardless of the degree of their sexual experiences, Emily and Lily, like Rachel Ray, whose only escape is the much better character of her lover, stray on the side of a paralyzing, maiming, and in Emily's case lethal notion of female virtue bound by religion and class prejudice, rather than on the side of transgressive behavior.

Only belatedly does Sir Harry acknowledge that his vacillations about George, with their fatal result, had to do with his own desire to keep title and property united. Trollope does not allow Sir Harry to get off without that dire realization, nor does he spare Sir Harry from condemnation for the crassness, not the nobility, of his desire, perhaps even the blasphemy of bartering his daughter so as to produce

---

[15] Markwick convincingly discusses Lily's charged language about her sexual experience in *Trollope and Women* (pp. 84–5); Nardin in *He Knew She Was Right* also argues that Lily had a "sexual involvement" with Crosbie (p. 112).

"true" male Hotspurs after the loss of his son. Emily comes to no such realization. Her sole virtue is her resistance to the uses to which her father would put her, except that she thoroughly embraces the very notions that make commodities of women. Unlike Maggie Tulliver, who, once swept away by passion, refuses to legitimize it because of the damage done to those around her, and even unlike Marianne Dashwood, who after her brush with death is appalled at the peril to her immortal soul caused by her selfish disregard for her own life, Emily, the "bonniest and the brightest and the most clever" (p. 80) of young women, wills herself to sink into an early grave. But is Sir Harry the only one to lose this daughter, "one of the finest girls that had ever been seen about London" (p. 112) who despite (or perhaps because) of little self-awareness and sense of her own life's worth would nonetheless have made a most loving wife? The desire for an unbroken line of aristocratic lineage for Trollope signals a sterile, stagnant social goal that sacrifices its most promising young women.

Mary Gresley's and Emily Hotspur's deaths are both foreshadowed and shocking. These young women, rigid in their notions of virtue inculcated by religion and class allegiance, respectively, anticipate the rigor mortis and annihilation with which they themselves have imbued their sense of duty to received, male-dominant ideals; Mary is bound to notions of religion whose simple-mindedness her own natural talent contradicts, and Emily binds herself to a historical chimera of aristocratic perpetuity. Is Trollope then blaming them? We have a feeling of waste as well as loss at the end of these tales, and it is not merely obeisance on Trollope's part to generic conventions of tragedy, since both plots could easily have been turned toward a comic ending. I would contend that Trollope mourns, at the same time as he is hastening, the passing of the proper Victorian heroine—the girl too good to live—as he begins, just begins, scratching an assay of the New Woman, someone who can survive a cad of a lover, refuse loyalty to an abusive father, and successfully adjust to life, even through a double exile. Dare I suggest it? Someone like the very non-Victorian and hardly lady—Marie Melmotte of *The Way We Live Now*.

PUNCH, OR THE LONDON CHARIVARI.—November 9, 1867.

FAGIN'S POLITICAL SCHOOL.

Fig. 15.1   "Fagin's political school," *Punch*, 9 November 1867

Conclusion
Gender, Liberalism, and Resentment[1]

Regenia Gagnier

Fifty percent of Margaret Thatcher's Cabinet and seven High Court Judges were members of the Trollope Society. I have a copy of a letter in which the Prime Minister herself declined to join the Society only because of prior commitments: "I certainly agree that Anthony Trollope was one of the greatest English novelists, and I have noted what you say about the position of the Cabinet. But I am already involved with so many organisations that I do not feel able to take on any more at the moment."[2] John Major is still the vice president of the Society, Norma Major a member, and the late Enoch Powell a devoted reader. The present Bishop of London and current Trollope Society President, Richard Chartres, claims to have read Trollope as a teenager, when, he says, he was so reactionary that he forced his parents to rebel against him. The day after Tony Blair's resignation, columnists concluded that "Blair's Britain has not had its Anthony Trollope."[3] Trollope famously defined himself as an "advanced, but still a conservative, Liberal."[4] In Britain, he is widely read by laypeople and often invoked by politicians on the radio, while in North America, as in many of the essays in this volume, his liberalism on issues of gender, race, reform, sexuality, and so on, is subtly appreciated by scholars. I want to conclude genealogically with the meanings of Trollope's liberalism and finally with what I take to be the necessary link in any society between gender flexibility and liberalism, or between gender flexibility and freedom as western societies know it.

Contrary to the Prime Minister's estimation of Trollope as certainly one of the greatest English novelists, Trollope has been second always in the great tradition of British novelists because his characters do not have the individual richness characteristic of the great authors of realism. From the beginning, he was known as a social novelist who presented everyday, phenomenal appearance "as the majority would see it." In Victorian terms, when realism was contrasted with idealism, he was compared unfavourably to Thomas Hardy's and George Eliot's "universal truths of humanity," Dickens's idealizations, or Meredith's inner

---

[1]   I am grateful to Margaret Markwick and Deborah Morse for comments on a draft of this essay and to Margaret for some helpful references on Trollope.

[2]   Letter from the Prime Minister to John Letts, Esq., O. B. E., 2 July 1987. Courtesy of David Skilton.

[3]   Caroline Michel, "In search of a Blair Zeitgeist," *Guardian*, 8 May 2007, p. 27.

[4]   Anthony Trollope, *An Autobiography* (London: Williams and Norgate, 1946), p. 257.

consciousness. Rather than developing his characters alone as individuals, Trollope took the interaction between them, using their complicated social strategies, as his means of characterization. Given that he wrote for an educated middle- to upper-class audience, the social, rather than the universal or introspective, was a major element of his realism. Richard Holt Hutton, Trollope's greatest Victorian critic, explained the difference with George Eliot as follows. Eliot represented the uneducated classes in her fiction and so was closer to the universal truths of humanity. "The habit of concealing … what is closest to our hearts, is … a result of education. It is quite foreign to the class of people whom George Eliot knows most thoroughly, and has drawn with the fullest power. All her deepest knowledge of human nature has probably been acquired among people who speak their thoughts with the directness … of Miss Bronte's Yorkshire heroes."[5]

Hutton also contrasted Trollope with Jane Austen, whose characters are "what they are by the natural force of their own nature and tastes": "You hardly see the crush of the world on any one. The vain man's vanity sedately flowers; the dull man's dullness runs to seed; the proud man's pride strikes its roots deep; even the fidgetiness of the fidgety persons appears to come from within, not from the irritation of external pressures."[6] But turn to Trollope, and "the atmosphere of affairs is permanent. The Church or the world, or the flesh or the devil, seem always at work to keep men going."[7] Trollope's modernity for Hutton consisted in this: "Everybody in Trollope is more or less under pressure, swayed hither and thither by opposite attractions, assailed on this side and on that by the strategy of rivals; … everywhere time is short … Mr. Trollope's people are themselves so far as the circumstances of the day will allow them to be themselves, but very often are much distorted from their most natural selves."[8]

Hutton described Trollope in fact as a

"social naturalist": "By which we mean not so much [depicting a character's] interior thoughts and feelings, but the outward habits in which these thoughts and feelings are expressed, the local and professional peculiarities of manner and habit in every place and in every trade, nay more, the minutiae of class demeanour, the value that is attached in particular situations to standing up rather than sitting down, to making a statement in one room rather than in another; in short, the characteristic dress in which the small diplomacies of all kinds of

---

[5]   Cited in David Skilton, *Anthony Trollope and his Contemporaries: A Study in the Theory and Conventions of Mid-Victorian Fiction* (London: Longman, 1972), p. 111. Skilton's essay in this collection, "Depth of Portraiture: What Should Distinguish a Victorian Man from a Victorian Woman," resumes this topic, now focussed on Trollope's women's actions "in position" in the world.

[6]   Skilton, p. 117.

[7]   Ibid.

[8]   Ibid., pp. 116–17.

social life clothe themselves.... Mr. Trollope makes one feel how great a social naturalist he is."[9]

Trollope, that is, represented the local and particular, rather than the universal, in the context of action and choice, as if everyday life were simply an evolving plot.

And that has been the historical consensus. Widely read in his own day, Trollope's reputation notoriously suffered with the posthumous publication of his autobiography at the height of Aestheticism, in which he confessed his professional—to some, mechanical—means of production. George Bernard Shaw favorably contrasted Trollope's realism to all the belletristic, aesthetic, romantic, and sensation schools of the day, pointing out that "Society has not yet forgiven that excellent novelist for having worked so many hours a day, like a carpenter or tailor, instead of periodically going mad with inspiration," and Shaw praised Trollope as "the first sincerely naturalistic novelist of our day" who "gave us a faithful picture of the daily life of the upper and middle classes."[10] The socialist Shaw had no trouble with Trollope's failure to "represent" the "lower" classes: "He, as an honest realist, only told what he knew; and, being a middle-class man, he did not and could not know the daily life of the slum and gutter."[11] The Victorian panoramic view, the omniscient narrator, was to Shaw a presumption.

Trollope wrote about the unleisured, modern, managerial class—the men and women who managed society and moved others. Arthur Schopenhauer had noted in 1819 that the modern individual's ability to plan and pursue his own interest gave rise to the possibility of dissimulation that further leads to the distance or lack of transparency between us, thereby increasing modern individuation. Accustomed to hide the springs of their own actions, the empowered class became individually opaque. Yet in his characters' very opacity, their being known only in their actions or ethos, Trollope's readers like Henry James saw "the surprise of recognition"[12] of English landed society in its essence, which was precisely its existence: the country estates, the location of the seats, the wealthy magnates, the less opulent squires, the parvenus of various ranks, the methods of estate management, the ample aristocratic entertainments, the sale of land, the problems of entail and inheritance, and the striving for social status through land-ownership. Hutton concluded that although phenomenal, dealing only with appearance "as the majority of the world see it," Trollope "pictured society of his day with a fidelity with which society has never been pictured before in the history of the world."[13]

---

[9] Cited in Skilton, p. 115.

[10] Cited in Philip Waller, *Writers, Readers, and Reputations: Literary Life in Britain 1870–1918* (Oxford: Oxford University Press, 2006), pp. 199–201.

[11] Ibid.

[12] Cited in Skilton, p. 144.

[13] Ibid., 105.

When the real returned with the First World War, Trollope regained a reputation literally for his "non-literariness" (Dorothy Richardson) and "world-creating" fidelity (Desmond MacCarthy). Siegfried Sassoon read him nostalgically in the trenches. Walter Raleigh at Oxford wrote positively that "Trollope understands affection"[14] and thereby could turn ordinary people "that bore you in life and in books" into epic (*epos* meaning a social fabric of events in which a hero is cultivated). The definitions of the novel expanded again beyond the aesthetic work of art to the satisfaction of curiosity about "life"—that most central term of New Liberalism. If one considers the evolution of the novel since antiquity as the inclusive representation of common life and action, Trollope provides an anthropology of upper-class Britain at the height of its empire. So let us take Trollope as an anthropological writer—not a universal humanist but rather as a specific fieldworker in a local environment asking, what kind of creatures are the governing class of British men and women in the second half of the nineteenth century?

When critics in this volume go to Trollope for nineteenth-century attitudes toward marriage, the empire, manhood and masculinity, Ireland, or women's independence, they tend to find a liberalism seemingly at odds with Trollope's standing among Tory politicians. With 47 novels and 34 short stories (plus 4 biographies, 4 sketch books, 2 plays, 5 travel books, 2 books of collected journalism, and 1 general rant), there is material to support all sides of the political spectrum. In Britain, Tories tend to read the Barsetshire series. In North America, progressive academics, currently concerned to protect liberalism in a larger society that seems determined to roll back the clock on enlightenment principles, focus on the political Palliser novels. In an essay that could not be included in this volume, Amanda Anderson explores the dual content of Victorian sincerity in Trollope's fiction: sincerity as critique and sincerity as embedded ethos, spanning both city and country novels.[15] The first focuses on the importance of liberal critique (argument, debate, and justification) and the second on the tacit ethos that supplies the worldly realism in which Trollope's characters live like fish in water. Anderson uses the way that Trollopian characters take distance on the embedded customs of their social milieux to model liberal proceduralism (critical reason, discourse ethics, "the moral point of view as embodied in an intersubjective praxis of argumentation which enjoins those involved to an idealized enlargement of their interpretive perspectives" [Habermas]),[16] which is her notion of liberalism.

In another excellent essay not included here, "Trollope and Anti-Semitism," Amarnick makes a persuasive case for Trollope's liberalism with reference to

---

[14]   Cited in Waller, p. 200.

[15]   Amanda Anderson, "Trollope's Modernity," *ELH*, vol. 74.3 (autumn 2007), pp. 509–34.

[16]   See also ch. 7, "Beyond Sincerity and Authenticity: the Ethos of Proceduralism," pp. 161–87 in Amanda Anderson (ed.), *The Way We Argue Now: A Study in the Cultures of Theory* (Princeton: Princeton University Press, 2006). Habermas quote p. 181.

his explicit use of characterization "for the expression of my political and social convictions."[17] Amarnick glosses Trollope's explicit definitions in Chapter XVI of *An Autobiography:* "The conservative sees inequalities in society and, believing they are of divine origin, is committed to preserving them" (p. 258). The Liberal, on the other hand, "is alive to the fact that these distances are day by day becoming less, and he regards this continual diminution as a series of steps towards that human millennium of which he dreams" (p. 259). The conservative Liberal, as Trollope describes himself, "believes that the changes must occur gradually so as to take hold properly." Amarnick argues that the sense of "conservative" in Trollope's self-description is as an adjective, not a noun, and has to do only with the speed of change. "Liberal," on the other hand, is a capitalized noun. Trollope is an advanced conservative liberal because his goals for social equality are radical but he believes that the change will take time.[18]

Amarnick further cites Trollope's travel book *North America* (1862) and a letter written to Kate Field during its composition to confirm his cosmopolitanism, which extends his liberal inclusiveness beyond his own nation.

> Any patriotism must be poor which desires glory or even profit for a few at the expense of many, even though the few be brothers and the many aliens. As a rule patriotism is a virtue only because man's aptitude for good is so finite, that he cannot see and comprehend a wider humanity. He can hardly bring himself to understand that salvation should be extended to Jew and Gentile alike.[19]

> One's country has no right to demand everything. There is much that is higher and better and greater than one's country. One is patriotic only because one is too small and too weak to be cosmopolitan.[20]

Trollope's acknowledgment of weakness is pragmatic. While his liberalism is as rational as Anderson would like, his conservatism is affective ("Trollope understands affection"). Rosalind Leveridge cites *An Autobiography*'s description of the self-consciously irrational pull of the past "with hearts which still love the old teachings which the mind will no longer accept": "We too cut our ropes, and go out in our little boats, and search for a land that will be new to us.... Who would not stay behind if it were possible to him."[21] In his most radical prose works, *The New Zealander*, drafted in 1855 but not published until 1972, and

---

[17]   Steven Amarnick, "Trollope and Anti-Semitism," preprint 2007 (Samarnick@aol.com).

[18]   Amarnick, p. 2.

[19]   Anthony Trollope, *North America* (New York: St. Martin's Press, 1986), p. 84.

[20]   Anthony Trollope, *The Letters of Anthony Trollope,* ed. N. John Hall (Stanford: Stanford University Press, 1983), p. 191.

[21]   Cited in Rosalind Leveridge, "'A Hairdresser's Estimate of Mankind': Anthony Trollope, Church, and Clergymen," MA Thesis, University of Exeter, 2007, p. 46. From *Clergymen of the Church of England* (London: The Trollope Society, 1993), pp. 128–9.

Clergymen of the Church of England (1866), Trollope espoused tolerance and condemned religious rivalry, denouncing both Evangelical fanaticism and Anglican formalism, or outward trappings that did not represent spirituality or religiosity and thus colluded in what in his angrier moments he considered the fundamental dishonesty of social life. It is well known that, throughout his works, Trollope consistently prized sincerity and tolerance. Yet while Anderson has well demonstrated sincerity as critique in Trollope, sincerity as ethos, the worldly realism in which his characters are embedded, is more difficult. Trollope's characters can be ardent critical proponents of communicative interaction or not. Most are not.

In *The Prime Minister* (1876) Trollope shows the full prejudice of the upper classes against an aspirant gentleman, Ferdinand Lopez, whose origins are unknown, except that his father was Portuguese. The Barrister Mr. Wharton makes it clear that no amount of explanation or revelation—of communication or new information—would change his mind about Lopez, as he equates Portuguese with Jewishness: "He had not explained to the man as he would wish to have done, that it was monstrous and out of the question that a daughter of the Whartons, one of the oldest families in England, should be given to a friendless Portuguese,—a probable Jew,—about whom nobody knew anything."[22] Elsewhere he says, "I dislike him particularly. For anything I know he may have sold pencils about the streets like any other Jew-boy" (p. 39), "One is bound to be very careful. How can I give you to a man I know nothing about,—an adventurer? What would they say in Herefordshire?" (p. 44), and "Nothing that she said altered in the least his idea about the man" (p. 46). In a book in which the Prime Minister is fit for purpose precisely because of his capacity for the ideals of "lucid explanation" and "debate" (p. 62), the lawyer is perceived even by his children as "prejudiced" (p. 45), "tyrannical and irrational" (p. 87). The narrator, meanwhile, simply points out that Wharton "was a Tory of the old school, who hated compromises" (p. 77) and upheld the status quo. Wharton prefers Lopez's rival because he is like himself: "because he is a gentleman of the class to which I belong myself; because he works; because I know all about him, so that I can be sure of him; because he had a decent father and mother; because I am safe with him, being quite sure that he will say to me neither awkward things nor impertinent things" (p. 88). References to Lopez multiply as "a Portuguese Jew" (p. 116), "a greasy Jew adventurer out of the gutter" (p. 126), "a black Portuguese nameless Jew" (p. 136), "a greasy, black foreigner" (p. 141). Wharton's son as well as his daughter perceive him and their family at large as "a stiff-necked, prejudiced set of provincial ignoramuses" (p. 108).

The trouble for the disgusted Victorian liberal—or the contemporary shocked politically correct—reader is that the provincial ignoramuses appear to be right. Not about Lopez's Jewishness, for there is never any evidence that he or his parents were Jewish. (He is simply an adventure capitalist and for the purposes

---

[22]   Anthony Trollope, *The Prime Minister*, ed. David Skilton, 1876 (London: Penguin, 1994), pp. 34–5.

of the other characters trades like a Jew: being Jewish here is an economic as much as a racial or religious category, as it is in most Victorian literature.)[23] But Wharton's prejudice against the proposed marriage between Lopez and his daughter seems to be justified. Emily Wharton's marriage to Lopez is a disaster. He is physically and psychologically abusive and a tyrant. She soon learns that he is "vulgar and damnable" (p. 338) and that while he possesses the external appearance of a gentleman he lacks the learned qualities (ethos) that her father valued and represented. The narrator explains:

> Though this man had lived nearly all his life in England, he had not quite acquired that knowledge of the way in which things are done which is so general among men of a certain class, and so rare among those beneath them. He had not understood that the Duchess's promise of her assistance at Silverbridge might be taken by him for what it was worth, and that her aid might be used as far as it went,—but that in the event of its failing him, he was bound in honour to take the result without complaining, whatever that result might be. He felt that a grievous injury had been done him, and that it behoved him to resent that injury. (p. 371)

I shall return to the key term, his resentment. As Lopez becomes viler, the narrator takes pains to explain that he did not know better:

---

[23]   There is a substantial literature on Jews in Trollope. In addition to the essay by Amarnick cited above and Richard Dellamora's treatment of *The Prime Minister* cited below, see Murray Baumgarten, "Seeing Double: Jews in the Fiction of F. Scott Fitzgerald, Charles Dickens, Anthony Trollope, and George Eliot," in Brian Cheyette (ed.), *Between Race and Culture: Representations of "the Jew" in English and American Literature* (Stanford: Stanford University Press, 1996), pp. 44–61; Everett Carter, "Realists and Jews" *Studies in American Fiction* 22.1 (1994): 81–91; Brian Cheyette, *Constructions of "the Jew" in English Literature and Society: Racial Representations, 1875–1945* (Cambridge, UK: Cambridge University Press, 1996); J. D. Coates, "Moral Patterns in *The Way We Live Now,*" *Durham University Journal* 71 (1978): 55–65; A. O. J. Cockshut, *Anthony Trollope: A Critical Study* (New York: New York University Press, 1968); Derek Cohen, "Constructing the Contradiction: Anthony Trollope's *The Way We Live Now*," in Derek Cohen and Deborah Heller (eds), *Jewish Presences in Literature* (Montreal: McGill-Queen's University Press, 1990); Paul Delany, "Land, Money, and the Jews in the Later Trollope." *Studies in English Literature, 1500–1900*, 32.4 (1992): 765–87; A. Abbott Ikeler, "That Peculiar Book: Critics, Common Readers, and *The Way We Live Now*," *College Language Association Journal*, 30.2 (1986): 219–40; Bill Overton, *The Unofficial Trollope* (Brighton: Harvester, 1982); Michael Ragussis, *Figures of Conversion: The Jewish Question and English National Identity* (Durham: Duke University Press, 1995); Edgar Rosenberg, *From Shylock to Svengali: Jewish Stereotypes in English Fiction* (Stanford: Stanford University Press, 1960); Michael Sadleir, *Trollope: A Commentary* (New York: Farrar Straus and Co., 1947). At the 2005 North American Victorian Studies Association Annual Meeting in Charlottesville, Anthony Wohl held a master class on anti-semitism in the 1870s in which Trollope was much discussed. I am grateful to Steven Amarnick, Margaret Markwick, Deborah Morse, and Anna Peak for the bibliography.

To give him his due, he did not know that he was a villain. When he was exhorting her to "get round her father" he was not aware that he was giving her lessons which must shock a well-conditioned girl. He did not understand that everything that she had discovered of his moral disposition since her marriage was of a nature to disgust her. And, not understanding all this, he conceived that he was grievously wronged by her, in that she adhered to her father rather than to him. (pp. 462–3)

Increasingly squeezed by financial constraints that his wife's father will do nothing to ameliorate, Lopez acts repeatedly in ways that disadvantage him socially. As his life rushes to crisis, the narrator returns once again to his deficiency of ethos:

He had no inner appreciation whatsoever of what was really good or what was really bad in a man's conduct. He did not know that he had done evil in applying to the Duke for the money. He had only meant to attack the Duke; and when the money had come it had been regarded as justifiable prey. And when after receiving the Duke's money, he had kept also Mr Wharton's money, he had justified himself again by reminding himself that Mr. Wharton certainly owed him much more than that. In a sense he was what is called a gentleman. He knew how to speak, and how to look, how to use a knife and fork, how to dress himself, and how to walk. But he had not the faintest notion of the feelings of a gentleman. He had, however, a very keen conception of the evil of being generally ill spoken of. (p. 497)

Bankrupt and universally held in contempt, Lopez suicides. After a decent period of abject (guilt-ridden) mourning, his widow marries a cousin of her own class, Arthur Fletcher, "the very pearl of the Fletcher tribe" (p. 125).[24] The Duke (Liberal Prime Minister) makes the speech that ventriloquized Trollope's views of Conservatism—the maintenance of social inequality—which had led to Lopez's marginalization:

---

[24]   Trollope presents Arthur Fletcher as consummate class privilege: "All the Fletchers and everything belonging to them were almost worshipped at Wharton Hall. There had been marriages between the two families certainly as far back as the time of Henry VII, and they were accustomed to speak, if not of alliances, at any rate of friendships, much anterior to that…. He looked like one of those happy sons of the gods who are born to success…. There was no one who in his youth had suffered fewer troubles from those causes of trouble which visit English young men,—occasional impecuniosity, sternness of parents, native shyness, fear of ridicule, inability of speech, and a general pervading sense of inferiority combined with an ardent desire to rise to a feeling of conscious superiority. So much had been done for him by nature that he was never called upon to pretend to anything. Throughout the country those were the lucky men—and those too were the happy girls,–who were allowed to call him Arthur. And yet this paragon was vainly in love with Emily Wharton, who, in the way of love, would have nothing to say to him, preferring,—as her father once said in his extremest wrath,—a greasy Jew adventurer out of the gutter!" (pp. 125–6).

> The Conservative wishes to maintain the differences and the distances which separate the highly placed from their lower brethren. He thinks that God has divided the world as he finds it divided, and that he may best do his duty by making the inferior man happy and contented in his position, teaching him that the place which he holds is his by God's ordinance. (p. 583)

Trollope's plot affectively recuperates the world that his politics rationally repudiate. In the course of reading the reader is appalled by the prejudice she reads, confused that the prejudice seems to be justified, and then enlightened as to the problem: Lopez's ignorance results from his exclusion and his resentment becomes a way of life of life-destroying action. Narratologically, as Frank O'Connor described, Trollope's "favorite device is to lead his reader very gently up the garden path of his own conventions and then to point out that the reader is wrong."[25] But while reinstituting the difference and distance between themselves and the likes of Lopez, Society feels guilty. The family of his ruined partner Sexty Parker is paid £2/week in perpetuity by Wharton (p. 593). The Duchess comes to "have a sort of feeling, you know, that among us we made the train run over him" (p. 659).

Trollope understands affection, and turns the lives of people who bore us into epic. Lopez is an accomplished example of Victorian resentment, an affect, rather than a rational idea, that becomes a way of life. He feels the injustice of uninformed prejudice and unearned status and cannot accept them. In *Friendship's Bonds: Democracy and the Novel in Victorian England* (2004), Richard Dellamora uses anti-Semitism in *The Prime Minister* to signal the end of the Liberal-Tory consensus.[26] Here I have not focussed on the high politics of that compromise (the plot of Plantagenet Palliser as Prime Minister) but rather on the social dimension: the final incompatibility of the worlds of Lopez and the Whartons. There is a representative sentiment in Victorian public school memoirs that the problem with men who had not been to public schools was that they were formless, constantly infringing on their betters' space, taste, and privacy. "I hate the lower classes," wrote Harold Nicolson in an extreme version, "People who have not endured the restrictive shaping of an English School are apt in after life to be egocentric, formless and inconsiderate."[27] Lacking recognition, Lopez does not know how to get it. Consumed with resentment, he can only feel the frustration of his desires and never learns to regulate them according to middle-class ideals of compromise and duty. What looks like egotism and selfishness is its opposite: the inability to

---

[25]   Frank O'Connor, "Trollope the Realist," *The Mirror in the Roadway: A Study of the Modern Novel* (New York: Knopf, 1956), p. 168.

[26]   Richard Dellamora, *Friendship's Bonds: Democracy and the Novel in Victorian England* (Philadelphia: University of Pennsylvania Press, 2004), ch. 4 "The Lesser Holocausts of William Gladstone and Anthony Trollope," pp. 102–26.

[27]   Harold Nicolson, *Some People* (1927), cited and discussed in Regenia Gagnier, *Subjectivities: A History of Self-Representation in Britain 1832–1920* (Oxford: Oxford University Press, 1991), p. 184.

be recognized by others and the consequent making a spectacle of oneself, which further disqualifies one from recognition.

"[Lopez] had, however, a very keen conception of the evil of being generally ill spoken of." Shame, as Sandra Bartky has said, involves the distressed apprehension of oneself as a lesser creature, and renders one less able to act within the social context of the world.[28] Resentment arises in a desire to dull the pain of frustration from an inability to carry out a desired action. It is a feeling, emotion, or affect that comes into being to cover the frustration, to numb the pain, of being unable to get what one wants. Resentment not only functions as a simple feeling or affect but becomes a form of agency that misguides and misjudges, blocking and frustrating desires. The man of resentment experiences a revaluation of his desires and devalues the desire he could not fulfil.

In the second half of the nineteenth century, a number of writers asked what kind of creatures humans were at home and answered: unfinished, willful, desiring, ungrateful, resentful. I do not have space to recount these philosophical anthropologies here, but elsewhere I discuss their evolution from Herder through Nietzsche. Whereas the spider and the bee were so closely fitted to their environments that they had one sole purpose, to spin or to hive, humans were so inadequate to theirs that they were forced to make many different ways of surviving, according to their cultures and climes. Because they had to, they created choice. Humankind's choice or freedom, while distinguishing it from nonhuman animals tied to their environments, is also a source of pain. Humankind, in Nietzsche's words, is the diseased animal—"the great experimenter with himself, the unsatisfied, the insatiate ... who finds no more any rest from his own aggressive strength".[29] This insatiability is a pain, and the pain of ceaseless will and choice can sometimes be assuaged by a physiological response: resentment. Resentment, that is, has a real physiological cause in "a demand for the deadening of pain through emotion."[30] Resentment seeks an object, a cause outside oneself, on which to blame one's pain. Nietzsche understood resentment not just as one agent's destructive path of frustrated desire but as a whole way of life-denying life, a whole culture that created values as a ruse to keep outsiders down. Ascetic ideals maintained the status quo by suppressing healthy intruders and diverting the course of resentment, what Nietzsche called "that most dangerous blasting-stuff and explosive [that] ever accumulates and accumulates."[31] Resentment could tear society apart, but it

---

[28]   Sandra Lee Bartky, *Femininity and Domination: Studies in the Phenomenology of Oppression* (New York: Routledge, 1990), p. 87, cited in Janet L. Borgerson, "Ressentiment, Decadence, and the Desire for Power," in L. Gordon and J. Borgerson (eds) *Heretical Nietzsche* (Boulder, CO: Paradigm Press, forthcoming). I am grateful to Borgerson for this preprint and for philosophical conversations on resentment.

[29]   Friedrich Nietzsche, *The Genealogy of Morals: A Polemic* Trans. Horace B. Samuel (London: Foulis, 1910), p. 155.

[30]   Ibid., p. 164.

[31]   Ibid., p. 163.

usually does not because the ascetic priest diverts that resentment back toward the sufferer: you are downcast, you are yourself to blame.

More than 20 years earlier, Dostoevsky had dramatized the quintessential man of resentment in *Notes from Underground* (1864), and then the ascetic priest who subdues the population and diverts resentment in "The Grand Inquisitor" section of *The Brothers Karamazov* (1881). (*The Prime Minister* [1876] falls between Dostoevsky and Nietzsche's *Genealogy of Morals* of 1887.) The Inquisitor berates Christ for asking too much of humanity and himself shoulders the burden of protecting them through mystery and authority, ruling them through lies but freeing them from their pain of freedom and choice. The Underground Man recognizes that Reason is only partial but the Will, of which resentment is an aspect, is a manifestation of all life. Our will, our choice, is our individuality, which is more humanly constitutive even than self-interest. The man of resentment knows that his action/choices are misapprehensions, tactless, and vulgar, but he commits them self-consciously, self-condemning for, above all, what he must assert is his choice: "punishment," wrote Dostoevsky, " is still better than nothing".[32] "Man," Nietzsche concluded in *The Genealogy of Morals*, "will wish Nothingness rather than not wish at all."[33] Nietzsche emphasized desire while Dostoevsky emphasized choice, but they are both stages in humankind's complex assertion of will, as its defining characteristic.

Trollope was no stranger to resentment. His *Autobiography* chronicles how he was called "dirty" at school (p. 24), his being accused (falsely) of some nameless crime (p. 24), his contemplating suicide, knowing "the misery of expulsion from all social intercourse" (p. 29), "the indescribable indignities" he endured (p. 30), how he was "odious to the eyes of those I admired and envied" (p. 30). "There were exhibitions from Harrow—which I never got. Twice I tried for a sizership at Clare Hall,—but in vain. Once I made a futile attempt for a scholarship at Trinity, Oxford,—but failed again … I bear in mind well with how prodigal a hand prizes were to be showered about; but I never got a prize" (pp. 34–5). "I feel convinced in my mind that I have been flogged oftener than any human being alive" (p. 35), he concludes Chapter 1, and he concludes of his first 26 years "of suffering, disgrace, and inward remorse", "There had clung to me a feeling that I had been looked upon always as an evil, an encumbrance, a useless thing,—as a creature of whom those connected with him had to be ashamed" (p. 68).

My point is not a psychological one about Trollope. As anyone who has studied the British public schools knows, the condition of shame and resentment was general, normal.[34] The point then was to make everyone feel deficient so that

---

[32]   Fyodor Dostoevsky, *Notes from Underground*, Trans. Ralph E. Matlaw (New York: Dutton, 1960), p. 31.

[33]   Op cit. p. 211.

[34]   Regenia Gagnier, *Subjectivities* (1991), see ch. 5 "The Making of Middle-Class Identities: School and Family," pp. 171–219. In *Imperial Masochism: British Fiction,*

they might aspire to transcend the feelings and then subject the next generation to them, in repetitive cycles. This is called governmentality.

While the conjunction of Dostoevsky, Nietzsche, and Trollope's works of the decades 1860s to 1880s may seem unlikely, it is no surprise to anyone who has thought seriously—genealogically—about liberalism: freedom and resentment have been inextricable in the democratization of human rights of the past 200 years.[35] These were the worldly authors, in their different ways realists fighting Idealism, whether in fiction or in philosophy. They were all concerned with the phenomenal and material worlds. There has been a tendency, particularly in North American work, to focus more and more on proceduralism as the essence of liberalism: freedom of speech, the press, debate, expression of lifestyle, and so on, in market democracy. I would agree that democratic procedures, especially rational debate, are absolutely essential to liberal society. But the human animal is not merely rational. The great anthropological traditions, asking what kind of creature the human animal is at home, whether philosophical anthropology in Nietzsche or novelistic anthropology in Dostoevsky and Trollope, had a deeper sense of freedom deriving it from our unfinished existence as human animals. This freedom is not just rational but *passional* and when frustrated gives rise to physiological conditions of resentment, which govern our actions even when they are life- and self-denying. Dostoevsky's influence on Nietzsche has been documented, and more recently ascetic ideals and resentment have been invoked in discussions of terrorism. My point has been that it makes little sense to talk about liberal "freedom" and "democracy" outside its historical companions of resentment and manipulation[36]—which is why Trollope's culminating political novel, where his defense of Liberalism is most explicit in the person of his favorite character, his "perfect gentleman" the Prime Minister *(Autobiography,* p. 314), is bifurcated, ripped through, with the story of the excluded and self-destructive Ferdinand Lopez. Both faces of masculinity, the Ideal and its negation, the Overman and the Underground Man, define the human animal as desiring and deficient.

Nor does it make sense to talk of freedom and liberalism without gender flexibility. It does not matter that Lopez is not a Jew; for the purposes of his

---

Fantasy, and Social Class (Princeton: Princeton University Press, 2007), John Kucich comes to similar conclusions.

[35] See, in a completely different philosophical register, P. F. Strawson, *Freedom and Resentment and Other Essays* (London: Methuen, 1974), esp. ch. 1, "Freedom and Resentment," pp. 1–25. "Much imaginative literature is devoted to exploring the complexities" of "punishing and moral condemnation and approval" (pp. 4–5), though Strawson does not discuss this literature. It is also worth noting that the other greatest Russian novelist of Trollope's time, Leo Tolstoy, also much admired *The Prime Minister.*

[36] This was Agamben's starting point in *Homo Sacer,* in which he explored the possible solidarity between democracy and totalitarianism (Giorgio Agamben, *Homo Sacer: Sovereign Power and Bare Life*, trans. Daniel Heller-Roazen [Stanford: Stanford University Press, 1998], p. 10).

exclusion he was born in Portugal and trades and travels like a Jew, and that is enough to mark him. Such categories are not more essential than women's roles. If one were to ask, anthropologically, what kind of creature is woman in the upper classes of Britain in the nineteenth century, one obvious answer is that, at least while young, she is also an economic as well as a sexual category: she is a commodity to be trafficked among men.[37]

Lopez did not marry Emily for her wealth, but having learned that it would be withheld from him due to Wharton's prejudice, he became a tyrant to his wife. The only good relationships in Trollope are those where husbands and wives are equal and women are freed from economic constraint.[38] Madame Max's first utterances are about politics. In her second, she offers Phineas her money. The second time she offers it and it is rejected, she offers Finn her hand. In the next volume, when Finn proposes to her, he does not need to make explanations or arguments, she just immediately accepts, with a plain-spoken testament that she has loved him always. The second best couple in Trollope, Glencora and Plantagenet Palliser, are also equal in wealth. When, in *Can You Forgive Her?*, Glencora tells him that she never loved him, he tells her that he has nonetheless loved her. In *The Prime Minister*, he tells her that he will resign and they are honest with one another. Yet even in this best of marriages, Glencora's resentment only fitfully sleeps: "Of course I know it would be wrong that I should have an opinion," she says to her husband, "As 'man' you are of course to have your own way" (p. 275). Two chapters earlier (Chapter 30), Emily Wharton had realized the same thing, that marriage "meant as much as that,—that a husband was to claim to dictate to his wife what opinions she was to form" (p. 262). This is not the difference between the vulgar Lopez and the gentleman Palliser. Both dominate their wives, with ensuing resentment. Mill published the *locus classicus* of liberalism, *On Liberty* (1859), within ten years of that of women's emancipation, *The Subjection of Women* (1869). Together they argued that freedom was incompatible with essentialist conceptions of any kind, ontological or epistemological, that choice was constitutive of human animals.

As essays by Morse, Polhemus, Michie, Noble, and Skilton establish, Trollope shows women's oppression, women's resentment, but also the effects of women's equality on their choices. Because it was Trollope's women—the divine Madame Max and the all too human Glencora Palliser— who first drew me to Trollope and then to a study of Trollope and gender, I shall conclude with David Skilton's words, on which, exceptionally, Lady Thatcher the former Prime Minister and I are in agreement: "Trollope gives his women mental lives analogous to those of

---

[37] See Deborah Denenholz Morse, *Women in Trollope's Palliser Novels* (Ann Arbor: UMI Research Press, 1987); reprinted University of Rochester/Boydell and Brewer, 1991).

[38] *Is he Popenjoy?* and *The Belton Estate* are explicit explorations of the issue of equality between husbands and wives.

his men, to the delight of the many intelligent women who are on record as very much admiring his women characters."[39]

---

[39]   David Skilton, original abstract.

Select Bibliography of Works on Trollope

Full bibliographic details of works cited can be found in our contributors' footnotes

apRoberts, Ruth. *Trollope: Artist and Moralist*. London: Chatto and Windus, 1971.

———, "Emily and Nora and Dorothy and Priscilla and Jemima and Cary," in Richard Levine (ed.), *The Victorian Experience: The Novelists*. Athens: Ohio University Press, 1976. pp. 87–120.

Bareham, Tony (ed.), *Anthony Trollope*. London: Vision Press, 1980.

— (ed.), *The Barchester Novels: A Casebook*. London: Macmillan, 1983.

Barickman, Richard, Susan MacDonald, and Myra Stark. *Corrupt Relations: Dickens, Thackeray, Trollope, Collins and the Victorian Sexual System*. New York: Columbia University Press, 1982.

Booth, Bradford. *Anthony Trollope: Aspects of his Life and Art*. London: Hutton, 1958.

Cockshut, A. O. J. *Anthony Trollope; A Critical Study*. London: Collins, 1955.

———, *Man and Woman: A Study of Love and the Novel 1740–1940*. London: Collins, 1977.

Cohen, Derek. "Constructing the Contradiction: Anthony Trollope's *The Way We Live Now*," in Derek Cohen and Deborah Heller (eds), *Jewish Presences in English Literature*. Montreal: McGill-Queens University Press, 1990, pp. 61–75.

Cohen, William A. *Sex Scandal: The Private Parts of Victorian Fiction*. Durham, NC: Duke University Press, 1996.

Collins, Philip. "Business and Bosoms; Some Trollopian Concerns," *Nineteenth Century Fiction*, 37 (December 1982): 293–315.

Dellamora, Richard. *Friendship's Bonds: Democracy and the Novel in Victorian England*. Philadelphia: Pennsylvania University Press, 2004.

———, "Stupid Trollope," *Victorian Newsletter* 100. Fall 2001: 22–6.

Donvan, Robert. "Trollope's Prentice Work." *Modern Philology*, 53.3 (Feb. 1956) 179–86.

Edwards, P. D., *Anthony Trollope: His Art and Scope*. Brighton: Harvester Press, 1978.

Escott, T. H. *Anthony Trollope: His Work, Associates, and Literary Originals*. London: John Lane, 1913.

Forrester, Mark. "Redressing the Empire: Anthony Trollope and British Gender Anxiety in "The Banks of the Jordan." *Imperial Desire: Dissident Sexualities and Colonial Literature*, Philip Holden and Richard J. Ruppel, eds. Minneapolis: Minnesota University Press, 2003.

Gilmour, Robin. *The Idea of the Gentleman in the Victorian Novel*. London: Allen and Unwin, 1981.

———, *The Novel in the Victorian Age: a Modern Introduction*. London: Arnold, 1986.

——, *The Victorian Period: The Intellectual and Cultural Context of English Literature, 1830–1890*. London: Longman's 1993.

Gindin, James. "Trollope" *Harvest of a quiet eye: The Novel of Compassion*. Bloomington: Indiana University Press, 1971.

Glendinning, Victoria. *Trollope*. London: Pimlico, 1993.

Hagan, John. "The Divided Mind of Anthony Trollope," *Nineteenth Century Fiction*, 14 (1959–60): 1–26.

Hall, N. John. "The Truth about Trollope's 'Disappearance'," *Trollopiana*, 22 (August 1993): 4–12.

——, *Trollope: A Biography*. Oxford: Clarendon Press, 1991.

——, *The Letters of Anthony Trollope*. 2 vols. Stanford: Stanford University Press, 1983.

——, *Trollope and His Illustrators*. London: Macmillan, 1980.

Halperin, John. ed. *Trollope Centenary Essays*. London: Macmillan, 1982.

——, *Trollope and Politics: a Study of The Pallisers and Others*. New York: Barnes and Noble, 1977.

Handley, Graham. *Anthony Trollope*. Stroud: Sutton Publishing, 1999.

Harrison, Frederic. *Studies in Early Victorian Literature*. 1895. London: Edward Arnold, 1910.

Harvey, Geoffrey. *The Art of Anthony Trollope*. London: Weidenfeld and Nicolson, 1980.

Herbert, Christopher. "*He knew He Was Right*, Mrs Lynn Linton, and the Duplicities of Victorian Marriage," *Texas Studies in Language and Literature*, 25 (1983): 448–69.

——, *Trollope and Comic Pleasure*. Chicago: University of Chicago Press, 1986.

——, "Trollope and the Fixity of the Self," *PMLA*, 93 (March 1978): 228–39.

——, "The Novel of Cultural Symbolism: Doctor Thorne." *Culture and Anomie: Ethnographic Imagination in the Nineteenth Century*. Chicago: Chicago University Press, 1991.

James, Henry. *The Critical Muse: Selected Literary Criticism*. ed. Roger Gard. London: Penguin Books, 1987.

Kendrick, Walter. *The Novel Machine: The Theory and Fiction of Anthony Trollope*. Baltimore and London: Johns Hopkins University Press, 1980.

Kincaid, James R. *The Novels of Anthony Trollope*. Oxford: Clarendon Press, 1977.

Lansbury, Coral. *The Reasonable Man: Trollope's Legal Fiction*. Princeton: Princeton University Press, 1981

Letwin, Shirley Robin. *The Gentleman in Trollope: Individuality and Moral Conduct*. London: Macmillan, 1982.

Levine, George. "Can You Forgive Him? Trollope's *Can You Forgive Her?* and the Myth of Realism," *Victorian Studies*, 18 (1974–75): 5–30.

McMaster, Juliet. *Trollope's Palliser Novels: Theme and Pattern*. London: Macmillan, 1978.

McMaster, R. D. *Trollope and the Law*. New York: St. Martin's Press, 1986.

Markwick, Margaret. *Trollope and Women*. London: Hambledon Press/Trollope Society, 1997.

——, *New Men in Trollope's Novels: Rewriting the Victorian Male*. Basingstoke: Ashgate, 2007.

Miller, Hillis. *The Form of Victorian Fiction*. Indiana: University of Notre Dame, 1968.

More, Paul Elmer. "My Debt to Trollope," *The Demon of the Absolute,* New Shelburne Essay, vol. 1, 89–125. Princeton, NJ: Princeton University Press, 1928.

Morse, Deborah Denenholz. *Women in Trollope's Palliser Novels*. Ann Arbor: UMI Research Press, 1987.

——, "Trollope's *Lady Anna*: Corrupt Relations or Erotic Faith?" *The Anna Book: Searching for Anna in History*. ed. Mickey Pearlman. Greenwood, CT: Greenwood Press, 1992, pp. 49–58.

——, "Educating Louis: Teaching the Victorian Father in Anthony Trollope's *He Knew He Was Right,*" in Regena Barreca and Deborah Denenholz Morse (eds), *The Erotics of Instruction*. Hanover, NH: University Press of New England, 1997.

Nardin, Jane. *He Knew She Was Right: The Independent Woman in the Novels of Anthony Trollope*. Carbondale: Southern Illinois University Press, 1989.

——, *Trollope and Victorian Moral Philosophy*. Ohio: Ohio University Press, 1996.

O'Connor, Frank. "Trollope the Realist." *The Mirror in the Roadway: A Study of the Modern Novel*. New York: Knopf, 1956.

Overton, Bill. *The Unofficial Trollope*. Brighton: Harvester Press, 1983.

Pei, Lowry. "*The Duke's Children*: Reflection and Reconciliation." *Modern Language Quarterly* 39 (1978): 284–302.

Polhemus, Robert M. "Being in love in *Phineas Finn* and *Phineas Redux*: Desire, Devotion, Consolation," *Nineteenth Century Fiction*, 37. 3: 383–95.

——, *The Changing World of Anthony Trollope*. Berkley and London: University of California Press, 1978.

——, "Trollope's Barchester Towers, 1857: Comic Reformation" in *Comic Faith: The Great Tradition from Austen to Joyce*. Chicago: Chicago University Press, 1980.

Pollard, Arthur. *Anthony Trollope*. London: Routledge and Kegan Paul, 1978.

Praz, Mario. *The Hero in Eclipse in Victorian Fiction*. Trans. Angus Davidson. London: Oxford University Press, 1956.

Riffaterre, Michael. "Trollope's Metonymies," *Nineteenth Century Fiction*, 37 (Dec. 1982): 272–92.

Sadleir, Michael. *Trollope: A Commentary*. London: Constable, 1927.

Sanders, Andrew. *Anthony Trollope*. Plymouth: Northcote House, 1998.

Skilton, David. *Anthony Trollope and his Contemporaries*. London: Longmans, 1972.

Smalley, Donald, ed. *Anthony Trollope; The Critical Heritage*. London: Routledge and Kegan Paul, 1969.

Stone, Donald D. *The Romantic Impulse in Victorian Fiction*. Cambridge, MA: Harvard University Press, 1980.

Super, R. H. *The Chronicler of Barchester: A Life of Anthony Trollope*. Ann Arbor: Michigan University Press, 1988.

——, *Trollope in the Post Office*. Ann Arbor: Michigan University Press, 1981.

——, "Truth and Fiction in Trollope's *Autobiography*," *Nineteenth Century Literature* 48.1 (June 1993): 74–88.

Surridge, Lisa. *Bleak Houses: Marital Violence in Victorian Fiction*. Athens: Ohio University Press, 2005.

Sutherland, John. *Victorian Fiction: Writers, Publishers, Readers*. London: Macmillan, 1995.

——, *Is Heathcliff a Murderer? Puzzles in Nineteenth Century Fiction*. Oxford: Oxford University Press, 1996.

——, *Victorian Novelists and Publishers*. London: Athlone Press, 1976.

Terry, R. C. ed. *Oxford Reader's Companion to Trollope*. Oxford: Oxford University Press, 1999.

——, *Anthony Trollope: The Artist in Hiding*. London: Macmillan, 1977.

——, "Three Lost Chapters of Trollope's First Novel," *Nineteenth Century Fiction*, 27 (June 1972): 71–80.

——, *Victorian Popular Fiction: 1860–1880*. London: Macmillan, 1983.

Tingay, Lance O. "Trollope's popularity: A Statistical Approach," *Nineteenth Century Fiction*, 11. 3 (December 1956): 223–9.

Tracy, Robert. "The Unnatural Ruin," *Nineteenth Century Fiction*, 37 (December 1982): 358–82.

——, *Trollope's Later Novels*. Berkeley and London: University of California Press, 1978.

Turner, Mark W. *Trollope and the Magazines: Gendered Issues in Mid-Victorian Britain*. London: Macmillan, 2000.

——, "Trollope Studies: 1987–2004," *Dickens Studies Annual*, 37 (2006): 217–49.

Wall, Stephen. *Trollope and Character*. London and Boston: Faber and Faber, 1988.

Woolf, Virginia. *Collected Essays*. vol. 2. London: Hogarth Press, 1966–67.

Wright, Andrew. *Anthony Trollope: Dream and Art*. Chicago: Chicago University Press, 1983.

Index